ASP.NET 3.5
A Beginner's Guide

About the Author

William B. Sanders has been developing software for the last 25 years, ranging from Basic to assembly language and everything in between. In 2001 he began developing back-end applications using ASP and then when it became available, ASP.NET 1.0. He is a founding faculty member of the Multimedia Web Design and Development major at the University of Hartford, where he teaches ASP.NET, C#, SQL, and ADO.NET, among other Internet languages and applications, to upper division students. He has consulted and developed software for major software companies as well other business clients.

About the Technical Editor

Chris Stewart has been working in the technology industry since 2001. He is a graduate of Virginia Commonwealth University and the founder of 913solutions, LLC. Chris has been involved with Microsoft .NET since the beginning and provides a number of consulting services around that technology platform. In addition to working with 913solutions, Chris actively maintains a number of technology blogs and co-hosts *Kill the Desktop,* a weekly technology podcast devoted to web-focused technology news.

ASP.NET 3.5
A Beginner's Guide

William B. Sanders

New York Chicago San Francisco
Lisbon London Madrid Mexico City
Milan New Delhi San Juan
Seoul Singapore Sydney Toronto

The McGraw·Hill Companies

Cataloging-in-Publication Data is on file with the Library of Congress

McGraw-Hill books are available at special quantity discounts to use as premiums and sales promotions, or for use in corporate training programs. To contact a special sales representative, please visit the Contact Us page at www.mhprofessional.com.

ASP.NET 3.5: A Beginner's Guide

1234567890 DOC DOC 0198

ISBN   978-0-07-159194-2
MHID   0-07-159194-X

Sponsoring Editor   Jane K. Brownlow

Editorial Supervisor   Janet Walden

Project Manager   Harleen Chopra, International Typesetting and Composition

Acquisitions Coordinator   Jennifer Housh

Technical Editor   Chris Stewart

Copy Editor   Jan Jue

Proofreader   Bhavna Gupta, International Typesetting and Composition

Indexer   Claire Splan

Production Supervisor   George Anderson

Composition   International Typesetting and Composition

Illustration   International Typesetting and Composition

Art Director, Cover   Jeff Weeks

This book is dedicated to Ricky, Olivia, Tess, John, and Jacob.

Contents at a Glance

Contents

Acknowledgments

This book was greatly influenced by my University of Hartford students, current and past, who have not been shy when it comes to providing feedback about what helps them learn ASP.NET. As they have tested ASP.NET 3.5 web sites with clients of their own, I was able to get a good feel for what clients typically require and developers need to understand to use this powerful Internet tool. Included in those who have added insight are Stephen Horbachuk, Dusan Ivanovic, James Lundell, Michael McGovern, Brendan Moriarty, MaryLynn Schaefer, and Destiny Uhlik.

The development of the book was aided immensely by the efforts of Chris Stewart. As the technical editor, Chris provided insights, righted wrongs, and has the knack for detail required to spot missing semicolons and other gremlins that can plague a program listing. He is a very talented C# programmer and is fully versed in ASP.NET and getting the most out of Visual Studio 2008. No author could ask for better, and I hope that his wisdom is reflected in the final result.

Takeshi Eto, the VP of marketing at DiscountASP.NET, provided me with a real-world server running ASP.NET 3.5. This allowed testing in an environment where the different web sites would ultimately be employed.

The overall ASP.NET community, both within and outside of Microsoft, is a wonder to behold. Microsoft provided rich and frequent materials for testing ASP.NET 3.5, C# 3.0, and Visual Studio 2008. Speakers at Microsoft-sponsored ASP.NET seminars gave invaluable presentations covering both the actual use of many of the new features in

ASP.NET 3.5 and clear explanations as to why the features were added. Additional materials available in *MSDN Events Developer Resource Kits,* of which I took full advantage, supported the seminars. All of the Microsoft support is further supplemented by ASP.NET enthusiasts around the world in the form of web sites and blogs.

My colleagues, John Gray and Chandima Cumaranatunge, in the Multimedia Web Design and Development program at the University of Hartford, were supportive as ever, and willing to listen to and contribute ideas. My gratitude to them is ongoing.

The editorial assistance at McGraw-Hill was always helpful and patient over a period where I broke my leg and had to readjust my writing schedule. Jane Brownlow, executive editor, worked to get the project off the ground and headed in the right direction in conjunction with Margot Hutchison, my trusted and efficient representative from Waterside Productions. Working with acquisitions coordinator Jennifer Housh was a pleasure as well. She was invaluable in getting all of the parts together and coordinating the several parts of the book.

Finally, I'd like to thank my kind and smart wife, Delia, for her patience and understanding. Also, I am grateful to our dogs, WillDe and Ruby, who guarded the writing room from squirrels and other critters who had the effrontery to venture into their space.

Introduction

What distinguishes the web hobbyist from the professional developer is the ability to store and retrieve data from a server over the Internet. Some readers may have made that step with PHP or Perl, and for them the journey has already begun. For others, ASP.NET 3.5 is just the next step in the growth and development of ASP.NET. For them, much will be familiar and some will be very new. If the transition is from ASP.NET using Visual Basic to ASP.NET with C#, then you will find even more new, and the transition to C# is going to be easier than many imagine. Still others are making the first step into the realm of server-side programming, so just about everything about ASP.NET 3.5 and C# 3.0 is new.

For those using ASP.NET for the first time, the good news is that the transition to the server side could hardly be easier. Everything in this book is set up to learn ASP.NET 3.5 and C# 3.0 using Visual Studio 2008. Using the tools built into Visual Studio 2008, you will quickly learn that most of what needs to be done can be accomplished by dragging controls into a visual editor. And with the "code behind" method, C# is added in a separate file, so when editing code, you will see a clear separation—the C# 3.0 code comes "behind" the ASP.NET 3.5 code. For the most part, though, you need only a minimum of coding skills in either ASP.NET, which feels a lot like HTML, or C#, which has many features recognizable from JavaScript. However, make no mistake about it, C# 3.0 is a full-fledged coding language with the power of any good object-oriented programming (OOP) language. Most of the C# you need is simply working with functions and subroutines called by ASP.NET events. As a result, learning C# is quite simple, and you'll get a lot of help from Visual Studio 2008 coding tips and built-in IntelliSense. However, if you wish not to use Visual Studio 2008, all of the code for both the ASP.NET and C# is provided as well. (You can program it all using Notepad if you like!) You can find a free Express version of Visual Studio 2008 at www.microsoft.com/express/download/, and it has much of the functionality of the full-fledged version. Likewise, you will find an Express Edition of SQL Server 2005, and with them both you can learn ASP.NET 3.5 and C# 3.0 on a budget while using a powerful development tool.

The main use of ASP.NET in conjunction with C# and Structured Query Language (SQL) is to store user input in a database and get it back again. If you've ever dealt with forms in HTML, you may know how frustrating it is to build a web site with data entry that cannot be stored. In fact, without some kind of storage facility and the tools required to place the data in storage, HTML forms have very limited use. However, not only can you use plain HTML forms, ASP.NET 3.5 has some web controls that are almost identical to HTML forms except they have far more functionality. In no time, you'll be working with tables and databases to store, fetch, change, and delete a wide variety of data.

In addition to the HTML-like controls, a whole other set of web controls is available to work with data and create objects that HTML cannot. For example, if your web site needs a calendar, all you have to do with ASP.NET 3.5 is add a calendar control by dragging it from the Toolbox and into the editor. Then you can use the Calendar properties to perform other functions, like reminding you of your upcoming anniversary. (Getting that right can be worth the price of this book!)

All in all, my hope is that you will enjoy working with ASP.NET 3.5 and C# 3.0 as much as I have. Not only is it very easy to develop rich interactive web sites using ASP.NET, but in conjunction with C# 3.0, the toolset is also a very powerful one. With it, you have the best of all worlds.

Who Should Read This Book

This book is written for the developer who wants to get started using server-side programming in ASP.NET 3.5 and C# 3.0. Ideally, the reader is familiar with HTML and has a good sense of the Internet and web pages. It is meant to be a *first* book for those who are serious about crafting Rich Internet Applications (RIAs) and want to get up and running as quickly as possible.

What This Book Covers

Because ASP.NET 3.5 and C# 3.0 are very large and powerful Internet tools, no attempt was made to look into every nook and cranny of these tools. Instead, the focus of this book is to begin with the absolute minimum requirements for accomplishing different tasks and to explain how to accomplish those tasks. The content leads to the primary goal of working with server-side databases so that web sites can store information that can be retrieved by administrators or users over the Internet.

While not every possible detail of ASP.NET 3.5 is covered, the important aspects are. New features such as LINQ and Ajax each have a chapter with explanations and examples that show the reader how to get started with these powerful tools. Likewise, important features such as validation, rich data controls, use of CSS with ASP.NET, data binding, importing text files, and security are all given ample attention. So while the primary focus is on getting data into and out of a database table, the book does not skimp when it comes to important supporting features in ASP.NET 3.5.

C# was selected as the language to use in conjunction with ASP.NET 3.5 rather than Visual Basic, J#, or one of the other languages that can be used with ASP.NET 3.5. This decision is based on the quality of the C# 3.0 language, the ECMA standard it meets, and the general compatibility with other OOP languages. Showing listings in multiple languages, such as C# and Visual Basic, is confusing and makes learning more difficult.

The following outline describes the contents of the book and shows how the book is broken down into task-focused chapters.

Part I: Getting Started

Part I provides an overview for getting started creating ASP.NET 3.5 web sites using Visual Studio 2008.

Chapter 1: Introduction to ASP.NET 3.5   The first chapter introduces the reader to the differences between client-side and server-side development with ASP.NET 3.5. Its purpose is to provide a general overview of what is happening on the server when using ASP.NET 3.5 in the context of the .NET framework. It explains how data is served back to the client after server-side interpretation and how to set up an IIS7 server on your computer. Finally, it introduces you to the ASP.NET language partners.

Chapter 2: ASP.NET 3.5 Tools and Development Environment   This chapter is a thorough introduction to installing and using Visual Studio 2008 for creating ASP.NET 3.5 applications using C#. Using the code-behind method for creating a ASP.NET 3.5 web site, Visual Studio 2008 generates multiple files and folders automatically. It can also act as a mini-server to develop and test applications. In addition, this chapter shows how to develop applications using non-Visual Studio 2008 tools.

Chapter 3: C# and ASP.NET 3.5   For both experienced and inexperienced developers, this chapter shows how to get up and running with C# in an ASP.NET 3.5 context. All of the basic elements of data types, statements, naming conventions, and expressions of C# are explained and illustrated. In addition, the chapter explores and provides examples for using the basic structures, including conditional statements, loops, and arrays.

Chapter 4: Doing More with C# and ASP.NET   The relationship between ASP.NET 3.5 and C# 3.0 is largely based on events ranging from the page loading to an event generated from a web control such as a Button. This chapter explains the process of event handling and setting up web sites based on the multiple files employing the code-behind development technique. It also covers some more advanced subjects that are meant for seasoned developers and are not necessary for basic development, but will be important for developers who want to tie in their application to other applications in C#.

Part II: Forms and Controls

The heart of ASP.NET 3.5 is the set of web controls it offers to create Rich Interactive Applications.

Chapter 5: HTML Forms: A Review   To tie in the known with the unknown, this chapter is a bridge from HTML forms to using those forms for server-side execution. In addition to being a review of HTML forms, it is also an introduction to the larger framework and working relationship between ASP.NET 3.5 and C# 3.0. For many, this will be the first time that HTML form data can be used to communicate with the server and get computed results back. A key element of this chapter is to show the reader how form attributes pass data to C# variables for processing.

Chapter 6: Standard Web Controls   Web controls are compared with HTML forms and shown to be both simpler and more powerful. At this point, the reader will see that ASP.NET 3.5 web controls are similar to HTML forms except that they have more properties and events to be used in conjunction with C# 3.0 programs. In addition to forms with counterparts in HTML, several other web controls are introduced that are unique to ASP.NET 3.5, along with how each works with different triggers to launch events that are picked up and used by C#.

Chapter 7: CSS for ASP.NET 3.5 Page Formatting   This chapter covers the design aspects of ASP.NET 3.5. For styling the web controls, designers can either use the properties of the web controls or use CSS, the universal styling language. Examples using different controls illustrate and explain how to get the design you want using CSS or design properties of the controls—or combining both. For dynamic styling, the chapter shows how to make style changes using C# 3.0.

Chapter 8: Control Events and Event Handlers   This chapter expands on earlier discussions of using events and event handlers. Of primary importance, it shows how to attach events that can be generated by different controls to event-handler operations in C#. The ease with which an event handler in C# 3.0 can be generated in Visual Studio 2008 is discussed briefly, because it's so easy that no lengthy discussion is required. Lots of examples provide illustrated explanations of what can be accomplished.

Chapter 9: Validation Controls   Data used in a web site are only as good as the information that users enter. To ensure the highest quality and accuracy of data entry, this chapter shows how to validate all data that a user types into a form or some other web control. The different web controls have properties for validation. Likewise, depending on the kind of data required, from making sure that an e-mail address is correctly entered to making sure that information is within an acceptable range, the validation controls built into ASP.NET make it very easy to validate a wide range of data.

Chapter 10: Rich Data Controls   ASP.NET 3.5 has a number of rich data controls that make the complex simple. Two key controls, the Calendar and AdRotator, show how easy it is for even a nonprogrammer to add sophisticated controls to a web site. In addition, a short XML tutorial shows how to add XML data to the controls.

Part III: ASP.NET and Databases
The big payoff for using a server-side application is its ability to communicate with a database table. This part looks at the different tools for working with databases using ASP.NET 3.5 and C#.

Chapter 11: A SQL Primer   This chapter shows how to use Structured Query Language (SQL), pronounced "sequel." Unlike some languages, SQL is very simple and is used to communicate with a database. As with everything else in Visual Studio 2008, the task is even easier because you can automatically generate SQL commands by selecting different queries simply by selecting them from a built-in tool. In this, not only is it easier to learn

the correct format for SQL queries, it is also easier to visualize what happens when a SQL query is made. Of course, you will learn the code for SQL commands so that you can write your own in any web development tool or text editor if you so choose.

Chapter 12: ADO.NET: Hello Database   In this chapter much of what has passed comes together in the process of creating a database and table and storing information in that database. With Visual Studio 2008 the process is very simple at all levels—connecting to a database, creating tables, storing data in the tables, retrieving data from the tables, and displaying the stored information. C# 3.0 uses the SQL commands learned in Chapter 11 to communicate with the database and server to deliver data entered anywhere in the world and to display it anywhere in the world.

Chapter 13: Data Binding   A crucial step in displaying data is to do so in a clear and coherent way. Data binding allows you to easily bind the data from the database table to an ASP.NET 3.5 web control. This chapter shows how to use many different options so that the data that have been carefully collected and stored are made available to the viewer with style, clarity, and consistency.

Chapter 14: LINQ   This chapter introduces a brand-new ASP.NET 3.5 technology—Language Integrated Query (LINQ). LINQ helps to ease and codify SQL commands into a language that C# can more easily handle and add functionality to. While the chapter only scratches the surface of a very deep well of functionality that is LINQ, it provides the basics for getting started with and using LINQ in web sites.

Chapter 15: Files   One of the often overlooked features of ASP.NET 3.5 and C# 3.0 is the ability to use plain text files placed on a web server. Without use of a database, information can be stored and easily retrieved. What's more, a simple text editor like Microsoft Notepad or Apple's TextEdit can be used to update the data that can be displayed. This is especially useful for clients who want to regularly update their sites but who do not program. In addition, ASP.NET 3.5 web controls can be used to enter and write data; so even knowledge of using a text editor is not required by the client. Finally, this chapter shows how to display files and directories on a remote server.

Chapter 16: Security   Very few web sites that gather and store information can afford not to have some kind of security. Fortunately, ASP.NET makes it very easy to create strong encryption that allows those who should have access to data to get them, and to keep out those who should not have access. The login and registration process is easy to create with the tools available in ASP.NET. Using both the web.config file and built-in ASP.NET 3.5 web controls, you can build web sites with maximum security and easy access.

Chapter 17: ASP.NET Ajax   One of the most-welcomed features of ASP.NET 3.5 is Ajax functionality. This chapter goes through the process of setting up Ajax in a web site so that the page has Ajax functionality that loads external materials—such as graphics and text—but does so without reloading the entire page. The result is a seamless update of everything from data to slideshows made up of web graphic files. For the developer who knows nothing about Ajax, the process is simply a matter of adding a couple of controls.

Part I

Getting Started

Chapter 1

Introduction to ASP.NET 3.5

Key Skills & Concepts

- Moving from client-side to server-side computing

- Understanding thin client

- Understanding stateless HTTP

- How ASP.NET 3.5 is an alternative to HTTP and CGI

- How server-side applications work with your browser

- Understanding the organization of the Microsoft .NET framework

- How to set up your computer or LAN to run ASP.NET applications

- The advantages of an ASP.NET hosting service

- What languages can be run with ASP.NET

In getting started with ASP.NET, you're entering the world of server-side programming. If you're familiar with languages like PHP or Perl, you already have some idea of what can be done with server-side processing. However, if you're beginning your journey to the server side of Internet computing, this book will show you just how powerful and enjoyable it can be. This book begins by assuming that you know HTML. You will find that ASP.NET has a lot in common with HTML. The core of the ASP.NET framework can be thought of as simply an extension of basic HTML form processing. The rest of the framework provides much richer functionality, which we'll get into later in this book. It is important as a newcomer to ASP.NET that you have a basic understanding of HTML form processing. For that reason this journey begins with HTML.

HTML Forms to Nowhere

In many respects the HTML tags available to create data input are a confusing and frustrating exercise in futility. Users can enter information for everything from responses to a questionnaire to an order for a product. Using a handy submit button, also available in HTML, you can then send the information to absolutely *nowhere*.

Try This   HTML Data Entry with No Exit

Open your favorite text editor, Notepad will suffice, and paste the following HTML code. Save the document as **nowhere.html**. Next, open the HTML file in your browser of choice. The following HTML code will set up a perfectly clear HTML form that sends information into the ether:

```
<!DOCTYPE html PUBLIC "-//W3C//DTD XHTML 1.0 Strict//EN"
"http://www.w3.org/TR/xhtml1/DTD/xhtml1-strict.dtd">
<html xmlns="http://www.w3.org/1999/xhtml">
<head>
<meta http-equiv="Content-Type" content="text/html; charset=ISO-8859-1" />
<title>HTML to Nowhere</title>
</head>
<body>
<form>
        Please enter your name:<br/>
        <input type="text" name="username"/>
         <p/>
         Press the button to receive all of your hopes and dreams:<br/>
         <input type="submit" value="Dream Button" />
</form>
</body>
</html>
```

When you test the code after you enter your name and click the Dream Button (a thinly disguised submit button), your output will look just like Figure 1-1.

Without some kind of mechanism to capture and store the information or pass it on to somewhere else, all you have is an HTML white elephant. What ASP.NET 3.5 offers is a way to store, retrieve, and process the information. Other than storing cookies on the visitor's computer, you can't do too much with HTML when it comes to controlling the state of your data.

Your Browser Is a Thin Client

Your browser's main job is requesting pages from the server and displaying what the server has processed. Using HTTP as a transfer protocol, your browser parses (interprets) the HTML code it gets from the server, but otherwise does little processing. Because your HTTP client (browser) leaves most of the processing work to the server, it is considered a *thin client*. There's nothing wrong with a thin client, and it can process JavaScript. With plug-ins, which virtually all browsers have built in, a thin client can also process certain

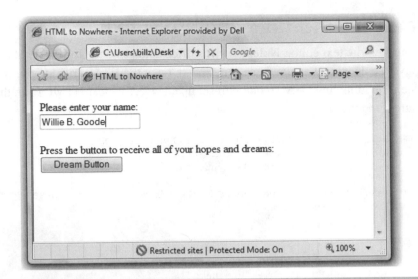

Figure 1-1 HTML data entry and submit form

kinds of files such as SWF (compiled Adobe Flash files), Java Applets, ActiveX Controls, as well as other files requiring that the browser have compatible plug-ins. For the most part, though, the thin client model is one where the server does the processing, and your browser's job is to display the contents it gets from the server.

A Protocol Without a Country: Stateless HTTP

In addition to being a thin client, your HTTP client browser is *stateless*. As soon as a web page reaches your computer, the connection between your browser and the server is broken. The browser does not remember the last page—it does not hold *state*. As soon as the next page arrives, it does not remember the last page.

You may be thinking that your cache holds lots of previous pages and that your browser's history feature remembers previous pages. That's not what *retaining state* means. You cannot use the data and information in your cache or the browser's history as states to use with the current page in memory. What is in *active memory* is the web page that the server has sent; the state of the previous page is not there. As soon as you load a page, the previous page is kicked out, and the new page is placed there. Just as the information you place in a text input box is sent to silicon oblivion when you click the Submit button, knowledge of the previous page (its *state*) is gone when the new page arrives. A well-organized web site may appear to maintain state as the links on pages connect to a set of related pages, but that is an illusion that the web designer has crafted by good planning.

Ask the Expert

Q: It seems that the term state **is used in different ways in programming. I've heard of everything from "State Machines" to "State Design Patterns." What is a simple explanation of** state?

A: An object's *state* refers to a condition of the object. For example, a Boolean can have two states—`true` or `false`. When you enter information into an input form, the information you enter reflects the current state of that form. To save that state, you have to put it somewhere that will hold that state until you need it. One place you can put state data is in a variable, and it can hold it for you temporarily. For permanent storage of a state, you can use a database or some other file you can store on a hard drive.

Cookies do maintain state in a sense. These are little text files stored on the client computer, and they can be read and used. However, these cookies only hold the Session ID, but typically the actual session data are stored on the server. So, while cookies can be used in very creative ways to emulate a state, they contain little information and are at the mercy of the user who can remove them whenever desired. Figure 1-2 shows the general model that developers use when creating standard web applications.

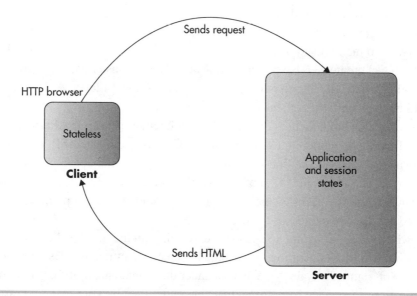

Figure 1-2   Client and server roles

Those who are more experienced with HTML may be aware of these limitations in working in an environment where you can do little more than present static elements in a stateless environment. The ASP.NET environment lets you move from a stateless HTTP environment to a state-preserved one.

ASP.NET 3.5 as an Alternative to CGI

Microsoft's alternative to a Common Gateway Interface (CGI) is ASP.NET, now in version 3.5. As a unified web platform, ASP.NET provides what you need to develop applications that hold state and use the information that you put into the HTML form. Instead of sending form information into a vacuum when you click a submit button, your data goes where it can be stored temporarily or permanently. Usually, when we think of saving state, we imagine writing the data to a storage device like a hard drive. Using a word processor, every time you save your file, you save its state. Using ASP.NET, you can do the same thing with information from *anyone* who uses your web application. This allows you to build applications where the information entered can be stored for use with either the next HTTP request or with a whole set of data entered by users all over the world—that's quite a feat compared with saving state in your word processor file. ASP.NET's state-management facilities provide you with the tools that you need to *control* state. You do not necessarily want to save all states of a web page, but you certainly want to save the state of data entered by users and perhaps the URL of a page. Having state management allows you to do this.

Microsoft's web server, Internet Information Services (IIS), uses the Internet Server API (ISAPI) to make function calls instead of using CGI scripts. By using ISAPI, developers can create web-based applications that execute faster and have greater extensibility than CGI, among other advantages. At the lowest level, ASP.NET interfaces with IIS through an ISAPI extension.

However, this book focuses on the high-level interaction with ISAPI in the form of ASP.NET and code written in C# (pronounced "C sharp") that use ASP.NET. So rather than having to deal with the fine-grained, low-level communications, ASP.NET allows you to write your scripts in C#. Another way of looking at ASP.NET is as a request-processing engine that takes incoming requests and sends them to a point where you can attach your C# script to process the request.

So while we are not going to spend time dwelling on the low-level operations, you can rest assured that those operations are handled in an efficient manner. Using *managed code,* the Microsoft name for code that executes under the management of the .NET framework, an application is executed by a virtual machine rather than by your own processor. Both C# and Visual Basic.NET (VB.NET) are languages for creating managed code that is efficiently run in the .NET environment.

From Client Side to Server Side

As you saw in Figure 1-2, all that the web browser does is make requests to the server and receive web pages in the form of HTML. The browser takes the HTML and constructs a page for viewing on your browser. For the most part, that's what will continue to occur when you adopt ASP.NET. The main difference is that by writing and executing server-side code, you can generate HTML that effectively handles dynamic states so that you can use and reuse a given state. Figure 1-3 shows the general flow when an ASPX file on a Microsoft server receives a call from the client.

In looking for an example, we need look no further than the original example of the HTML page with the form. With a server-side program to *catch* the data that is sent to the server, lots of processes on the server are possible. Suppose the user enters the name, *Willie B. Goode.* The server-side file can use the property name, username, to extract a value. In this case, it would extract the name Willie B. Goode and do something with it. It might run a SQL script to store the name in a database, compare it with a password, or it could pass information about Willie B. Goode back to the browser in HTML.

To get an idea of the differences and similarities between HTML and ASP.NET, we can take the HTML form and add a calculated response from the server. In this next example, you will see two scripts. One is the ASP.NET script and the other is the C# code using a *code behind* file to serve as the event engine for the application. The form tag includes a name and the code

```
runat="server"
```

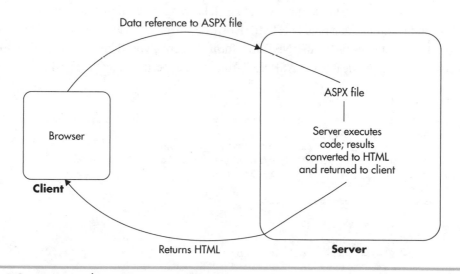

Figure 1-3   Server-side script

This little code line means that everything will be taken care of by the server. So, unlike the HTML file that does all of the work in the client (browser), the processing is done on the server and returned to the client as HTML. However, the server can do a lot more, including sending and retrieving data from a database. While getting HTML from the server is nothing new, what's new is the fact that the HTML being returned originated in the browser and is generated by files executed on the server that you wrote.

The example we'll look at is saved in an ASP.NET file named Dreamer.aspx. In the Dreamer.aspx file, the `<form>` container includes an input text window just like the HTML file-to-nowhere file, with only a slightly different format:

```
<asp:TextBox...
```

instead of

```
<input type ="text"...
```

Likewise, the `<form>` container has a button using the script

```
<asp:Button...
```

rather than

```
<input type ="submit"...
```

found in HTML. For the time being don't worry about the headers and the `using System` statements. We'll get to that in Chapter 3 when discussing C#. Here, look at the ASP.NET forms elements—the text box, button, and label, keeping in mind that they are analogous to the text and submit button tags in HTML. However, there's no label. Once you begin seeing that a lot of what goes on in ASP.NET uses form elements, you'll be able to see that you already know a good deal about ASP.NET from your experiences with HTML.

Dreamer.aspx

```
<%@ Page Language="C#" AutoEventWireup="true" CodeFile="Dreamer.aspx.cs"
Inherits="_Dreamer" %>
<!DOCTYPE html PUBLIC "-//W3C//DTD XHTML 1.0 Transitional//EN"
"http://www.w3.org/TR/xhtml1/DTD/xhtml1-transitional.dtd">
<html xmlns="http://www.w3.org/1999/xhtml">
<head runat="server">
<title>Server Side Dreamer</title>
</head>
<body>
<form id="form1" runat="server">
      <div> Please enter your name:<br />
            <asp:TextBox ID="DreamBox"
```

```
                     runat="server"> </asp:TextBox>
            <p />
            Press the button to receive all of your hopes and dreams:<br />
            <asp:Button ID="Dreamer"
              runat="server"
              Text="Dream Button"
              OnClick="DoDream" />
            <p />
            <asp:Label ID="Dreams" runat="server"
    Text="Dreams Here"></asp:Label>
            </div>
    </form>
    </body>
    </html>
```

Along with the ASP.NET code, the C# code is generated in a separate CS file known as *code behind*. As you will see, the C# code is primarily used to trigger events that launch an ASP.NET script. The following C# code largely has been generated by Visual Studio 2008, and the only line that the developer needs to add is a statement telling the application to take the input from the asp:TextBox and put it into the asp:Label. The code also deletes the default launch event of Page_Load that launches any actions as soon as the page is loaded. This script waits until the user clicks the button to launch the action that adds content to the asp:Label form.

Dreamer.aspx.cs

```csharp
using System;
using System.Data;
using System.Configuration;
using System.Linq;
using System.Web;
using System.Web.Security;
using System.Web.UI;
using System.Web.UI.WebControls;
using System.Web.UI.WebControls.WebParts;
using System.Web.UI.HtmlControls;
using System.Xml.Linq;

public partial class _Dreamer : System.Web.UI.Page
{
    protected void DoDream(object sender, EventArgs e)
    {
        Dreams.Text = DreamBox.Text + "'s dreams are big ones!";
    }
}
```

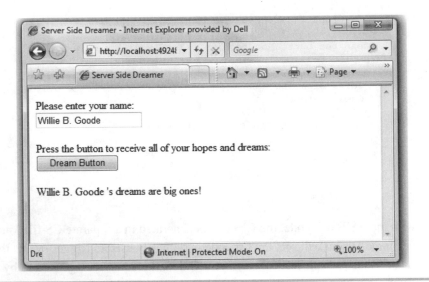

Figure 1-4 Server-side operations can do more.

If that code looks daunting, it is only because of all of the `using System` statements. However, if you keep in mind that all of those were automatically generated in Visual Studios 2008, you're really only looking at just a few lines of code. Figure 1-4 shows what you can expect to see once you enter a name and click the Dream Button.

At this point, don't expect to understand how ASP.NET or C# works. As you delve deeper, you'll understand more, but the primary goal is to show how to accomplish tasks using ASP.NET. As with driving a car, you may know little about how the internal combustion engine or hydraulics work; however, you just want to get to your destination. In the case of ASP.NET, that means creating useful applications.

.NET Organization

Probably the best way to think of .NET is as a big control system with two key elements. First is the .NET framework class library. This library has thousands of classes organized into *namespaces*. This large set of classes was designed to provide all the class support for virtually any application a developer would want to create. This library is a repository of reusable types for object-oriented development. For example, System.Web.UI Namespace allows you to create several different ASP.NET server controls and user interfaces. A *namespace* can be understood as an organizing concept for classes. Each namespace contains a collection of classes, most of which you do not need for any single application.

The following represent a *few* of the classes in this namespace:

- Control
- Data Binder
- PageParser
- UserControl

To use the classes as well as other structures such as interfaces, you need to include the namespace in your program.

Second, and at the core of .NET, is the *common language runtime.* The runtime is a management agent for code as it executes. All of the services, such as memory and thread management and remoting, are handled by the .NET framework. For example, VB.NET (Visual Basic) has access to the same family of classes as does C#. It is designed to aid in strict type safety and other structures that secure both robustness and security. Microsoft refers to code that targets the common language runtime as *managed code* and refers to code that does not target the runtime as *unmanaged code.* Figure 1-5 illustrates managed code running in different environments.

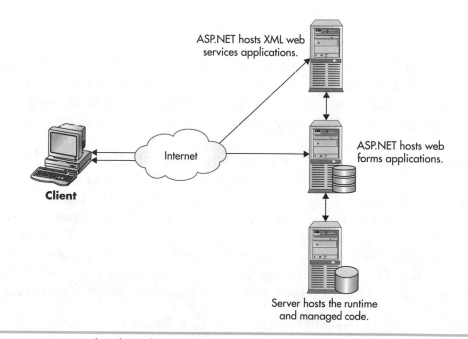

ASP.NET hosts XML web services applications.

Internet

Client

ASP.NET hosts web forms applications.

Server hosts the runtime and managed code.

Figure 1-5 Managed code in the servers

ASP.NET is one of the main frameworks provided by the .NET framework. The same ASP.NET forms that are integrated into a VB.NET program can be developed with J#, JScript.NET, or C#. All are processed using the .NET framework. So once you learn how to develop applications in one language, such as C#, you will find development in the other languages very simple and similar.

Development Contexts

If you've never developed server-side applications, the process may appear daunting, but it's really not. You can develop in a simple HTML environment, adding both C# scripts and ASP.NET forms. In the Dreamer.aspx example, we could have developed the C# script within the same context as the HTML code and ASP.NET forms. For example, the following code in the HTML page would do the same thing as the Dreamer.aspx.cs file:

```
<%@ Page Language="C#" AutoEventWireup="true" %>
<!DOCTYPE html PUBLIC "-//W3C//DTD XHTML 1.0 Transitional//EN"
"http://www.w3.org/TR/xhtml1/DTD/xhtml1-transitional.dtd">
<script runat="server" language="C#">
protected void DoDream(object sender, EventArgs e)
    {
        Dreams.Text = DreamBox.Text + "'s dreams are big!";
    }
</script>
…rest of ASP.NET page
```

To make it easier to learn, however, this book will use the code generated when you use Visual Studio 2008 as a development tool. If you prefer to use another tool, feel free to do so. In the next chapter, you will see how to use Visual Studio 2008 and to provide code by use of alternative tools—including tools as simple as Microsoft's Notepad.

Running ASP.NET Files on Your Computer or LAN

When you save a file as an ASPX file, you can save the C# right in the file with the ASP.NET forms using the `<script>` tags, or you can use the code-behind method described earlier. This does not mean that you can just place ASPX files and the code behind C# files on a web server and everything will work. You need to place your files on the right kind of hosting service running IIS7, which can be your very own computer.

You can do this on your own computer where you have Visual Studio 2008 set up, so you're not faced with an "either/or" alternative. You can have the best of both worlds.

Installing and Using an IIS7 Server on Your System

If you want to work with a more realistic environment with the files you create either with Visual Studio 2008 or some other tool, you can set up a working ASP.NET system right on

Ask the Expert

Q: Why are ASP.NET and C# developed in separate windows if they are part of the same program? Aren't most programs developed in a single file?

A: ASP.NET is a set of forms and controls, while C# is a dynamic language that communicates not only with ASP.NET but also with databases and outside links. Think of the separation as you would an automobile. The car without the engine focuses on the arrangement of seats and the different controls that make a car ready to be used for transportation. That is the ASP.NET aspect of the code behind. The car's engine is what makes it go. It is a different element than the car's body and takes a different kind of thinking to work on it. Nevertheless, the engine interacts with the car body and responds to its controls. C# is like the engine, and by keeping it separate during development, you can clearly focus on what you want it to do.

your own computer and use it on your LAN. Depending on the version of Windows Vista that you have, you may or may not have IIS7 available to you, and if you do not, you can upgrade your version of Windows Vista. The following steps show how to do this:

1. Go to Start | Control Panel.

2. In the Control Panel select Programs.

3. When the Programs window appears, under Programs And Features select Turn Windows Features On Or Off. A User Account Control window appears. (These steps are slightly different on Windows Vista Ultimate.)

4. Click the Continue button. You will see a "please wait" notice. Wait until you see the check boxes and their folders as shown in Figure 1-6.

5. Expand Internet Information Services | World Wide Web Services | Application Development Features. Check the .NET Extensibility, ASP.NET, ISAPI Extensions, and ISAPI Filters boxes as shown in Figure 1-7.

6. Once you've checked all of the options indicated, click the OK button. You'll have to wait while all of the changes are made to your system.

7. To make sure it is installed correctly, open your browser (Internet Explorer, Firefox, or any current browser will work fine). Type **http://localhost/** in the URL window on your browser. Figure 1-8 shows what you will see if the IIS7 installation worked successfully.

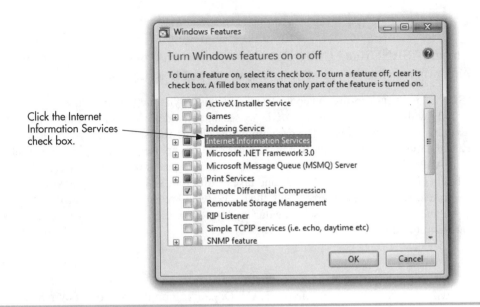

Click the Internet Information Services check box.

Figure 1-6 Selecting the Internet Information Services option

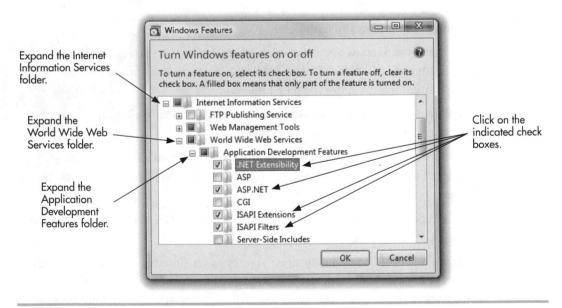

Expand the Internet Information Services folder.

Expand the World Wide Web Services folder.

Expand the Application Development Features folder.

Click on the indicated check boxes.

Figure 1-7 .NET, ASP.NET, and ISAPI options selected

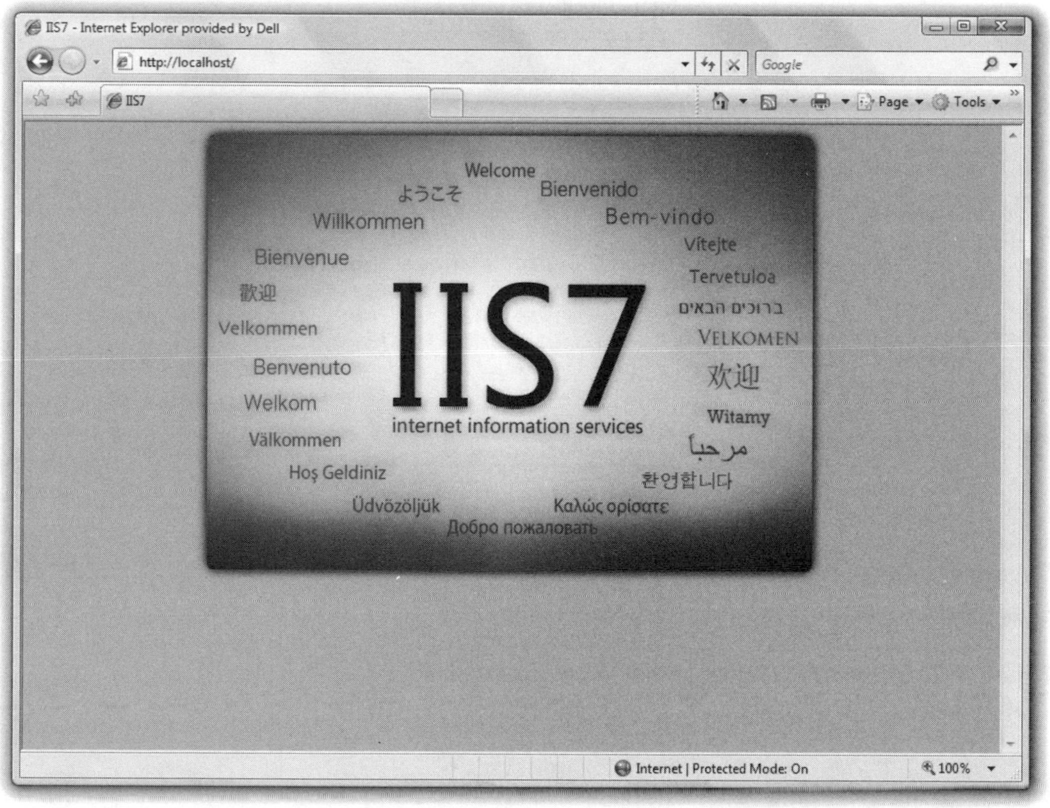

Figure 1-8   Welcome page for IIS7

8. After activation, you will find some important new folders. Click your Start icon in the lower-left corner of your screen. Select Computer I OS (C:) and find the inetpub folder. Open the inetpub folder and then find the wwwroot folder. The wwwroot folder is where you place your ASP.NET applications as shown in Figure 1-9. The Dreamer folder contains ASPX and CS application files. You can place the application files directly in the wwwroot folder, but with other supporting files and folders used for the application, things will get messy and confused very quickly if you do. It's best to place each application in a separate folder in the wwwroot folder.

This is the directory where you
place your application folders.

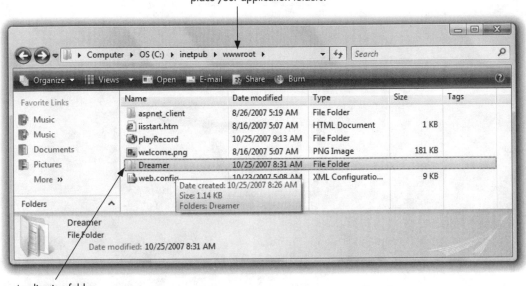

Application folder

Figure 1-9 Application folder in the ASP.NET root directory

Using Visual Studio 2008, each web application generates an application folder, an ASPX file, a C# (CS) file, a web.config file, and an App_Data folder. Place the web.config XML file in the root directory if you do not have one there. If you leave it in the application folder, you will be unable to run your application over the Internet, including on a LAN. Figure 1-10 shows the contents of a typical application folder. The web.config file was removed and placed in the wwwroot folder.

When you run an ASP.NET application from your computer-turned-into-an-ASP.NET server, you will be able to see a good deal about the way ASP.NET works. Using a simple ASP.NET application that displays the users' IP address, the application was run from different environments in a LAN composed of three computers with Microsoft Windows Vista, Microsoft Windows XP, and a Macintosh OS X. The Vista computer contained Visual Studio 2008 and acted as a web server with ASP.NET available. First, Figure 1-11 shows what you can expect to see when you test the application in Visual Studio 2008.

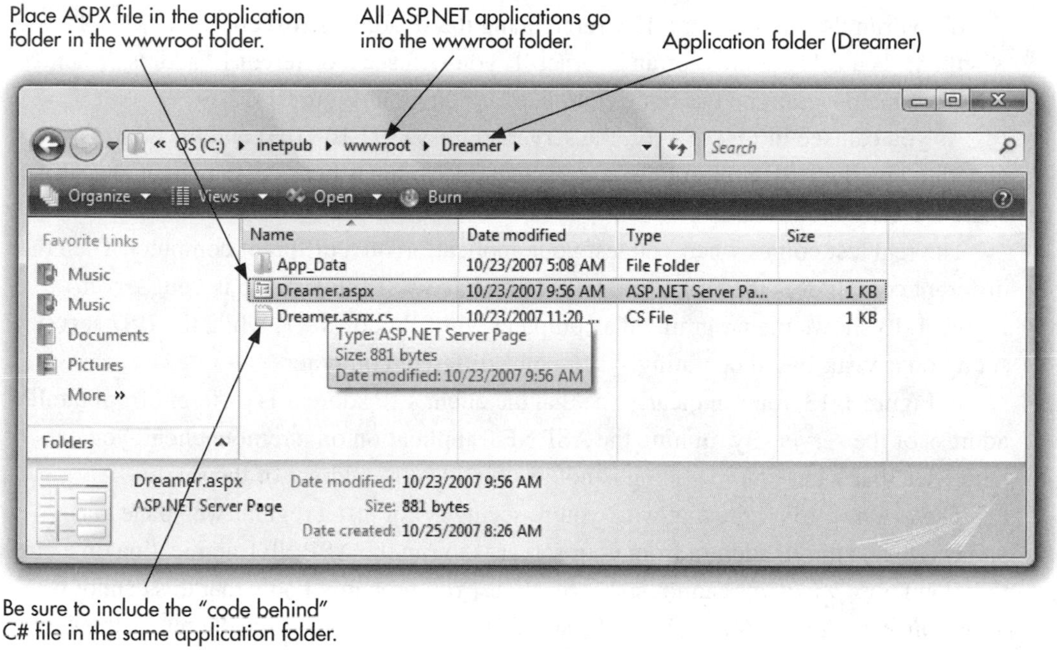

Place ASPX file in the application folder in the wwwroot folder.

All ASP.NET applications go into the wwwroot folder.

Application folder (Dreamer)

Be sure to include the "code behind" C# file in the same application folder.

Figure 1-10   Both ASP.NET and C# files are in the application folder.

Address automatically called when CTRL-F5 is pressed in Visual Studio

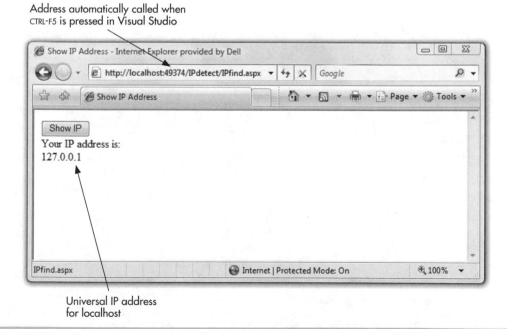

Universal IP address for localhost

Figure 1-11   Local IP address

If you run the same program by referencing the IP address (except for 127.0.0.1), whether it is a LAN address or an Internet IP, you will see a different IP address when you run the same program on the same computer, as shown in Figure 1-12.

As you can see in Figure 1-12, the server address (192.168.0.3) and the address generated by the ASP.NET application are identical. This is because the client and server share the same IP address.

The real test comes when you test your application on a different computer. Then the different computer is the client, and where you have ASP.NET set up is your server. Figure 1-13 shows the program on a computer with Windows XP, while the IIS7 server is set up on a Vista-based operating system on a different computer.

In Figure 1-13 you can clearly see that the client's IP address is different from the IP address of the server. By running the ASP.NET application on a remote client, you can better see that what you're getting is not just the local IP address of the server.

The acid test to ensure that what you're seeing is not just a regular web page that somehow gets the IP address from your server is to run the ASP.NET application on a client that you know *positively* cannot host ASP.NET. (You probably know that this cannot be accomplished with HTML or XHTML alone.) Fortunately, one of the clients on the LAN is a Macintosh, and if we call the .aspx file up on a Mac, we know that the only way to see that Mac's IP address is if we're dealing with a true server-side application. Figure 1-14 shows what you will see in a Safari browser on a Macintosh.

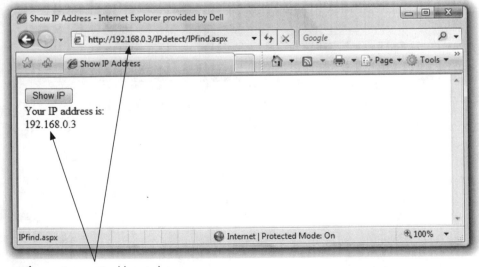

Reference to own IP address in browser

Figure 1-12   Addressing LAN IP address

LAN (IP) address of server

LAN (IP) address of client

Figure 1-13   Remote client on Windows XP

Figure 1-14 shows beyond any doubt that what's doing all of the work is the server-side ASP.NET combined with a C# program generated on the remote server. Does this mean that you can develop applications on a Mac just as on your Windows PC? Not exactly. You can write your C# and ASP.NET applications on a Mac using a simple text editor or something more sophisticated like Dreamweaver. Then by transferring the code to an ASP.NET host, you can see the same thing as you do in Figure 1-14. However, you cannot host the code on a Mac because ASP.NET cannot be set up on a Mac. Still, as you will see in the next section, you can work with any kind of system you want if you have an ASP.NET hosting service.

Server address on LAN

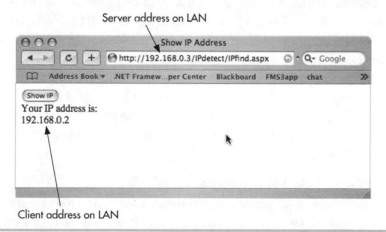

Client address on LAN

Figure 1-14   Macintosh browser showing results from processing on Windows Vista ASP.NET system

ASP.NET in the Real World

One of the best options available is to develop your applications using either Visual Studio 2008 or your favorite web development tool, and to place the applications on a production server. A *production server* is one where you place your applications for actual use on the Internet. Several hosting companies provide ASP.NET 3.5 along with the necessary server software you need to run ASP.NET files. Discount ASP.NET has an offer that provides a 50 percent discount for a one-year contract. Within the first 30 days, if you decide you do not want the service you can get a full refund. After you're comfortable with developing some applications using either Visual Studio 2008 or on your own system with IIS7, you might want to give Discount ASP.NET a try to see what development on a hosting service is like.

The advantage of using a production hosting service is that your application can be tested in the same environment in which you will eventually be placing the completed files. Using a LAN is a close equivalent, and if you have multiple computers, it's the best alternative to a hosting service. However, with big databases and other space-consuming elements, you can't beat a hosting service. So while Visual Studio 2008 is the recommended development environment, the ultimate testing environment is a production server.

Language Partners with ASP.NET

Examples for this book are written in C# because Microsoft recommends it. Also, C# is an ECMA 334 standard language. That means the syntax is similar to other ECMAScript languages such as ActionScript 3.0, and if you understand one of the other ECMAScript languages, learning others is far easier. So even though ActionScript 3.0 is developed along the lines of ECMA 262 standards, it has far more in common with C# than with earlier versions of ActionScript. Likewise, JavaScript 2.0 will be developed as an ECMAScript language, and picking up JavaScript 2.0 when it becomes available should prove to be less of a challenge if you already know C#.

Readers who are familiar with C, C++, or Java will find C# very similar as well. So using C# not only will help you latch onto an Internet language standard (ECMAScript), but it will also help you learn something about other languages on which ECMAScript is based. If you see a program written in Java, for example, you'll find many structures that you recognize from C#.

VB.NET—Not Quite VB Anymore

If you are comfortable with Visual Basic, you may want to develop in that language. Using Visual Studio 2008, you can select the option to use VB.NET. However, the Visual Basic of yore is not much like VB.NET, and you may not be saving as much time and as many brain cells as you might think by sticking with a language you know. Further, C# is used lightly with ASP.NET, so it might be a good time to learn C# with ASP.NET while you can get it in small doses.

J# and JScript.NET—Still Feels Like a Scripting Language

If you're familiar with JavaScript but know nothing about either Visual Basic or C#, you might want to try using either J# or JScript.NET. Both have the feel of JavaScript but are different from each other. However, unless you have a good reason to do so, such as working in an environment where J# or JScript.NET is used, C# is recommended. First, you will find many similarities between these languages and C#, so it's not a big leap. Also, as with VB.NET, if you learn using C# with ASP.NET, you'll be getting it in light doses.

Chapter 2

ASP.NET 3.5 Tools and Development Environment

Key Skills & Concepts

- Using tools to aid in creating ASP.NET applications

- Understanding Visual Studio 2008

- Installing Visual Studio 2008

- Creating ASP.NET 3.5 applications

- Testing applications

- Using other web development tools

- Entering code in text editors

At some level in coding, just about everything can be done with a simple text editor. Using a text editor to write code gives you an enormous amount of flexibility and a deeper understanding of what your program is doing. In working with ASP.NET 3.5, the same is true, but creating ASP.NET applications with Notepad or TextEdit will put the learning curve pretty high. As you saw in Chapter 1, an ASP.NET program is actually a combination of ASP.NET coding and C#. So, keeping track of things with a text editor is a little tricky. In this chapter you'll be learning about a wonderfully powerful tool that will not only aid in your learning all about building applications, but also will help your learning about the code in the files you will be building.

Visual Studio 2008

The sheer size of ASP.NET 3.5 is such that you need a powerful tool that can provide access to the over 7,000 classes that now make up ASP.NET. As you know from Chapter 1, the classes are organized into namespaces, but with so many classes that finding each in the right namespace is a daunting endeavor. To make life simple, Microsoft has devised a tool as powerful as the language itself in Visual Studio 2008. If you are familiar with earlier versions of Visual Studio, you'll probably find this latest version familiar. However, be sure you're using Visual Studio 2008 for creating all of the different applications you will find in this book. Visual Studio 2008 includes many new properties and classes that are not available in Visual Studio 2005 or earlier versions. All examples in this book have been developed using Visual Studio 2008, and while they can be duplicated using either a simple text editor or other web development tool such as Dreamweaver, you will find the development process far more tedious and prone to bugs. Likewise, you may be able to develop a good many of the simpler applications using Visual Studio 2005, but I would not recommend it, because sooner or later you will encounter new features that are not available in Visual Studio 2005. The best alternative to using the full version of Visual Studio 2008 is to use the Express edition. While Express Visual Studio 2008 does not have all the functionality of the full version, you will be able to follow this book and create the examples.

Installing Visual Studio 2008

Before installing Visual Studio 2008, I would recommend installing IIS7 web server as described in Chapter 1. You can simulate running ASP.NET 3.5 applications with Visual Studio 2008, but with IIS7 set up, you can actually run ASP.NET applications in a web environment using server-side compilation and a more realistic testing environment. However, that is strictly optional. Installing Visual Studio 2008 is straightforward and simple. Before beginning the installation process, check available space on your hard drive to make sure that you have enough room. Defragment your hard drive as well before installing Visual Studio 2008. The software will take up several gigabytes of hard drive, and you don't want to be 90 percent through the installation process only to find that you have insufficient space on your computer. Click the install icon, whether you have downloaded Visual Studio 2008 from Microsoft or have received it on a CD-ROM. Be patient; installation takes a long time.

The Visual Studio 2008 Environment

Once you've got Visual Studio installed and begin using it, you will find many different options. The main option you want to be aware of is the C# development one. You will find other languages available for use with ASP.NET as discussed in Chapter 1. All example applications will be done with code connected to a C# script. It is not difficult to keep your applications in the C# ASP.NET environment, but if things are not looking the same in your application as those in the book, it may be due to having accidentally set Visual Studio 2008 for VB.NET or for some other program language that works with ASP.NET.

While writing code is pretty straightforward, you will find that Visual Studio 2008 gives you a lot of help in getting it right. As you begin entering code, different context menus will pop up and help you complete the line of code or segment. Microsoft calls this feature *IntelliSense,* and for learning all of the different features of both ASP.NET and C#, you'll find these menus invaluable. As noted, ASP.NET has over 7,000 classes, and those classes have properties—some have events and methods. The IntelliSense menus will drill-down several different layers and provide help as you develop your applications, and if you're not used to context menus popping up unbidden, you may find these a bit annoying with the simple examples. However, as you go further, you will see that they are sorely needed.

As with most endeavors that require learning something new, the best way is to jump in and actually do something once you have the basics completed. In the next section, you will be jumping in and writing and testing a simple ASP.NET application using C# as the firing mechanism. As you go through the steps, the features are described for you, and you'll see that using Visual Studio 2008 is easy and helpful.

Creating a Simple ASP.NET Application

The kick-off application using Visual Studio 2008 is similar to the "Hello World" examples found in just about every other language. The application will use an ASP.NET form (Label), and the C# code will place the text value of the Label form on the screen when the page opens. So, without further ado, select Start | Microsoft Visual Studio 2008 and launch it.

When you open Visual Studio 2008 for the first time, you will see the latest news from MSDN and Recent Projects. Later, as you configure your Visual Studio 2008 to the way you like it, it will launch with the settings you last used. Figure 2-1 shows a typical setup

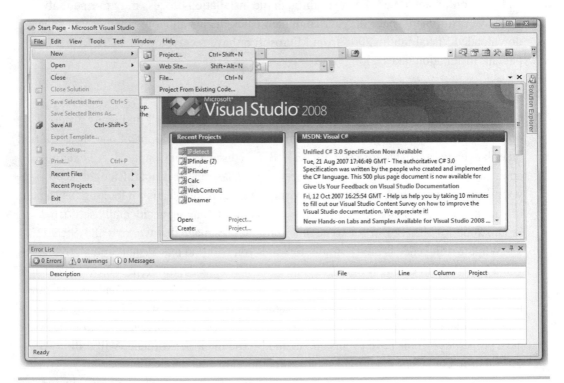

Figure 2-1 Visual Studio Start page and File menu

for Visual Studio 2008. At the bottom, you can see the Error List window, and along the (upper) right edge of the Visual Studio 2008 window, you can see the docked and closed Solution Explorer. All of the settings for viewing different tools and windows are found in the View menu.

The best way to get started with ASP.NET is to create a little application that does something. The following steps walk you through creating an application and at the same time point out a number of tools you can use. Before starting, though, you need to understand that creating an ASP.NET application is a little different from creating a C# application. In the File | New submenu, you will see four choices:

- Project
- Web Site
- File
- Project From Existing Code

For the great bulk of this book, you will be selecting Web Site and saving an ASPX file that works with the CS file you will be creating simultaneously. Figure 2-1 shows all of the menus and submenus selected and opened. Given that information, let's get started:

1. Open Visual Studio 2008 and select File | New | Web Site. Look at Figure 2-1 to make sure that you are making the right selections. It will be a little different depending on any configuration you have made on Visual Studio 2008.

2. After you have made your selection in Step 1, you should see the New Web Site menu as shown in Figure 2-2. The Visual Studio–installed templates should show the ASP.NET Web Site is selected. In the Language pop-up menu, select Visual C#. (Note that the pop-up menu item in the upper-right corner is .NET Framework 3.5. If it is something other than that, open the menu and select .NET Framework 3.5.)

3. Either type in the path where you want to store your application, or click the Browse button and select the location for your file. Using Visual Studio 2008, you can put your files anywhere, but you will definitely want to organize them in some way so that they can easily be retrieved. The storage path in Figure 2-2 shows that the files will be stored on the Desktop in a folder named ASP.NET Book in subfolders ch02 and FirstApp. Once you have your storage path entered, click OK.

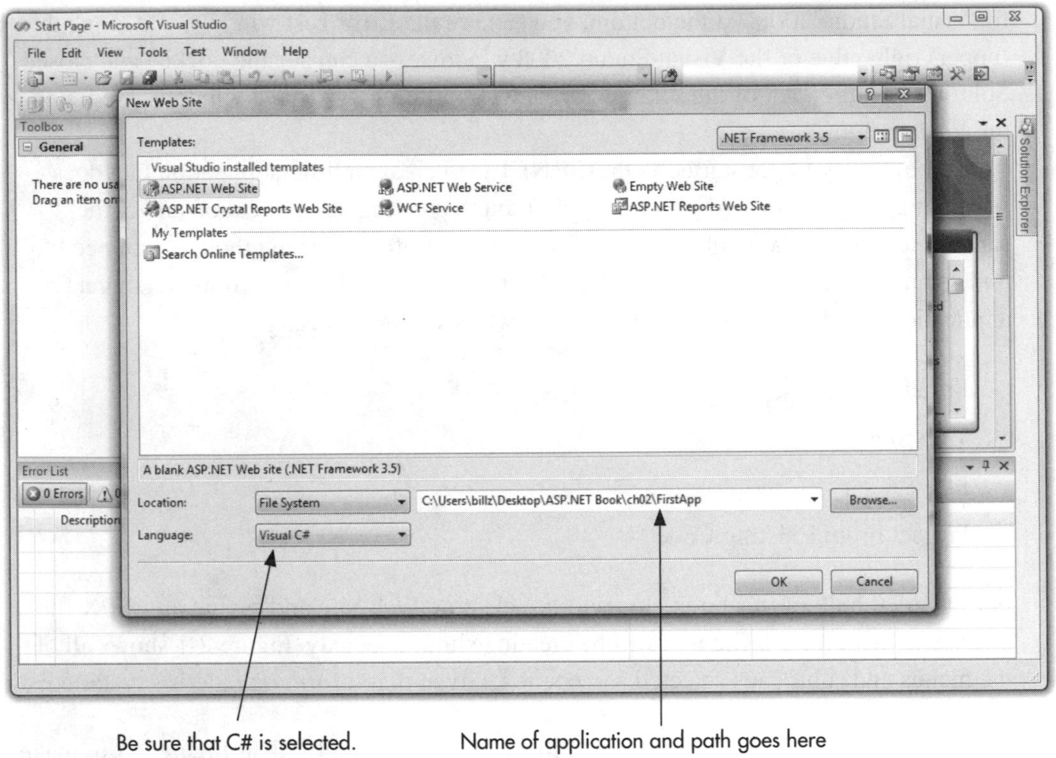

Be sure that C# is selected.   Name of application and path goes here

Figure 2-2 Selecting the storage folders for your application

4. After you click OK, a tab showing "Default.aspx" appears. First, choose the Source view by clicking on the Source button at the bottom of the tab's page. Figure 2-3 shows the page in the Source view. Visual Studio 2008 automatically generates code for you to get started.

5. From the menu bar select View | Toolbox, and when it opens, click on the Standard folder to open it. Figure 2-3 shows the Toolbox open on the left side of the work area. Just about everything visual you'll need is in the Toolbox, and most of the ASPX coding is done by dragging an object from the Standard Toolbox to the code window. (This would also be a good time to select View | Error List so that your main debugging window will be available when needed.)

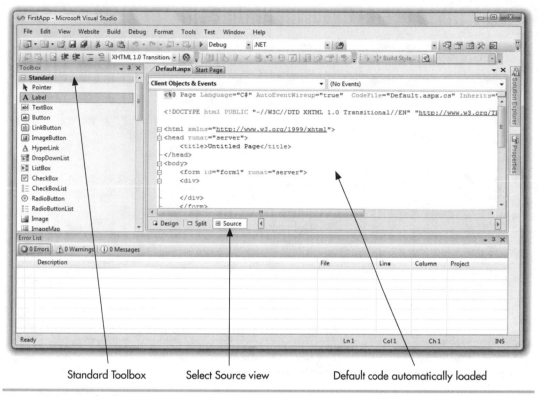

Standard Toolbox   Select Source view   Default code automatically loaded

Figure 2-3 Code showing in Source view

6. Select the Label object in the Toolbox window, and drag it to the code window between the `<div>` `</div>` tags as shown in Figure 2-4. As soon as the Label is in place and you release the mouse button, the ASP.NET code appears automatically. (Later you will see what happens from the Design view, but for now, the focus will be on the code only.)

7. Next, you need to add a little C# code to your application. To open the C# code window, select View | Code from the menu bar as shown in Figure 2-5 or press F7. You will see where the "code behind" is located and used in conjunction with the ASP.NET code.

8. Note that the name of the C# code is the same as the ASP.NET (ASPX) file except that it includes a .cs extension. So, the Default.aspx and Default.aspx.cs files can be seen as "going together," and when you begin placing files on your server, you'll need to see that they are placed together in an application folder. (Later you will see how to use names other than "Default" for your applications.)

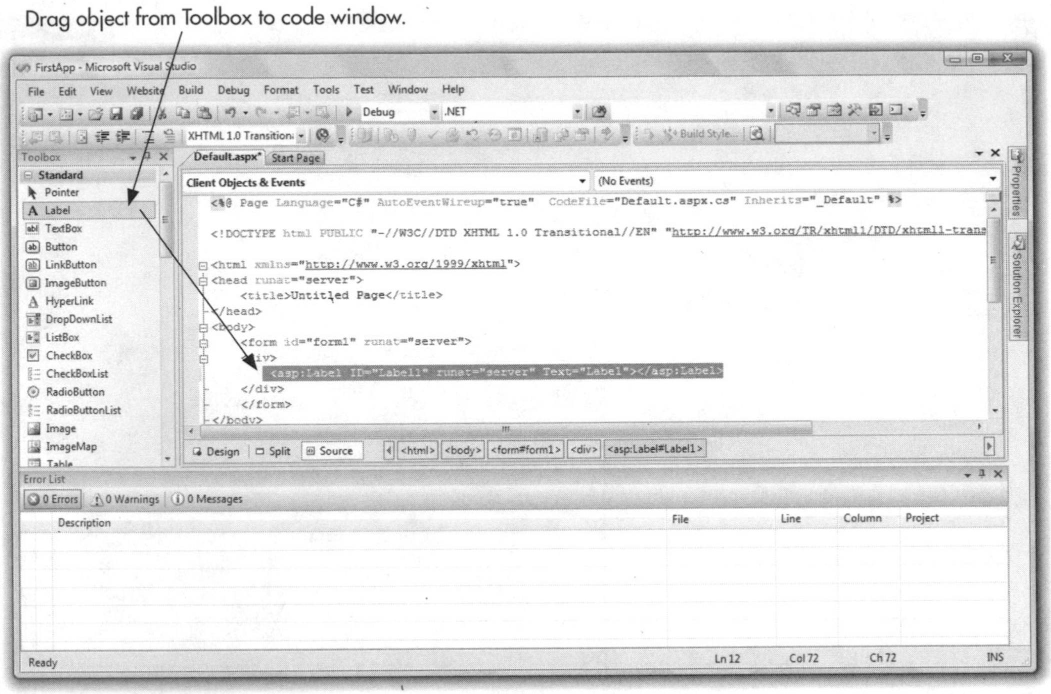

Drag object from Toolbox to code window.

Figure 2-4 Dragging objects from the Toolbox to code window

9. In the C# code window find the line that begins with:

```
protected void Page_Load(object sender, EventArgs e)
```

Insert a line after the curly brace ({) on line 16, and begin typing **Label1** on line 17. When you begin typing Label1, a window appears as shown in Figure 2-6. This is the *IntelliSense* window, which recognizes objects from the ASP.NET file. When you dragged the Label object to the stage, it was automatically given the ID of "Label1" in the ASPX code (see Figure 2-4). The IntelliSense feature recognizes all objects and instances in the ASPX code and uses the existing form IDs to help create the necessary code in the C# window. Use your arrow keys to highlight Label1 in the list, and press ENTER for the word to automatically appear in the code.

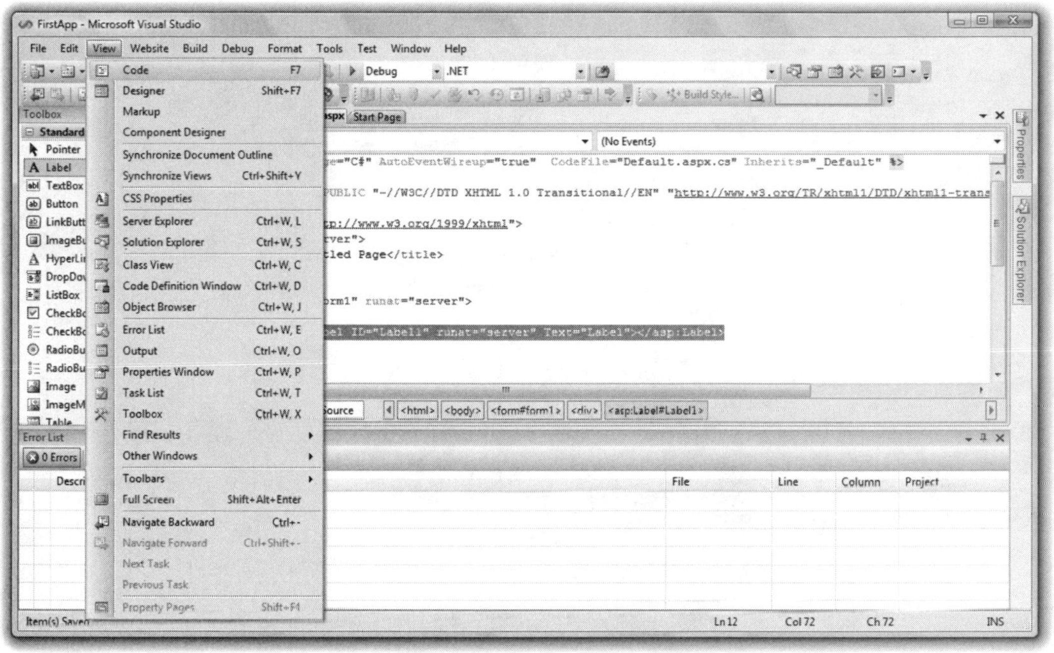

Figure 2-5 Open the C# code window.

NOTE

Unfortunately, it's easy to confuse **Label** (a form object) and the automatic ID of **Label1**. Note in Figure 2-6 that the IntelliSense window shows both the *Label* object and the *Label1* ID names.

Ask the Expert

Q: Why do errors appear in the Error List window when I'm typing code?

A: I like to think of the Error List as a worrywart that is always *on the job*. Once you get the whole line completed, if it is correctly formatted, the error messages go away. Rather than viewing the Error List as a fussy nag, keep in mind that it's really your best friend and will save hours in debugging your code.

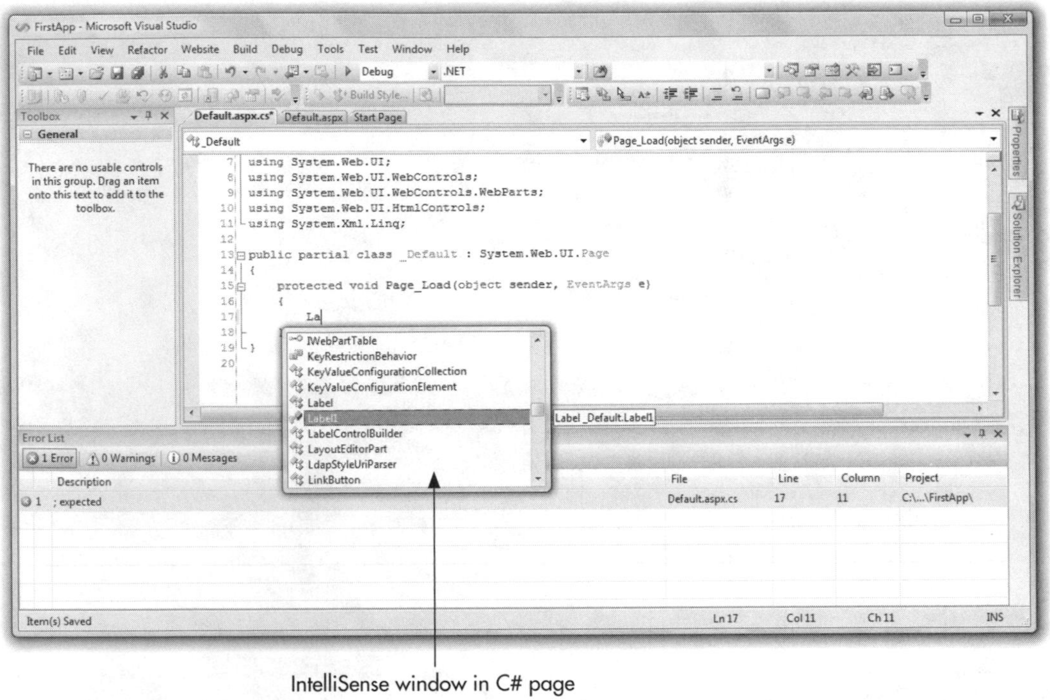

IntelliSense window in C# page

Figure 2-6 IntelliSense window automatically opening in C#

10. Once that `Label1` appears in the code window, type in a period (**.**). As soon as you type in the period (sometimes called a *dot*), the IntelliSense menu appears again and displays all of the different properties and other elements associated with the Label class as shown in Figure 2-7.

11. Use the arrow keys to scroll to `Text` in the IntelliSense window and press ENTER. You will now see `Label1.Text`.

Properties associated with Label control

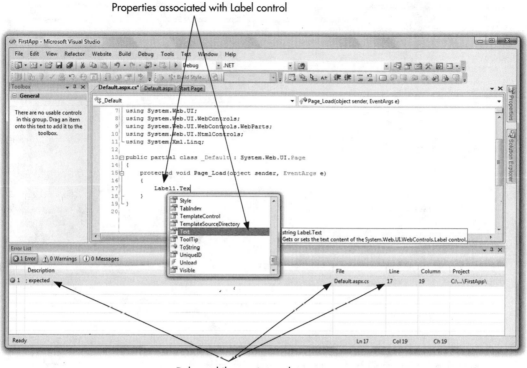

Debug while creating code

Figure 2-7   IntelliSense window displaying Label object properties

12. Following `Label1.Text` add
`="This ASP.NET 3.5 application written by <Your Name>";`
as shown in Figure 2-8. In C# you need to add a semicolon at the end of each
statement, but you do not put them at the end of ASP.NET lines.

13. Select File | Save All or press CTRL-SHIFT-5. This action saves both your CS and ASPX
files. You will always need both files saved when you test your program. Figure 2-9
shows the sequence.

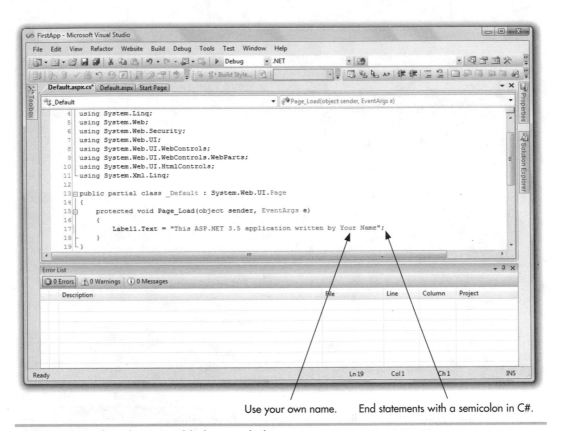

Use your own name.   End statements with a semicolon in C#.

Figure 2-8 A literal string added to a Label Text property

NOTE

In Figure 2-9 the string shows <Your Name> indicating that you should put your name in. However, if you place arrow brackets around your actual name, nothing appears after the word "by" in the output. That's because C# treats arrow brackets as HTML tag delimiters.

14. To test your application, select Debug | Start Without Debugging or press CTRL-F5. (Alternatively you can just click the green arrow button to test your application.) Figure 2-10 shows what you should see, except that your name should appear.

While this application is little more than a "Hello World!" example, it shows the essential procedures for creating both ASP.NET and C# scripts using Visual Studio 2008. To get a better overview, this next section will look at the code files of both the ASPX and CS files.

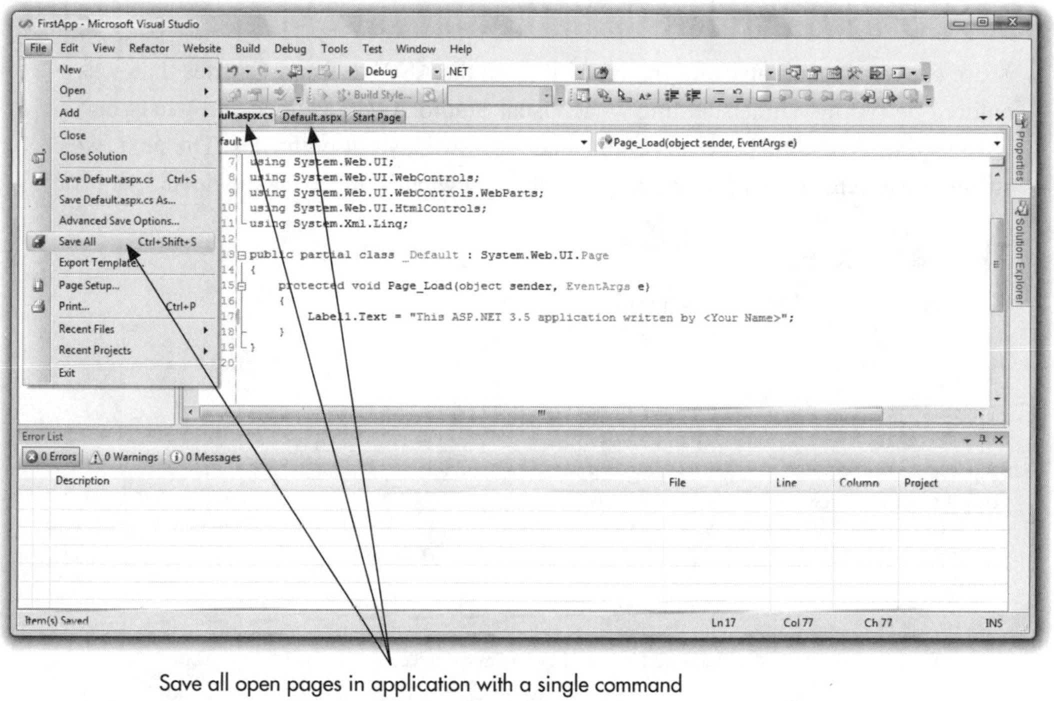

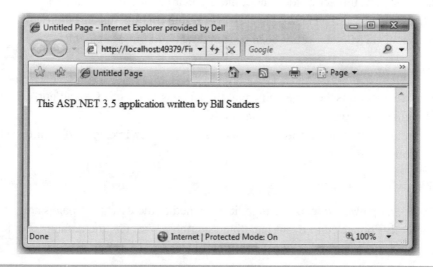

Save all open pages in application with a single command

Figure 2-9   Save all files with a single command.

Figure 2-10   A Label form showing the string from the C# script

ASPX and C# Files

More code was generated automatically in both the ASP.NET and C# files than was entered by typing. Understanding what Visual Studio 2008 has done and what you will need to do can be better accomplished when we lay out both files. The next two subsections explain all of the code generated and what is added by the developer (you).

The ASPX File

First, look at the ASP.NET as a whole.

```
<%@ Page Language="C#" AutoEventWireup="true"  CodeFile="Default.aspx.cs"
Inherits="_Default" %>
<!DOCTYPE html PUBLIC "-//W3C//DTD XHTML 1.0 Transitional//EN"
"http://www.w3.org/TR/xhtml1/DTD/xhtml1-transitional.dtd">
<html xmlns="http://www.w3.org/1999/xhtml">
<head runat="server">
    <title>Untitled Page</title>
</head>
<body>
    <form id="form1" runat="server">
    <div>
        <asp:Label ID="Label1" runat="server" Text="Label"> </asp:Label>
    </div>
    </form>
</body>
</html>
```

For the most part, this script looks a lot like standard XHTML. In fact, it looks pretty much like a plain-vanilla HTML page. However, the first line has far more information than a typical HTML one. It has been broken down into three segments:

```
<%@ Page Language="C#"
```

This first segment lets the page know that the language in use is C# and not VB or some other language. It's pretty self-explanatory.

The next segment has a special Boolean, `AutoEventWireup`, and requires a bit more explanation:

```
AutoEventWireup="true"
```

The `AutoEventWireup` Boolean indicates whether the ASP.NET pages are automatically connected to event-handling functions. With C#, the default is set to `true`, so the pages are connected to event-handling functions.

The final section indicates the name of the C# file and what it inherits. As we saw earlier, Visual Studio 2008 automatically assigns the ASP.NET filename to the code file to use, and since the name of the ASP.NET file is `Default.aspx` the `CodeFile` is `Default.aspx.cs`. That part is fairly straightforward.

```
CodeFile="Default.aspx.cs" Inherits="_Default" %>
```

The `Inherits` attribute refers to the name of the class that the code inherits. This may be a little confusing because in C# the reference for one class inheriting another is simply a colon (:). For example, in the C# code you will see the line

```
public partial class _Default : System.Web.UI.Page
```

That means that the `_Default` class inherits the `System.Web.UI.Page` class. In the ASPX file, the `Inherits` attribute simply points to the class that the page inherits.

The C# File

The first 11 lines of the C# script are all `using` directives that tell which namespaces to make available. Because they are part of a template, it's an all or none proposition when opening the C# code file in the template. In fact, if you remove all but the first `using` directive, the application works perfectly fine. In the general overview of the script, keep in mind that all of the default directives are unnecessary. For the time being, though, leave them as they are.

```
using System;
using System.Data;
using System.Configuration;
using System.Linq;
using System.Web;
using System.Web.Security;
using System.Web.UI;
using System.Web.UI.WebControls;
using System.Web.UI.WebControls.WebParts;
using System.Web.UI.HtmlControls;
using System.Xml.Linq;

public partial class _Default : System.Web.UI.Page
{
    protected void Page_Load(object sender, EventArgs e)
    {
        Label1.Text = "This ASP.NET 3.5 application written by Your Name";
    }
}
```

The C# class definition begins with the line

```
public partial class _Default : System.Web.UI.Page
```

This statement announces that the *name* of the class is `_Default` and that it inherits `System.Web.UI.Page`. From a strictly C# point of view, the partial class allows you to break up a class into more than a single file. This is useful where you have a big class or you have multiple developers working on a single class with different assignments. The compiler thinks that multiple partial class files are just a single class, so the internals are unchanged.

When working with ASP.NET (ASPX) files and C#, you can think of the ASPX file and CS files as the source code for multiple parts of the partial class. Strictly speaking that's not wholly accurate, but for all practical purposes it's a useful way of thinking about the value of a partial class in C# with an ASP.NET file. More accurately, the partial class allows C# to declare all the server-side controls you have declared in your ASPX file. Also, the partial class allows automatically generated code to be stored in a temp file from the code you generate. So, throughout this book, you will see the *partial* type modifier in a class definition.

The **public** keyword specifies the accessibility of the class as available to any other class. Most of the classes are initially defined as public, and if you want to delegate the class to another class, it will be accessible. (You will find more on class and object modifiers in Chapter 3, where C# is reviewed in more detail.)

In the class declaration, the class inherits everything in the `System.Web.UI.Page` class. That means that all of the properties in `System.Web.UI.Page` are available in the class named, `_Default`. Throughout the book, you will see many properties and other elements from the `System.Web.UI.Page` class (`Page` class) at use. For example, `IsPostBack`, which is discussed later, is a property you will use that is part of the `Page` class.

The key function in the C# code works with a built-in function that acts as an event handler, `Page_Load()`.

```
protected void Page_Load(object sender, EventArgs e)
```

The event simply waits until the page is loaded to launch whatever the code tells it to. By default, the `Page_Load()` function is in all of the C# scripts, and if you ignore it, nothing happens. If you are going to be using other event handlers, such as clicking a button, you can remove the function. The parameters are standard and are used to pass any information you will need. As the examples that require the parameters appear in the book, their use will be illustrated.

As you know from working through the example, the line

```
Label1.Text = "This ASP.NET 3.5 application written by Your Name";
```

is what you added using Visual Studio 2008. Remember that the Label form is an ASP.NET web form, and Text is one of the form's properties. Also, keep in mind that the form runs on the server, and the only way for the code from the ASPX file to execute is through the links that the ASPX file has to the C# file and inheritance of its class.

At this point, you need not expect to understand everything. The example used is to show how to use Visual Studio 2008 and not how C# and ASP.NET work in concert. However, you should be able to see a general picture of the process for developing applications using Visual Studio 2008. Also, keep in mind that Visual Studio 2008 is *huge,* and as you progress through the book, you will find more and elements of this important development tool. In the next section, you will see a bit more of what you can do with Visual Studio 2008 and how it can be used to give you exactly what you want.

More Visual Studio 2008 Tools

To see more helpful tools in Visual Studio 2008, you can change the ASP.NET coding on the example you have developed in this chapter. The next set of steps begins with your ASP.NET (Default.aspx) page and adds properties to the eventual output.

1. If it's not open, open the Default.aspx page in Visual Studio 2008. To open a single file, select File | Open | File, navigate to Default.aspx, and click the Open button.

2. Place the cursor right after `<asp.Label ID="Label1"` and press ENTER to add a line break. Then replace the current code with the following:

   ```
   runat="server"
   ```

   Text="Label" />

3. Delete the following tag:

   ```
   </asp: Label>
   ```

4. Select View | Properties Window from the menu bar or press CTRL-W, P to open the Properties window.

5. Select Label in the tag `<asp:Label` as shown in Figure 2-11. When you do that, the Properties window displays the object's properties.

6. Place the cursor between Text="label" and /> and press ENTER.

7. Select ForeColor, type **"AntiqueWhite"** in the Properties window, and press TAB. You should see ForeColor="AntiqueWhite" /> in the code window, and in the Properties window you will see AntiqueWhite in the right column next to ForeColor.

Object instance   Click button for color choices

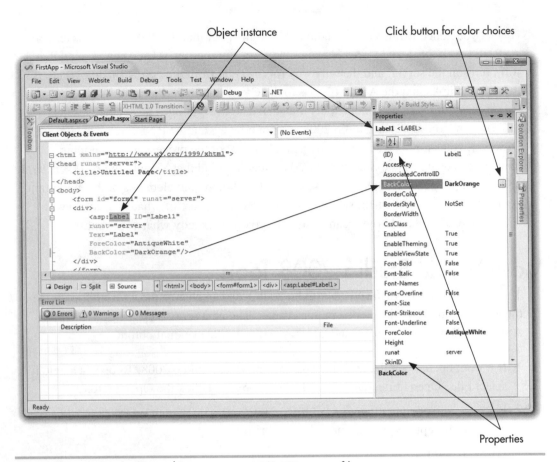

Figure 2-11   Properties window open in ASP.NET source file

8. Place the cursor between ="AntiqueWhite" and /> and press ENTER.

9. Select BackColor in the Properties window. You should see a button with three dots on it as shown in Figure 2-11. Click the button. The Color window opens and gives you several ways to choose a color as shown in Figure 2-12.

10. Click on the color you want and then click OK. Sometimes when you select a color, you will see a name in the Name window such as DarkOrange in Figure 2-12. Other times you will see no name. If you see no name, as is the case for color value 990000, you will see the hexadecimal value in the Properties window expressed as #990000 (or whatever the hex value is).

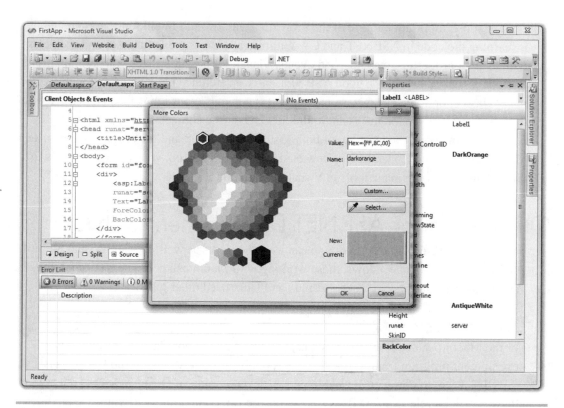

Figure 2-12   Color window shows hex value, name (if one is available), and color box with selected color

When you test the application by pressing CTRL-F5, you will see the same message as you saw before making the changes, but this time, you will see the background color you selected and the font color. Using the colors in the example, you will see an orange background with an off-white text displaying your message.

Ask the Expert

Q: Why do some colors have names and others not, and how were the color names selected?

A: The .NET colors with names were selected from a standard set known as X11. I'm still trying to figure out why names like "aqua" were selected rather than "cyan," and where in the world they got the name "papaya whip."

The most important purpose of the Properties window and IntelliSense pop-up menus is learning the code in ASP.NET and C#. With literally thousands of classes and each class with its own properties, methods, and events, Visual Studio 2008 saves you an immense amount of time. Obviously a good ASP.NET and C# reference book helps, but with so many classes, options, parameters, events, and statements, your job is made far easier with the computerized version in Visual Studio 2008. Over the course of this book, you will be shown how to get the most out of both Visual Studio 2008 and the programs you write using ASP.NET and C#, and as the new elements are introduced, you will also see how it's done using one of the many tools in Visual Studio 2008.

Other Tools for ASP.NET Development with C#

Besides using Visual Studio 2008, you can use other tools as well. Because Visual Studio 2008 is only made for Windows, those working with Macintosh computers or other non-Windows operating systems such as Linux and Unix need other tools.

Dreamweaver

For the Macintosh and Windows systems, you will find the popular Dreamweaver web development program from Adobe that has support for both ASP.NET and C#. Because ASP.NET 3.5 is so new, you'll need to get whatever version of Dreamweaver is released after the official release of ASP.NET 3.5 to ensure full compatibility. If you have an older version of Dreamweaver, though, you can still get some valuable help from Dreamweaver. For example, Figure 2-13 shows how Dreamweaver has a context menu that displays selections of ASP.NET web forms and other available options.

You should also note in Figure 2-13 that rather than placing the C# code in a separate CS file using a partial class, Dreamweaver uses the embedded script method beginning on Line 4. Depending on how you like working with code-behind C#, this alternative embedded style may or may not be your preference. Using Dreamweaver, you will have to use an online ASP.NET hosting service because you cannot test your applications as you develop them as with Visual Studio 2008.

POTE—Plain Old Text Editor

If you have nothing more than a simple text editor (or you prefer writing your own code with no help), you can do so with any editor that saves code as plain text. For systems such as Mac OS or Linux, you may not have any other choice, so using a text editor works

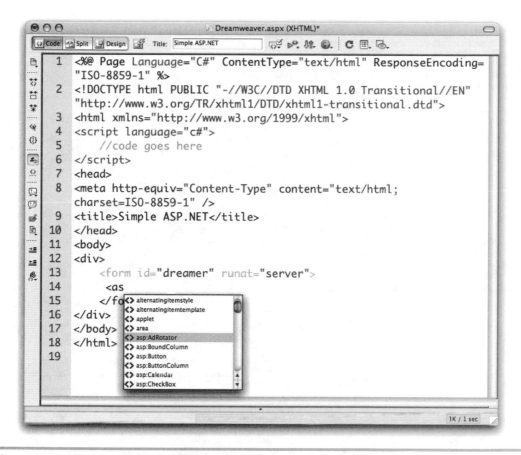

Figure 2-13 Dreamweaver ASP.NET context menu

fine for developing code. You can just write it and save it as an ASPX file with embedded C#. In fact, you can write the C# using code-behind if you like, but you cannot compile the C# unless you place your applications on a hosting service that will compile your C# and ASP.NET together.

If you are using a Mac and the TextEdit text editor, you will need to change the default preferences in your editor. TextEdit defaults to Rich Text Format (RTF), and you have to change it to plain text. To do so, select TextEdit | Preferences | Plain Text (radio button) as shown in Figure 2-14.

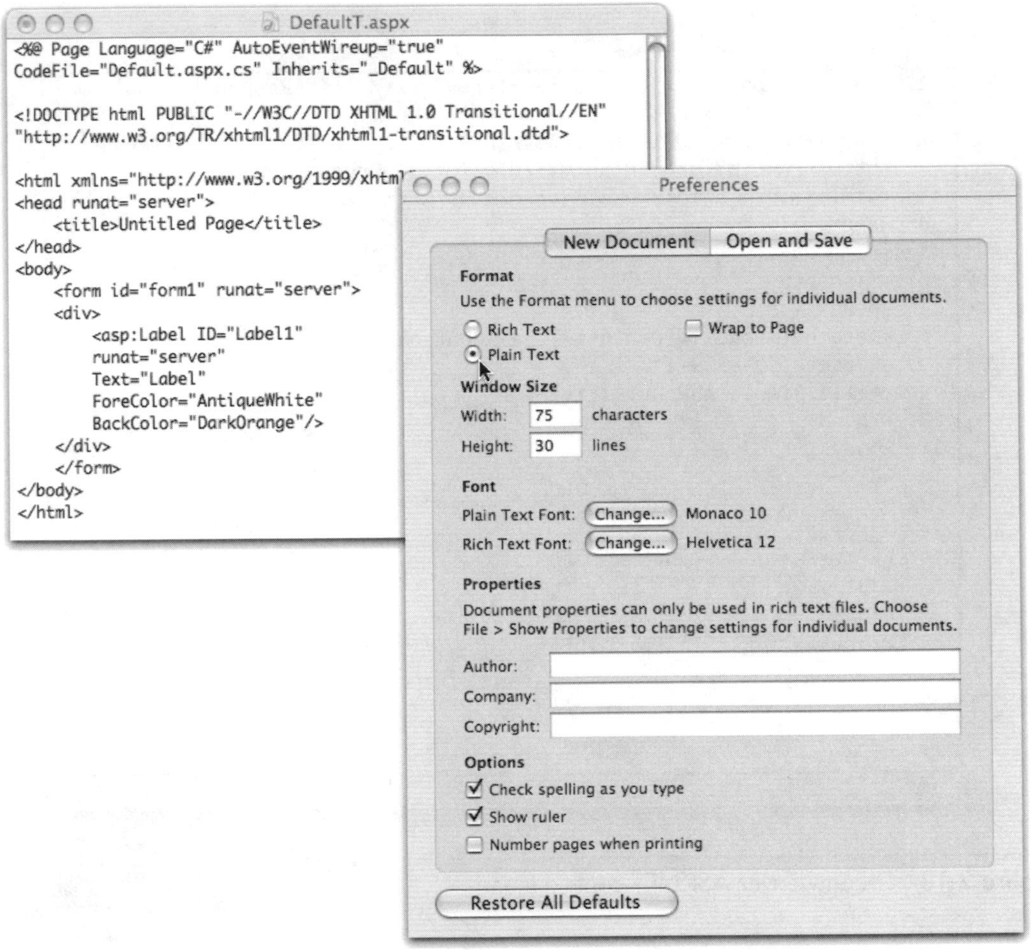

Figure 2-14 Resetting preferences in TextEdit

As you can see in Figure 2-14, the code is identical to that generated with Visual Studio 2008, and a separate C# file is referenced. If you save the source code as an ASPX and CS file, respectively, they should work fine with a hosting service running IIS7 and ASP.NET 3.5. So, while possible, it does involve more work and access to an IIS7 server.

Chapter 3

C# and ASP.NET 3.5

Key Skills & Concepts

- The relationship between C# 3.0 and ASP.NET basics

- C# 3.0 and ECMAScript Rev 4 standards

- Class structure

- Statements

- Types

- Variables and constants

- Defining assignments

- Strings

- Writing expressions

- Operators

- Conditional statements

- Loops

- Arrays

This chapter provides you with the rudiments of C#—pronounced "see-sharp." A very small subset of C# is used with most ASP.NET applications, but if you understand C# basics, you will be able to do much more with the C# you need to use. Even though Visual Studio 2008 writes a good deal of the C# for you, knowing what C# is doing will aid in your ASP.NET development.

C# 3.0 and ASP.NET 3.5

As you saw in Chapters 1 and 2, Visual Studio 2008 creates a partial class in C# when you begin developing ASP.NET web pages. Coming to understand what C# is doing and how it is structured can be accomplished by beginning with the fundamentals of C#, even though these fundamentals may not immediately be seen in the little code that you'll be using in the basic ASP.NET applications.

Case and Naming Variables and Instances

The first thing to understand about C# is that unlike some languages C# is *case sensitive*. That means whenever you reference a variable or class instances in C#, you need to be sure that the reference names take into account the case of the name. For example, the following three variables are all different:

```
merryWidows
MerryWidows
merrywidows
```

So, if you want to reference `MerryWidows`, you *cannot* use

```
merryWidows
MERRYWIDOWS
merrywidows
```

You must use `MerryWidows` and nothing else.

For the most part, you probably do not want simply to change the case of different characters to create different variable names. For example, if you have two different variables for hound dogs named

```
houndDog
Hounddog
```

you're likely to confuse yourself and anyone who is working with you in developing an application. Because case sensitivity allows you to differentiate between variable names does not mean you have to do so. Just keep in mind that all labeling needs to be clear in the context of its use, and names like

```
houndDog1
houndDog2
houndDog3
```

are far clearer than simply using different combinations of cases.

However, you can make life simpler by naming instances using lowercase for initial names of classes. For instance, suppose you have developed a class and named it `Monitor`. When you wish to declare an instance of the Monitor class, you may want to use the following:

```
Monitor monitor = new Monitor();
```

Later, when you are using the `monitor` object (instance), it's easy to remember it as an instance of the `Monitor` class. If you need several instances of the `Monitor` class, then you'll want to have some way of distinguishing between instances, such as

```
Monitor redMonitor = new Monitor();
Monitor greenMonitor = new Monitor();
Monitor blueMonitor = new Monitor();
```

The guiding rule in all labeling is to use common sense in the context of the project. Given that, just remember that your labels are case sensitive.

NOTE

If you are familiar with JavaScript, Java, C++, or ActionScript 3.0, you will find many of the same structures and formats that you will in C#. In time, Internet languages like C# and JavaScript will have a common underlying set of structures in meeting certain European Computer Manufacturers Association (ECMA) standards. You will find differences still, but ECMA is emerging as *the* language standard. For the full standard on C#, see www.ecma-international.org/publications/standards/Ecma-334.htm.

Types, Statements, and Expressions

Like most programming languages, C# deals with different types of data. For example, you may be familiar with *numeric* and *string* types. Numbers can be used for math calculations, and strings, for text storage. Assigning a value to a variable requires the data type to be included in the declaration of the variable. For example, the following two variables represent an integer declaration and a string declaration:

```
string myString;
int myNumber;
```

A language that requires a type for variables, constants, and objects is a *strictly typed language*, so C# can be considered strictly typed. Each complete instruction, whether it is simply to declare a variable or some more complex operation, is called a *statement*. Every statement is terminated by a semicolon (;), and if the semicolon is left out, an error is thrown.

Once you have declared a variable, you can then assign it a value. For example, using the variables we just declared, we could write

```
myString = "Happy programming";
myNumber = 45;
```

and the variables would now contain the values that we assigned. Any kind of statement that results in a value being assigned to a variable, constant, or object is called an *expression*. An expression can either be a simple assignment, or can be more complex and involve calculations and even the variable typing. For example, the following statements are expressions that *type* a variable (declare a variable type) and assign it a value made up of calculated values and another variable (`anotherNumber`) and a combination of string literals and a string variable (`anotherString`):

```
int myNumber = 45 + (anotherNumber - 3);
string myString = "Name: " + anotherString + " Smith";
```

Once you have set up your variable, you can run into problems as you attempt to assign the wrong kind of value to a variable. For example, the following assignments would throw errors:

```
int myNumber = "Calculate this: 2 * 10";
string myString = 33 * 22;
```

In the first case, the numeric variable is assigned a string literal. (A *literal* is an actual value.) Any expression enclosed in quotes is treated as a string literal. In the second case, not only are the values for a string numeric values, but also the expression contains a numeric operator (*) for multiplication.

Type Details

Differentiating between numbers and strings is pretty easy. Thing get a little tricky when you begin looking at the different data types. With text, the two basic data types are `string` and `char`. The `char` data type holds a single text character such as *a, b, c, 5,* or *@.* (Each character is a *Unicode character.*) A `string` data type contains a series of Unicode characters, such as "My dog Fred lives @ home!" The `char` data type requires less memory reserved because each value is the same length. The `string` data type requires more memory because the amount of memory depends on the number of characters. Also, just as numbers and strings are different, so are `char` and `string` types. For example, the following would throw an error:

```
char myCharacter = "Top of the morning!"; //Error!
```

because more than a single Unicode character is in the value assigned to a `char` type variable. Most of the C# examples you will see in this book use the `string` type.

With numeric types, you will find far more types. In the most basic sense, you can divide number types into whole numbers (integers) and floating-point numbers (contain fractions). You can also divide numeric types into *signed* (may have both positive and negative values) and *unsigned* (positive numbers only). Finally, the types you encounter either are built-in (*intrinsic*) or as created from classes and interfaces. You will be using intrinsic and class-based types.

C# Type	.NET Type	Description	Bytes (8-bit)
byte	Byte	Unsigned integers (0–255)	1
bool	Boolean	True or false	1
short	Int16	Signed integers from −32,768 to 32767	2
ushort	UInt16	Unsigned integers from 0 to 65,535	2
long	Int64	Signed integers from −9,223,372,036,854,775,808 to 9,223,372,036,854,775,807	8
ulong	UInt64	Unsigned integers from 0 to 18,446,744,073,709,551,615	8
int	Int32	Signed integers from −2,147,483,648 to 2,147,483,647	4
uint	UInt32	Unsigned integers from 0 to 4,294,967,295	4
float	Single	1.5×10^{-45} to 3.4×10^{38}, 7-digit precision (requires *f* or *F* at end of literal)	4
double	Double	5.0×10^{-324} to 1.7×10^{308}, 15-digit precision (requires *d* or *D* at end of literal)	8
decimal	Decimal	1.0×10^{-28} to 7.9×10^{28}, 28-digit precision (requires *m* or *M* at end of literal)	12

Table 3-1   Sample of C# and .NET Numeric Types

Table 3-1 outlines the common intrinsic numeric types you're likely to use.

You will find that data typing helps you organize your program. However, because you will be dealing with data coming from input from ASP.NET structures, you need to consider the translations from data input using ASP.NET forms and C# data analysis. This next section shows a typical example.

Passing Values Between ASP.NET and C#

Using the partial class format that connects ASP.NET to C#, you must be aware that names created in ASP.NET are used by C#. Therefore, in any discussion of C# and ASP.NET, you have to understand how the naming works. In examples in Chapters 1 and 2, you saw some examples of C# code assigning values, and here we'll take a close look at the connection between what the ASP.NET sets up and how C# can use structures from ASP.NET.

Take, for example, the following task:

User inputs two values. The first value is multiplied by .85 and the second by .15. The output shows the sum of the products.

That's a pretty simple problem. On the ASP.NET side, set up two `TextBox` forms to enter the values and a `Label` form to show the total. In addition, you will need a `Button` to set off an event to total the two values and add them together. So, in ASP.NET you'd have something like the following setup:

```
<asp:TextBox ID="ScoreA" runat="server"/>
<asp:TextBox ID="ScoreB" runat="server"/>
<asp:Button ID="Calc" onclick="Do_Calc" runat="server"/>
<asp:Label ID="Total" runat="server"/>
```

All the user has to do is to enter two values; the C# portion of the partial class has to use the input values, do the math, and then output the results to the ASP.NET `Label` form named `Total`. First, look at the C# listing (minus the unnecessary `using` statements automatically included), and then consider how C# first took information and then sent it back from ASP.NET.

```
using System;
public partial class _Default : System.Web.UI.Page
{
        private double s1;
        private double s2;

        protected void Do_Calc(object sender, EventArgs e)
        {
        s1 = Convert.ToDouble(ScoreA.Text) * .85;
            s2 = Convert.ToDouble(ScoreB.Text) * .15;
        Total.Text = Convert.ToString(s1 + s2);
        }
}
```

The first thing that is done in the C# portion is to declare two variables to handle the input. Both variables are typed as `double` (an intrinsic numeric type) and set up with a `private` modifier. (Variables with a `private` modifier are accessible only from code in the class where they are declared.) Next, the code sets up a method for the class that is initiated by a button-click.

```
protected void Do_Calc(object sender, EventArgs e)
```

This code uses the `Do_Calc` from the event handler in the ASP.NET line

```
<asp:Button ID="Calc" onclick="Do_Calc" runat="server"/>
```

The rest of the method converts data entered as string to real numbers to be used in the calculations. For example, the C# line

```
s1 = Convert.ToDouble(ScoreA.Text) * .85;
```

takes whatever was entered into the TextBox in the ASP.NET portion of the class into a number (a double) and assigns the value to the variable s1. Included is the multiplication of the text from ASP.NET that has to be converted to a floating-point number (the double type in this case) by .85. The TextBox field with the reference name (ID) of ScoreA originated in the line

```
<asp:TextBox ID="ScoreA" runat="server"/>
```

in ASP.NET.

Going in the opposite direction, to output the results of the multiplication and addition to the *Total* Label field, the numeric values have to be re-converted to text as the following C# line shows:

```
Total.Text = Convert.ToString(s1 + s2);
```

So, in the same way that the Convert class uses the ToDouble method to convert from a string to a number, ToString converts back to a string that can be used in a Label output form. Think of it as a roundtrip beginning with the ASP.NET structures and the C# engine kick-starting the user events or events from some other state in the program.

Basic C# Structures

In this section, we're going to look at the basic C# structures independent of ASP.NET. Then in the examples, you will see how these structures are used in conjunction with ASP.NET in a partial class. However, for the time being this section focuses on the C# structures.

Variables and Constants

As implied in the previous sections in this chapter, a *variable* is a container-like structure used to store data. The data in the container can change in value—it varies; hence, the term *variable*. As you saw in the previous discussion, you need to provide variables with a type, and you cannot pass the value of one variable type to a variable of a different variable type. So, if you place a decimal value into a decimal type variable, you'll find everything works fine. Further, if you place the value of one variable into another of the same type, your program works.

A *constant* is like a variable in that it stores values, but unlike a variable, a constant represents an unchanging value. For example, the value of the mathematical constant *pi* is unchanging, and by placing its value into a constant, you're assured that some other value will not creep in. Actually, any value can be placed into a constant whether it's absolute like the value of pi or the freezing point of water or some other value that you want for your program. Let's say you have a program to check for the legal voting age of 18 that calculates age based on current date and birthday. The voting age needs to be constant, while you expect the current date and birthday to change. Then, suppose that the voting age changes from 18 to 21 because your calculation is based on a different country. The only value you would need to change is the constant that holds the voting age.

Using constants and variables *of the same type* together works well. For example, the following statements will calculate values fine:

```
const int VAGE = 18;
int yourAge = 35;
int legalAge;
legalAge = yourAge - VAGE; //Expression using both constant and variable
```

The important aspect of the script is not whether an element is a variable or constant, but whether the *types* of the variables and constants are the same. In this case, both variables and the constant are of the same type, `int`; therefore, they work together. The following script pair illustrates how C# and ASP.NET use constants and variables in concert.

ASP.NET ConVar

```
<%@ Page Language="C#" AutoEventWireup="true" CodeFile="ConVar.aspx.cs"
Inherits="ConVar" %>
<!DOCTYPE html PUBLIC "-//W3C//DTD XHTML 1.0 Transitional//EN"
"http://www.w3.org/TR/xhtml1/DTD/xhtml1-transitional.dtd">
<html xmlns="http://www.w3.org/1999/xhtml">
<head runat="server">
 <title>Constants and Variables</title>
</head>
<body>
 <form id="form1" runat="server">
 <div>
  <asp:Label ID="YourAge" runat="server" Text="19" />

 </div>
 </form>
</body>
</html>
```

C# ConVar

```
using System;
public partial class ConVar : System.Web.UI.Page
{
 private const int VAGE = 18;
 private int yourAge;
 private int legalAge;

 protected void Page_Load(object sender, EventArgs e)
 {
  yourAge = Convert.ToInt16(YourAge.Text);
  legalAge = yourAge - VAGE;
  YourAge.Text = Convert.ToString(legalAge);
 }
}
```

That exact script returns the value of 1. That's because the `Label` object named `YourAge` has a `Text` value of "19," and while a string, it is converted to an integer by the C# portion of the class. Try changing the value of 19 to something else relative to the constant's value of 18. You can then get a negative number.

Naming Conventions

Naming conventions are just that—*conventions*. They are not *rules*, so your name selection may be unique, not follow conventions, and everything may still work just fine. However, I find that a consistent set of naming conventions is quite helpful, and you will find that once you have a standard set, you and others can understand your code much better. One of the areas where things get murky in naming conventions is with constants. In most languages, constants have been written in all caps. In the previous example, `VAGE` is an example of a constant name following the convention of using all uppercase for constants. Depending on which convention article you read and the date, you will find different conventions suggested for constant names in C#. The following are some different applied conventions:

- **All caps** This convention uses all uppercase letters. It is only to be used for constants and SQL commands. For example, `FREEZEPOINT` is a typical identifier when using constants.

- **Camel case** Also called "mixed case" or "inter case," this naming convention joins words without using spaces or underscores. The first letter is lowercase, hence the name *camel* for the hump where an uppercase letter appears. For example, `firstName` is a variable that uses camel case.

● **Pascal case**   Very similar to the camel case, the Pascal case begins with uppercase and then joins words with capital letters. You will find that classes and constructor functions typically use the Pascal case. For example, `CustomerList` is an example of the Pascal case where two words are joined into one.

These conventions can be helpful, and Microsoft tries to help out by the more-than-occasional white paper on the topic. In this age of languages converging around ECMA standards, you might want to use more general conventions that you're comfortable with or that will most clearly communicate meaning among a team of developers.

Some conventions may not be to your taste and/or not be used consistently. For example, several developers prefer to use a leading underscore for private variable names (for example, `_apples`, `_fruitcake`); however, the default name of all partial classes generated by Visual Studio is a class name beginning with an underscore (that is, `_Default`), and in this book you will see that rather than using the default name, the name of the partial class is more descriptive and does not begin with an underscore. The decision not to use underscores for the class name of a partial class is based on the fact that the naming practice of the leading underscore is ingrained in some programmers as indicating a private class, method, or variable.

Definite Assignments

Before a variable can be used, it must be initialized in some way. From what I've seen, this rule seems to operate a little differently from a pure C# program and a hybrid ASP.NET/C# one. Generally, a definite assignment means that a variable needs to be initialized prior to use. In some cases, you can just assign a data type such as

```
private string myString;
```

and then use the variable even though it has not been assigned a value. For example, suppose you have the following ASP.NET script:

```
<%@ Page Language="C#" AutoEventWireup="true" CodeFile="DefiniteAssn.aspx.cs"
Inherits="DefAssn" %>
<!DOCTYPE html PUBLIC "-//W3C//DTD XHTML 1.0 Transitional//EN"
"http://www.w3.org/TR/xhtml1/DTD/xhtml1-transitional.dtd">
<html xmlns="http://www.w3.org/1999/xhtml">
<head runat="server">
 <title>Definite assignment</title>
</head>
<body>
 <form id="form1" runat="server">
 <div>
```

```
  <asp:TextBox ID="Show" runat="server" />
 </div>
 </form>
</body>
</html>
```

All this ASPX file does is to provide a convenient TextBox form for output for a variable to be defined in the C# portion. The C# portion is where you can see definite assignment at work (or not). First, look at a perfectly well-formed *definite assignment* for the string variable stVar.

```
using System;
public partial class DefAssn : System.Web.UI.Page
{
 private string stVar;
protected void Page_Load(object sender, EventArgs e)
  {
   stVar = "Test";
   Show.Text = stVar;
  }
}
```

When that runs, you will see the value Test appear in the text box window. If you comment out the line

```
//stVar = "Test";
```

everything still works fine. Nothing appears in the text box window, but the compiler doesn't throw an error. However, if you comment out the line

```
//private string stVar;
```

and leave in the statement that provides the variable with the value Test, you will get an error. That's because the variable has not been declared. If you declared a variable in C# but did not assign it a value (initialize it) prior to using it, you will get an error. So, while it's an important practice to keep in mind, output to an ASP.NET form is a bit more forgiving than to a C#-only program that outputs to the System.Console.WriteLine or some similar non-ASP.NET structure.

Operators and Punctuators

C# uses a full set of operators to state the relations between elements in expressions. Likewise, a set of punctuators sets demarcations between different units in statements. Those unfamiliar with operators can think of them as *verbs* and the different elements that they handle as *nouns*. That's not wholly accurate, but might be helpful for getting started with operators. Similarly, if you think of punctuators exactly like normal language punctuation, you will have a good idea of how they are used.

Basic Operators

The most basic operators are those that deal with either assignment or math. If you have experience with other programming languages, you may be aware that operators can differ for different languages. C# is no different. Some of the operators you're used to using may be identical in C#, but some may be different; so pay close attention.

Assignment Operator

The *assignment* operator is the most used and is fairly simple. Represented by a single equal sign (=), the assignment operator is used to assign a value to program elements including properties, variables, and constants. The basic structure is the following:

```
someProperty (operand) = (assignment variable) someValue (operator)
```

As you've seen in this and previous chapters, the value that can be assigned to a variable depends on the type, but otherwise, the use of the assignment operator is pretty simple and standard. The following is an expression showing a typical assignment:

```
string myString = "A string of pearls";
```

In some cases you may want more than one property to be assigned the same value. For example, the following assigns the horizontal and vertical properties to the same value:

```
objHorizontal = objVertical = 55;
```

Using chained assignments can save you time and even help organize assignments.

Mathematical Operators

The mathematical operators do pretty much what you'd expect—add, subtract, and other mathematical operations. The one exception is the add sign (+). If the variables or literals are numbers, the add sign sums one or more values. (As with assignment operators, you can have multiple operators in an expression.) If the elements you are working with are strings, then the add sign concatenates them. For example, the following shows where the add symbol in an expression would lead to concatenation:

```
private string morning = "Good morning ";
private string night = "Good night";
private string allDay = morning + night;
//results Good morning Good night
```

Symbol	Description
+	Add (and string concatenation)
–	Subtract
*	Multiply
/	Divide
%	Modulo (whole numbers remaining after division)
++	Increment by 1, may be pre- or post-increment
--	Decrement by 1, may be pre- or post-decrement
Compound Operators	
+=	Takes current value and adds to assigned value
–=	Takes current value and subtracts from assigned value
*=	Takes current value and multiplies by assigned value
/=	Takes current value and divides by assigned value
%=	Takes current value and performs modulo of assigned value

Table 3-2 Mathematical Operators

Otherwise, the math operators behave as described in Table 3-2.

The increment and decrement operators are commonly found in loop structures (described later in this chapter). They are used to automatically add or subtract 1 from the current variable's value.

The compound operators are a combination of a math operator and an assignment operator. They are used to automatically take the value of the variable and then do the math in relationship to the variable's value. For example, the following shows how a compound operator could be used to add an 8 percent tax to an item:

```
using System;
public partial class CompoundOp : System.Web.UI.Page
{
  private decimal cost;
  private decimal tax;
  protected void Page_Load(object sender, EventArgs e)
  {
    cost = 29.95m;
    tax = .08m;
    cost += (cost *= tax);
    Total.Text = Convert.ToString(cost);
  }
}
```

Ask the Expert

Q: What are the *m* characters doing in the literals for the cost and tax values?

A: When assigning literal values to decimal type variables or constants, you have to add the *m* character to distinguish the value from integers, doubles, or some other kind of nondecimal type literal. Note, however, that the variables containing decimal values need not include the *m*.

The cost variable uses an *addition compound operator* to add itself to the value of the cost multiplied by the tax variable using a *multiplication compound operator*.

Relational Operators

When two or more elements in an expression are compared, relational operators generate Boolean `true` or `false` values. Generally, values of the same type are evaluated as being equal to one another or somehow different. Table 3-3 shows the primary relational operators and a brief description of what they do.

Relational operators are used widely with conditional statements both within and apart from loops. They can also be used to establish the value of Boolean constants or variables. The important fact to remember is that relational operators *always* evaluate to `true` or `false`. Consider the following code:

```
int first = 10;
int second = 20;
bool same;
same= (first == second);
//same resolves to false
```

Symbol	Description
==	Equal to
!=	Not equal
>	Greater than
<	Less than
>=	Greater than or equal to
<=	Less than or equal to

Table 3-3   Relational Operators

Basically, the script asks if 10 and 20 are equal, and because they are not, the Boolean variable, same, evaluates to `false`. Further in this chapter, you will see how Boolean results are used in conditional statements to control conditional and loop structures.

String Comparisons

In some languages, you can compare strings using the same operators used to compare numeric values. If you try that in C#, you'll quickly run into an error. For string comparisons, you use `String` class method `Compare`. The `Compare` method has the following format:

```
int numVal = String.Compare(String1, String2);
```

In evaluating whether one string is greater than another, the `String.Compare()` method uses the placement of the first letter in the string relative to its position in the alphabet. If a letter is before another letter, it is considered *less than.* So, the letter *a* is less than the letter *b* and the rest of the alphabet. Also, a lowercase letter is less than its counterpart in uppercase. However, if a lowercase letter is greater in the alphabet than an uppercase one, it is resolved to greater than. Furthermore, the same letters in different cases are not equal. Only letters of the same case *and* value are considered equal. Table 3-4 shows the three outcomes and their meaning.

As you can see, this kind of relational outcome using the `String.Compare()` method is very different from the Boolean outcomes found when comparing numbers.

Logical Operators

In many respects logical operators are similar to relational operators because they also have Boolean resolutions. Table 3-5 shows the three logical operators used in C#.

As with relational operators, you will find logical operators used a good deal in conditional statements. They are essential when you want to test more than a single condition. For example, if you want to plan a ski trip, you might want to know whether

Result	Meaning
−1	The second string is greater than the first string.
1	The first string is greater than the second string.
0	Both are equal.

Table 3-4 String Relational Using the `String.Compare` Method

Symbol	Description
&&	logical AND
||	logical OR
!	logical NOT

Table 3-5 Logical Operators

the temperature is cold enough to sustain snow and whether snow is actually on the ground. So you might have code like the following:

```
bool temp = true;
bool snow = true;
bool both = (temp && snow);
//both resolves to true
```

If you only wanted one or the other to be true, you would use the statement

```
bool either = (temp || snow);
```

For the most part, you will be using the kinds of basic operators discussed in this section. C# also has bitwise operators that you're unlikely to use unless you're familiar with binary math.

Symbols in Grammar and Punctuators

The grammar and punctuator symbols are similar to those found in other modern computer languages. Table 3-6 shows the main symbols not used as operators and how they are used in C#.

Symbol	Description
;	Statement terminator; also element delimiter in `for` statement
,	Element separator in arrays
{}	Open and close conditional statements, loops, functions, and classes
[]	Array element delimiter
()	Parameter delimiters
//	Single-line comment
/* ... */	Block comment
:	Case delimiters in `switch` statement. Also used in class declaration to inherit a super class

Table 3-6 Key Punctuation and Grammar Symbols

Most of the grammar and punctuation are best understood in the context of their use, even when using a partial listing of all grammar and punctuation symbols as in Table 3-6. In looking at the different structures in C#, note how these symbols are correctly employed.

Conditional Statements

From looking at the different operators, you can see that the bulk of the outcomes, when comparisons are made, are going to be Boolean. Essentially, a conditional statement uses a Boolean to take one path or another. Often, the condition is nothing more than to do something or not to do something. However, at other times a conditional statement needs to choose between one branch or another.

If and Else

The most basic conditional statement is the `if` statement. Its format is the following:

```
if(condition)
{
     //do something
}
```

The condition is an expression using a relational operator such as `varA > varB` or Boolean. For example, the following uses a Boolean to determine whether Mary is younger than Jake:

```
int Mary = 20;
int Jake = 21;
bool compare = (Mary < Jake);
if(compare)
{
     //output Mary is younger than Jake
}
```

With a single condition to test, you can set up two specific outcomes using the `else` statement in the following format:

```
if(condition)
{
     //take path A
}
else
{
     //take path B
}
```

The following example uses two ASP.NET text boxes, and depending on the outcome, in the C# portion of the script an `if/else` statement determines which of the two values is greater.

ASP.NET# SimpleIf

```
<%@ Page Language="C#" AutoEventWireup="true" CodeFile="SimpleIf.aspx.cs"
Inherits="SimpleIf" %>
<!DOCTYPE html PUBLIC "-//W3C//DTD XHTML 1.0 Transitional//EN"
"http://www.w3.org/TR/xhtml1/DTD/xhtml1-transitional.dtd">
<html xmlns="http://www.w3.org/1999/xhtml">
<head runat="server">
 <title>Simple Conditional</title>
</head>
<body>
 <form id="form1" runat="server">
 <div>
  <asp:TextBox ID="TextBox1" runat="server"/>
  Number 1
 <p/>
  <asp:TextBox ID="TextBox2" runat="server"/>
  Number 2
  <p/>
<asp:Button ID="Compare" runat="server"
                  Text="Compare" onclick="DoCompare" />
 <p/>
 </div>
 </form>
</body>
</html>
```

C# SimpleIf

```
using System;
public partial class SimpleIf : System.Web.UI.Page
{
 private int n1;
 private int n2;

 protected void DoCompare(object sender, EventArgs e)
 {
  n1 = Convert.ToInt16(TextBox1.Text);
  n2 = Convert.ToInt16(TextBox2.Text);

  if (n1 > n2)
  {
   TextBox1.Text = n1 + " is greater";
  }
```

```
else
{
 TextBox2.Text = n2 + " is greater";
}
}
}
}
```

When you test the script, enter two different integers; which one is greater shows in the text box, as shown in Figure 3-1.

To handle more than a single condition, you can use a series of `if` or `else if` statements using the following format:

```
if(conditionA)
{
     //do A
}
else if (conditionB)
{
     //do B
}
```

When faced with more than a single condition to resolve, the `else if` statement will do the trick. It can get a little messy when you have several alternative outcomes to evaluate.

Switch

When you have several different outcomes, `else if` becomes a bit cumbersome, but it works fine. A better alternative than `else if` is the `switch` statement, which can handle any number of conditional values. The `switch` statement takes the value of a single variable and then examines several different cases to decide which to use. Most `switch` statements also contain a `break` statement at the end so that when the matching case is

Ask the Expert

Q: In the last example, nothing happens if the numbers are equal. How do you deal with values that are equal?

A: If you only use a single condition, use the *greater-than* or *equal-to* operator (>=) so that the equal condition can be included.

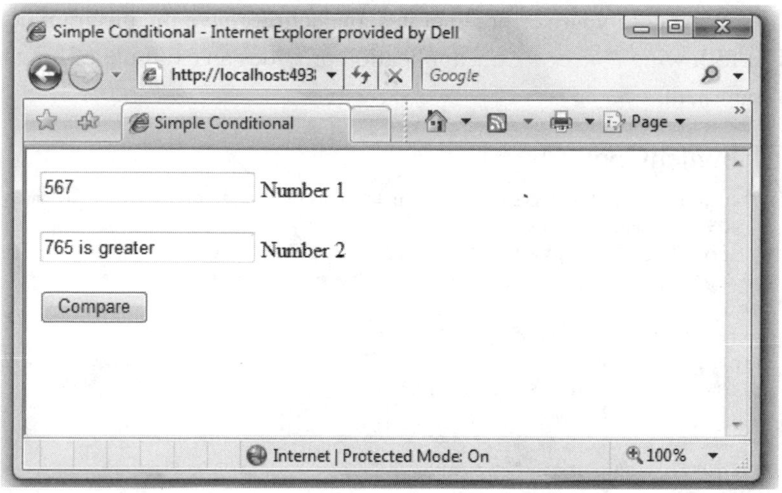

Figure 3-1 The conditional statement determines which number is larger.

found, the search stops immediately. The switch statement has the following general format:

```
switch (someVar)
{
      case value1:
            //do action A
            break;
      case value2:
            //do action B
            break;
}
```

The switch statement allows you to easily deal with several conditional values. Depending on the case value, you can have your program take a wide range of desired actions. This comes in handy when you need to have more than a single or just a few options available to launch.

One use you can put the switch statement to is in sorting out the outcomes generated by the String.Compare values shown in Table 3-4. Each of the possible three values that the String.Compare method generates is treated as a separate case. So the cases would be

```
case 1:
case -1:
case 0:
```

Depending on the case your script generates, the actions have the program do different things. The following `SwitchCom` application provides an example of how to apply the switch statement.

ASP.NET SwitchCom

```
<%@ Page Language="C#" AutoEventWireup="true"  CodeFile="SwitchCom.aspx.cs"
Inherits="SwitchCompare" %>
<!DOCTYPE html PUBLIC "-//W3C//DTD XHTML 1.0 Transitional//EN"
"http://www.w3.org/TR/xhtml1/DTD/xhtml1-transitional.dtd">

<html xmlns="http://www.w3.org/1999/xhtml">
<head runat="server">
    <title>Switch Compare Strings</title>
</head>
<body>
    <form id="form1" runat="server">
    <div>
        <asp:TextBox ID="TextBox1" runat="server"/>
         Enter first string</div>
    <p/>
        <asp:TextBox ID="TextBox2" runat="server"/>
      Enter second string
    <p/>
        <asp:Button ID="Compare"
            runat="server"
            Text="Compare Strings"
            onclick="DoCompare"
            />
    <p/>
    <asp:Label ID="Output" runat="server" Text="Results" />
    </form>
</body>
</html>
```

C# SwitchCom

```
using System;

public partial class SwitchCompare : System.Web.UI.Page
{
    private int n1;

    protected void DoCompare(object sender, EventArgs e)
    {
        //In using String.Compare the following outcomes
        //are possible:
        //-1 means that the first string is less than the second
        //1 means that the second string is less than the first
        //0 means the values are equal
```

```
n1 = String.Compare(TextBox1.Text, TextBox2.Text);
switch (n1)
{
    case -1:
        Output.Text = TextBox1.Text + " is less than " + TextBox2.Text;
        break;
    case 1:
        Output.Text = TextBox2.Text + " is less than " + TextBox1.Text;
        break;
    case 0:
        Output.Text = "The two strings are identical";
        break;
}
}
}
```

Figure 3-2 shows that two strings with the same casing are resolved as identical. However, the output in Figure 3-3 indicates that the first string is *less than* the second string. Note that the only difference between the two is that the first string is all lowercase, and the second string has a single uppercase character.

In the example, you can see exactly what's going on with the `String.Compare` method and better use it in your own applications.

Loops

Loops generate repeated actions until some condition is met. Like most languages, C# has different kinds of loops, depending on the situation of its use. Each complete loop is

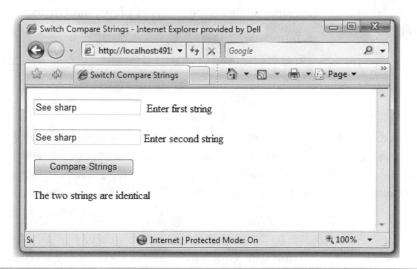

Figure 3-2 Equality requires identical case.

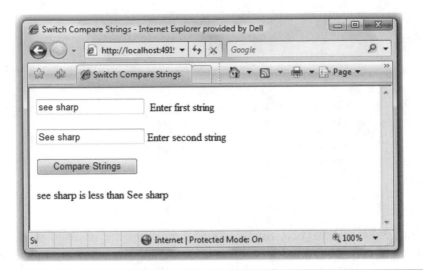

Figure 3-3 Similar strings with different cases are resolved as different.

called an *iteration,* and loops can have as many or as few iterations as needed. However, you must be careful to have some kind of condition that will terminate the loop. Different kinds of loops have different ways of setting up termination conditions, and in the next subsections, you will see the primary loops you'll use in C#.

For Loop

When you want to set a specific number of iterations in a loop, the for loop has a simple structure:

```
for (loop variable initial; termination condition; change loop variable)
{
    //statements
}
```

Generally, you will see the loop begin with an integer variable, followed by a termination statement using a relational operator, and ended by an increment or decrement of the variable. For example, the following loop sets the beginning value of the loop variable to 0 and checks to see that as long as it is less than 12, it continues iterations:

```
for (int loopvar = 0; loopvar < 12; loopvar++)
```

In this case, it has 12 iterations with loopvar values of 0–11. To see a visual use of the for loop, the following application illustrates how the loop variable changes with each iteration.

ASP.NET Loop.aspx

```
<%@ Page Language="C#" AutoEventWireup="true" CodeFile="Loop.aspx.cs"
Inherits="LoopTest" %>
<!DOCTYPE html PUBLIC "-//W3C//DTD XHTML 1.0 Transitional//EN"
"http://www.w3.org/TR/xhtml1/DTD/xhtml1-transitional.dtd">
<html xmlns="http://www.w3.org/1999/xhtml">
<head id="Head1" runat="server">
 <title>For Loop</title>
</head>
<body>
 <form id="form1" runat="server">
 <div>
 <asp:TextBox ID="Output"
 runat="server"
 Width="450"
 Height="30" />
 </div>
 </form>
</body>
</html>
```

C# Loop.aspx.cs

```
using System;
public partial class LoopTest : System.Web.UI.Page
{
 private int loopcount;
 protected void Page_Load(object sender, EventArgs e)
 {
  for (loopcount = 0; loopcount < 25; loopcount++)
  {
      Output.Text += loopcount + "-";
  }
  Output.Text += "End of loop";
 }
}
```

When you test this application, you will see a long, narrow text box with the values from 0 to 24 and then the message that the end of the loop has been reached. The key line in the loop is the following:

```
for (loopcount = 0; loopcount < 25; loopcount++)
```

The loopcount integer variable begins at 0, and each time through the loop, the statement checks to see if loopcount is less than 25. If it is, then one is added to the

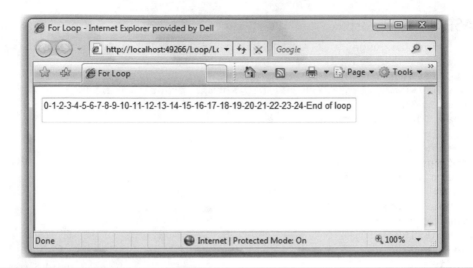

Figure 3-4 Output of simple `for` loop

`loopcount` variable (`loopcount++`) and the loop executes again. Figure 3-4 shows the output you can expect to see.

You can perform the same action with each iteration, or you can use the loop variable to generate different outcomes.

foreach Loop

The `foreach` loop is a favorite of mine because you can loop through an object with an unknown and/or changing collection of elements. For example, an array object contains any number of elements of specified types. (See the section on arrays later in this chapter.)

Ask the Expert

Q: In the example the loop variable is initialized as a private variable outside of the loop statement. Why is that?

A: This is more a matter of style than either convention or necessity. I like to gather up all of my variables and put them in one place. Then when I set up the loop, I don't have to enter the type, reducing clutter. The only problem with that style is that when you have several different loops and you want to keep each local and reuse your favorite loop variable name, you may generate conflict.

Using the `foreach` loop, you provide a typed variable you want to pull out of the object, and the loop iterates through the object until it gathers up all of the elements and makes them available to you. The general format is the following:

```
foreach (type myLoopVar in myObject)
        {
            //do something
            //myLoopVar is treated as a
            //standard variable
        }
```

The powerful feature of this kind of loop is its ability to look at an object's properties and send them out until the object is empty. Typically, you will find this kind of loop used with an array object, and the following example uses a string array to illustrate its use. Further, in a `for` loop, you need to type the iteration variable, but not in a `foreach` loop.

ASP.NET ForEach.aspx

```
<%@ Page Language="C#" AutoEventWireup="true"  CodeFile="ForEach.aspx.cs"
Inherits="ForEach" %>

<!DOCTYPE html PUBLIC "-//W3C//DTD XHTML 1.0 Transitional//EN"
http://www.w3.org/TR/xhtml1/DTD/xhtml1-transitional.dtd">

<html xmlns="http://www.w3.org/1999/xhtml">
<head runat="server">
    <title>Foreach</title>
</head>
<body>
    <form id="form1" runat="server">
    <div>
        <asp:TextBox ID="Output"
        height="100"
        runat="server"
        TextMode="MultiLine" />
    </div>
    </form>
</body>
</html>
```

C# ForEach.aspx.cs

```
using System;
public partial class ForEach : System.Web.UI.Page
{
    private string[] myArray;
```

```
protected void Page_Load(object sender, EventArgs e)
{
    myArray = new string[5];
    myArray[0] = "More memory";
    myArray[1] = "Sound card";
    myArray[2] = "Monitor";
    myArray[3] = "Terabytes drive";
    myArray[4] = "Faster processor";

    foreach (string s in myArray)
    {
        Output.Text += s + "\n";
    }
}
}
```

As you can see in the output, the `foreach` loop marched right through the array and plucked out all of the strings and placed them in a `TextBox` field. Also note the ASP.NET portion of the application where the `TextMode` property is set to `"MultiLine"`. This setting allows the output to be placed on separate lines as shown in Figure 3-5.

Keep the `foreach` loop in mind for digging through a set of data that has been sent to an array. Generally, the different controls in ASP.NET can do a good job of dealing with data displays from a database, but for certain types of data analysis, you'll be glad you know how to work with the `foreach` loop.

Figure 3-5   Loop displaying element values from an array

While Loop

The while loop has two different implementations. The first is as a loop that checks the condition at the top of the loop.

ASP.NET While LoopWhile.aspx

```
<%@ Page Language="C#" AutoEventWireup="true" CodeFile="LoopWhile.aspx.cs"
Inherits="WhileLoop" %>
<!DOCTYPE html PUBLIC "-//W3C//DTD XHTML 1.0 Transitional//EN"
"http://www.w3.org/TR/xhtml1/DTD/xhtml1-transitional.dtd">
<html xmlns="http://www.w3.org/1999/xhtml">
<head runat="server">
 <title>While Loop</title>
</head>
<body>
 <form id="form1" runat="server">
 <div>
 <asp:TextBox ID="Output"
        runat="server"
        Width="450"
        Height="30" />
 </div>
 </form>
</body>
</html>
```

C# LoopWhile.aspx.cs

```
using System;
public partial class WhileLoop : System.Web.UI.Page
{
    private int loopcount;

    protected void Page_Load(object sender, EventArgs e)
    {
        loopcount = 25;
        while (loopcount > 0)
        {
            Output.Text += loopcount + "-";
            loopcount--;
        }
        Output.Text += "End of Loop";
    }
}
```

This loop has the condition right at the beginning. If the loopcount variable is 0 or less, it will *not* iterate through the loop a single time, but will go immediately to the End Of Loop message. However, because the counter variable is set to 25, it takes 25 iterations before the variable is 0. Figure 3-6 shows what you will see counting backwards.

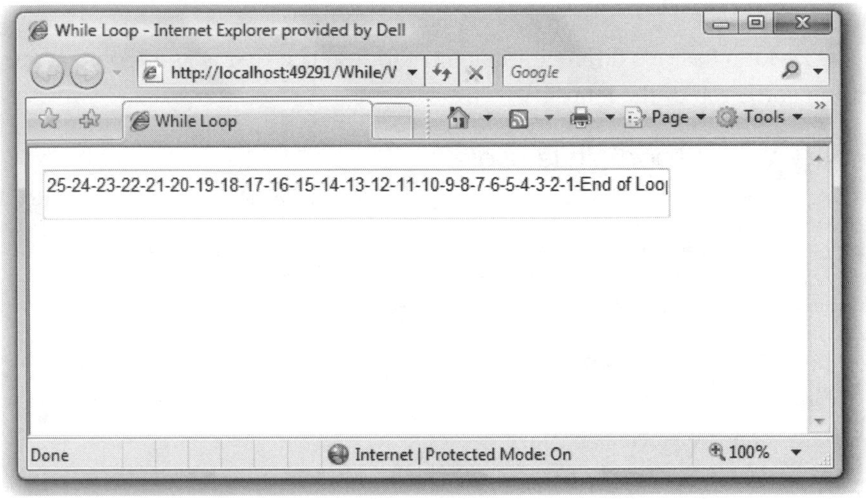

Figure 3-6 Output of `while` loop counting backwards

The important feature to keep in mind when using a `while` loop is that it will *not iterate at all* if the condition resolves to false on the first attempt to go through the loop. The next section shows a similar loop but with one important difference.

Do Loop

On some occasions, you need a loop that will iterate *at least once,* and this is where the `do while` (or just `do`) loop comes in handy. The condition for checking termination is *at the bottom of the loop,* while the actions for the loop are at the top of the loop. It has the structure

```
do
  {
     //Loop actions
  }
  while (condition);
```

As you can see, the actions occur before the `while` condition that evaluates a Boolean value. So where you want some kind of action taken, even if the Boolean value resolves as `false` the first time through the loop, use the `do` loop. The following example illustrates how this works.

ASP.NET DoWhile.aspx

```
<%@ Page Language="C#" AutoEventWireup="true" CodeFile="DoWhile.aspx.cs"
Inherits="DoWhile" %>
<!DOCTYPE html PUBLIC "-//W3C//DTD XHTML 1.0 Transitional//EN"
"http://www.w3.org/TR/xhtml1/DTD/xhtml1-transitional.dtd">
<html xmlns="http://www.w3.org/1999/xhtml">
<head runat="server">
 <title>Do Loop</title>
</head>
<body>
 <form id="form1" runat="server">
 <div>
 <asp:TextBox ID="Output"
        runat="server"
        Width="450"
        Height="30" />
 </div>
 </form>
</body>
</html>
```

C# Do DoWhile.aspx.cs

```
using System;
public partial class DoWhile : System.Web.UI.Page
{
        private int loopcount;
        protected void Page_Load(object sender, EventArgs e)

        {
            do
            {
                Output.Text += loopcount + "-";
                loopcount++;
            }
            while (loopcount < 25);
            Output.Text += "Loop Ends";
        }
}
```

When you test the program, you will see the output in Figure 3-7. It looks like the others, but it has a significant difference. The value in the first iteration is 0, the default value of an initialized integer type. That occurred because the loopcount variable did not increment until *after* its value is placed in the text box that outputs the value to the screen. Further, no matter what, in the first iteration it will put a value of the counter variable, *even if it exceeds the conditional value.* That is, if the loopcount variable were

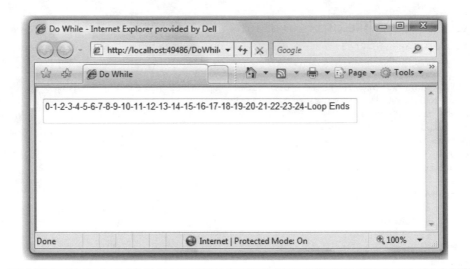

Figure 3-7 The first value of the loop is 0 because 0 is the default value of the counter variable before the loop increment.

set to 75 initially, it would still show up in the output text box because the do while loop *always* iterates at least once.

Basically, the difference between the do while and the while loop is the conditional Boolean being at the beginning or the end of the loop. For all practical purposes that means your application either needs to iterate at least once or not at all.

Arrays

Arrays are data structures that contain multiple elements. Each element of an array is itself an object or variable with values. Each of the values in each of an array's elements must be of the same kind. For example, an integer type array can only contain integers, and a string type array can only contain strings. (See Figure 3-5 and the discussion of the foreach loop previously in this chapter.)

By way of orientation, arrays in C# actually come in more than one flavor including the simple array that will be discussed here. However, C# also has ArrayLists and Stacks that have features familiar to you from using arrays in other programming languages. For example, the push() and pop() methods are used in arrays in other languages to add or remove elements from the array. You will not find those methods in the standard C# array, but you will find both methods in the Stack class. So, if you are familiar with arrays from other languages, you're certain to understand the general array concept, but because of the precise way they are used in C#, you might want to pay close attention to this discussion.

Creating Arrays

You can use different methods to instantiate an array. Likewise, assigning values to arrays can be done in different ways. Probably the best way to think about setting up an array is to imagine a stack of safe-deposit boxes. Each box is considered an array element, and the stack itself is the array. Furthermore, you need to specify the number of boxes you need and the type of contents each box will hold. For instance, one stack of boxes can hold only jewels and another stack, only money. However, the stack with the jewels cannot hold money and *vice versa.* With that in mind, let's look at how an array can be instantiated.

The general form for declaring an array is as follows:

```
type[] arrayLabel;
```

For instance, the following creates a string array named `stringSlots`:

```
string[] stringSlots;
```

Unlike a variable, arrays need some kind of indication of how many elements will reside, so when they are instantiated, you need to indicate how big they will be. The following creates an array with 44 elements available for data:

```
stringSlots = new string[44];
```

When no values are assigned to a string array, each has a value of null. Integer arrays default to 0. However, you can assign values to array elements on initialization. For example, the following two examples assign three element values to a string array:

```
string[] stringSlots = new string[3] { "apples" , "oranges" , "pears" };
string[] stringSlots = { "apples" , "oranges" , "pears" };
```

The first initialization requires an extra step, so most developers use the second. The array length is implied by the three element values that are in curly braces ({ }).

If you do not know what the values are going to be, you can assign values by a direct reference to an array index after the array has been initialized. For example, the following sequence shows a string array that is declared, initialized, and has data added to specific elements:

```
string[] stringSlots; //declared
stringSlots = new string[44]; //initialized
stringSlots[28] = "Nancy"; //value added to element 28
stringSlots[43] = "Joe"; //value added to element 43
```

As you saw in the foreach example in the C# code listing (`ForEach.aspx.cs`) and in Figure 3-5, tools are available for looping through the array elements both for adding and retrieving data.

NOTE

Array elements are zero-based indexes. So, the first element is 0, and the last is the array length minus 1. Thus with a length of 44, the last index value for the array would be 43. So the statement
`stringSlots[43] = "Joe";`
would be the highest element number in the `stringSlots` array.

Array Methods

Arrays look and act a lot like built-in types, and for the most part that's how they will be treated. However, they are in fact an object of `System.Array`, which has the set of methods and a single property that can be used with the simple array. Table 3-7 shows a sample of the available `System.Array` methods and how they are used.

Method	Use
AsReadOnly	Returns a read-only wrapper for the specified array.
BinarySearch	Binary search algorithm used to find element.
Clear	Resets all elements to 0 or null.
ConvertAll	Array type is changed (e.g., converts integer type to string).
Copy	Range of elements copied from one array to another.
CopyTo	Like `Copy()` method but copies *all* elements.
CreateInstance	New instance of Array class initialized.
Find	Search method for finding element that matches search criteria. Finds first instance.
FindAll	Like `Find()` except it finds all elements.
GetType	Used to get the *type* of current instance.
GetValue	Used to get the element value of array.
IndexOf	In one-dimensional array, returns index of first occurrence of value.
LastIndexOf	In one-dimensional array, returns index of last occurrence of value.
Resize	Changes the size of an array to the specified new size.
Reverse	Reverses order of elements in an array.
SetValue	Sets a value to a given element in array.
Sort	All array elements sorted.

Table 3-7 Commonly Used `System.Array` Methods

Array Length Property

The lone property in a `System.Array` is `length`. The length of an array refers to the number of elements it *can possibly* contain, but more generally it refers to the actual number of elements in the array. Keep in mind that array elements are zero-based, meaning that the first element is 0. For example, an array with three elements would have the following:

```
myArray[0]  =  "First"
myArray[1]  =  "Second"
myArray[2]  =  "Third"
```

The length is one-based. So while an element may be referenced as 0, it is the first of any number of elements in the array.

Using Arrays

Now that you've seen the major elements of arrays, their methods and property, this next example illustrates their use in an application. The purpose is to take a simple example with both numeric and string arrays and to add key methods to show how to work with them. Note in particular how the array methods are used. The format

```
Array.Method(stringLabel)
```

helps remind us that the simple arrays are really part of the `System.Array` class rather than a built-in feature independent of the `System.Array` class. Look for the `Reverse()` and `Sort()` methods in the C# portion of the following example.

ASP.NET ArrayTest.aspx

```
<%@ Page Language="C#" AutoEventWireup="true"  CodeFile="ArrayTest.aspx.cs"
Inherits="ArrayTest" %>
<!DOCTYPE html PUBLIC "-//W3C//DTD XHTML 1.0 Transitional//EN"
"http://www.w3.org/TR/xhtml1/DTD/xhtml1-transitional.dtd">
<html xmlns="http://www.w3.org/1999/xhtml">
<head runat="server">
    <title>Untitled Page</title>
</head>
<body>
<form id="form1" runat="server">
    <div>
    <asp:TextBox ID="Output"
        runat="server"
        TextMode="MultiLine"
        Height="170"
```

```
            Width="180" />
        </div>
        </form>
    </body>
    </html>
```

C# ArrayTest.aspx.cs

```csharp
using System;
public partial class ArrayTest : System.Web.UI.Page
{
    string[] stringBox = { "Hope", "Charity", "Peace", "Prudence" };
    int[] integerBox = new int[3] { 1944, 1492, 711 };

    protected void Page_Load(object sender, EventArgs e)
    {
        Array.Sort(stringBox);
        Array.Reverse(integerBox);

        Output.Text += stringBox[0] + "\n";
        Output.Text += stringBox[1] + "\n";
        Output.Text += stringBox[2] + "\n";
        Output.Text += stringBox[3] + "\n";

        Output.Text += integerBox[0] + "\n";
        Output.Text += integerBox[1] + "\n";
        Output.Text += integerBox[2] + "\n";

        Output.Text += stringBox.Length + "=String Array size\n";
        Output.Text += integerBox.Length + "=Integer Array size\n";

    }
}
```

When you run the example, Figure 3-8 shows what you will see on the screen. The Sort() method changed the order of the array element values from

- Hope
- Charity
- Peace
- Prudence

to the output in alphabetical order that you see in Figure 3-8. Likewise, the Reverse() method reversed the order of the three integers from "1944, 1492, 711" to "711, 1492, 1944."

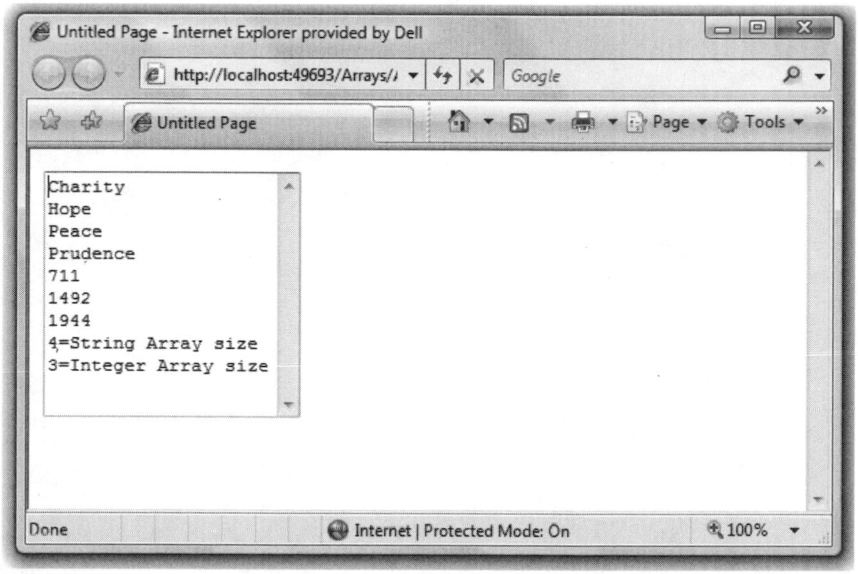

Figure 3-8   String and Integer Array output and array length

The length of the two arrays shown in the output in Figure 3-8 is based on the values in the initiated array in the example. Each element is given a value in both arrays. However, if you initiated an array with 250 and did not assign a single value to any of the elements, assigned values to some elements and not others, or assigned 250 values for the 250 elements, the array length would be the same. That is, the array length is based on the number of reserved slots and not whether each slot has an actual nondefault value.

Chapter 4

Doing More with C# and ASP.NET

Key Skills & Concepts

- Events

- Subroutines and functions

- Object-oriented programming (OOP)

- Creating classes

- Accessing C# classes from a web application

B ecause you need just a little C# to successfully work with ASP.NET does not mean that you cannot use the full power of C# with your ASP.NET applications. This chapter delves a little deeper into the events that can be generated by different ASP.NET tools and handled by C#, and also shows how to access a full C# class from the partial classes made up of C# and ASP.NET. However, neither the previous chapter nor this chapter does more than touch the surface of what can be done with C#. To learn more about C#, see *C# 3.0: A Beginner's Guide* by Herbert Schildt (McGraw-Hill, 2009).

Events and Handling Them

In the previous chapters, you have seen a couple of different ways that C# handles events connected to ASP.NET forms either on loading a page or with a button form. However, different ASP.NET objects generate different kinds of events, and this section examines how this is done and provides some examples aside from those you've seen.

Adding ASP.NET Controls Events to C#

Using Microsoft Visual Studio 2008 makes adding ASP.NET event handlers to C# code very easy. Ironically, rather than generating C# code from the ASP.NET Source mode, you do it from the Design mode. This next example shows how to generate the C# event handlers using the following steps:

1. Open a new web site saving it as the application named **EventWork**.

2. Change the mode to Design, and drag a TextBox, Button, and ListBox from the Toolbox to the editor and use the labels shown in Figures 4-1 to 4-3.

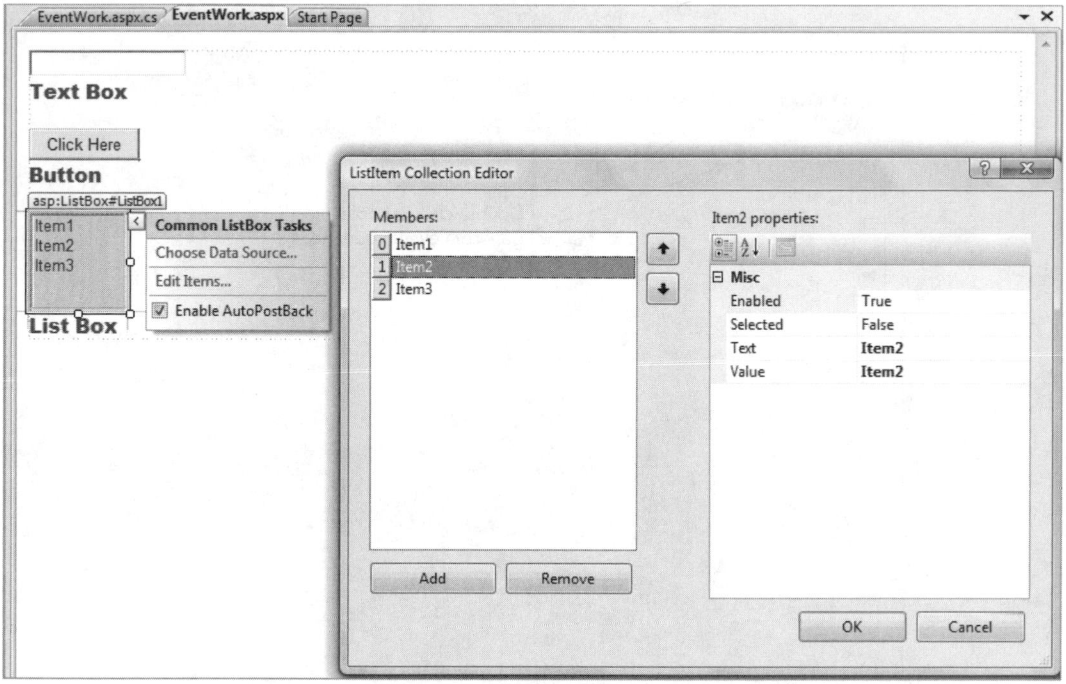

Figure 4-1   Adding items to the ListBox object in the Design mode

3. Click on the ListBox control, open the CommonListBox Tasks menu, and select Edit Items. This will open the ListItem Collection Editor as shown in Figure 4-1.

4. Click the Add button at the bottom of the ListItem Collection Editor until you have added three items as shown in Figure 4-1. Select each item in the Members column and in the Item Properties column, and set the Text and Value properties to Item1, Item2, and Item3 respectively.

5. Double-click the TextBox control. When you do so, you will be switched into the C# editor, and you will see the following code generated:

```csharp
protected void TextBox1_TextChanged(object sender, EventArgs e)
    {

    }
```

By inserting code between the curly braces, you can tie that code to an event in the TextBox that launches the code when the text in the box is changed and ENTER is pressed.

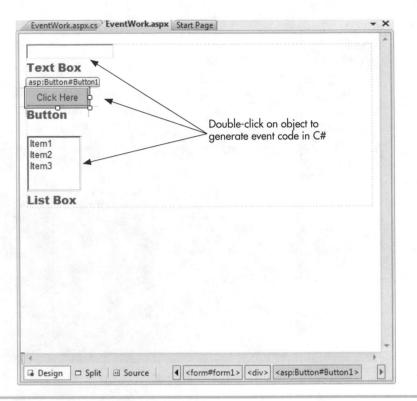

Figure 4-2 Add object event handlers by double-clicking objects.

6. Repeat Step 5 for the Button and ListBox objects as shown in Figure 4-2.

7. In addition to the page load event, your C# code should include three more event handlers—one each for the Button, the TextBox, and the ListBox.

Adding Statements to the Event Handlers

Without our engaging in hyperbole, the great majority of the C# event coding you will be doing with ASP.NET involves adding statements to the events generated in the manner just described. Depending on the nature of the project, you will have different statements. In the following example, you can see different kinds of C# statements and structures you may want to add.

Figure 4-3   Different events generate different output.

ASP.NET EventWork.aspx

```
<%@ Page Language="C#" AutoEventWireup="true"  CodeFile="EventWork
.aspx.cs" Inherits="EventWork" %>
<!DOCTYPE html PUBLIC "-//W3C//DTD XHTML 1.0 Transitional//EN"
"http://www.w3.org/TR/xhtml1/DTD/xhtml1-transitional.dtd">

<html xmlns="http://www.w3.org/1999/xhtml">
<head runat="server">
    <title>Event Work</title>
    <style type="text/css">
        .abGrey
        {
            font-family: "Arial Black";
            color: #555555;
        }
        .grey
```

```
        {
            color: #555555;
        }
    </style>
</head>
<body>
    <form id="form1" runat="server">
    <div>
        <asp:TextBox ID="TextBox1" runat="server"
            ontextchanged="TextBox1_TextChanged"
            CssClass="grey" AutoPostBack="True" />
      <br />
       <span class="abGrey">Text Box</span>
       <p />
      <asp:Button ID="Button1" runat="server"
          onclick="Button1_Click" Text="Click Here" />
      <br />
       <span class="abGrey">Button</span>
       <p />
       <asp:ListBox ID="ListBox1" runat="server"
           AutoPostBack="True" Height="80px"
           onselectedindexchanged="ListBox1_SelectedIndexChanged"
           Width="80px">
           <asp:ListItem Value="Item1"></asp:ListItem>
           <asp:ListItem Value="Item2"></asp:ListItem>
           <asp:ListItem Value="Item3"></asp:ListItem>
      </asp:ListBox>
      <br />
      <span class="abGrey">List Box</span></div>
    </form>
</body>
</html>
```

NOTE

To control the style of ASP.NET applications, you can add CSS just as you would in HTML or XHTML. The two CSS classes added in the EventWork.aspx file simply illustrate how to add CSS code. This includes adding CSS to style the TextBox ASP.NET control, which requires using the `CssClass` property:

```
<asp:TextBox ID="TextBox1" runat="server"
            ontextchanged="TextBox1_TextChanged"
            CssClass="grey" />
```

The C# portion of the application should have the event methods all set to go except for the code that directs the method what to do. The simple directives in the event methods indicate what's going on.

C# EventWork.aspx.cs

```csharp
using System;

public partial class EventWork : System.Web.UI.Page
{
    protected void Page_Load(object sender, EventArgs e)
    {
        TextBox1.Text = "Page Loaded";
    }
    protected void Button1_Click(object sender, EventArgs e)
    {
        TextBox1.Text = "Button Pressed";
    }

    protected void TextBox1_TextChanged(object sender, EventArgs e)
    {
        TextBox1.Text += "*";
    }

    protected void ListBox1_SelectedIndexChanged(object sender,
EventArgs e)
    {
        switch(ListBox1.SelectedItem.Value)
        {
            case "Item1":
                TextBox1.Text = "#1 Selected";
                break;
            case "Item2":
                TextBox1.Text = "#2 Selected";
                break;
            case "Item3":
                TextBox1.Text = "#3 Selected";
                break;
        }
    }
}
```

When you test this application, you will see all outcomes presented in the TextBox window, as shown in Figure 4-3. To see how the event in the TextBox works, type in anything and press ENTER, and you will see "PageLoaded*" in the output. The event reloads the page and then adds the asterisk as required in the event code for the TextBox.

As you use more and more ASP.NET controls, you will be introduced to more C# event handling functions. For the most part, though, all you will have to do is to double-click the control in Microsoft Visual Studio 2008 Design mode for the correct method shell to appear in the C# code listing.

Creating and Using Classes

Both ASP.NET and C# have a wealth of built-in classes, but you can build your own classes in C#. In C#, as in all object-oriented programming (OOP) languages, a class is a way of abstracting something. For example, you can abstract an animal like a cat. All cats have certain characteristics that are similar, but the actual cats have unique values for those general characteristics. Actual cats in our example would be referred to as *instances* of the Cat object. For example, the same cat abstraction applies to both housecats who rely on their owners to feed and house them and to cheetahs fending for themselves in the wild. Each time you need a cat, you can use the cat class to provide the general properties, and then all you have to do is to specify the characteristics of those properties. Both housecats and cheetahs have running speeds, but the cheetah can exceed speeds of 60 mph, while the housecat has a top speed of something significantly less. Other cat-like characteristics and actions are contained in the class so that when you actually instantiate a cat, it has both the general characteristics and the specific characteristics you include for a particular cat.

Making a Simple C# Class

An actual class is a very flexible entity in programming. Up to this point in the book, you have seen several examples of partial classes in C#, and they are indeed a type of class. Generally, the partial classes you've seen simply have a single event that defaults to Page_Load. The rest of the class usually involves nothing more than placing some statements into the event handling function.

A basic class typically has the following:

- List of **using** statements
- The class *name*
- The class *constructor*
- Variables (private instance variables)
- Properties (public accessors for the variables)
- Methods

The classes you will create are *public* ones. That means they can be accessed from other classes, including partial classes such as you've seen up to now. The following shows the generic features of a simple class (the key elements have been placed in boldface):

```
using System;
public class MyClass
```

```
{
     private string myProperty;

     public MyClass()
     {
          myProperty = "Some value";
     }
     public string MyMethod(string paramName)
     {
          return myProperty + paramName
     }
}
```

If you've used Java, the format should be fairly familiar. Some other languages, like ActionScript 3.0, use the keyword **function** for methods, but the general approach is the same. To get a better idea of how to create a pure C# class in an ASP.NET environment in Microsoft Visual Studio 2008, the next section provides a simple example.

Mutators and Accessors

In general, you should use mutators and accessors (also known as "getters" and "setters") with private properties. You would use accessors to get the value of a property and mutators to set a value. By doing so, you further encapsulate a variable. However, to keep the C# functions in the ASP.NET 3.5 web sites relatively short, accessors will not be used here. To employ a getter/setter model, use the format:

```
MyVar
{
     get
     {
          return myVar;
     }
     set
     {
          myVar = value;
     }
}
```

However, as a reminder of good practices, most of the variables are defined as private even though the getter/setter functions are not used.

Creating the ASP.NET Module

To get started, create a new ASP.NET web site in the same way as you would normally do. The following ASP.NET script only has a single text box for output, so start by creating it as listed in ClassOut.aspx.

ASP.NET ClassOut.aspx

```
<%@ Page Language="C#" AutoEventWireup="true" CodeFile="ClassOut.aspx
.cs" Inherits="ClassOut" %>
<!DOCTYPE html PUBLIC "-//W3C//DTD XHTML 1.0 Transitional//EN"
"http://www.w3.org/TR/xhtml1/DTD/xhtml1-transitional.dtd">
<html xmlns="http://www.w3.org/1999/xhtml">
<head runat="server">
    <title>Using Outside Class Resources</title>
</head>
<body>
    <form id="form1" runat="server">
    <div>
        <asp:TextBox ID="Output" width=200
        runat="server"/>
    </div>
    </form>
</body>
</html>
```

As you can see, the ASP.NET elements look pretty much like the ones that have been covered thus far. You do not need to do anything for the ASP.NET file (.aspx) other than you would were you only using a partial C# class.

Adding a C# Class

Once your ASPX file is ready, select File | New | File in Microsoft Visual Studio 2008, and you will see the Templates window shown in Figure 4-4. Select the C# Class icon, and add a name for the class with the .cs extension, also shown in Figure 4-4 in the Name window. Once you have that done, click the Add button.

As soon as you click the Add button, you will get an Alert dialog box as shown in Figure 4-5. Click the Yes button. This action creates an App_Code folder where the C# file is placed.

As soon as you click the Yes button, you will see the C# class template appear in your code window as shown in Figure 4-6.

The C# class template lists the same using elements as you see in the C# partial class when it first appears. Now, add what you want to your class, and then you'll see how to instantiate an instance of the class in the C# partial class. The following listing shows a simple C# class that you can use.

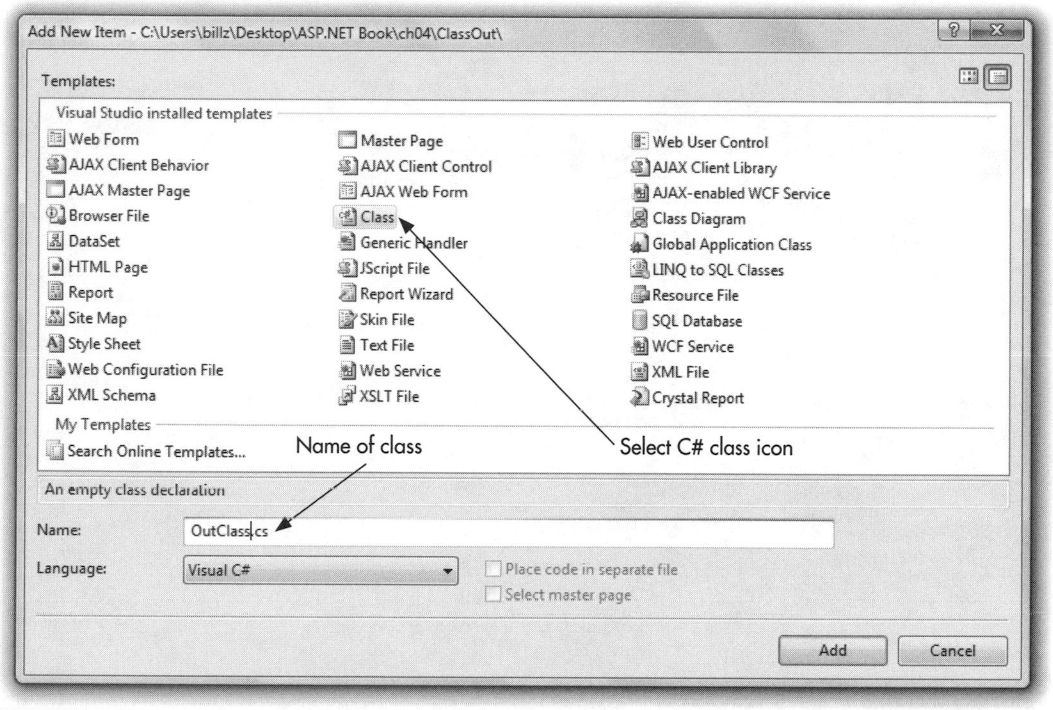

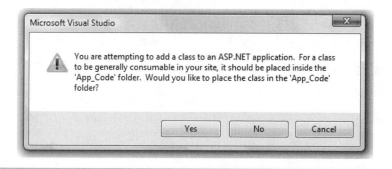

Figure 4-4   Selecting C# class template

Figure 4-5   Alert box to create folder for C# class

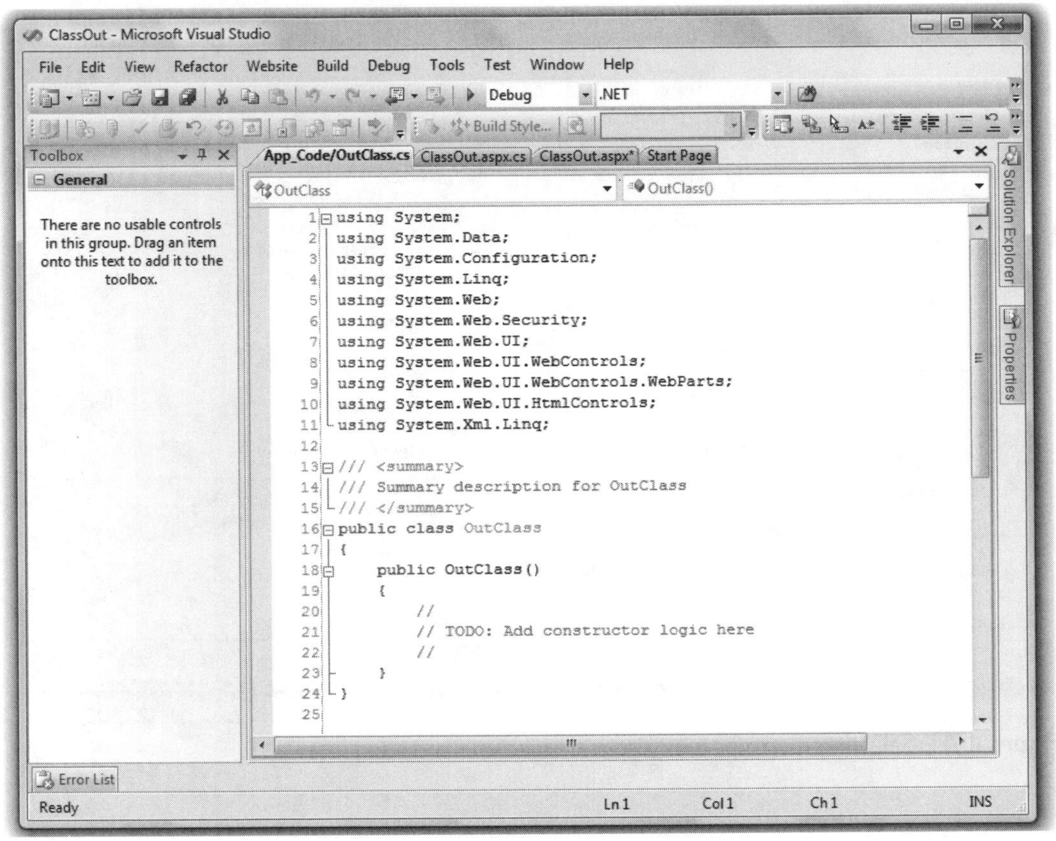

Figure 4-6 C# class template

OutClass.cs

```
using System;

/// <summary>
/// Class with single method to send string
/// </summary>
///
//Declaring a class with the class label
public class OutClass
{
    //Property of the class
    private string header;
```

```
  //Constructor function has the same name as the class
    public OutClass()
    {
      header = "From your class:";
    }

  //Class method
  public string sendMsg(string fromClass)
  {
      return header + fromClass;
  }
}
```

This class has a single method, sendMsg(), and a single property, header. Because the sendMsg() method is public, you can access it from another class.

Accessing the C# Class from the C# Partial Class

The final step is to modify the C# partial class that is automatically generated. Open the partial C# class, and within the Page_Load function, begin adding code as shown in Figure 4-7. To instantiate an instance of the OutClass within the partial class, simply declare the class and then instantiate it as shown in Line 9 in Figure 4-7. Once you have instantiated the class, IntelliSense recognizes the OutClass method, making it very easy to develop with user classes you've developed yourself.

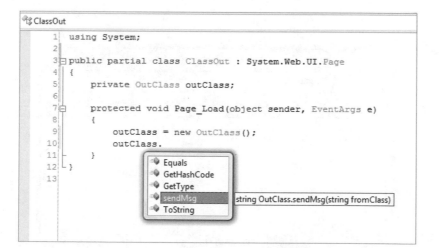

Figure 4-7   IntelliSense recognizes methods from instantiated classes.

In looking at the entire partial C# class, you can see the instantiated user class represents a gateway to any class in C#, no matter how simple or complex. In fact, if you've created sophisticated design patterns in C#, you can instantiate them in the C# partial class connected to ASP.NET just as you would using the C# project editor or any other tool of choice. The following listing shows how the partial class is linked both to the user class (OutClass) and to the ASP.NET TextBox form, Output.

C# OutClass.cs

```
using System;

public partial class ClassOut : System.Web.UI.Page
{
    private OutClass outClass;
    private string fromClass;

    protected void Page_Load(object sender, EventArgs e)
    {
        outClass = new OutClass();
        fromClass = outClass.sendMsg("The ClassOut class");
        Output.Text = fromClass;
    }
}
```

Once you have finished and saved the three modules, test the application. You will see the output shown in Figure 4-8.

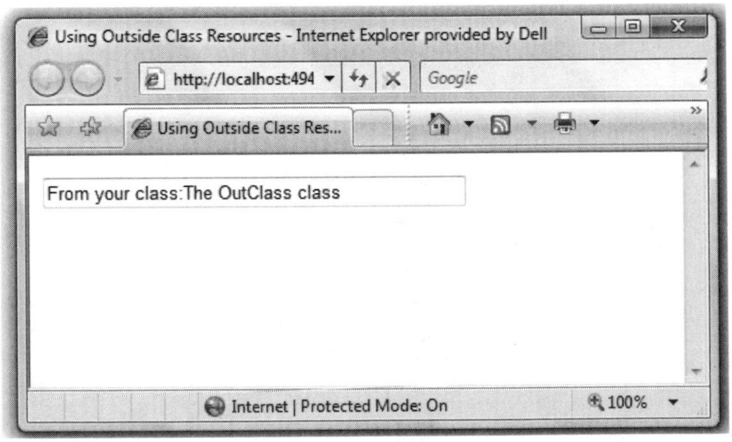

Figure 4-8 Output using ASP.NET, C# partial class, and C# class

In looking at Figure 4-8, you can see the contributions of each of three main elements:

- The window displaying the text (**TextBox** from ASP.NET)
- "From your class:" (content of the C# class property, **header**)
- "The OutClass class" (text in the parameter of the **sendMsg** method from the ClassOut class instance in the partial class)

As you can see, each of the three scripts made a contribution. The main lesson from this, though, is that you can access C# classes and structures from the partial class associated with the ASP.NET controls and forms.

Using Interfaces

Like classes, interfaces in C# can be used in conjunction with an ASP.NET application. Generally, interfaces are used in more sophisticated structures, and while you may not need them to learn ASP.NET, knowing how to use them with ASP.NET may prove to be valuable with more advanced structures found in object-oriented programming or in design patterns.

Like a class, an *interface* is an abstraction to be employed concretely in specific implementations. Generally, interfaces *describe a group of related functionalities.* You might think of a class as an abstraction of an object and of an interface as an abstraction of a method. An interface cannot be directly instantiated, but must be instantiated from concrete classes that implement an interface. Moreover, a key good practice is to program to an interface and not to an implementation. For the most part, this means that the typing will be to the interface, but the instantiation is to the class that implements the interface.

To better understand interfaces and their use, look at a good book on OOP or C#. Here, you will see how an interface can be used with an ASP.NET web application. In this next sample application, you will see a simple interface with output to an ASP.NET form. The following steps show how:

1. Create a new web site in Visual Studio 2008 using the name **Interface Test**.

2. Change the default name of the ASPX file to **Iface** and then enter the following code.

ASP.NET Iface.aspx

```
<%@ Page Language="C#" AutoEventWireup="true" CodeFile="Iface.aspx.cs"
Inherits="Iface" %>
<!DOCTYPE html PUBLIC "-//W3C//DTD XHTML 1.0 Transitional//EN"
```

```
"http://www.w3.org/TR/xhtml1/DTD/xhtml1-transitional.dtd">
<html xmlns="http://www.w3.org/1999/xhtml">
<head runat="server">
    <title>Interface Example</title>
</head>
<body>
    <form id="form1" runat="server"/>
    <div>
        <asp:Label ID="Label1" runat="server" />
        <asp:Label ID="Label2" runat="server"/>
    </div>
    </form>
</body>
</html>
```

3. In the partial class, you will be implementing the interface. The name of the interface
is IfaceIt. The script types two objects named iA and iB as IfaceIt types. Then,
using the IfaceIt objects, it instantiates two classes that implement the interface.
Because both of the classes implement the interface, you can use the objects typed to
the interface to instantiate each of the different classes as shown in the following script.

C# Iface.aspx.cs

```
using System;

public partial class Iface : System.Web.UI.Page
{
    private String showMe;
    private IfaceIt iA;
    private IfaceIt iB;

    protected void Page_Load(object sender, EventArgs e)
    {
        iA = new UseIfaceA();
        iB = new UseIfaceB();
        Label1.Text = iA.Show();
        Label2.Text = iB.Show();
    }
}
```

4. Next, build a simple interface. The interface has a single method that does nothing
more than return a string. The actual string it returns can be just about anything, and the
details of the method are left to the actual implementation of the interface in concrete
classes. All they have to do is return a string and use the name of the method specified
in the interface; the method, Show, has *no content,* only a return type (String).

Just open a new C# class file exactly as though you were creating a class instead of an interface. (Remember, you'll be asked if you want Visual Studio 2008 to create an App_Code folder for you—you will respond in the affirmative.)

C# IfaceIt.cs

```
using System;

/// <summary>
/// This is a simple interface example
/// </summary>
public interface IfaceIt
{
    String Show();
}
```

5. To make a concrete class that implements the interface, you code it just like an inheritance—using the colon (:) to indicate implementation. Also, you have to provide the specific content for the method. In this example, the method, Show(), returns a string literal indicating the identity of the implementation. Note that the string literal contains an XHTML tag that can be read by the ASP.NET form.

C# UseIfaceA.cs

```
using System;

/// <summary>
/// Summary description for UseIfaceA
/// </summary>
public class UseIfaceA : IfaceIt{
public String Show()
    {
        return "First Implementation<br />";
    }
}
```

6. The second implementation of the interface is similar, but it has a different string literal as a return value for the method.

C# UseIfaceB.cs

```
using System;

/// <summary>
```

Ask the Expert

Q: What exactly is meant by *inheritance*?

A: When one class or partial class inherits another class, the inheriting class gets all of the characteristics of the class it inherits. That means that the inheriting class, called the *child* or *subclass* of the inherited class, can use all of the methods and properties of the parent class.

```
/// Summary description for UseIfaceB
/// </summary>
public class UseIfaceB : IfaceIt
{
    public String Show()
    {
        return "Second Implementation";
    }
}
```

You might want to make sure that the files for the interface and the two classes that implement the interface are in the App_Code folder before you test your application. When everything is ready, go ahead and test it by selecting the Iface.aspx file in the Solution Explorer and pressing CTRL-F5.

Figure 4-9 shows the different results generated by the same interface implemented in two different classes. The partial class that you're accustomed to using with ASP.NET code is able to instantiate objects based on the interface with no problems. The same is true with larger structures in C# that use interface.

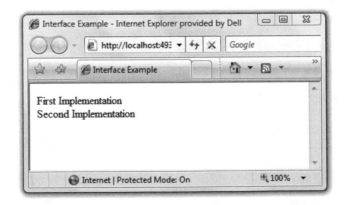

Figure 4-9 ASP.NET Label displays strings from two different classes implementing a single interface.

Doing More with C# and Object-Oriented Programming

This chapter is actually a long footnote about using more sophisticated structures in C#, but you will need to look at a complete book on C#, such as *C# 3.0: A Beginner's Guide,* to get into the kinds of details you will need to really employ OOP. You will find C# to be an incredibly powerful language. If you already know that and feel frustrated by using partial classes instead of full-blown C# classes and OOP structures, I hope you have seen how to use full classes in this chapter, and that you need not fear that you are limited to partial classes when using C# with ASP.NET 3.5. Everything you want to do with C# can be fully accomplished by C# partial classes. What's more, because the partial classes are woven into ASP.NET, you can use all of the ASP.NET structures as well.

For beginners who just want to learn how to get a back-end working for their sites using ASP.NET, fear not. Throughout this book, you will quickly see that the focus is on ASP.NET forms and controls you can use. This is most important when it comes to using databases and SQL structures to move data into and out of stored data sources. Once you've got the basics down, you'll probably want to use the more powerful features of C# to develop your ASP.NET applications.

Part II

Forms and Controls

Chapter 5

HTML Forms: A Review

Key Skills & Concepts

- Working with form tag and attributes

- Reviewing HTML user input: Text, Submit Radio, and Checkbox

- More form formats: Textarea, Select, Option

- What's in a name attribute: HTML names and variable names

One of the frustrations of working with HTML forms is that they cannot work by themselves. Unless some other programming language is working with the HTML page, user entry goes nowhere. Therefore, this chapter reviews HTML forms to show how data and form names can be passed in ASP.NET applications. If you're already familiar with HTML forms and their attributes, still take a look at the subtle differences between using them with HTML and with ASP.NET.

Working with Form Tags and Attributes

All forms in HTML begin with the `<form>` tag. If you're working with some kind of other code or external file where you want to pass on data entered in the form, you will see something like the following:

```
<form id="myForm" action= "someURL" method = "post">
```

The form's `id` acts something like a variable name to distinguish it from any other forms that might be in the page. The action calls a URL invoking the called program. If you're familiar with the original ASP or with PHP, you know that the data in the HTML forms can be passed to these other programs that are called. The final common attribute is a method with one of two values, `post` or `get`. The method used depends on whether the form is *idempotent* or not. For all practical purposes, an idempotent method is one where the values are unmodified even when multiple calls are made. Non-idempotent methods are ones where the values may change. When the forms are idempotent, use the `get` method; otherwise use the `post` method. Because non-idempotent methods are more frequently used, developers tend to use the `post` method. The selection of method can cause heated debate in an HTML environment, but in ASP.NET, you will not see a value assigned to a method attribute. Instead, you will see something like the following:

```
<form id="myForm" runat="server">
```

As you've seen in previous chapters, all of the Web pages in ASP.NET contain `<form runat="server">` somewhere in the ASPX file. For the most part, that is the primary difference (and it's a big one!) between HTML forms in either HTML or XHTML and in ASP.NET.

HTML Tag Properties

HTML tags have several different attributes or properties. The easiest way to see a tag's attributes or properties is with Visual Studio 2008. To get started looking at HTML tags in a Web form, we'll create a simple project using some HTML forms.

NOTE

You can find HTML tag attributes at www.w3.org, the World Wide Web Consortium's main site. For the most recent draft, see www.w3.org/html/wg/html5/.

Try This Using HTML Forms with ASP.NET Web Sites

To get the ball rolling, use the following steps to create a site using HTML forms:

1. Open Visual Studio 2008, create a new Web Site, and make sure that the Properties window is open (View | Properties Window).

2. Once you've opened a new Web Site, select the word "form" in the line `<form id="form1" runat="server">` and open the Properties window. When you do, you will see the attributes shown in Figure 5-1.

(continued)

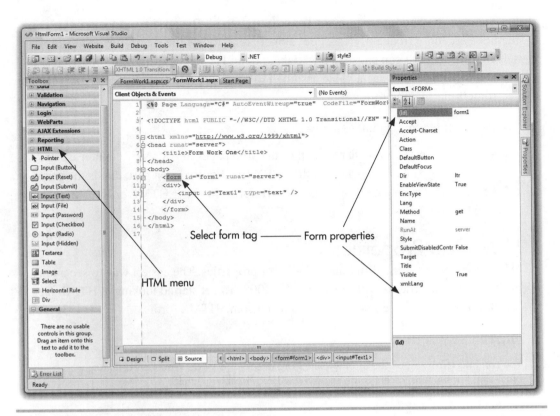

Figure 5-1 Form properties

3. In the Toolbox, click on the HTML menu, and then drag an Input (Text) form to the stage and place it in the <div> container. Then include the attribute **runat="server"** as shown in Figure 5-1.

4. Input (Text) forms do not have a Text attribute (or property) as does the ASP.NET control, TextBox. Instead they have a value attribute that can be used to add some kind of content to the form. Add the value "My message" to the input text form using the code **value="My message"** within the tag. The line should now be

```
<input id="Text1" type="text" runat="server" value="My message" />
```

5. Finally, add **
** to the end of the line to create a new line where the next HTML element will go.

6. Select a `Textarea` form and drag it to the stage right under the `Input (Text)` element. Add **`runat="server"`** at the end, and delete the `</textarea>` tag and place the closing slash at the end of the tag as shown in the following line:

```
<textarea id="TextArea1" cols="20" rows="2" runat="server" />
```

Once you have made the changes, your code should look like the following:

FormWork1.aspx

```
<%@ Page Language="C#" AutoEventWireup="true" CodeFile="FormWork1.aspx.cs"
Inherits="FormWork1" %>
<!DOCTYPE html PUBLIC "-//W3C//DTD XHTML 1.0 Transitional//EN"
"http://www.w3.org/TR/xhtml1/DTD/xhtml1-transitional.dtd">
<html xmlns="http://www.w3.org/1999/xhtml">
<head runat="server">
 <title>Form Work One</title>
</head>
<body>
 <form id="form1" runat="server">
 <div>
 <input id="Text1" type="text" runat="server" value="My message" /> <br/>
 <textarea id="TextArea1" cols="20" rows="2" runat="server" />
 </div>
 </form>
</body>
</html>
```

Once you've got everything in the ASPX file saved, you will need to deal with HTML elements from the C# side. That's what we'll do next.

C# and HTML Tags

This next step is pretty simple because all it does is transfer the string literal in the Input (Text) form to the Textarea form. (Further on in this section, you will see what happens if you attempt to use an HTML button to wait for user input.) For now, though, just edit the C# partial class to the following.

C# FormWork1.aspx.cs

```
using System;
public partial class FormWork1 : System.Web.UI.Page
{
 protected void Page_Load(object sender, EventArgs e)
 {
 TextArea1.Value = Text1.Value;
 }
}
```

(continued)

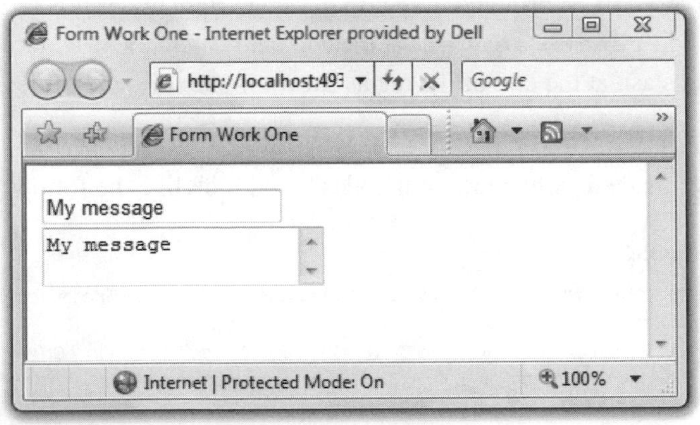

Figure 5-2 Assigned values can be shared

As you can see, the script simply transfers the value of the input text form to the textarea. Both forms use the value attribute, and C# is able to use those HTML form elements to place the contents of one form into another as you can see in Figure 5-2.

Obviously, transferring data from a text input form to a textarea form isn't too useful unless the user has a chance to enter data. Therefore, we need to look at using something to hold the transfer until it is ready to be used.

HTML Buttons

Now that you've seen that C# can pass values between HTML forms, let's take a look at HTML buttons. The bad news is that HTML buttons do not automatically generate the C# code for event handling. With Standard buttons, all you have to do is to switch to the Design mode and double-click on the button to generate the C# event handler. However, when you double-click an HTML button, you get JavaScript code instead.

Try This Using HTML Buttons

The following steps give you a quick view of what happens when you use an HTML button rather than a Standard button from the Toolbox.

1. Open a new Web Site by selecting File | New | Web Site. Give it the name **junk** because you'll be throwing it out when you're done.

2. In the Source mode, drag an Input (Button) from the Toolbox to the `<div>` container (between the `<div>` and `</div>` tags).

3. Switch to the Design mode, and double-click the Button icon. (You may remember from previous chapters that this action automatically generates a C# function for button event-handling.) However, instead of generating code for C# to handle, it generates the following JavaScript code:

```
<script language="javascript" type="text/javascript">
// <!CDATA[
function Button1_onclick() {
}
// ]]>
```

That may be a handy piece of JavaScript code, but it's not what you need in your C# partial class to set up an event handler using the code-behind method. So, when creating applications using HTML forms, you're going to need a different approach for triggering the C# events.

Standard Buttons and HTML Forms

As you've seen, you can use HTML forms, but when we try to put an HTML button in an application, Visual Studio 2008 automatically generates JavaScript code. Is it possible to use Standard ASP.NET buttons with a Standard button? In other words, can C# handle a mix of both Standard controls and HTML forms? Fortunately, the answer is yes.

Try This Using Standard ASP.NET Buttons

This next application illustrates mixing ASP.NET standard controls with HTML forms that are set to `runat="server"` so that they can work with ASP.NET and be read as forms by the C# code behind. While we're at it, let's add an image so that we can see if it's possible to mix in tags like `<img>` to the application. The following steps show how to create the application:

1. Open a new Web Site by selecting File | New | Web Site. Give it the name **HtmlForm2**.

2. Select the Source mode and the HTML Toolbox menu, and drag an instance of the Input (Text) form and a Textarea form into the `<div>` container.

3. Select the Standard menu in the Visual Studio 2008 Toolbox, and drag an instance of a Button to the source page and place it right below the `<textarea>` tag.

4. Place an image in the HtmlForm2 folder as shown in Figure 5-3. In this case, I used a clip-photo example in JPG format.

5. Switch to the Design mode, and drag the image from the folder to the position you want it on the page. When you drag the image, a dialog box appears and prompts for an Alternate text name and a Long description. Provide the requested names and click OK.

(continued)

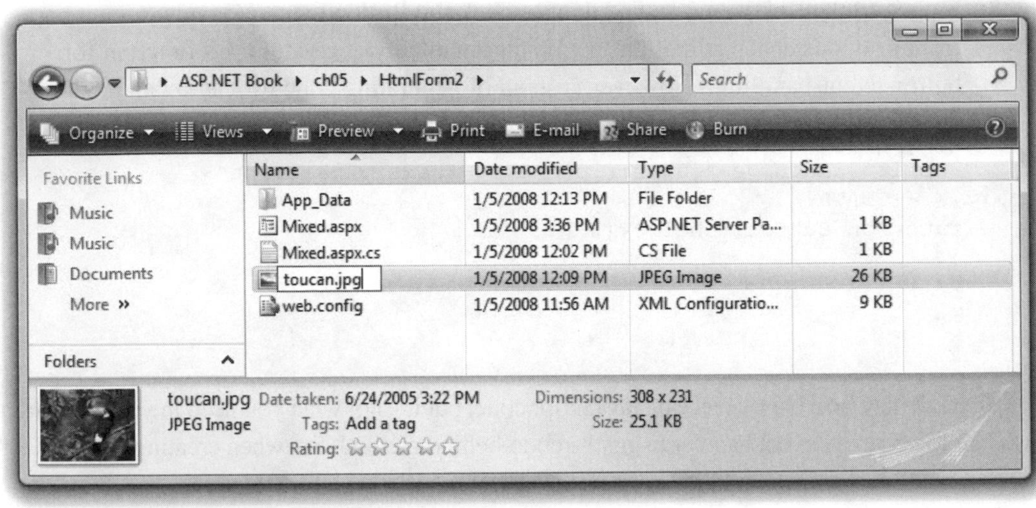

Figure 5-3 Image file placed with C# and ASP.NET files

Once you're finished, your ASP.NET code should appear as the following:

Mixed.aspx

```
<%@ Page Language="C#" AutoEventWireup="true" CodeFile="Mixed.aspx.cs"
Inherits="Mixed" %>
<!DOCTYPE html PUBLIC "-//W3C//DTD XHTML 1.0 Transitional//EN"
"http://www.w3.org/TR/xhtml1/DTD/xhtml1-transitional.dtd">
<html xmlns="http://www.w3.org/1999/xhtml">
<head runat="server">
 <title>Mixed Controls</title>
</head>
<body>
 <form id="form1" runat="server">
 <div>
 <input id="Text1" type="text" runat="server"/><br >
 <textarea id="TextArea1" cols="20" rows="2" runat="server" /><br />
 <asp:Button ID="Button1" runat="server" Text="Button" onclick="Button1_Click" />
          <br />
 <img alt="bird" longdesc="big bird" src="toucan.jpg"
style="width: 308px; height: 231px" />
 </div>
 </form>
</body>
</html>
```

An equally important part of this exercise is to see if the different mixed types of
HTML forms and the Standard ASP.NET button will work together. Also, remember that

the objects include a JPEG file, and the image file must play nicely in the sandbox with the other elements that are set up using `runat="server"` in their tag containers. Note, however, that nowhere in the `Mixed` partial class is there any reference to the `<img>` tag.

C# Mixed.aspx.cs

```
using System;

public partial class Mixed : System.Web.UI.Page
{
 protected void Button1_Click(object sender, EventArgs e)
 {
 TextArea1.Value = Text1.Value;
 }
}
```

Once you've entered the code, go ahead and test it. As you can see in Figure 5-4, the two different HTML forms appear along with the Standard ASP.NET button and the image of the bird.

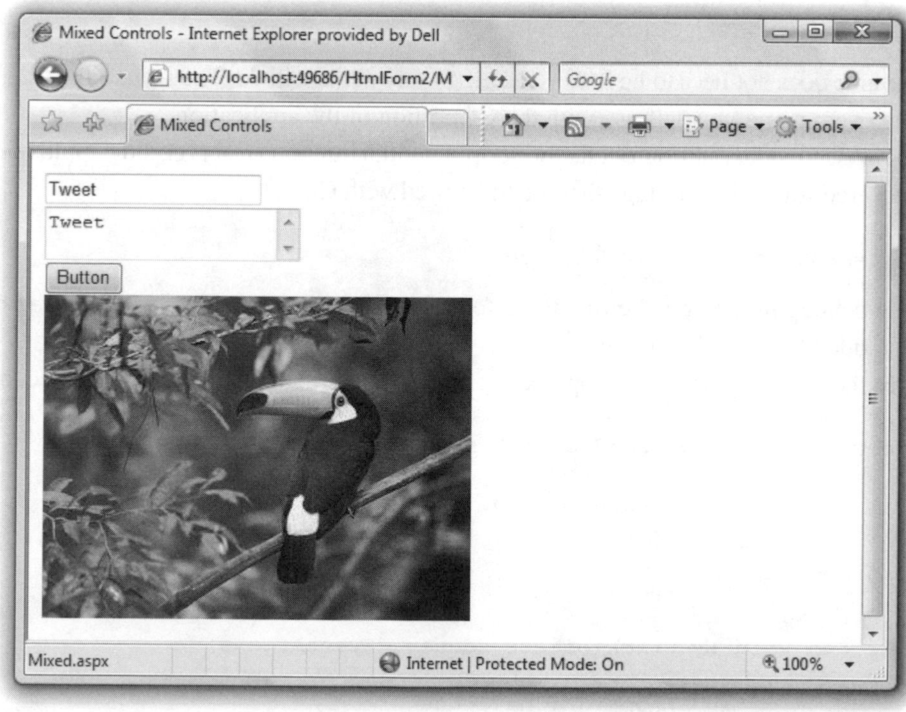

Figure 5-4   Different types of tags in a single ASP.NET application

(continued)

Enter text in the top HTML text field and click the button. You will see that the value of the top text box is passed to the bottom text box without a problem.

Using HTML Forms Interactively

You can use the HTML forms for data input in an ASP.NET application, but to use HTML buttons, we're going to have to put in some special code rather than relying on good old Visual Studio 2008 to do all the work. First of all, you will need to use a submit button when you're setting up your button to fire a C# event handler. Second, you'll need a special format to specify an event. The following shows the key elements you will need to enter by hand after you have dragged the Input (Submit) button from the Toolbox to the stage:

```
<input id="MyButton" type="submit" value="Button" OnServerClick=
"My_Click" runat="server" />
```

Two key attributes must be included. First, you need the attribute

```
OnServerClick="My_Click"
```

The value does not need to be "My_Click"—any name will do. The value ("My_Click") is the event name you will use with the C# portion of the application.

The second key attribute tells the script that this button is a server-side application. It is required for all HTML tags that are to be used with C#.

```
runat="server"
```

In the debugging process the first thing to check is whether the runat="server" has been added to your HTML tag.

In the C# code the easiest approach is to change the default C# event handler code from

```
protected void Page_Load(object sender, EventArgs e)
  {
                //Operational code
  }
```

to

```
protected void My_Click(object sender, EventArgs e)
  {
                //Operational code

  }
```

Ask the Expert

Q: Can you use any event handler name you want? What if I wanted to use "Page_ Load" as an event handler name for a button? I know it doesn't make much sense, but I'm just curious.

A: Because `Page_Load` is a page event, it will not respond to a button-click event. In fact, ASP.NET 3.5 and C# 3.0 have several page events such as `Page_Unload`, `Page_Init`, and `Page_LoadComplete` that will not respond to the button click. However, if you use an event handler name like `Page_Click` with a button, it responds just as well as any other name associated with a Button control. Until you learn more, though, I'd suggest that you not preface your event name with `Page_` unless it is one that you want to have respond to a page event.

As you can see, the change is minimal. You're just substituting your own handler name for the default `Page_Load`. All C# will be looking for is the right event name based on the attribute `OnServerClick="My_Click"` in your button tag and `runat="server"`.

Extracting Values from HTML Forms

Up to this point, we've been using the `value` attribute of different types of HTML text forms to pass values. However, in addition to HTML text forms, you have a much richer selection from which to choose. Included are drop-down menus (Select forms), radio buttons, and checkboxes. Each of these has a place in the UI (user interface) for several different kinds of sites. Each of these HTML forms is discussed along with how data can be pulled from the different forms. Then, using several different HTML forms, we'll look at how to make a political polling application that uses a sample of HTML data input forms.

HTML Select Forms

The HTML Select forms are often called *pop-up* or *drop-down* menus. They are used when the user must select from a long list of options, and you don't have much room on the page to display them. If you've ever selected from a country list beginning with Afghanistan and ending with Zimbabwe, you have a good idea of how much room such a list takes. However, by using a Select form, you can store all the countries in the world and take up only a single line.

ASP.NET Setup HTML Select   Setting up a Select form is a little different than some of the other HTML forms because you add several lines. Initially when you drag a Select form from the HTML Toolbox menu to the editor, you will see the `<select>` container, and within that is a single `<option>` container. You can add as many option elements as you want. Typically the top option is the name of the menu, and then each selectable option is a category or case within that set. For example, the following shows how a Select form is set up in ASP.NET:

```
<select id="Select1" runat="server">
 <option>Country</option>
 <option>Afghanistan</option>
 <option>Albania</option>
 <option>Algeria</option>
</select>
```

An important attribute to include in the HTML Select object is `runat="server"`. If you forget to add that attribute, it will not be recognized by the C# script. Also, you have to decide whether the Select list is going to allow multiple choices at once or is mutually exclusive. If you want the user to select multiple options, then you must add the attribute and value

```
multiple="multiple"
```

within the `<select>` tag. Of course, you may want to add some of the other properties as well, and further on in the book you will be looking at some properties useful when working with specific kinds of data.

C# Reading and Writing HTML Select Forms
The easiest way to think of an HTML Select form is as an array. The name of the array is the value assigned to the `id` attribute. In the example, the default name `Select1` is the `id` value. Each option in the form can be treated as an array element. You may reference the options as `Items` in an array. For example, if we take the second item in the Select form, on a zero-based array, we could get *Afghanistan* as the string variable in the following line:

```
String someCountry = Select1.Items[1];
//someCountry would have the value Afghanistan
```

Of course when you are programming in C#, the only values that you want are those selected by the user. One of the properties, `Selected`, is a Boolean. So, if the user selects the fourth element, for example, the value of that item would be `true`. In the preceding listing, the value of the fourth item would be *Algeria*. The good thing about arrays is that you can use a loop to iterate through them. In that way if you have a long list, it's easy to check each one with a minimum of code. In the case of the Select form, you will be looking to see if the option is selected. If it is selected, then your code can pass it on to wherever you want it to go. The following shows a typical loop for inspecting the contents of an HTML Select form and then sending it out to a textarea form:

```
for (int state = 0; state <= Select1.Items.Count -1;state++)
 {
 if (Select1.Items[state].Selected)
 {
 TextArea1.Value += Select1.Items[state].Text + "\n" ;
 }
 }
```

Note that the `Count` property of the `Select.Items` object is used to determine the length of the array (number of options.) Also note that 1 is subtracted from the number of options because like all arrays, this one is zero-based. Figure 5-5 shows a typical pop-up menu using an HTML Select form.

As a user interface, the Select form is handy for saving room; however, Select forms need to be used judiciously. Often users will overlook a pop-up menu as the correct category for a selection. If they do, they may miss something they're trying to find. (That definitely *is not* something that you want to happen in an e-business application!) You're pretty safe using them with well-known categories like states and countries, though.

HTML Check Boxes

Check boxes are great for situations where you want the user to make one or several selections. Not only is it easy for the user to make the selections, but also the check box is a way to let the user know what her options are. As you will see, they're easy to use for data collection and are another handy UI.

ASP.NET Setup HTML Checkbox   Each check box you place in your application needs a separate `id`, `value`, and `runat="server"` attribute. Unlike the HTML Select form, the HTML Checkbox does not store values in an `<option>` container, but rather is assigned to a `value` attribute. The following shows a typical check box setup in an ASPX file:

```
<input id="Checkbox1" type="checkbox" runat="server" value="Economy"/>
```

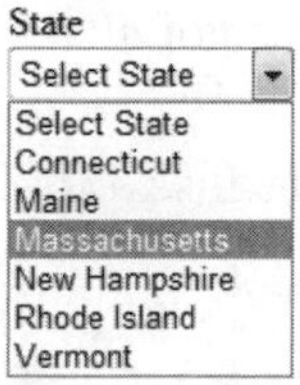

State

Select State	▼

Select State
Connecticut
Maine
Massachusetts
New Hampshire
Rhode Island
Vermont

Figure 5-5   The Select forms are pop-up menus.

For the user to know the reference to the check box, after the closing tag character, you need to type in the value. For example, the following shows what would typically follow the closing tag character:

```
... runat="server" value="Economy/>Economy<br/>
```

If the check boxes are arranged vertically, as is typically the case, each check box will be followed by some kind of line break tag.

C# Reading and Writing HTML Checkboxes   The check box has two states: Checked or Not Checked. Like the `Selected` property of the HTML Select form, the `Checked` property is a Boolean. Working out the state of each check box using standard conditional statements both can be time-consuming and can clutter your code. Using a C# ternary operator greatly simplifies and condenses the process of tricking out the check box's current state. The following line shows a simple example:

```
SendValue=Checkbox1.Checked == true ? Checkbox1.Value: null;
```

That line simply queries whether the check box is true or not, and if it is, it assigns the check box's value to the variable `SendValue`. If it's not true, `SendValue` is assigned a null value. Using the ternary operator, the entire process only takes a single line rather than several lines using an `if...else` sequence.

Figure 5-6 shows a typical use for check boxes. The user is provided with several different options and can choose as many or few as he wishes.

As you can see, the choices are clear and visible. All the user has to do is to click the check box to select the option or click it to unselect.

HTML Radio Buttons

HTML Radio buttons are virtually identical to the HTML Checkbox forms with one important exception. Radio buttons are for mutually exclusive selections (if you select one, you cannot select others), and check boxes are for multiple selections. For example, if you ask for a person's gender, it's going to be male or female, not both. Sometimes questionnaire designers want to force a single response, such as what the user believes is the *single most important choice* instead of *all the choices* that are believed to be important.

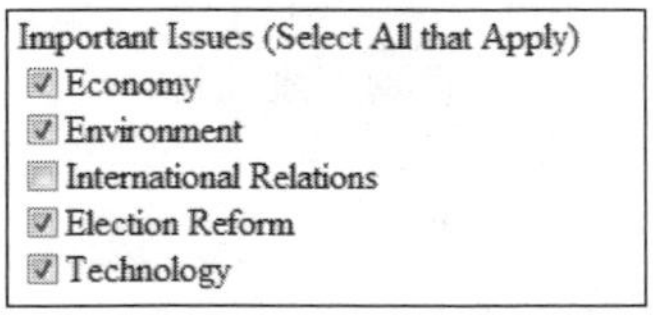

Figure 5-6   More than one Check box can be checked at the same time.

ASP.NET Setup HTML Radio Buttons   As with check boxes, you need to include with radio buttons a unique `id`, `value`, and `runat="server"` attribute. However, the HTML Radio form also has a `name` attribute. The `name` attribute with radio buttons is actually a *group name* in that several different radio buttons with unique `id` values can all have the same name. Otherwise, the format is the same as with the HTML Checkbox. The following example shows two typical radio buttons with the same `name` but with different `id`s and values:

```
<input id="Radio1" type="radio" name="party" value="Democratic"
runat="server" />
<input id="Radio2" type="radio" name="party" value="Republican"
runat="server" />
```

As you can see, both have the `name` value of *party*. When the user clicks on one radio button, all the others *with the same name* are unchecked. They can have as many different `id` values as you want, but only a single radio button in a `name` group can be selected at any onc time.

C# Reading and Writing HTML Radio Buttons   When C# reads a radio button, it reads it just like check boxes. The Checked property is a Boolean attached to the radio button's `id` value. As a result, you can use the same C# ternary operator as with HTML Checkbox forms. The following shows an example:

```
SendValue = Radio1.Checked == true ?  Radio1.Value: null;
```

Notice that the `name` attribute is not used. As a result, when checking to see if a radio button is checked, you will need to check each `id` separately.

   Figure 5-7 shows a typical use of the radio button. When you create a query using radio buttons, be sure to provide all possible categories. The *Other* category would be useful for picking up users who are Libertarian, Green, or some other party not listed.

   In Figure 5-7, if the user chooses any of the other radio button categories, the currently selected one would be unchecked. (The filled circle in a radio button doesn't look like a check, but that's the name of the property.)

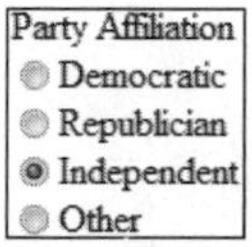

Figure 5-7   Radio buttons are for mutually exclusive categories.

Try This A Political Poll Using HTML Forms

For a practical view of how you might incorporate HTML forms, this next example uses several different forms. Once the user completes the form, the output is presented in an HTML textarea form. For data entry and calculation, the application is not very different from one you might develop for entering data into a database.

The following steps show how to get the application up and running:

1. Open Visual Studio 2008 and select File | New | Web Site.

2. Enter the name **PoliticalPoll** for your application and click OK.

3. Open the Solution Explorer, rename the ASPX file **Poll**, and enter the following code. (By this point, you know that you can save time by dragging the different HTML forms to the editor to generate some of the code automatically.)

ASP.NET Poll.aspx

```
<%@ Page Language="C#" AutoEventWireup="true" CodeFile="Poll.aspx.cs"
Inherits="Poll" %>
<!DOCTYPE html PUBLIC "-//W3C//DTD XHTML 1.0 Transitional//EN"
"http://www.w3.org/TR/xhtml1/DTD/xhtml1-transitional.dtd">

<html xmlns="http://www.w3.org/1999/xhtml">
<head runat="server">
 <title>Political Poll</title>
</head>
<body>
<center><h1>New England Voter Poll</h1></center>
 <form id="form1" runat="server">
 <div>

 State<br />
 <!-- Select Menu -->
 <select id="Select1" runat="server">
 <option>Select State</option>
 <option>Connecticut</option>
 <option>Maine</option>
 <option>Massachusetts</option>
 <option>New Hampshire</option>
 <option>Rhode Island</option>
 <option>Vermont</option>
 </select>
       
 <!-- Input Text -->
 <input id="Town" type="text" value="Town Name" runat="server"/>
 <br />

 Party Affiliation
 <br />
```

```
<!-- Radio Buttons -->
<input id="Radio1" type="radio" name="party" value="Democratic" runat="server"
/>Democratic<br />
<input id="Radio2" type="radio" name="party" value="Republican"
runat="server"/>Republican<br />
<input id="Radio3" type="radio" name="party" value="Independent"
runat="server"/>Independent<br />
<input id="Radio4" type="radio" name="party" value="Other" runat="server"/
>Other<p />

Important Issues (Select All that Apply)<br />
<!-- Checkboxes -->
<input id="Checkbox1" type="checkbox" runat="server" value="Economy"
/>Economy<br />
<input id="Checkbox2" type="checkbox" runat="server" value="Environment"
/>Environment<br />
<input id="Checkbox3" type="checkbox" runat="server" value="International
Relations" />International Relations<br />
<input id="Checkbox4" type="checkbox" runat="server" value="Election Reform"
/>Election Reform <br />
<input id="Checkbox5" type="checkbox" runat="server" value="Technology"
/>Technology<p />

<!-- Buttons -->
<input id="Reset1" type="submit" value="Clear" runat="server"
OnServerClick="Reset_Click" />
<input id="Submit1" type="submit" value="Send Data" runat="server"
OnServerClick="Submit_Click"/>
<p />
<!-- Textarea -->
<textarea id="TextArea1" cols="40" rows="10" runat="server"></textarea>
</div>
</form>
</body>
</html>
```

4. Once you have completed entering the ASP.NET code, open the Poll.aspx.cs file and enter the following C# code:

C# Poll.aspx.cs

```
using System;
public partial class Poll : System.Web.UI.Page
{
protected void Reset_Click(object sender, EventArgs e)
  {
  Radio1.Checked = false;
  Radio2.Checked = false;
  Radio3.Checked = false;
  Radio4.Checked = false;
```

(continued)

```
TextArea1.Value = "";
Town.Value = "Town Name";

for (int state = 0; state <= Select1.Items.Count - 1; state++)
{
Select1.Items[state].Selected = false;
}


Checkbox1.Checked = false;
Checkbox2.Checked = false;
Checkbox3.Checked = false;
Checkbox4.Checked = false;
Checkbox5.Checked = false;
}


protected void Submit_Click(object sender, EventArgs e)
{
//Handle Input (Text)
TextArea1.Value ="You vote in " + Town.Value + ", ";
//Handle Select
for (int state = 0; state <= Select1.Items.Count -1;state++ )
{
if (Select1.Items[state].Selected)
{
TextArea1.Value += Select1.Items[state].Text + "\n" ;
}
}


//Handle Radio Buttons
TextArea1.Value += Radio1.Checked == true ? " Your affiliation is:" +
Radio1.Value + "\n" : null;
TextArea1.Value += Radio2.Checked == true ? " Your affiliation is:" +
Radio2.Value + "\n" : null;
TextArea1.Value += Radio3.Checked == true ? " Your affiliation is:" +
Radio3.Value + "\n" : null;
TextArea1.Value += Radio4.Checked == true ? " Your affiliation is:" +
Radio4.Value + "\n" : null;


//Handle Checkboxes
TextArea1.Value += "These Issues are important to you:\n";
TextArea1.Value += Checkbox1.Checked == true ? " " + Checkbox1.Value + "\n" :
null;
TextArea1.Value += Checkbox2.Checked == true ? " " + Checkbox2.Value + "\n" :
null;
TextArea1.Value += Checkbox3.Checked == true ? " " + Checkbox3.Value + "\n" :
null;
TextArea1.Value += Checkbox4.Checked == true ? " " + Checkbox4.Value + "\n" :
null;
TextArea1.Value += Checkbox5.Checked == true ? " " + Checkbox5.Value + "\n" :
null;
}
}
```

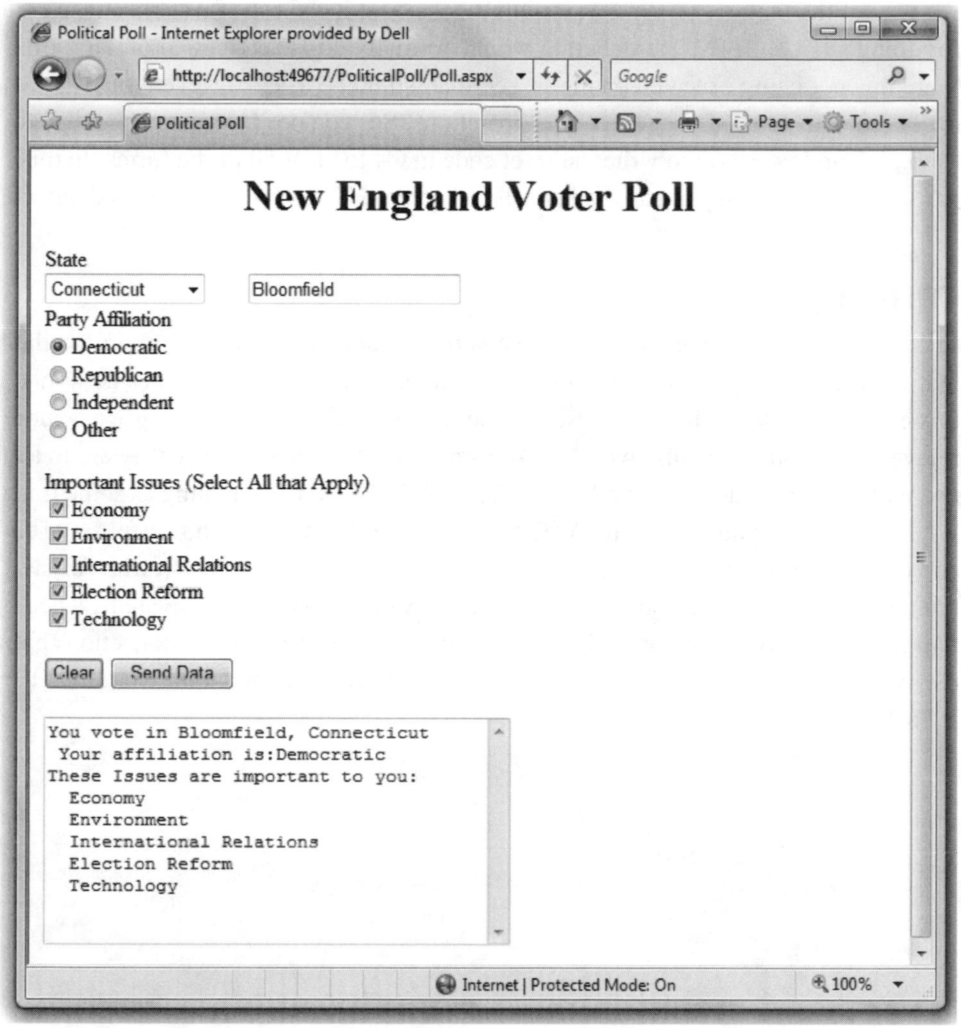

Figure 5-8   HTML forms and C# polling application

Once you have entered both the ASP.NET and C# code and saved them, test your application. Figure 5-8 shows how the data selected by the user is reflected in the HTML textarea form.

One of the features you may have questions about is the use of a submit-type button for doing what an HTML reset button would normally do—clear out all of the forms. Were this not being executed on the server, that would be true. However, the reset type is not recognized by C# or server-side operations. So, you need to change the type to "submit," and you have to write the reset code in C# to clear all of the forms. In this particular application you can see how five different HTML forms are cleared out.

Summary

In completing this chapter, you may have noticed that other HTML forms are available that were not covered; either their use has a common feature with the ones described in this chapter, or they will be discussed further on in the book where their use has more relevance. If you're familiar with HTML forms, you can see how easy they are to adapt to use with ASP.NET and C#. In other words, ASP.NET is not as daunting as some imagine.

In Chapter 6, you will see the Web Server Controls, a far more powerful set of forms and controls you can use with ASP.NET. Not only are they easier to use with ASP.NET, but they also work more cohesively with Visual Studio 2008 and the related C# code you will be using throughout the book. You should be able to see several connections between the Web Server Controls and what you learned in this chapter about the more familiar HTML forms.

Chapter 6

Standard Web Controls

Key Skills & Concepts

- Data entry: TextBox, CheckBox, RadioButton, DropDownList, ListBox, RadioButtonList, CheckBoxList

- Data display: TextBox (as a data display), Label, Literal, Panel

- Triggers, links, and images: Button, ImageButton, LinkButton, HyperLink, Image, ImageMap

In Chapter 5 you saw how to use a wide range of HTML forms to capture and temporarily store data and to pass values through C# to different forms. You will likely find this chapter using standard ASP.NET forms to be much simpler—or at least as simple— because you will be using web controls that were build specifically to use ASP.NET in conjunction with C#. ("Web Form controls" is the official Microsoft term, but "web controls" is a less awkward term.) For example, instead of having to hand-code the event handler for a standard web control Button object, you can use Visual Studio 2008 so that all you need to do is double-click on the Button icon in the Design view to generate the event handler function in the C# partial class.

In working with the web controls, you will find that the properties are far richer than the attributes available in the HTML forms. As a result you can do more with a web control than with an HTML form. Nevertheless, you should find the procedures for sending data from one place to another very similar, so what you learned in using HTML forms can be applied to ASP.NET web controls.

Data Entry

This section looks at the main standard web controls whose primary mission is to receive user input. These controls are essentially UI controls, and in most respects they are no different from the HTML forms discussed in the previous chapter. Included are the following web controls:

- TextBox
- CheckBox
- RadioButton

- DropDownList
- ListBox
- RadioButtonList
- CheckBoxList

All of these controls have a host of properties; for example, we're going to take a close look at how to use the properties associated with the TextBox. In looking at the TextBox, you can see how to apply properties to different data entry controls. What's more, we'll be looking at how the same control can be used in more than a single way simply by changing the properties.

TextBox Control for Data Entry

To get started, we'll take a look at the different TextBox control properties arranged by category. These categories can quickly tell you which kind of functionality you can add to your control.

In Visual Studio 2008 use the following steps to get started:

1. Open a new Web Site and name it **DataEntry**.

2. Set the editor to Source mode. Open the Toolbox for ASP.NET.

3. Drag a TextBox control to the editor, and place it within the `<div>` container.

4. Select the `TextBox` portion of the code, and open the Properties window.

5. In the Properties window, click on the Categorized icon.

Now you're all set to start working with the TextBox control and its properties. Organizing the control tasks into categories lets you work more efficiently. You will see the following categories:

- Accessibility
- Appearance
- Behavior
- Layout
- Misc

Depending on which category you need, you can keep the Properties window focused by toggling between the + and – signs next to each category name, so that only the ones you will be using are expanded (have the – sign displayed). The Appearance and Behavior categories have the most property options, so they will be used to illustrate how to work with ASP.NET properties.

Appearance

Close all of the categories in the TextBox Properties window except for Appearance. ("Appearance" will have a – sign next to it, and the others will have a + sign.) You will see several different options available in the Properties window as shown in Figure 6-1.

As long as the `TextBox` keyword on Line 12 is selected, you will be able to see the TextBox properties in the Properties window. You can both see the properties and make changes from there that show up in the code.

To get started making changes, select the `BackColor` property in the Properties window and type

```
#FFFF80
```

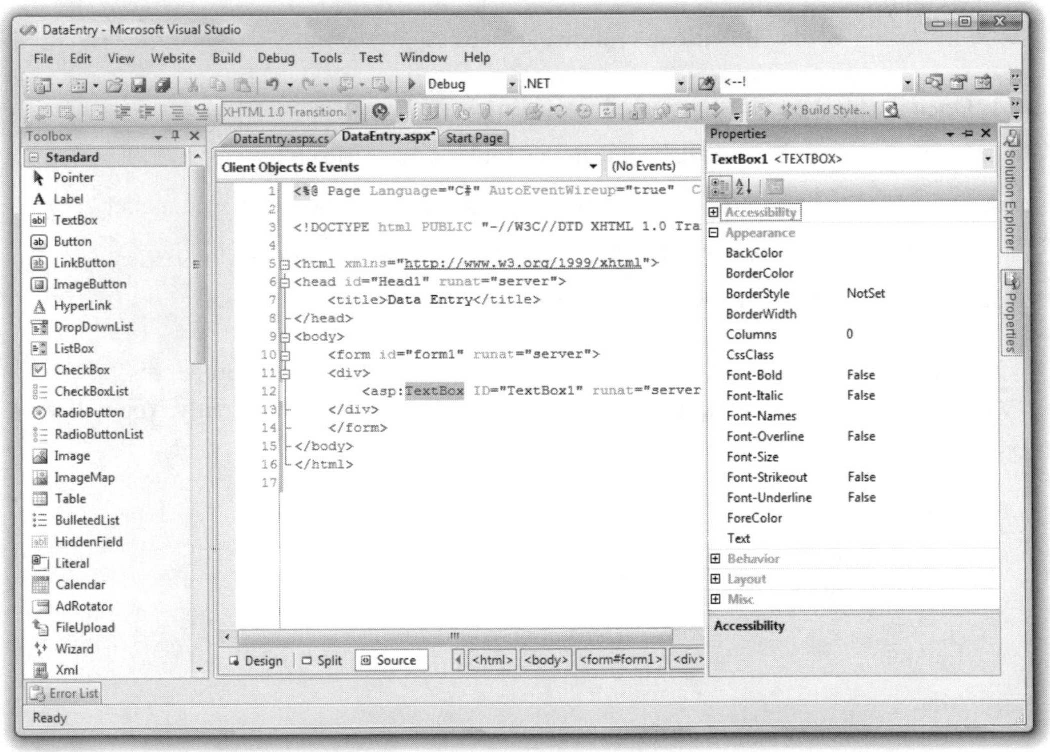

Figure 6-1 TextBox Appearance properties

as shown in Figure 6-2. When you make the change, you will see that the code in the TextBox control changes as well to include

```
BackColor="#FFFF80"
```

The hexadecimal values give you exactly the color you want from a choice of over a million combinations. However, whenever you open a color property, a small icon appears to the right of the property as shown in the circled icon in Figure 6-2. If you click the icon, a color selection palette appears, and you can simply click on the default palette or select from others in the window that opens.

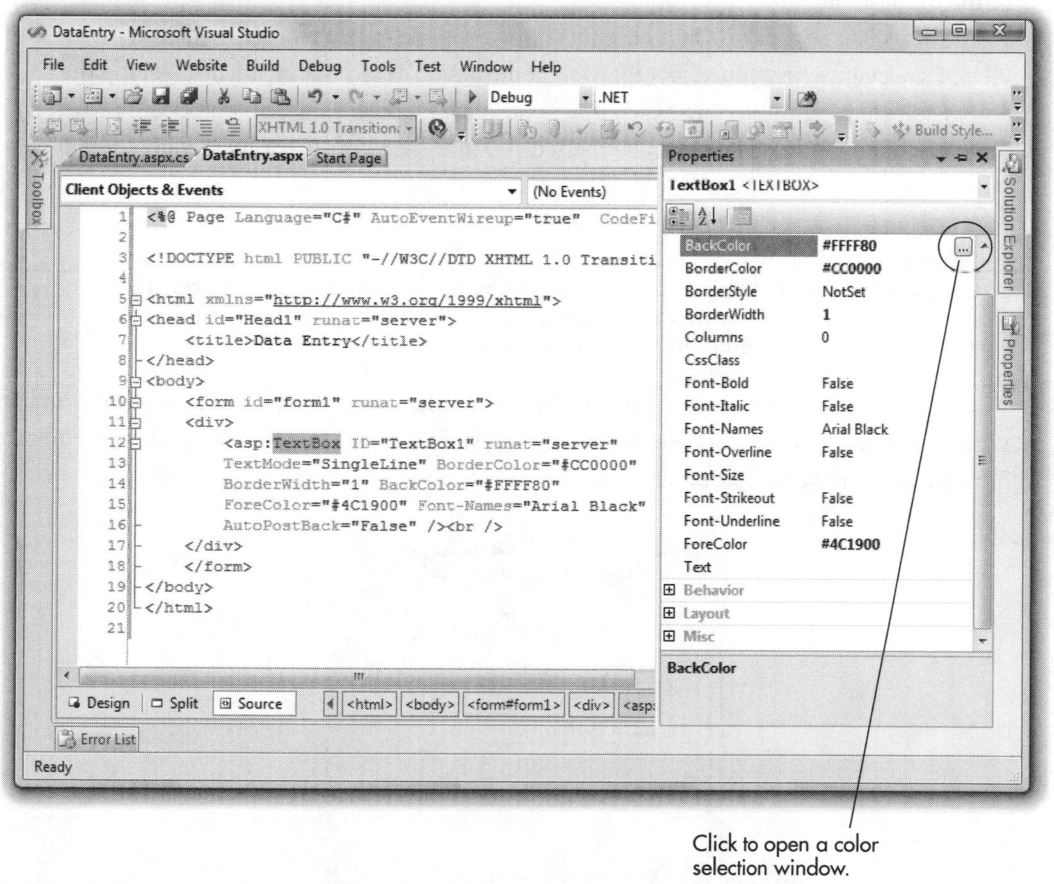

Click to open a color selection window.

Figure 6-2   Changing Appearance property values in TextBox control

In addition to changing the value of the `BackColor` property, change the following as well:

Property	Value
BorderColor	#CC0000
BorderWidth	1
Font-Names	Arial Black
ForeColor	#4C1900

Once you're finished, go ahead and test it. You should see your TextBox control as pictured in Figure 6-3. When you enter text, you will see the bold Arial Black font instead of the default one.

Using Visual Studio 2008, you may also view appearance changes when in the Design view. However, when you select the web control, you'll see that instead of seeing the colors selected in the Properties window, you'll see the color change that occurs when an object is selected. Just click outside the web control, and you'll see the actual colors.

NOTE

In setting up color schemes, designers typically use CSS, and that method is favored for constancy in site design. Using CSS is covered in Chapter 7. The `CssClass` property requires a CSS. However, for smaller applications, you can make changes to one control and use the same property values for the other controls without CSS.

The best way to become accustomed to the TextBox control appearance is to experiment with it. It's pretty simple to use, but even with simple tools, trying out different elements now prevents unwanted surprises later.

Figure 6-3 Appearance property changes in TextBox

Behavior

The behavioral properties of a web control can influence *appearance,* but generally add or delete an *action* associated with the web control. The Behavior properties can also transform a web control from one functionality to another. For example, in Chapter 5, you saw that both an Input (Text) form and a TextArea form were used in an application. However, you will not find a TextArea form in the standard web control menu. You could use an HTML TextArea form, or you could change the TextBox control so that it behaves like a TextArea form; in the "Data Display" section you'll see how that can be done.

To see how you can usefully change a TextBox control's behavior for a data entry interface, a useful tool is the `ToolTip` property. Using Visual Studio 2008, you see several different kinds of tool tips when you pass the mouse pointer over an area containing a tool tip. For example, when you pass the pointer over the Save icon in the menu bar, you get a little message—a tool tip—that lets you know that the icon is for saving your file. You can do the same thing for your applications; users appreciate any help they can get. Figure 6-4 shows the properties for the TextBox control, and you can see that the `ToolTip` property has a value set to Data Entry Box.

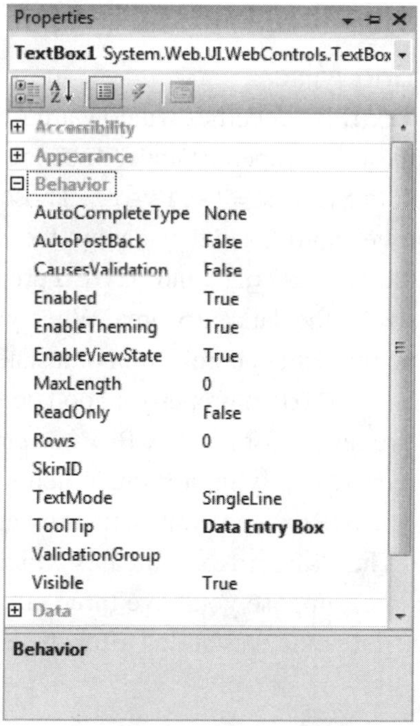

Figure 6-4   Behavior properties change the way a web control acts

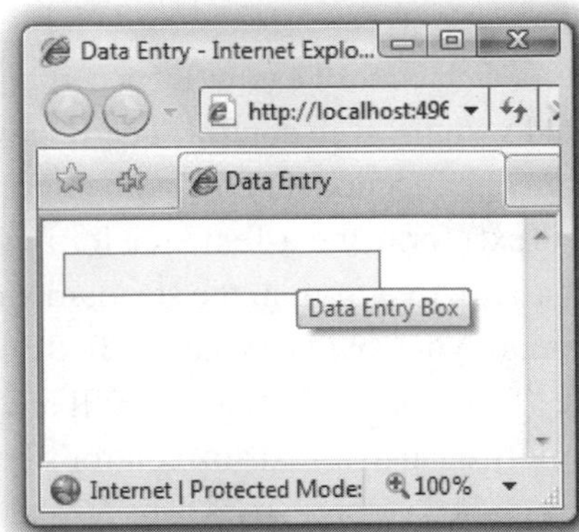

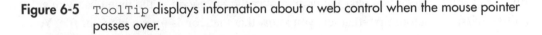

Figure 6-5 `ToolTip` displays information about a web control when the mouse pointer passes over.

You can add any message you want to a `ToolTip` property, so if you prefer to change the tool tip, just type in any text you want. Figure 6-5 shows the different *behavior* caused by adding a tool tip.

Accessibility, Layout, and Misc

The final categories in the TextBox Properties window are Accessibility, Layout, and Misc. Of these categories all of the properties under *Misc* are automatically filled with the object's ID, and they default to `runat ="server"`. Those under *Layout* for the TextBox are for changing the size of the control, and they default the `Wrap` option to `true`, which is generally preferred. The default `Height` and `Width` properties for the `TextBox` are good for changing the size of the data entry area. When you have different-size input requirements, such as for the two-letter abbreviation of a state, or for something longer like a street address, you will use the `Width` property a good deal.

The final category of properties for the TextBox is *Accessibility*. With data entry, the `TabIndex` property can be vitally important. When you design a page with several different data entry TextBox web controls, you want to make it easy for the user to type in a response. The `TabIndex` indicates which data entry box the cursor focuses on next. For example, suppose you have three entries—last name, first name, and e-mail address. If the first name was added after the e-mail address TextBox, tabbing will place the e-mail address entry between the last name and first name. The TabIndex order will be

Control	TabIndex
Last Name	0
Email	1
First Name	2

To change it so that the *second* tab focuses on the First Name entry, all you have to do is to change the Email TabIndex value to 2 and the First Name TabIndex to 1. (As with array elements, the TabIndex is zero-based.)

In some cases you may want to give the user additional access support by providing an AccessKey value. The AccessKey property allows you to place a key value that when used in combination with the ALT key (or OPTION key on the Mac) will automatically give focus to the TextBox. For example, Figure 6-6 shows the settings for the AccessKey property set to (lowercase) *p*.

NOTE
The default setting for tags is that as each property is added, the tag is extended to the right. Very soon, the tag requires a horizontal scroll—from California to New York, it may seem. As you can see in Figure 6-6, the added properties are easily visible because the tag beginning with <asp: TextBox... has been clarified by adding line breaks within the tag.

Be sure to experiment with different properties in different contexts with the web controls. Using Visual Studio 2008, all you need to do is to select the web control name in the editor and open the Properties window.

CheckBox and CheckBox List Controls
In the previous chapter, you learned about using the HTML Checkbox form. The web controls have both checkboxes and checkbox list controls. In this section you will learn how to use both and where they are most appropriate to use.

To some extent deciding to use individual CheckBox web controls is a matter both of how you like to work with the code and of personal preference, but I have found a rule of thumb that seems to work based on the number of checkboxes needed for any grouping. For example, when I have just a *few* checkboxes, such as ones I may include at the end of an order where the user can check to decide if she wants to receive mailed or e-mailed information, the CheckBox web control suffices. However, if I have a longer list of items, I'll use the CheckBoxList. Also, you will want to look at the kind of coding required in C#, and if one is preferable to the other for the task, that will guide your choice.

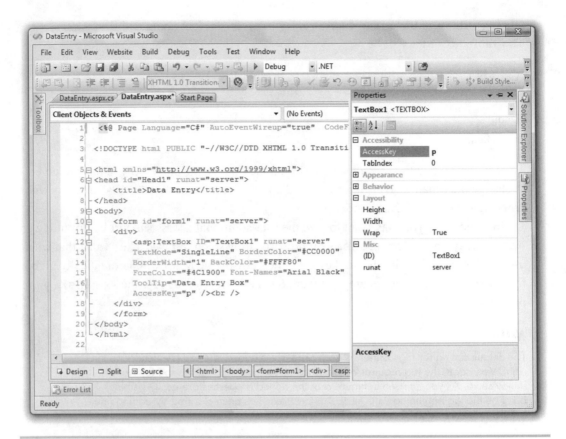

Figure 6-6 Changing the `AccessKey` for keyboard focus

Try This CheckBox Web Control

When you're working with the CheckBox web control, the C# that is handling the checkboxes looks a lot like what you see when working with HTML Checkbox forms. However, you also will find some important differences, especially when you look at the properties. For example, the web control uses a `Text` property for displaying and finding information, while the HTML form uses the `Value` property.

This next example shows a simple display of selected CheckBox web controls. Use the following steps to set it up:

1. Open a new Web Site in Visual Studio 2008, naming it **SingleCkBx**. In the Source view, open the Solution Explorer and change the name from Default.aspx to **Cbox.aspx**.

2. In the ASP.NET editor begin by dragging four CheckBox web controls from the Toolbox to between the `<div>` tags in the editor.

3. Drag one Button and one Label web control beneath the four checkboxes.

4. Once you have the basic parts in place, edit the file so that it matches the Cbox.aspx file shown next:

ASP.NET Cbox.aspx

```
<%@ Page Language="C#" AutoEventWireup="true"  CodeFile="Cbox.aspx.cs"
Inherits="Cbox" %>

<!DOCTYPE html PUBLIC "-//W3C//DTD XHTML 1.0 Transitional//EN"
"http://www.w3.org/TR/xhtml1/DTD/xhtml1-transitional.dtd">

<html xmlns="http://www.w3.org/1999/xhtml">
<head runat="server">
<style type="text/css">
  .head
  {
      font-family:Arial Black;
      color:Blue;
  }
</style>
    <title>Single Check Boxes</title>
</head>
<body>
    <form id="form1" runat="server">
    <div>
    <p class="head">Pick a Presidential Cabinet</p>
        <asp:CheckBox ID="CheckBox1" runat="server" Text="Mo"/><br />
        <asp:CheckBox ID="CheckBox2" runat="server" Text="Larry"/><br />
        <asp:CheckBox ID="CheckBox3" runat="server" Text="Curly"/><br />
        <asp:CheckBox ID="CheckBox4" runat="server" Text="Shemp"/><p />
```

(continued)

```
        <asp:Button ID="Button1" runat="server" Text="Choose Cabinet"
onclick="Button1_Click" /><p />

        <asp:Label ID="Label1" runat="server" Text="Cabinet"></asp:Label>
    </div>
    </form>
</body>
</html>
```

Once you have the ASP.NET portion complete, open the Cbox.aspx.cs file from the Solution Explorer. As you will see, just as with the HTML Checkbox form, you can use the same algorithm with the ternary conditional to extract the data from the web control. However, note that the property is Text instead of Value as it is in the HTML version. The following code snippet shows the basic line of code for data extraction:

```
myVariable = CheckBox1.Checked == true ? CheckBox1.Text: null;
```

The rest of the C# portion of the application is likewise similar to the CheckBox's HTML cousin:

C# Cbox.aspx.cs

```
using System;

public partial class Cbox : System.Web.UI.Page
{
    private String cabinet;

    protected void Button1_Click(object sender, EventArgs e)
    {
        cabinet = "Your cabinet is:<br/>";
        cabinet += CheckBox1.Checked == true ? "--" + CheckBox1.Text +
"<br />" : null;
        cabinet += CheckBox2.Checked == true ? "--" + CheckBox2.Text +
"<br />" : null;
        cabinet += CheckBox3.Checked == true ? "--" + CheckBox3.Text +
"<br />" : null;
        cabinet += CheckBox4.Checked == true ? "--" + CheckBox4.Text +
"<br />" : null;
        Label1.Text = cabinet;
    }
}
```

Once you finish, test the application. Figure 6-7 shows what you should see.

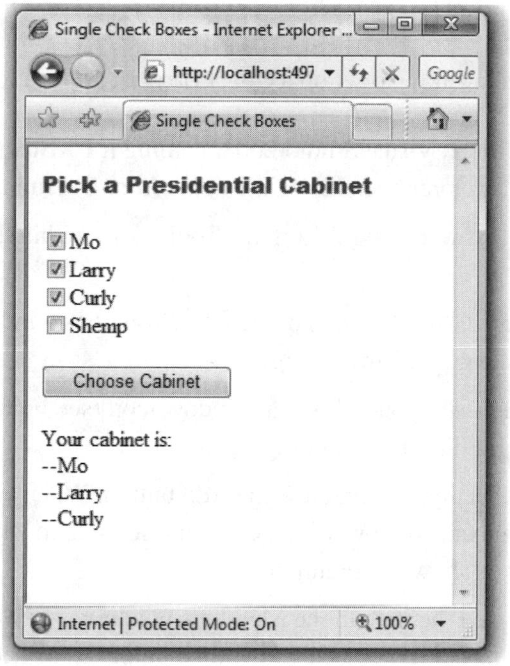

Figure 6-7 Single CheckBox Web forms

You may have noticed that a little CSS was slipped into the code to provide a header for the application. Also, you probably noticed that it's plain vanilla CSS. However, in the next chapter you'll see some properties in web controls that use special properties specifically for ASP.NET applications.

CheckBoxList Web Control

While the CheckBox web control is similar to the HTML Checkbox, the CheckBoxList is not related at all to an HTML form. Using a single CheckBoxList web control, you can enter as many checkboxes as you want, but instead of using individual objects, the CheckBoxList uses a property called Items.

Try This Creating CheckBoxList Web Control

The following steps show how to set up a CheckBoxList application:

1. Open a new Web Site in Visual Studio 2008, naming it **CkBoxes**. In the Source view, open the Solution Explorer and change the name from Default.aspx to **CkBoxes.aspx**.

2. Drag a CheckBoxList web control from the Toolbox to within the `<div>` container of the editor.

3. Select the code `CheckBoxList` and open the Properties window. Under the Misc category select `Items` as shown in Figure 6-8.

4. When you select `Items`, you will see a Window icon (see Figure 6-8) that opens the ListItem Collection Editor shown in Figure 6-9.

5. In the ListItem Collection Editor, click the Add button. When you do, an untitled line appears in the Members window. Change the untitled line to whatever you want, for example, Oranges as shown in Figure 6-9.

6. Once you have named the item in the Members window, you will see its properties in the panel at its right. The `Text` you add will be output as a checkbox with the name next to it. The `Value` can be a numeric or string value. (In Figure 6-9, you can see the Orange properties displayed.)

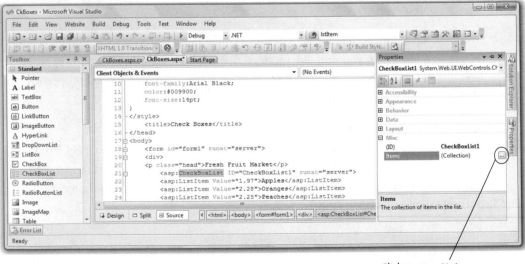

Click to open ListItem
Collection Editor

Figure 6-8 CheckBoxList `Items` property

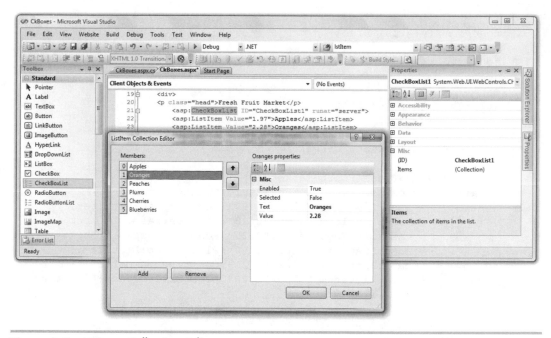

Figure 6-9 ListItem Collection Editor

7. Add Members for Apples, Peaches, Plums, Cherries, and Blueberries. The Member name and `Text` property values are the same. The value, in this case, is a rough estimate of the prices of the different fruits. In the accompanying script (CkBoxes.aspx), you will see the values employed, but you can use your own. Just be sure to use numeric values.

8. Drag a Button and a Label web control to the editor beneath the CheckBoxList. The following code shows how the ASP.NET file appears when completed:

ASP.NET CkBoxes.aspx

```
<%@ Page Language="C#" AutoEventWireup="true"  CodeFile="CkBoxes.aspx.cs"
Inherits="CkBox" %>

<!DOCTYPE html PUBLIC "-//W3C//DTD XHTML 1.0 Transitional//EN"
"http://www.w3.org/TR/xhtml1/DTD/xhtml1-transitional.dtd">

<html xmlns="http://www.w3.org/1999/xhtml">
<head runat="server">
<style type="text/css">
.head
```

(continued)

```
{
        font-family:Arial Black;
        color:#009900;
        font-size:14pt;
}
</style>
    <title>Check Boxes</title>
</head>
<body>
    <form id="form1" runat="server">
    <div>
    <p class="head">Fresh Fruit Market</p>
        <asp:CheckBoxList ID="CheckBoxList1" runat="server">
                <asp:ListItem Value="1.97">Apples</asp:ListItem>
                <asp:ListItem Value="2.28">Oranges</asp:ListItem>
                <asp:ListItem Value="2.25">Peaches</asp:ListItem>
                <asp:ListItem Value="1.50">Plums</asp:ListItem>
                <asp:ListItem Value="4.21">Cherries</asp:ListItem>
                <asp:ListItem Value="1.80">Blueberries</asp:ListItem>
        </asp:CheckBoxList>
        <br />
        <asp:Button ID="Button1" runat="server" Text="Calculate Total"
onclick="Button1_Click" />
        <p />
        <asp:Label ID="Label1" runat="server" Text="Total" />
    </div>
    </form>
</body>
</html>
```

The beauty of the CheckBoxList web control is that it works like an array; each item is an array element of the CheckBoxList instance. Because of this, setting up a loop to iterate through each of the items is easier than doing so with separately named CheckBox controls. In the C# section, you will see a helpful use for the `foreach` loop. Rather than having a separate line of code for each different checkbox, all you need to do is add a loop. The advantage of this is most pronounced where several checkboxes are required and each does not require a separate statement for data analysis.

A subtle but important difference between a list item and a CheckBox object is that the ListItem has a `Selected` property while the CheckBox has a `Checked` property. This is a minor difference, but one that could be confusing when writing code for one or the other object. The following C# code handles the data in the CheckBoxList:

C# CkBoxes.aspx.cs

```csharp
using System;
using System.Web.UI.WebControls;

public partial class CkBox : System.Web.UI.Page
{
    private double accumulator;

    protected void Button1_Click(object sender, EventArgs e)
    {
        foreach (ListItem ckLstItm in CheckBoxList1.Items)
        {
            if(ckLstItm.Selected==true)
            {
                accumulator += Convert.ToDouble(ckLstItm.Value);
            }
        }
    Label1.Text = "Your total is: $"+ accumulator;
    }
}
```

When you test your application, you should see that the values of the different list items in the CheckBoxList have been totaled and presented in the output (see Figure 6-10).

Ask the Expert

Q: Why is it that you had to convert the text to a **double** type when getting it from a string but did not have to convert it back to a string for output in the **Label1 .Text** web control?

A: One of the ways to convert a numeric type to a string type is to concatenate the number with a string. Adding "Your total is: $" to the numeric variable named accumulator automatically changes the number to a string. Try this to better see how it works. Remove the code ("Your total is: $" +) from the line and see what happens. It will throw an error because you're attempting to assign a numeric type (double) to a string (Text) web control.

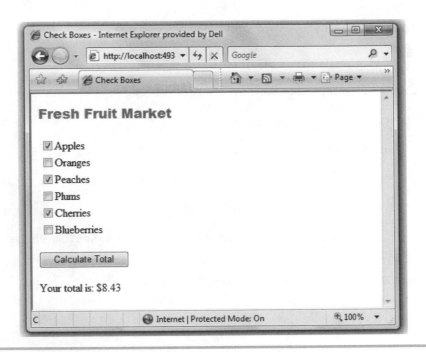

Figure 6-10 CheckBox List items used in numeric calculation

All of the calculations are handled by the C# script to generate the total cost. The important feature of this application to remember is that it's very easy for the user to make selections of multiple items. Keep this in mind the next time you're building an e-business application.

RadioButton and RadioButtonList Controls

As you may recall from the previous chapter on HTML controls and forms, the key feature of the radio button control is that it is generally used with mutually exclusive choices—where you can have only a single choice from a group of selections. When you look at the radio button controls from the Standard menu, you see the same set as with checkboxes. You can select either individual RadioButton or RadioButtonList objects. We'll take a look at radio button controls separately, but use a single sample application to see how to work with them both.

RadioButton Web Control

The RadioButton web control resembles the HTML version, but because it is set up specifically for ASP.NET applications, it's a little different. When you add a RadioButton object to the source editor, you see the following:

```
<asp:RadioButton ID="RadioButton1" runat="server" />
```

Using either the Properties window or typing in code, you need to add two key properties, GroupName (Behavior category) and Text (Appearance category). The GroupName property causes the selection of any single radio button to automatically deselect all of the others in the group. After adding both elements, you will see something like the following:

```
<asp:RadioButton ID="RadioButton1" runat="server" GroupName="OS"
Text="Windows XP" />
```

As you can see, the properties are similar to the HTML radio button.

For the C# portion the radio button's value in the Text property is accessed very much like one for the CheckBox web control in the previous section. The following C# code snippet illustrates how a value is passed from a checked radio button to a variable:

```
radVar += RadioButton1.Checked ? RadioButton1.Text : null;
```

The += compound operator is a way of not getting a null where you don't want it. If your last radio button in a group is null and assigned to a variable, it wipes out the value of a previous assignment. However, if you use +=, the null is just added to whatever is stored and does not really affect the non-null value stored.

RadioButtonList Web Control

Working with the RadioButtonList is almost identical to working with the CheckBoxList discussed in the last section. Each single RadioButtonList can have several items added to it, and when addressing the selected value, the reference is to the ListItem property where the data are stored. Adding items is the same as working with CheckBoxList items (shown earlier in Figure 6-9) in the previous section.

When it comes to working with the RadioButtonList with C#, you'll find it very easy because the user selects only a single ListItem. So instead of looping through the object, you can just assign the value of the selected item as shown in the following snippet:

```
radVar = RadioButtonList1.SelectedItem.Text;
```

The key here is the SelectedItem property. Only one list item can have that property.

Try This **Making Mutually Exclusive Selections**

To see how the RadioButton web controls work, this next application employs both the Standard RadioButton and RadioButtonList. Note that the lists are set up for handling a single order, forcing the user to first make a selection of one mutually exclusive group and then to make a second selection from a different mutually exclusive group. Enter the following two scripts in a new web site.

ASP.NET RadioControl.aspx

```
<%@ Page Language="C#" AutoEventWireup="true"  CodeFile="RadioControl
.aspx.cs" Inherits="RadioControl" %>

<!DOCTYPE html PUBLIC "-//W3C//DTD XHTML 1.0 Transitional//EN"
"http://www.w3.org/TR/xhtml1/DTD/xhtml1-transitional.dtd">

<html xmlns="http://www.w3.org/1999/xhtml">
<head runat="server">
<style type="text/css">
.os, .model
{
      font-family:Copperplate Gothic Bold;
      font-size:18px;
      color:#990000;
}

.model
{
      color:#009900;
}

</style>
    <title>Radio Controls</title>
</head>
<body>
    <form id="form1" runat="server">
    <div>
    <h1>Choose Your Computer</h1>
    <span class="os">Select OS:</span><br />
        <asp:RadioButton ID="RadioButton1" runat="server" GroupName="OS"
Text="Windows XP" />
        <br />
        <asp:RadioButton ID="RadioButton2" runat="server" GroupName="OS"
Text="Windows Vista" />
        <br />
     <span class="model">Select Model</span>
```

```
        <asp:RadioButtonList ID="RadioButtonList1" runat="server">
            <asp:ListItem Value="Lap 1000">Laptop 1000</asp:ListItem>
            <asp:ListItem Value="Laptop 2000">Laptop 2000</asp:ListItem>
            <asp:ListItem Value="Laptop 3000">Laptop 3000</asp:ListItem>
            <asp:ListItem Value="Desktop 1000">Desktop 1000</asp:ListItem>
            <asp:ListItem Value="Desktop 2000">Desktop 2000</asp:ListItem>
            <asp:ListItem Value="Desktop 3000">Desktop 3000</asp:ListItem>
        </asp:RadioButtonList>
        <br />
        <asp:Button ID="Button1" runat="server" Text="Confirm and Ship"
            onclick="Button1_Click" /><p />
        <asp:Label ID="Label1" runat="server" Text="Your Order"></asp:Label>
    </div>
    </form>
</body>
</html>
```

The C# portion of the application is very simple compared with the checkbox example, especially the portion dealing with the RadioButtonList.

C# RadioControl.aspx.cs

```
using System;

public partial class RadioControl : System.Web.UI.Page
{
    private string packUp;

    protected void Button1_Click(object sender, EventArgs e)
    {
        packUp = "OS: ";
        //Individual Buttons
        packUp += RadioButton1.Checked ? RadioButton1.Text : null;
        packUp += RadioButton2.Checked ? RadioButton2.Text : null;

        //List
      packUp += "<br/>System: " + RadioButtonList1.SelectedItem.Text;
        Label1.Text = packUp;
    }
}
```

Figure 6-11 shows what you can expect to see when you test the application in Visual Studio 2008.

(continued)

Figure 6-11 RadioButton and RadioButtonList output to a Label object

After working with both RadioButton and RadioButtonList, you may find that using the RadioButtonList is far easier than dealing with several RadioButton objects. The RadioButtonList web control automatically includes a "group name"—the list itself is the "group"; so that's one less property to set. Also, data access with C# is easier using RadioButtonList compared with RadioButton.

DropDownList and ListBox Controls

Chapter 5 shows how to use the HTML Select form, and in this chapter you'll see a close cousin, the DropDownList web control. In addition, you'll also see how to work with the ListBox control.

Before going on to examine the DropDownList and ListBox separately, you need to know a few things about the two list web controls. First, when dealing with the ListItem settings, you will not find the items as a property of either the ListBox or DropDownList. What you need to do is to set up the ListBox or `DropDownList` container, and then within the container begin adding a tag by adding the tag arrow (<). As soon as you begin the tag, you get an automatic completion menu from IntelliSense with the necessary starting code as shown in Figure 6-12.

Once you have begun the ListItem, you can *now* open the Properties window and fill in the properties for the ListItem as shown in Figure 6-13. This is very different from the other web controls you've worked with using Visual Studio 2008.

Even though getting to the Properties window from within a DropDownList or ListBox is a two-step process, once the ListItem properties appear in the Properties window, changing them is identical to any other object properties you may change.

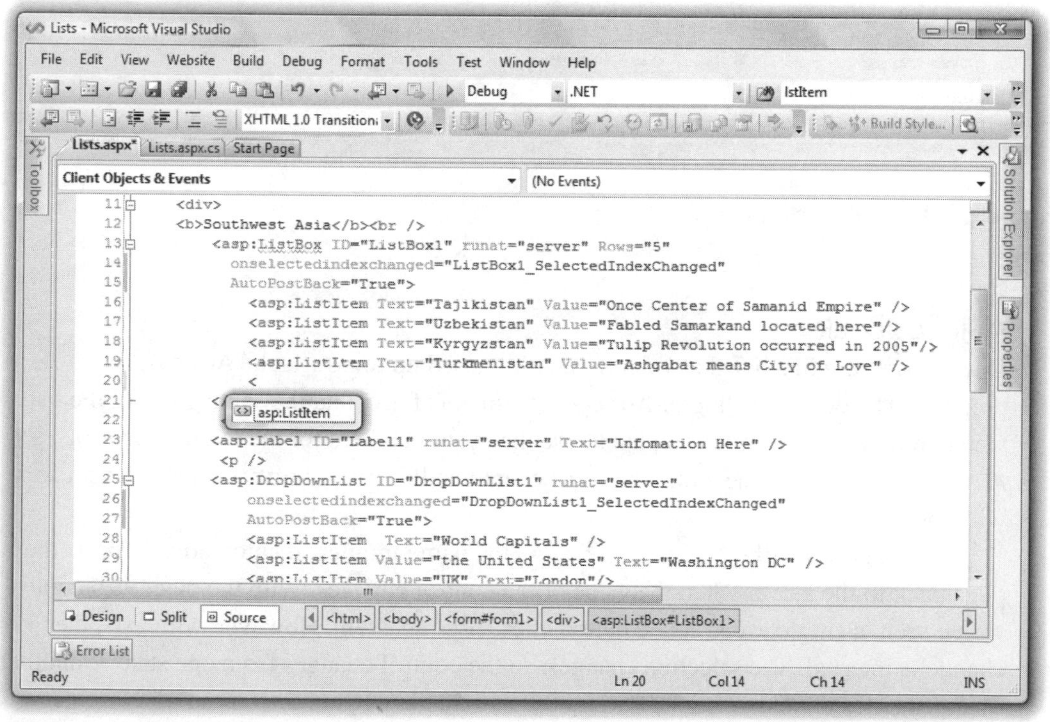

Figure 6-12 IntelliSense with code for ListItem

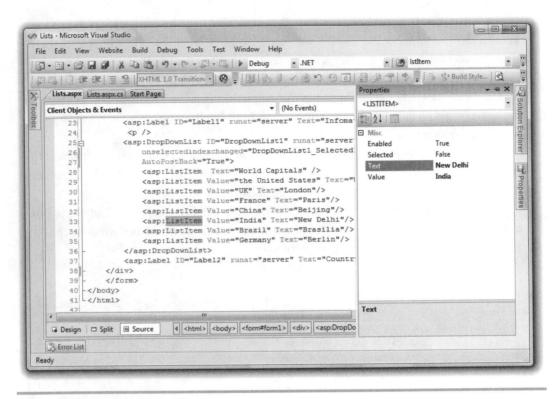

Figure 6-13 ListItem properties

AutoPostBack

One feature of ASP.NET that we have not discussed up to now is the `AutoPostBack` property. The default setting of `AutoPostBack` is false, and the same goes for the list web controls. However, if you plan to use the event handlers for the list web controls, set `AutoPostBack` to true. Otherwise, the event handler `onSelectedIndexChanged` will not work.

So, what does `AutoPostBack` do? As the name implies, it automatically posts the page back to the server when the value of the control changes. With the other web controls we've seen, a single event, like a button click, fires an event. However, with lists, the change is internal. The selection changes; so the control changes from one state to another. This generates an additional server request, and that is why on the other web controls we've left the property setting at the default of false. Figure 6-14 shows where to find the `AutoPostBack` property in the Properties window and set it to true.

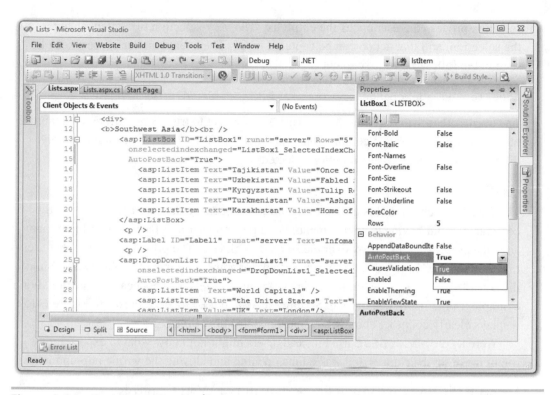

Figure 6-14 Setting AutoPostBack to true

When we look at the two list web controls, you will see that both have identical event handlers in the ASP.NET portion of the code. The `AutoPostBack` built into the web controls allows the events to trigger.

DropDownList

The `DropDownList` is almost identical to the HTML Select form. The `DropDownList` container holds different ListItem elements used to hold the text and value of the item. These values then can be passed to a variable or output in the C# portion of the application. In Figure 6-15, you can see that a single selection is visible at any one time, but in the

Figure 6-15 ListBox web control displays choices clearly

selection process the user opens the entire list. The very selection of an item changes the selection, and that action can be captured in C#. The event handler property can be seen in the following code segment:

```
...onselectedindexchanged="DropDownList1_SelectedIndexChanged"...
```

The event, other than requiring `AutoPostBack` be set to true, is no different from any of the other events used in conjunction with other Web forms. Its invocation is simply different—it happens when an item is selected.

ListBox

The ListBox web control is an important addition because the user can easily see the contents without having to open a menu. For a general user interface, you will find many advantages of using a ListBox over the `DropDownList`. The primary reason is that users may not know what to expect or where to look for something that they may want. While the `DropDownList` is useful for saving space on a page, it can conceal information. For example, in the list of countries in Southwest Asia, the `ListBox` shown in Figure 6-15 displays clearly countries about which most people know little.

Were a `DropDownList` used instead, users might not know what to expect and might make up the choices and waste time opening and closing the wrong pop-up menus.

Using Both Text and Value Properties in List Web Controls

The two list web controls are displayed in this next example. However, more importantly, you can see how both the `Text` and `Value` properties are used in the ListItem elements. In previous examples, either both properties were the same, or only one was used. However, in this next example, the `Value` property provides information about the `Text` value that can be passed on to a variable or to some other storage source by C#.

ASP.NET Lists.aspx

```
<%@ Page Language="C#" AutoEventWireup="true"  CodeFile="Lists.aspx.cs" Inherits="Lists" %>

<!DOCTYPE html PUBLIC "-//W3C//DTD XHTML 1.0 Transitional//EN"
"http://www.w3.org/TR/xhtml1/DTD/xhtml1-transitional.dtd">

<html xmlns="http://www.w3.org/1999/xhtml">
<head runat="server">
    <title>List Menu & Boxes</title>
</head>
<body>
    <form id="form1" runat="server">
```

```
    <div>
    <b>Southwest Asia</b><br />
        <asp:ListBox ID="ListBox1" runat="server" Rows="5"
          onselectedindexchanged="ListBox1_SelectedIndexChanged"
          AutoPostBack="True">
            <asp:ListItem Text="Tajikistan" Value="Once Center of Samanid Empire" />
            <asp:ListItem Text="Uzbekistan" Value="Fabled Samarkand located here"/>
            <asp:ListItem Text="Kyrgyzstan" Value="Tulip Revolution occurred in 2005" />
            <asp:ListItem Text="Turkmenistan" Value="Ashgabat means City of Love" />
            <asp:ListItem Text="Kazakhstan" Value="Home of Borat!" />
        </asp:ListBox>
         <p />
        <asp:Label ID="Label1" runat="server" Text="Information Here" />
         <p />
        <asp:DropDownList ID="DropDownList1" runat="server"
          onselectedindexchanged="DropDownList1_SelectedIndexChanged"
          AutoPostBack="True">
            <asp:ListItem  Text="World Capitals" />
            <asp:ListItem Value="the USA" Text="Washington DC" />
            <asp:ListItem Value="the UK" Text="London" />
            <asp:ListItem Value="France" Text="Paris" />
            <asp:ListItem Value="China" Text="Beijing" />
            <asp:ListItem Value="India" Text="New Delhi" />
            <asp:ListItem Value="Brazil" Text="Brasilia" />
            <asp:ListItem Value="Germany" Text="Berlin" />
        </asp:DropDownList>
        <asp.Label ID="Label2" runat="server" Text="Country" />
    </div>
    </form>
</body>
</html>
```

C# Lists.aspx.cs

```csharp
using System;
using System.Web.UI.WebControls;

public partial class Lists : System.Web.UI.Page
{
    private string info;

    protected void ListBox1_SelectedIndexChanged(object sender, EventArgs e)
    {
        info = ListBox1.SelectedItem.Value;
        Label1.Text = info;
    }
    protected void DropDownList1_SelectedIndexChanged(object sender, EventArgs e)
```

Figure 6-16 Two list web controls

```
    {
        info = DropDownList1.SelectedValue;
        Label2.Text = "is the capital of "+info;
    }
}
```

Once you have completed the code, test the application. Each web control displays information in two different Label web controls. Figure 6-16 shows what you can expect to see when you test the application.

Data Display

At some point whatever data are gathered from a database or calculated from online data entry must be displayed. This last section examines the web controls for showing the user the information he needs. However, at this point you will not see one of the most important display tools for data—the table. Data display in a table is most useful where your application displays data stored in a database table. To discuss tables at this point would be premature, but in the chapters after the introduction of ADO.NET, you will see several different table-related tools.

TextBox (as a Data Display)

For the most part the TextBox web control examples have been used for the purpose of data entry. The default TextBox is very similar to an HTML Input (Text) form. However, you may also use the TextBox for data display. You have a lot of text and only enough space on your page for a limited view of the text; your display needs a scroll bar. Using the HTML TextArea form, you saw how a large amount of text fit into the form because of the form's ability to be scrolled. The TextBox can do the same thing, and all you have to do is change the size and a few properties. The following list shows the key properties to change to create a TextBox that can be used to display and scroll large amounts of text:

Property	Value
Height	N px
Width	N px
TextMode	MultiLine
ReadOnly	True

The `Height` and `Width` properties are set to fit the design. More importantly, the `TextMode` property needs to be changed to `MultiLine`. Finally, because the TextBox is to be used for data display instead of data entry, change the status of the `ReadOnly` property from false to true.

In addition you can apply any of the other TextBox properties, such as color, font, and other features of the object. The upcoming Figure 6-18 shows that the text inside the TextBox is different from the other text in the application and includes a shaded background. So in addition to data entry, it's easy to reconfigure the TextBox object to act as a data display tool.

Label and Literal Web Controls

The Label and Literal web controls are very similar, and the differences that have been attributed to them are almost the stuff of urban legends. Both are used for placing text on the page, both can be used with CSS, and both use the `Text` property for output. To best see the differences between the two web controls, look at Figure 6-17. On the left, you will see that the Literal only has a few properties in the Properties window, while the Label at right has many.

If your output is plain vanilla text or numbers, either is fine. However, if your design needs more properties, you'll be better served by the Label web control. In the sample application DisplayInfo.aspx (later in the chapter), you will see that they both display data through the Text property with assigned strings containing CSS encoding. In Figure 6-18 you can see that the output from the two web controls is identical except for the string values and color.

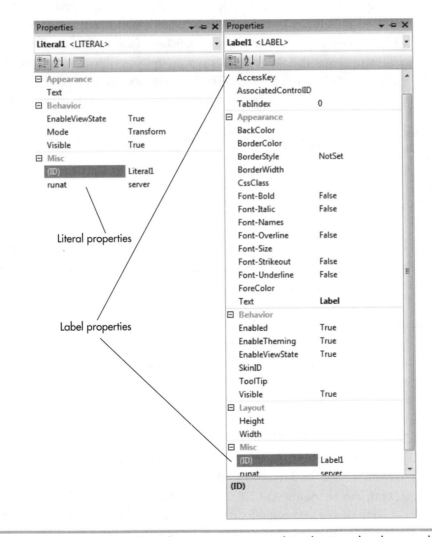

Figure 6-17 Label web control has far more properties than the Literal web control.

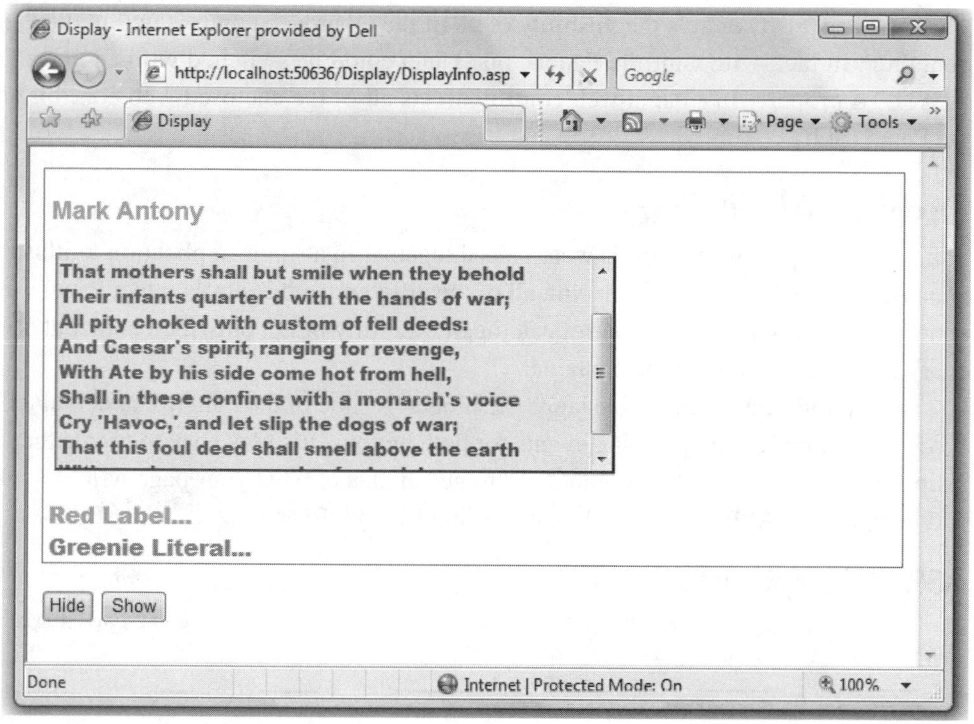

Figure 6-18 Display objects within Panel web control

Panel

When using multiple display web controls, you may wish to place them within a Panel web control container. Any elements within the Panel take on the properties set in the panel. The individual settings of the web controls override the Panel control's settings, but if undefined, they will take on the characteristics of the Panel. For styling a group of web controls, this can be very handy. Rather than setting the values for the different web controls, all of the controls can automatically be styled by the Panel web control's setting. For example, in the following <Panel> tag, you can see that the font color will be red (ForeColor), and the font will be Arial rather than the serif default.

```
<asp:Panel ID="Panel1" runat="server"
        ForeColor="Red" Font-Names="Arial"
            BorderStyle="Solid" BorderColor="#CC0000"
            BorderWidth="1px">
```

The Panel also controls the visibility of all of the other web controls within the Panel container. In fact, with multiple Panels, one Panel could be switched with another. The `Visible` property in a Panel web control affects all of the enclosed web controls and the Panel itself.

Display All at Once

The several display web controls were placed together in a single application to illustrate what each looks like. Also, by placing all of the different web controls into a Panel web control, you can see how the control can toggle visibility of not only the Panel, but also every other web control in the container.

Two buttons are included to change the property value of the Panel. The default is `Visible=True`, and by having events for both buttons, it's very easy to toggle the visibility. First, take a look at Figure 6-18 to get an idea of what your page will look like, and then add the ASP.NET code shown next in DisplayInfo.aspx.

ASP.NET DisplayInfo.aspx

```
<%@ Page Language="C#" AutoEventWireup="true"  CodeFile="DisplayInfo
.aspx.cs" Inherits="DisplayInfo" %>

<!DOCTYPE html PUBLIC "-//W3C//DTD XHTML 1.0 Transitional//EN"
"http://www.w3.org/TR/xhtml1/DTD/xhtml1-transitional.dtd">

<html xmlns="http://www.w3.org/1999/xhtml">
<head runat="server">
    <title>Display</title>
</head>
<body>
    <form id="form1" runat="server">
    <div>
        <asp:Panel ID="Panel1" runat="server"
        ForeColor="Red"
        Font-Names="Arial" BorderStyle="Solid"
        BorderColor="#CC0000" BorderWidth="1px">

        <h3> Mark Anthony</h3>
          <asp:TextBox ID="TextBox1" runat="server"
        TextMode="MultiLine" Width="400" Height="150"
        BorderColor="#999999" BackColor="#EEEEEE"
        ForeColor="#990000" Font-Names="Arial Black"
        ReadOnly="True" BorderStyle="Outset" /><p />

         <asp:Label ID="Label1"
        runat="server" Text="Label" />
        <br />
```

```
 <asp:Literal ID="Literal1" runat="server" />
</asp:Panel>
<br />
<asp:Button ID="Button1" runat="server" Text="Hide"
    onclick="Button1_Click" />
<asp:Button ID="Button2" runat="server" Text="Show"
onclick="Button2_Click" />
</div>
</form>
</body>
</html>
```

The web control ID values and event handlers are the default ones.

The C# portion of the code looks busier than it really is. To get a long chunk of text, a single string variable keeps adding more text to a base value. Eventually a chunk of text from Shakespeare's *Julius Caesar* is big enough to fill up the TextBox to allow scrolling. Otherwise, the events generate simple changes of state by assigning values to display elements. The exceptions, of course, are the two buttons that change the visibility of the Panel.

C# DisplayInfo.aspx.cs

```csharp
using System;
using System.Web.UI.WebControls;

public partial class DisplayInfo : System.Web.UI.Page
{
    private string anthony;

    protected void Page_Load(object sender, EventArgs e)
    {
        Label1.Text = "<span style='color:#ff0000;font-family:Arial
Black'>Red Label...</span>";
        Literal1.Text = "<span style='color:#009900;font-family:Arial
Black'>Greenie Literal...</span>";

        antony+="Blood and destruction shall be so in use \n";
        antony+="And dreadful objects so familiar\n";
        antony+="That mothers shall but smile when they behold\n";
        antony+="Their infants quarter'd with the hands of war;\n";
        antony+="All pity choked with custom of fell deeds:\n";
        antony+="And Caesar's spirit, ranging for revenge,\n";
        antony+="With Ate by his side come hot from hell, \n";
        antony+="Shall in these confines with a monarch's voice \n";
        antony+="Cry 'Havoc,' and let slip the dogs of war;\n";
        antony+="That this foul deed shall smell above the earth \n";
        antony+="With carrion men, groaning for burial.\n";
```

```
        TextBox1.Text = antony;
    }
    protected void Button1_Click(object sender, EventArgs e)
    {
        Panel1.Visible = false;
    }
    protected void Button2_Click(object sender, EventArgs e)
    {
        Panel1.Visible = true;
    }
}
```

When you test the application, you will see all of the different display elements as shown in Figure 6-18.

In looking at Figure 6-18, you may conclude that the displays of "Mark Antony" and "Red Label" are identical. They look it, but "Mark Antony" is a string within an <h3> tag making it appear bolder and the approximate size of "Red Label." Both are red, but the "Mark Antony" color and font (Arial) are controlled by the `Panel` property, while the "Red Label" color and font (Arial Black) are due to a CSS color designation.

To see what happens when you change the Panel's `Visible` property from true to false, test the application and click the Hide button. Figure 6-19 shows the same page when the Panel's visibility is negated.

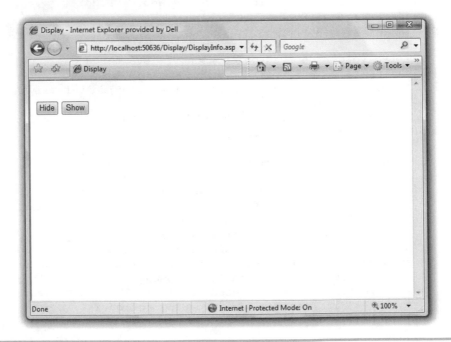

Figure 6-19 All web controls in the `Panel` are affected by its visibility state

As long as both buttons are outside of the Panel web control container, they will be visible. Only those web controls inside the Panel web control are not visible. As soon as the `Visible` property is changed back to true, all of the objects inside the `Panel` will appear again.

Triggers, Links, and Images

This last group of web controls is divided into Triggers, with a focus on buttons; Links, looking at the HyperLink form; and Images, which examine both the Image and ImageMap web controls. Other triggers, such as those caused by selections in lists, are discussed in the earlier sections about the list web controls. Here the focus will be on triggers whose main purpose is to launch an event that changes a behavior.

Buttons

Buttons have a purpose of bringing about change and are the perfect trigger because nobody expects them to do anything else but fire off some kind of event. You saw in this and previous chapters that buttons are simple and effective ways to generate events that fire methods in C#. In most respects, the different kinds of button web controls behave similarly; they just look different from one another. The following three web control buttons are available in ASP.NET 3.5:

- **Button**   The plain vanilla button has properties to control different aspects of the button such as the text, color, and dimensions of the button.

- **ImageButton**   An imported graphic image is used to stand in place of the button image. Any GIF, JPEG, or PNG image can be listed as a value of an `ImageUrl` property and be displayed as the button.

- **LinkButton**   This web control looks like a default underlined link, but in fact is a button in all respects. It does *not* have a URL property for links (a `NavigateURL` property), but just looks like a default HTML link.

Any of these buttons can be displayed in the Design mode, double-clicked, and then will generate C# code for a method that fires when the button is clicked. Their main unique features involve their appearance and not their functionality.

HyperLink

If you want a simple way to set up a link with another page, use the Hyperlink web control. This control has a `NavigateURL` property, and the string (containing a URL) assigned to the `NavigateURL` property launches the targeted URL just as an HTML link would. Likewise, a `Target` property lets you specify the kind of target to one of the following HTML-type targets:

- _search
- _top
- _self
- _blank
- _parent

As you can see, the targets let you assign the same variety of web document elements as you can with an HTML link.

The HyperLink web control has the default appearance of HTML links. When it first appears on the page, the underlined text is blue; after you visit the linked web page, its "visited" color is purple. You can change this with either the properties or CSS. However, you can also use an image like the ImageButton by assigning the URL of an image file to the `ImageUrl` property. The result is exactly the same appearance as an ImageButton, but you have the functionality of a linking object. Figure 6-20 shows a HyperLink with the default formatting.

Image

The Image web control is a placeholder for images you want on your page, but it is much more. In the sample application, Trigger.aspx, you will see that the Image web control is placed in the code, but it is not assigned a value. Rather, when the ImageButton is pressed, the C# portion of the application assigns values to both the `Visible` and `ImageUrl` properties. The following code snippet shows the values assigned dynamically to the Image web control:

```
Image1.Visible = true;
Image1.ImageUrl = "LgOlivia.jpg";
```

In this way, not only can you keep the empty Image off the page, but also it shows a box with a red *x* that indicates no graphic is assigned to the web control. When you're ready to add an image, all you have to do is change the `Visible` property to true and assign a URL to the `ImageUrl` property. The larger of the two images in Figure 6-20 shows the image brought to the page by the C# code initiated by the ImageButton.

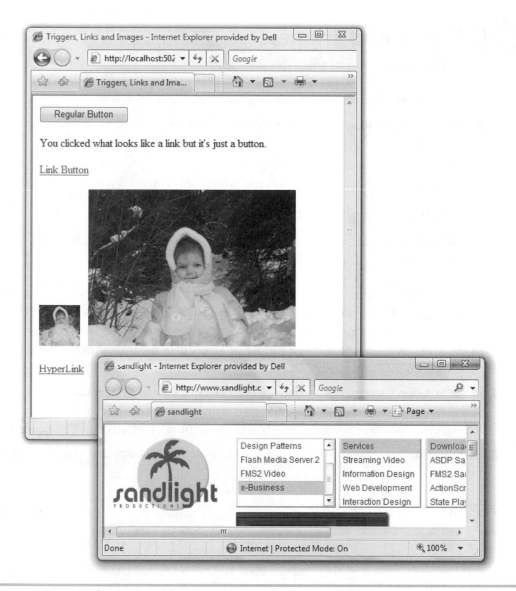

Figure 6-20 You have several button style and appearance options

Trigger, Image, and Link Application

Rather than have separate small applications to look at the features of the web controls, placing them into a simple application helps you to better see what they look like and to operate in reality relative to one another.

Try This   Events and Triggers

The following steps show you how to get started:

1. Open a new Web Site using the name **Triggers** as an application name.

2. In the Source view, drag the following from the Toolbox to the editor between the `<div>` tags:

   - Button
   - Literal
   - LinkButton
   - ImageButton
   - Image
   - HyperLink

3. In the Triggers folder, add an image for the ImageButton. The image should be a GIF, JPEG, or PNG image and of the size you want for your button. Add a second image to the Triggers folder. This image should be larger than the image for the button. (See Figure 6-20 to get a rough idea of the relative sizes of the images.)

4. In the Solution Explorer rename the file from Default.aspx to **Triggers.aspx**. In the Triggers.aspx.cs file, change the partial class name from _Default to **Triggers**. Rename the `Inherits` value in the Triggers.aspx from _Default to **Triggers**.

5. Edit the code in the Source view to that shown in the Triggers.aspx and Triggers.aspx.cs listings.

ASP.NET Triggers.aspx

```
<%@ Page Language="C#" AutoEventWireup="true" CodeFile="Triggers
.aspx.cs" Inherits="Triggers" %>

<!DOCTYPE html PUBLIC "-//W3C//DTD XHTML 1.0 Transitional//EN" "http://www.
w3.org/TR/xhtml1/DTD/xhtml1-transitional.dtd">

<html xmlns="http://www.w3.org/1999/xhtml">
<head runat="server">
    <title>Triggers, Links and Images</title>
</head>
<body>
    <form id="form1" runat="server">
    <div>
```

```
        <asp:Button ID="Button1" runat="server" Text="Regular Button"
onclick="Button1_Click" />
        <p />
        <asp:Literal ID="Literal1" runat="server" />
        <p />
        <asp:LinkButton ID="LinkButton1" runat="server" onclick="LinkButton1_
Click"
        Text="Link Button" />
        <p />
        <asp:ImageButton ID="ImageButton1" runat="server" ImageUrl="olivia.jpg"
            onclick="ImageButton1_Click" />  
            <asp:Image ID="Image1" runat="server" Visible="False" />
            <p />
        <asp:HyperLink ID="HyperLink1" runat="server" Target="_blank"
        NavigateUrl="http://www.sandlight.com">HyperLink</asp:HyperLink>
    </div>
    </form>
</body>
</html>
```

C# Triggers.aspx.cs

```csharp
using System;

public partial class Triggers : System.Web.UI.Page
{
    protected void Button1_Click(object sender, EventArgs e)
    {
        Literal1.Text = "You clicked the plain vanilla button";
    }

    protected void ImageButton1_Click(object sender, System.Web.UI
.ImageClickEventArgs e)
    {
        Image1.Visible = true;
        Image1.ImageUrl = "LgOlivia.jpg";
    }

    protected void LinkButton1_Click(object sender, EventArgs e)
    {
        Literal1.Text = "You clicked what looks like a link but it's
just a button.";
    }
}
```

Once you've entered the code and are all set, test the application. Figure 6-20 shows what you should see.

(continued)

The Regular Button and the Link Button both add text to a Literal web control by firing a C# method. The ImageButton works like a thumbnail enlarger. The small image on the button appears in a larger format in the Image web control when the user clicks the button with the same image. The HyperLink web control simply brings up a linked web page in a separate window.

ImageMap

The final web control to be discussed in this chapter is the ImageMap. This control works very much like an HTML image map. Different areas on the graphic are made into *hotspots*. The hotspots act like little buttons or links. When you mouse over the hotspots, they can present tool tips or alternative text, and when you click a hotspot, it can launch a linked site. You can use any graphic you want. For example, you might want to have an image of a skeleton, and make the different bones hotspots that identify each bone by its medical term. Alternatively you might make a news site covering a country and use an image of an actual map.

TIP

One of the best sources of digital graphic maps on the Web can be found at www.cia.gov. In the *World Factbook* on the CIA site you will find maps of every country in the world. You can freely download and use them with the CIA's blessing. About the only graphic on the site that you cannot use is the CIA seal. Otherwise, your tax dollars have already paid for the great assortment of digital maps available on the site.

Try This   Using the ImageMap

To get started on creating an image map using the ImageMap web control, follow this next set of steps:

1. Create a new Web Site named **ImgMap**.

2. Place an image (JPEG, GIF, or PNG) you want to use for an image map in the ImgMap folder. For this example, I went to the CIA site and got a map of Sudan. This map was modified to highlight the Darfur region and placed on Wikipedia Commons (see Tip about CIA site).

3. Drag an ImageMap web control into the `<div>` container.

4. Click on the ImageMap line, and click on the Properties window. In the Properties window select `ImageUrl` and enter the image name, including the graphic extension.

5. In the Source mode within the `ImageMap` container, type in **<** to begin a tag. As soon as you do, you will be presented with a menu of different hotspot options as shown in Figure 6-21.

6. Once you have added your hotspots to the code, switch to the Design mode.

7. Select the Image Map icon, and open the Properties window.

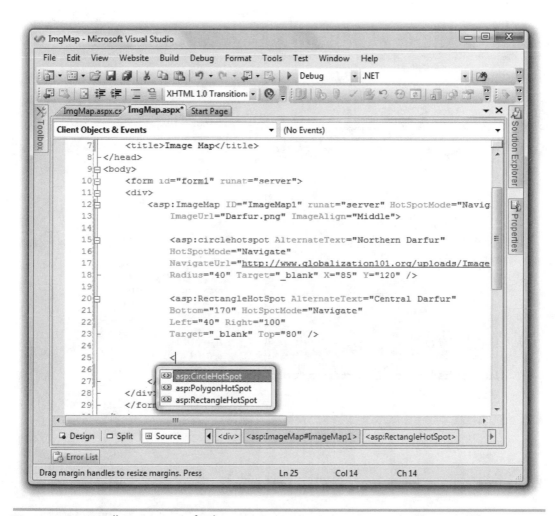

Figure 6-21   IntelliSense menu for hotspots

(continued)

8. Select the `HotSpots` property and a button will appear next to the `(Collection)` value as shown in Figure 6-22. Click the button.

9. Clicking the `(Collection)` button opens the HotSpot Collection Editor. Using this editor, you can create hotspots and their related behaviors. Figure 6-23 shows the open editor.

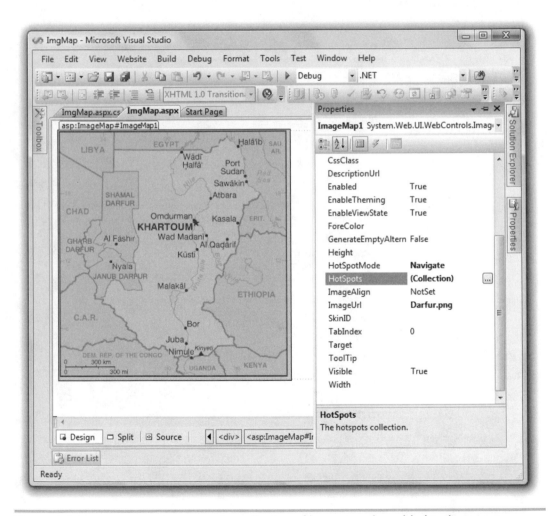

Figure 6-22   `HotSpots` represents the collection of hotspots to be added to the image map.

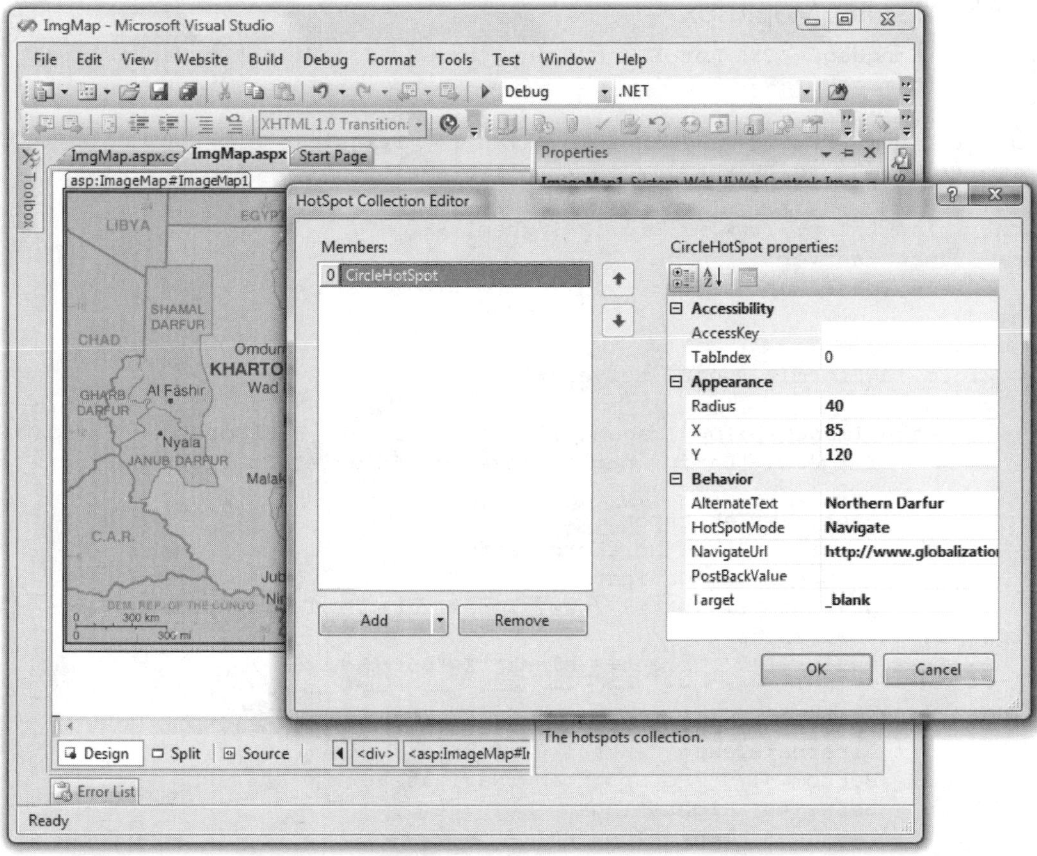

Figure 6-23   HotSpot Collection Editor

10. Depending on the kind of hotspot you have selected, different Appearance properties appear. In Figure 6-23 with a CircleHotSpot, the `Radius` of the circle and it's `X` and `Y` starting positions provide a circle in the position defined by the X and Y locations on the image map with a specified radius. You can include `AlternateText`, `HotSpotMode`, a URL to link, and a `Target` type if you plan to set up a link.

11. To finish the application, add as many hotspots as you want. The following code shows different hotspots added to the image. All of the hotspots were able to use an ASP.NET link form instead of one generated through C# code.

(continued)

ASP.NET ImgMap.aspx

```
<%@ Page Language="C#" AutoEventWireup="true"  CodeFile="ImgMap.aspx.cs"
Inherits="ImageMp" %>

<!DOCTYPE html PUBLIC "-//W3C//DTD XHTML 1.0 Transitional//EN"
"http://www.w3.org/TR/xhtml1/DTD/xhtml1-transitional.dtd">

<html xmlns="http://www.w3.org/1999/xhtml">
<head runat="server">
    <title>Image Map</title>
</head>
<body>
    <form id="form1" runat="server">
    <div>
        <asp:ImageMap ID="ImageMap1" runat="server" HotSpotMode="Navigate"
            ImageUrl="Darfur.png" ImageAlign="Middle" ToolTip="Darfur">

            <asp:circlehotspot
            AlternateText="Northern Darfur"
            HotSpotMode="Navigate"
            NavigateUrl="http://www.globalization101.org/uploads/Image/
darfur/darfur-women.jpg"
            Radius="40" Target="_blank" X="85" Y="120" />

            <asp:RectangleHotSpot
            AlternateText="Central Darfur"
            Bottom="170" HotSpotMode="Navigate"
            Left="40" Right="100"
            Target="_blank" Top="80" />

            <asp:CircleHotSpot
            AlternateText="Southern Darfur"
            Radius="40" X="80" Y="200" />

        </asp:ImageMap>
            </div>
    </form>
</body>
</html>
```

C# ImgMap.aspx.cs

```
using System;

public partial class ImageMp : System.Web.UI.Page
{
//Nothing from the C#
}
```

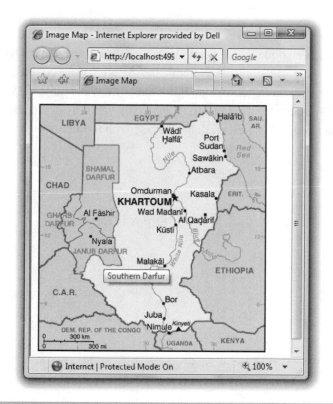

Figure 6-24   Image map displaying Alternate Text for Southern Darfur

As you can see, the C# portion was unused. That's not a problem, even when using code-behind. However, I like to leave the C# in place just in case I want to update my site and need to add a little C#. Figure 6-24 shows the Alternate Text that appears when the mouse is over the Janub Darfur region (Southern Darfur).

To see how a link works, move the mouse over the Shamal region (Northern Darfur), and click when you see the Alternate Text or the Hotspot icon (a hand). As you do, you will see the linked page appear in a separate window.

Summary

This chapter has been quite lengthy, but the web controls are at the center of ASP.NET 3.5. In fact, not all of the web controls available in ASP.NET were covered, but you will find that by working with these controls and their properties, it's quite easy to use others as well. As we delve deeper into ASP.NET, especially when using databases, you will find that further properties are available for use with the many web controls seen in this chapter.

Chapter 7

CSS for ASP.NET 3.5 Page Formatting

Key Skills & Concepts

- Styling control properties

- Controlling ASP.NET format with CSS

- Using the `cssClass` property in Web forms

The clarity and style of a page require both a good designer and good structure. The good structure can be found in Cascading Style Sheets (CSS). It has become the default styling standard, and CSS can be usefully employed with ASP.NET pages and assigned values with C#. Of course the whole process is made easier with the built-in CSS features in Visual Studio 2008.

Styling with the Properties Window

To get started, instead of jumping right into CSS, this first section looks at working with styles by using the simple Properties window. When any control or form is placed in the ASP.NET editor, the Properties window provides the elements in the control that can be assigned directly to the object. In the Design or Split mode in Visual Studio 2008, you can see exactly how your control or form appears once a style has been added.

Styling Web Controls

For example, if you place a Button web control in the editor, in the Properties window you will see several different options in the Appearance directory. The following steps walk you through a simple example:

1. Open a new Web Site, and select the Design mode.

2. Drag a TextBox control to the editor.

3. Drag a Button control to the editor, and place it directly beneath the TextBox.

4. Select the TextBox and open the Properties window. Find the Appearance directory and open it if it is not already opened.

5. Set the `BorderWidth` to **3px**.

6. Open the Font directory and set the `Font` to **Courier New** and the size to **Larger**. Set the `ForeColor` to **#CC3300**.

7. Select the Button control, set the `BackColor` to **#FFCC00**, `BorderStyle` to **Groove**, `BorderWidth` to **7px**, `ForeColor` to **Red**, and `Text` to **Styled Button**.

8. Open the Font directory and set the `Font` to **Verdana**, `Bold` to **True**, and `Size` to **Larger**. Figure 7-1 shows what you will see in the Design window while making these changes.

Whenever you select an object in the Design mode, its appearance is slightly different than you will see when you test the application. Save and test the application, and you will see that the button looks a bit different, and that the text in the TextBox is styled as italicized (see Figure 7-2).

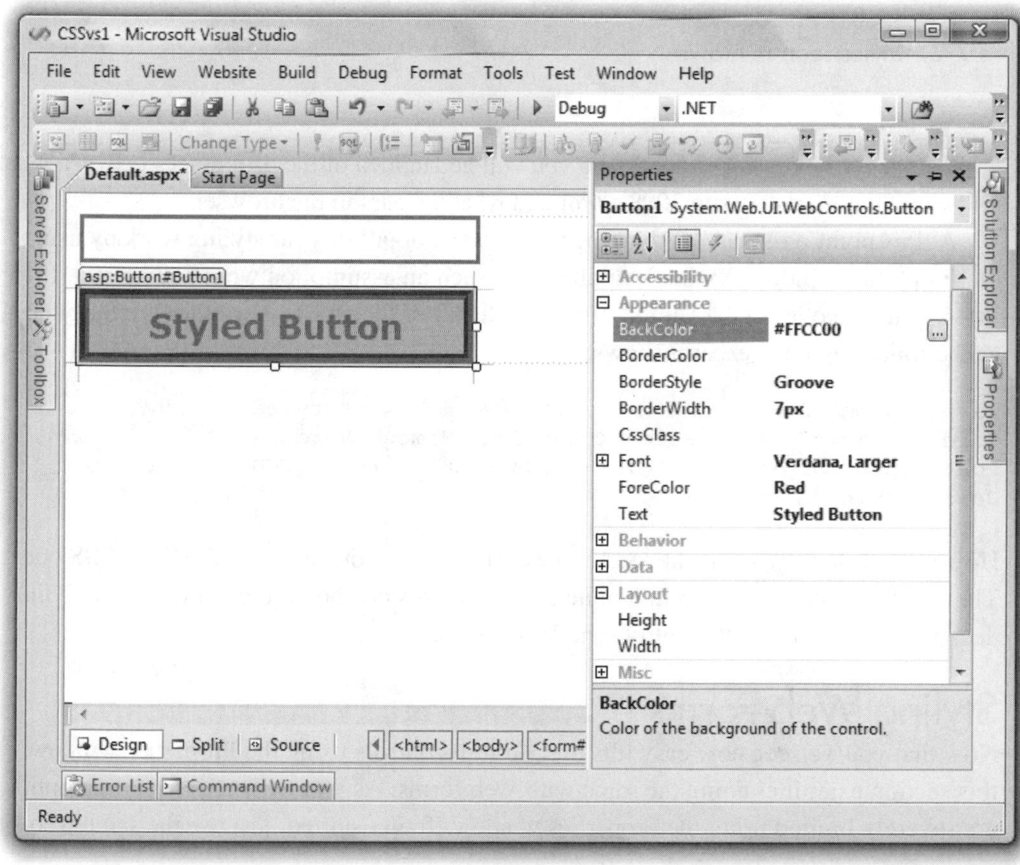

Figure 7-1 Using the Properties window to style web controls

Figure 7-2 Styles seen in browser

Compare Figures 7-1 and 7-2, and you will get an idea of the differences between what you see in the Visual Studio 2008 editor and what appears in the browser.

At this point, you may be thinking that you can do all of your styling work by using the Properties window; for some applications such an assumption would be correct. In looking at the code for the Button, for example, all of the styling attributes are fairly clear, as the following code excerpt shows:

```
<asp:Button ID="Button1" runat="server" Text="Styled Button"
BorderWidth="7" Font-Bold="True" Font-Names="Verdana"
Font-Size="Larger" ForeColor="Red" BackColor="#FFCC00"
BorderStyle="Groove" />
```

However, close inspection shows that the attributes are not standard HTML or CSS ones. They look similar but they're not quite the same. This can be problematic, especially in designs that use both web controls and Web forms.

Styling Web Forms

Now that you've seen how easy it is to style web controls using the Properties window, this section examines doing the same with Web forms. As you will see, the styling options are severely limited using the Properties window. To get started, just use the same web site used earlier for styling the web controls. The following steps, continued from the previous section, walk you through steps that illustrate the differences:

1. Open the HTML menu in the Toolbox.

2. Drag an Input (Text) form to the Design editor, and place it directly below the Button web control.

3. Drag an Input (Submit) button to the Design editor, and position it directly below the Input (Text) form.

4. Select the Input (Submit) button form and open the Properties window. As you will see, it looks very different from the web control. You see no Appearance directory, but you have a very long Misc directory with a few style choices. However, you will see a Style option.

5. Click to the right of the Style option in the menu, and you will see a button that opens a Modify Style window as shown in Figure 7-3.

6. Fill in the values shown in Figure 7-3, or use your own selections.

7. Select the Input (Text) form, and style it as well to suit your own taste.

At this point, stop and take a look at the Source view. You will see that both of the HTML forms have been styled with inline CSS. For example, the following shows the style code for the button:

```
<input id="Submit1" name="SubBtn" size="250"
style="font-family: Verdana, Arial, Helvetica, sans-serif;
font-size: 12px;
font-weight: bold;
font-style: inherit;
font-variant: small-caps;
text-transform: capitalize;
color: #800000;
text-decoration: none"
type="submit" value="Send Information" />
```

All of the style code added inline is not only messy in the ASP.NET portion of your application, but it also is poor practice. Styles should integrate a web site by having a common style source. A single style class or an external style sheet could do the same thing with only a reference to the class in use rather than using inline CSS in individual forms.

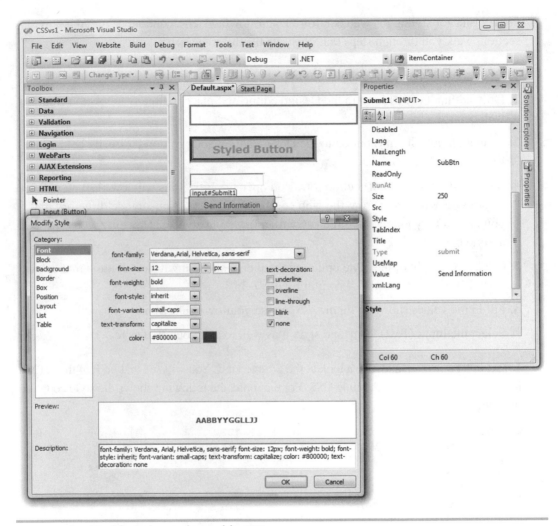

Figure 7-3 Modify Style window adds CSS

Before continuing, test the application. The materials added in the Modify Style window using CSS should show up. Figure 7-4 shows that both web controls and forms can be styled using the Properties window.

Aside from the fact that when both web controls and Web forms are used in the same application, you would have to use the Properties window for styling web controls and CSS for the Web forms, doing so is wasted effort and can lead to a jumbled design. A much better solution is to use CSS throughout your application.

Figure 7-4   CSS-styled Web forms added to web controls

Designing with CSS

Most of the work done with ASP.NET will be to set up forms and controls that users do one of two things with: enter data or extract data. A user *enters* data when she types in her name, the product she wants, and her payment information. By *extracting* data, a user usually just looks at the information made available on the web site, but extraction also includes interactive data that respond to data input or stored data. Along with those two key functions, users will be clicking buttons, making selections from lists, and selecting links. However, the key role of ASP.NET and C# is to get and give information.

TIP

If you're reading this book, you're probably not a designer. (If you are, bless you, and skip the remainder of this tip.) While there are exceptions, most developers need to face the fact that they'd probably not make very good designers. One of the best tips I got from a designer was to get ideas from what other designers have done. When it comes to CSS, you can find some first-rate designs in CSS style sheets. Here are a few URLs where you can freely (and legally) download designs created with CSS:
www.templateworld.com/free_templates.html
www.opensourcetemplates.org/
www.oswd.org/
By comparing your designs with a designer's design, you'll see what I mean.

Visual Studio 2008 CSS Design Tool

Visual Studio 2008 has a very powerful CSS design tool. To get started, this section will take two different objects—a Web TextBox and an Input (Text) form—and apply a single CSS class to both.

Try This Designing CSS with Visual Studio 2008

This is both a CSS refresher and a step-by-step guide for working with the Visual Studio 2008.

1. Open a new Web Site, and select the Source mode.

2. From the Standard Toolbox menu, add a TextBox web control to the editor between the <div></div> tags, and put a **<p/>** tag after it.

3. From the HTML Toolbox menu, add an Input(Text) Web form beneath the <p/> tag.

4. Switch to Design mode.

5. Select View | Manage Styles to open the CSS Manage Styles tool. (Note: For readers familiar with previous versions of Visual Studio, the CSS Manage Styles tool is accessed through a different set of menus now.)

6. Once the CSS style tool is open, click on New Style at the top of the window. The New Style window opens.

7. In the Selector box, type **.input**. This is the class name.

8. In the Define In box, choose Current Page from the drop-down list.

9. Select Font from the Category menu. Make the settings shown in Figure 7-5.

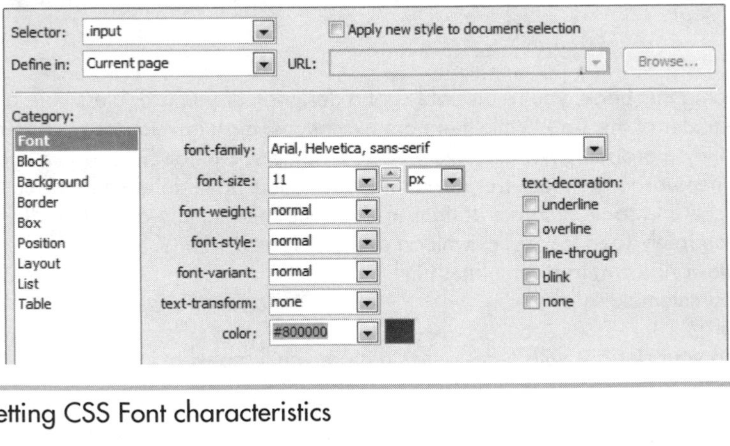

Figure 7-5 Setting CSS Font characteristics

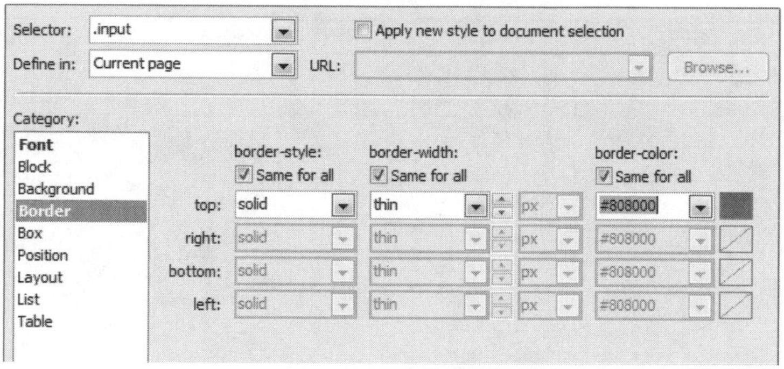

Figure 7-6 Setting CSS Border values

10. Select Border in the Category menu. Enter the settings shown in Figure 7-6.

11. Select Position in the Category menu, and enter the values shown in Figure 7-7.

12. Click OK. Switch to the Split view, and move the mouse cursor over the .input class in the Current Page directory in the Manage Styles window. Scroll to the style definition in the Source view. Both views now show the code for the .input class just created. Figure 7-8 shows what you can expect to see.

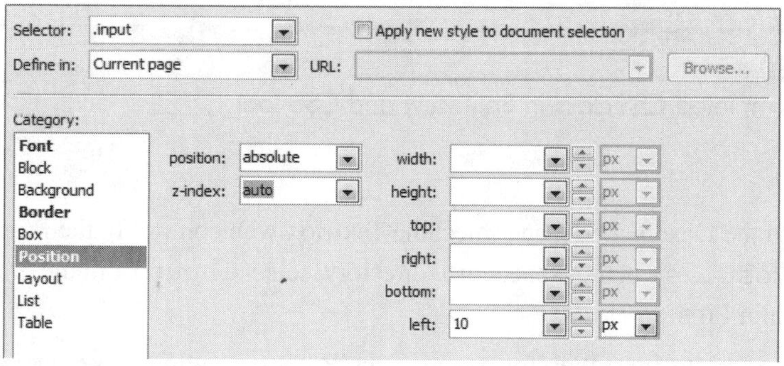

Figure 7-7 Setting Position values

(continued)

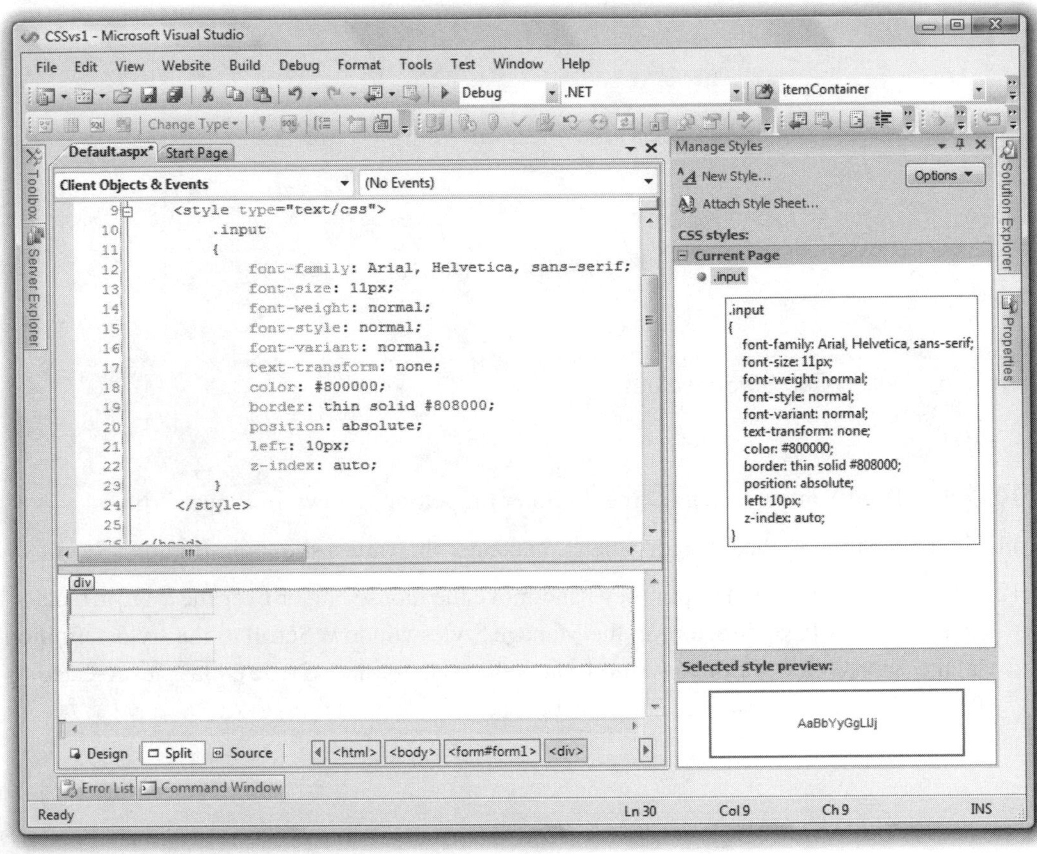

Figure 7-8 Completed CSS class in Split view and CSS tool

13. Switch to the Design mode, and select the TextBox web control. In the Properties window, next to `CssClass` in the Appearance directory, select `input` from the drop-down menu as shown in Figure 7-9.

14. Select the Input (Text) Web form, and in the Properties window select `input` from the drop-down menu next to the `Class` property. (Note that with the web control, the property was `CssClass`.) Figure 7-10 shows what you will see.

15. Test the application by pressing CTRL-F5. Figure 7-11 shows what you can expect to see.

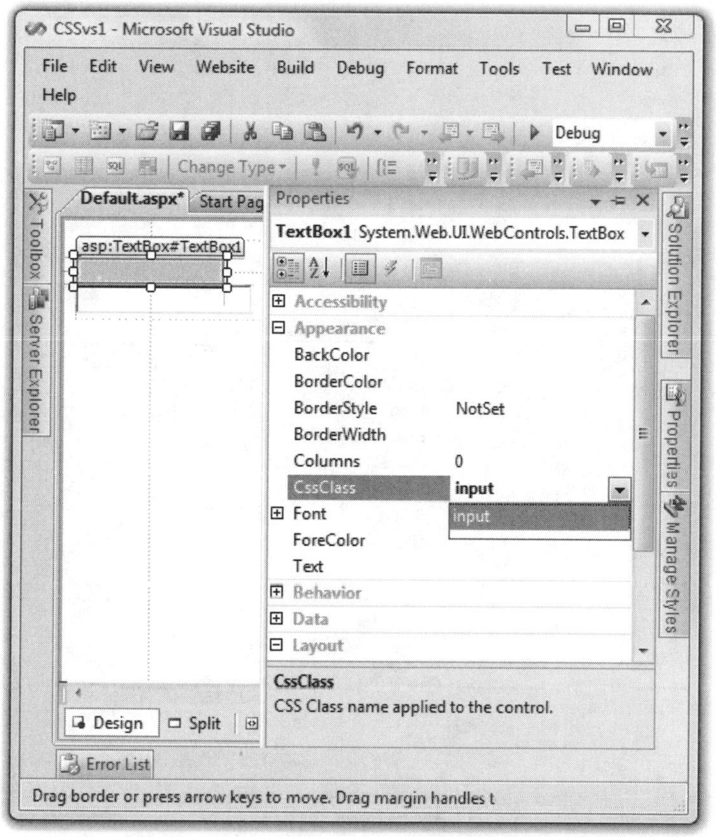

Figure 7-9   Web controls use `CssClass` property to set style class

That may have seemed like a lot of work to get two input forms to look the same, but the point is that with CSS, once the style is completed, you can apply it to any web control *or* Web form and achieve a consistent design. To see how this works, add a CheckBoxList and a Button from the Standard Toolbox menu. Apply the `CssClass` property `input` to both, and test the application. Figure 7-12 shows them all to have the same design now.

This should give you a better idea of what can be done with CSS and your application.

(continued)

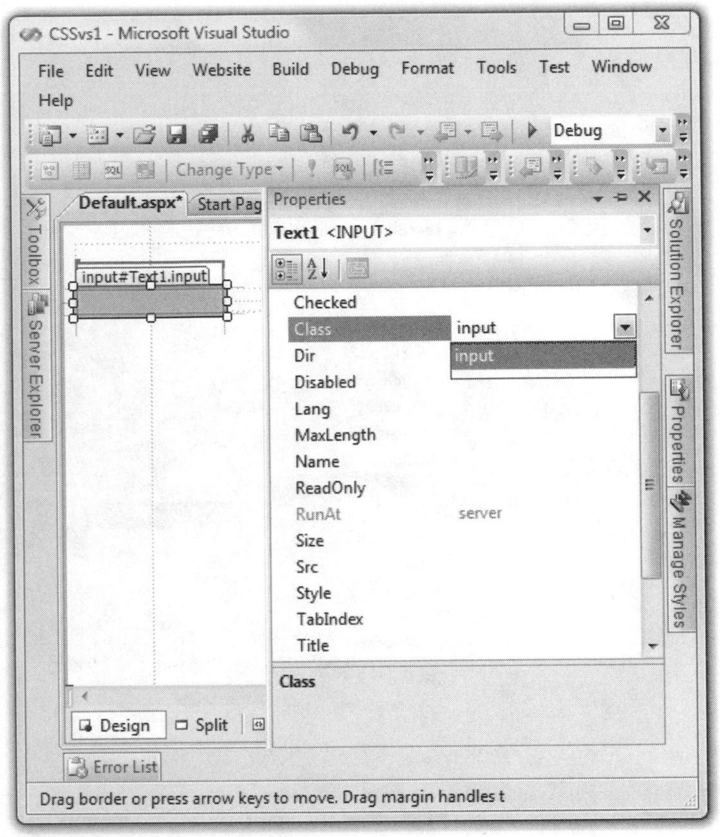

Figure 7-10 Web forms use `Class` property to set style class

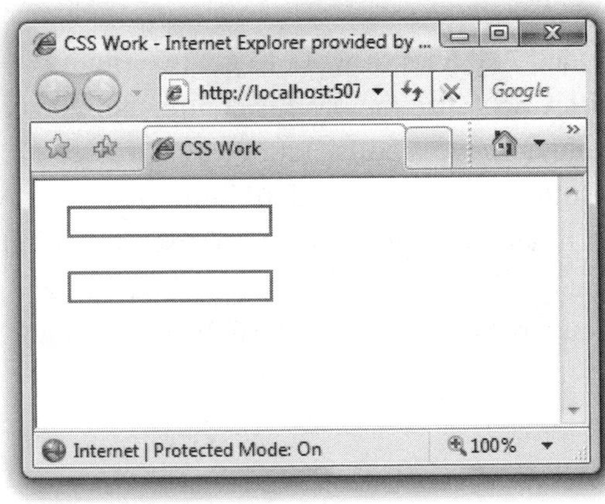

Figure 7-11 Web form and web control with identical CSS class

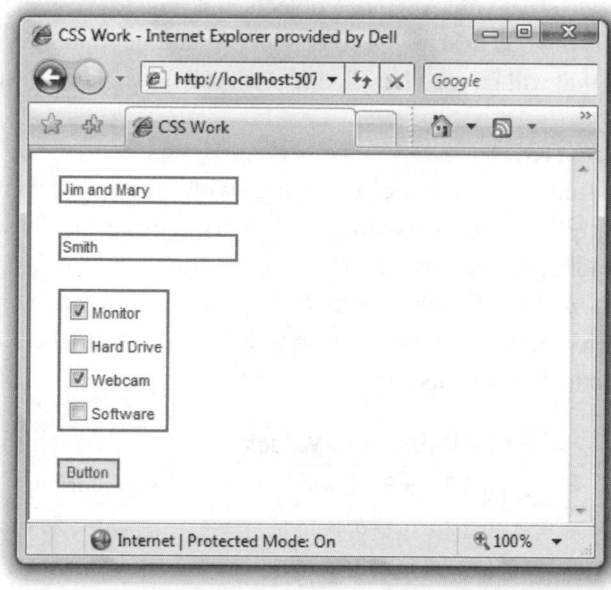

Figure 7-12 Additional web controls with identical CSS style applied

CSS External Style Sheets

If you look at the CSS behind even simple designs, you will find quite a bit of CSS code. Designers have excellent tools for generating CSS code for their designs, and they attend to every single detail. When attending to such detail, though, you need to have a plan so that when you begin making those applications, everything goes together.

NOTE
Whether or not you're accustomed to creating external style sheets, you might want to keep in mind the simple tag

```
<link href="MyStyle.css" rel="stylesheet" type="text/css" />
```

The style sheet itself is nothing but a text file with the CSS code. If you have some style sheets from previous work, all you need to do is to add the `<link>` tag inside the `<head>` container in the ASP.NET portion of the web site. Place the CSS text file in the same folder with your ASPX file, and you're good to go. Sometimes it's just easier to use what you have rather than reinvent it with sophisticated tools like Visual Studio 2008.

To see how to create and use an external style sheet, this next project walks you through the process. The style sheet is relatively small, but the purpose is to show how to create and use a style sheet with ASP.NET objects, not how to create a perfect sheet. One of the key elements of good design is a color scheme, and in building a style, you need to get a set of colors that will go together. So the project begins with getting a color scheme.

The Color Scheme

The first step is to find a color scheme. You can go with something simple or elaborate, but be careful, especially if you're a developer. The colors in this example were extrapolated from a book on color combinations, *The Designer's Guide to Color Combinations: 500+ Historic and Modern Color Formulas in CMYK* by Leslie Cabarga (North Light Books, 1999). First, the CMYK values were changed to RGB values and then to hexadecimal. The following palette makes up the color schemes:

Hex Value	RGB (Decimal Values)	Descriptive Name
#C1272D	(r:193, g:39, b:45)	Brick red
#C3B06F	(r:195, g:176, b:111)	Medium tan
#D8CAA1	(r:216, g:202, b:161)	Light tan
#000000	(r:0, g:0, b:0)	Black
#FFFFFF	(r:255, g:255, b:255)	White

Once you have the color scheme, use the Manage Styles tool to integrate your style into your style sheet. The following steps show you how to set your color scheme:

1. Set your mode to Design, and place all of the objects and text you want to style in the editor.

2. Open the CSS style tool.

3. Select New Style and in the Define In box, select New Style Sheet and click OK. At this point, it doesn't really matter whether you have entered a style. If you have, be sure to name the style in the Selector box with a dot (.) definition—a period prefix needs to be placed in the Selector window. For example, `.inputData` is an acceptable style name.

4. When the Microsoft Visual Web Developer window appears, click Yes if you have a style you want in the style sheet. Otherwise click No.

5. As soon as you click Yes or No, you will see a new style sheet next to your ASPX file. It will be named StyleSheet#.css, where # is a number. If this is your first style sheet, you will see it named StyleSheet1.css. Select File | Save StyleSheet#.css As, and you will see the default path to a StyleSheet folder and the default name of your style sheet. Change the default name to **Simple.css**.

6. In the Manage Styles window, click on New Style, and when your New Style window opens, select Existing Style Sheet in the Define In box. Then click the Browse button and select Simple.css. It will appear in your URL window as shown in Figure 7-13.

In the Selector window, type in **.header1**, and enter the following values by selecting the different menus and entering the values:

```
border-style: none;
font-family: Arial, Helvetica, sans-serif;
font-size: 16px;
font-weight: bold;
font-style: normal;
font-variant: small-caps;
text-transform: capitalize;
color: #C1272D;
background-color: #FFFFFF;
```

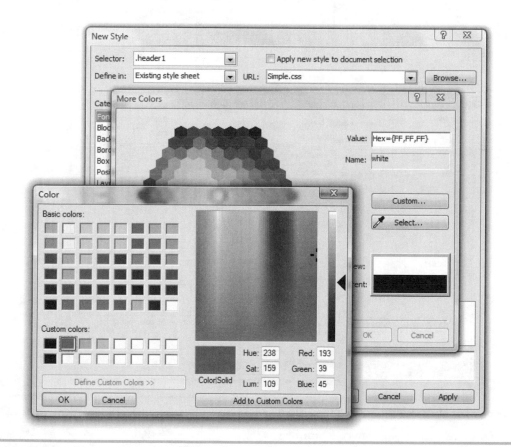

Figure 7-13 Creating a custom color palette

7. When you get to the color entry, click on the Color box (or the menu and then the More Colors button), and the More Colors window opens. Then click on the Custom button that opens the Color window as shown in Figure 7-13.

8. Click in one of the empty boxes in the Custom Colors group shown in Figure 7-13. Then in the Red, Green, and Blue boxes, enter decimal values for your color. Once you have all of your custom colors entered, you can then color all of your other styles simply by clicking on the Color drop-down menu and selecting your color from your palette as shown in Figure 7-14.

9. Complete all of the entries for all of the categories you want. Figure 7-15 shows one of the styles completed.

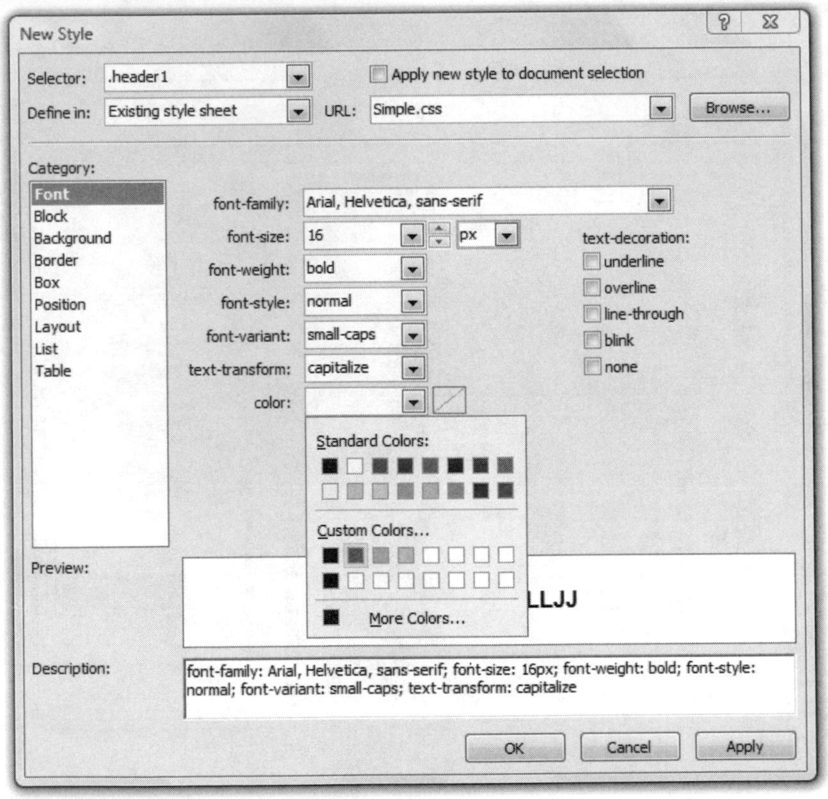

Figure 7-14 Choosing colors from Custom Colors

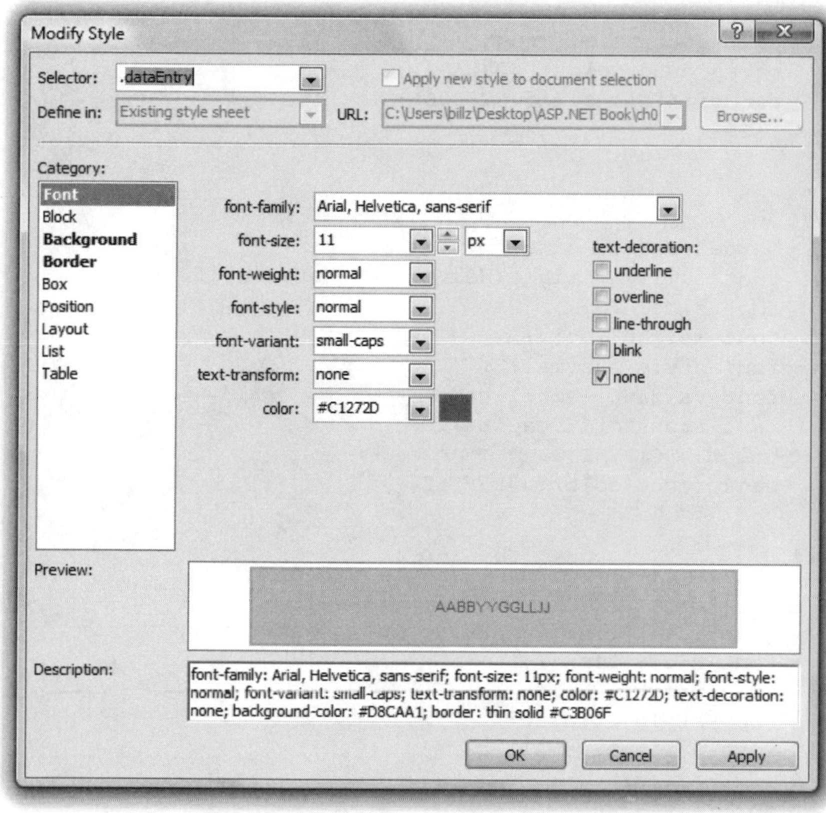

Figure 7-15 Completed style with a Preview and Description of all settings

10. The following shows the completed style sheet saved as Simple.css.

```
body {
     border-style: none;
     background-color: #ffffff;
}
.dataEntry
{
     font-family: Arial, Helvetica, sans-serif;
     font-size: 11px;
     font-weight: normal;
     font-style: normal;
     font-variant: small-caps;
     text-transform: none;
```

```
        color: #C1272D;
        text-decoration: none;
        background-color: #D8CAA1;
        border: thin solid #C3B06F;
}

.header1
{
        border-style: none;
        font-family: Arial, Helvetica, sans-serif;
        font-size: 16px;
        font-weight: bold;
        font-style: normal;
        font-variant: small-caps;
        text-transform: capitalize;
        color: #C1272D;
        background-color: #FFFFFF;
}

.header2
{
        font-family: Arial, Helvetica, sans-serif;
        font-size: 14px;
        font-weight: bold;
        font-style: italic;
        font-variant: small-caps;
        text-transform: none;
        color: #C3B06F;
        text-decoration: none;
        background-color: #FFFFFF;
        background-image: none;
        background-repeat: no-repeat;
}
.btn
{
        font-family: Arial, Helvetica, sans-serif;
        font-size: 10px;
        font-weight: bold;
        font-style: normal;
        font-variant: small-caps;
        text-transform: capitalize;
        color: #C1272D;
        border: thin solid #C1272D;
        background-color: #D8CAA1;
}
.inputLabel
```

```
    {
        font-family: Arial, Helvetica, sans-serif;
        font-size: 12px;
        font-weight: normal;
        font-style: normal;
        font-variant: small-caps;
        text-transform: capitalize;
        color: #C1272D;
    }
```

11. Open the Manage Styles tool, and select Attach Style Sheet.

12. When the Select Style Sheet window opens, select Simple.css. As soon as you make the selection and click OK, the styles appear in the CSS Styles area in the Manage Styles window as shown in Figure 7-16.

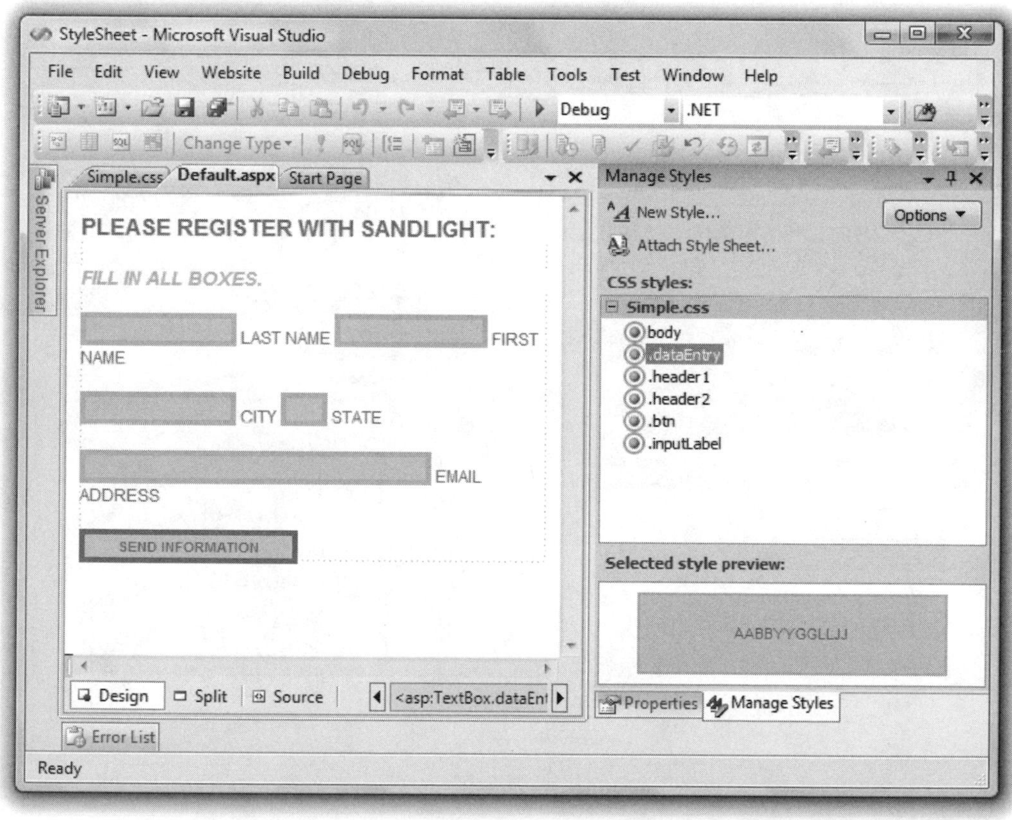

Figure 7-16   Style sheet in Manage Styles window

13. Place text and web controls in the Design window with the Design mode selected as shown in Figure 7-16.

14. To style the text and controls, select each control and text, right-click the style you want to use, and choose Apply Style as shown in Figure 7-17.

Once you have applied all of the styles to all of the forms, test your application. As you will see in Figure 7-18, the Design window and the running application are a little different. The Design window does not show the small caps, but instead, shows all caps. However, when the actual application launches, you see the correct font style display shown in Figure 7-18.

Besides showing the correct font style, the borders around the button and textboxes are slightly thinner in the application than in the Design window.

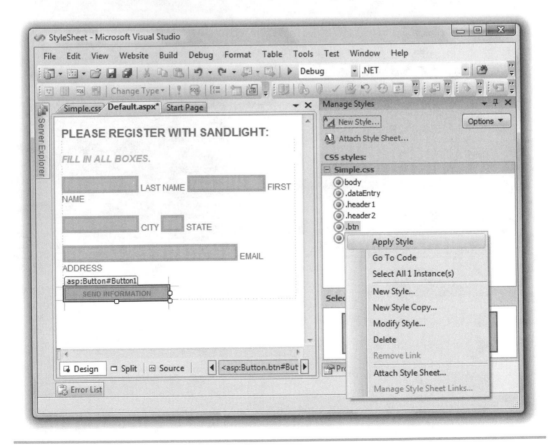

Figure 7-17 Applying styles from style sheet

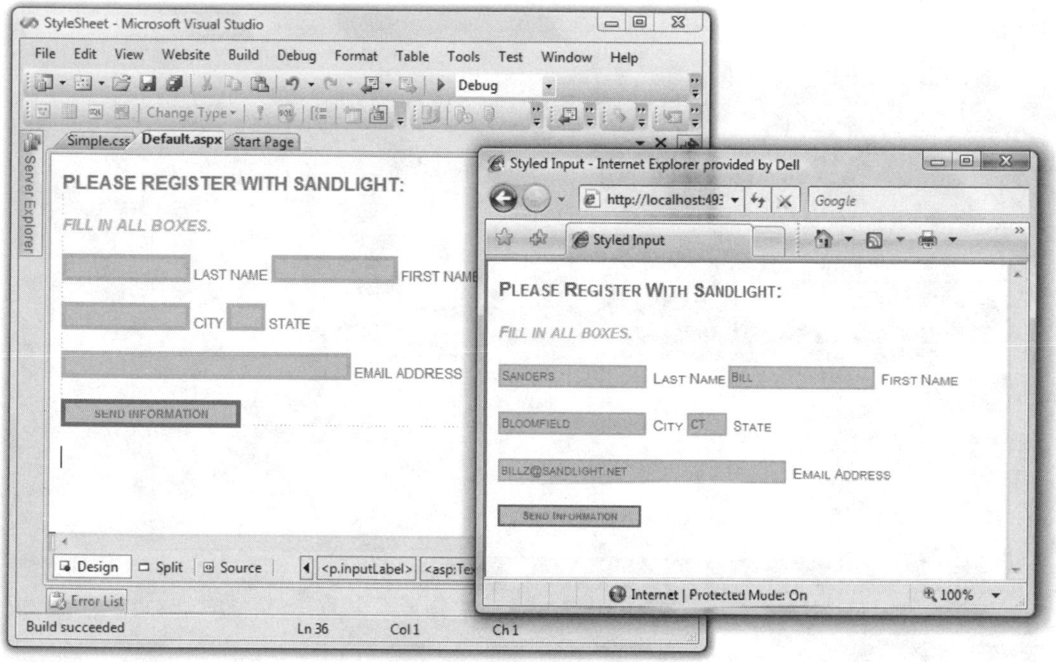

Figure 7-18 Design mode display and the actual application have some differences.

As any designer can tell you, far more is involved in design than getting the colors right. However, poor colors can ruin an otherwise good design. As mentioned, take a look at some designs created by designers to see all of the different considerations you might want to think about when creating your style sheets.

Ask the Expert

Q: My colors never work right. They look bad, and I want to be able to find good color combinations quickly, online if possible.

A: The mother lode of color combinations can be found at http://kuler.adobe.com/. You can choose from over 50,000 color combinations (and growing), with all of the information about each color set. The information includes HSL, RGB, and Hexadecimal values that you can use in specifying the colors in the Color window that is part of the Manage Styles tool. Figure 7-19 shows a sample of what you can see.

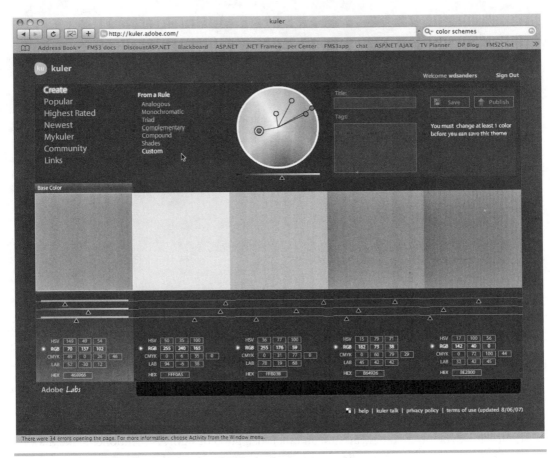

Figure 7-19 Color combination and color information

C# Style

In addition to creating styles for your objects by using ASP.NET, you can also add style classes to web controls directly from C#. Suppose your style sheet is set, and you do not want to change it. However, a single Input form needs to be tweaked because the users are entering nicknames instead of their given first names. For example, you need to have "James" instead of "Jim" and "Victoria" instead of "Torrie" to verify credit card information. So rather than change your style sheet, you decide to add a little C# styling. The format is

```
ControlName.Style["css attribute"] = "css value";
```

For example, the control instance, `TextBox2`, is where users enter their first name, and the default style for the text is a normal-weight red font. To get users' attention, you add a green bold font and a reminder not to use a nickname. The following code excerpt shows how you can change the style and add the warning:

```
TextBox2.Style["color"]="#00cc00";
TextBox2.Style["font-weight"] = "bold";
TextBox2.Text = "Do not use a nickname.";
```

By and large, you will not be using C# for any of the styling work when dealing with ASP.NET because all of your styles should be handled by a style sheet. However, if you run into a problem, in a pinch you can quickly solve it with C# coding.

Summary

When working with a technology such as ASP.NET that can be used for both gathering and dispensing information, developers sometimes lose sight of the fact that users interact with the interface setup to give and get information. The more consideration given to the design of input and output, the greater the chances that you will get the data you need and that the user will get what he needs. Just because ASP.NET and C# are powerful development tools does not mean that design should be ignored.

For the most part, in dealing with real-world clients, graphic designers will be creating the style sheets used in applications. However, designers may not be familiar with applying these designs and layouts to ASP.NET objects. Therefore, while you may not have to create the actual designs used in an application you develop with ASP.NET and C#, you should know how to apply them and communicate with designers about the styling options available with ASP.NET 3.5.

Chapter 8

Control Events and Event Handlers

Key Skills & Concepts

- Automatic event generation

- Working with Change events

- Button Command events

The ASP.NET controls interact with C# primarily through events. A function (or method) in C# has a name associated with some web control event assignment. This chapter looks further into events, exploring how to find what events are associated with a given web control and how they can be used in ASP.NET/C# applications. Much of the material in this chapter will be familiar because virtually every ASP.NET/C# application up to this point in the book has included an event—if nothing more than a Page Load event. However, we look further in this chapter to better use events and the web controls associated with them.

Automatic Events

Whenever you open a new web site, the C# portion of the application has a function beginning with the line

```
protected void Page_Load(object sender, EventArgs e)
```

The name of the *method* is actually `Page_Load`, and the event that assigns the name `Page_Load` is part of C# and ASP.NET assignment. In other words, the *event name* is *not* `Page_Load` but something else. In this case, it's a built-in `OnLoad` event assigned the value that `Page_Load` associated with the page object. Because the name "Page_Load" sounds like an event, often developers just assume it's an event, but it's not. It could have been named anything—"Hip_Hop," if the designers so desired.

Double-Click in the Design Mode

The main shortcut for generating an event associated with a web control has been to double-click a web control in the Design mode and to use the default function name that appears in the C# code. For example, if you double-click a TextBox control, you can expect to see the C# method beginning

```
protected void TextBox1_TextChanged(object sender, EventArgs e)
```

If you click on the page and the default `Page_Load` method has been removed from the C# code, a new one will appear. Visual Studio 2008 is pretty smart and knows that if you have one page-loading event, another would just conflict with it. In a single page-loading event function or subroutine, you can enter as many statements as you want, so having more than a single event handler for a single event does not make any sense even for multiple statements.

Some web controls like the Label do not generate event code when double-clicked in the Design mode. The Label web control can be a useful information source, and with the right design you may well want labels with events and event handlers. Fortunately, you can add certain events to virtually any web control if you want. You just don't do it by double-clicking the object in the Design mode, as you will see in the next two sections.

Selecting Events in the Properties Window

In the Design or Split mode, if you select a web control, you can see the available events in the Properties window. When you open the Properties window, click the Lightning Bolt icon. All of the events for the selected web control appear. The following steps provide a simple example:

1. In a new Web Site add a Label web control to the Design portion while in the Split mode.

2. Select the Label control and open the Properties window.

3. Click on the Lightning Bolt icon. You will see a list of all events that can be used with the Label web control as shown in Figure 8-1.

4. Next to the Init event, type **LabelEvent** as shown in Figure 8-1.

When working with web controls and events, do not depend on the "double-click" method in the Design or Split mode. Some web controls that can have events do not generate them automatically in ASP.NET and C# by double-clicking them in the Design window. However, working with the Properties window, as soon as you enter an event name such as `LabelEvent` as shown in Figure 8-1, the code for both the ASP.NET and C# portions of the application are automatically coded.

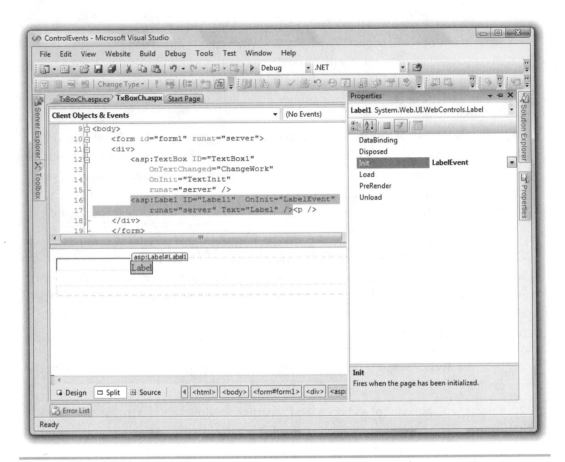

Figure 8-1 Label web control events displayed in the Properties window

IntelliSense and Events

A third way to easily get your events into your application is to use the IntelliSense context menus that pop up in the Source mode. The following simple steps show how:

1. Add a TextBox web control to your application in the Source mode.

2. Click inside the `<TextBox>` tag and press SPACEBAR. A context menu opens.

3. Type the letter **o** and you will see all of the events associated with the TextBox web control. Notice that every event has a lightning bolt next to it. (Also, events all begin with "On"—`OnInit`, `OnLoad`.) Figure 8-2 shows what you can expect to see.

Unlike using either the double-click method in the Design mode or selecting events in the Properties window, when using IntelliSense in the Source mode, you will have

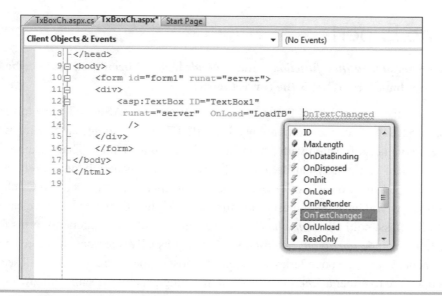

Figure 8-2   IntelliSense context menu showing TextBox events

to assign a value to the event and write your own function in C#. This method might be handy where you want to add multiple events in the same web control. Note in Figure 8-2 that in addition to the OnTextChanged event, the same TextBox web control also has an OnLoad event included in the same tag. Both events require that you write a C# routine to handle them.

Events and Event Handling

Every ASP.NET object that has an event associated with it needs an event handler. The name assigned to an event in a tag is the name of the event handler. So, the code segment

```
OnTextChanged="ChangeWork"
```

names the C# function that handles the event ChangeWork. In the C# portion of the application, you will see the method that handles the OnTextChanged event as

```
protected void ChangeWork(object sender, EventArgs e)
{
      //Statements go here
}
```

If you plan to use more than a single event with a tag, the names assigned to the events must all be unique unless you plan to have two different events launch the same function.

Ask the Expert

Q: The terms *subroutines, functions,* and *methods* have all been used to describe the C# event handlers. What is the correct term?

A: The dual histories of Visual Basic and C# associated with ASP.NET have left an unusual legacy of function terminology. In ASP.NET, a *subroutine* is a function with no return value. A function with a return value is called a *function.* That makes a lot more sense if you're a Visual Basic user, but with C# you generally do not reference a void-typed function as a *subroutine.* The term *method* is a reference to a C# class function. As you have seen, most of the functions that handle the events are clearly part of a class, so the term *method* is appropriate as well. More general terms for functions include *operations* and *routines,* but they usually reference the more specific statements within the boundaries of a method. Most of the references you will see in this book are to either a *function* or *method,* meaning exactly the same thing without regard for whether they include a return value. A few *subroutines* references are added to make those with a Visual Basic background feel comfortable.

Adding multiple events is as simple as adding one. Using the Properties window and Design view or just with code, all you have to do is add the event to the target web control's properties.

Try This   Using Multiple Web Controls

To show how multiple web controls and events applications work, this next simple example uses a single TextBox and Label. Follow this set of steps to create the application:

1. Open a new Web Site.
2. Add a TextBox control in the <div> container.
3. Next to the TextBox add a Label.
4. In the Design mode window select the TextBox web control and open the Properties window.
5. Click the Lightning Bolt icon and type **ChangeWork** next to the TextChanged event and **TextInit** next to the Init event.

6. Select the Label icon, open the Properties window, and click the Lightning Bolt icon.

7. Next to the Init event, type **LabelEvent**. The following ASP.NET listing shows what you should see in the Source mode:

ASP.NET TxBoxCh.aspx

```
<%@ Page Language="C#" AutoEventWireup="true"  CodeFile="TxBoxCh.aspx.cs"
Inherits="TxbxChange" %>
<!DOCTYPE html PUBLIC "-//W3C//DTD XHTML 1.0 Transitional//EN"
"http://www.w3.org/TR/xhtml1/DTD/xhtml1-transitional.dtd">
<html xmlns="http://www.w3.org/1999/xhtml">
<head runat="server">
    <title>Change Text Box</title>
</head>
<body>
    <form id="form1" runat="server">
    <div>
        <asp:TextBox ID="TextBox1"
            OnTextChanged="ChangeWork"
            OnInit="TextInit"
            runat="server" />

        <asp:Label ID="Label1"  OnInit="LabelEvent"
            runat="server" Text="Label" /><p />
    </div>
    </form>
</body>
</html>
```

8. Open the C# window and add the following code:

C# TxBoxCh.aspx.cs

```
using System;
public partial class TxbxChange : System.Web.UI.Page
{
    protected void TextInit(object sender, EventArgs e)
    {
        TextBox1.Text = "Original";
    }
    protected void ChangeWork(object sender, EventArgs e)
    {
        TextBox1.Text = "Changed";
        Label1.Text = "Goodbye Ms. Label";
    }
```

(continued)

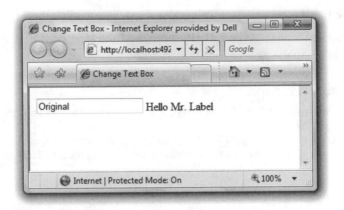

Figure 8-3 The Init events generate text for the web controls

```
protected void LabelEvent(object sender, EventArgs e)
{
    Label1.Text = "Hello Mr. Label";
}
}
```

Those few events and two web controls tell a very big event story. When you test the application, you should first see the page shown in Figure 8-3.

Both the TextBox and Label web controls contain text that is generated by the Init event. The Load and Init events are part of the life cycle an ASP.NET page goes through when it launches. For all intents and purposes, you will find very few differences between using initialization and Load events because they both occur when the page first appears.

The only user event is changing the text in the TextBox from "Original" to anything else—the event is a Change event. As soon as you make a change, the TextBox and Label change as shown in Figure 8-4.

The events in this example are mostly automatic, occurring as the page loads. The only event that fires otherwise is when the user makes a change to the original contents of the TextBox and presses ENTER. Pressing TAB will not fire the event, so if you want it to work effectively with users, you need to clearly specify to press ENTER when they have entered their information.

Now that you have a general idea of setting up events and event handlers, the next several sections look at various web controls dealing with different kinds of events and at handling those events. You will be familiar with some of the event issues because in

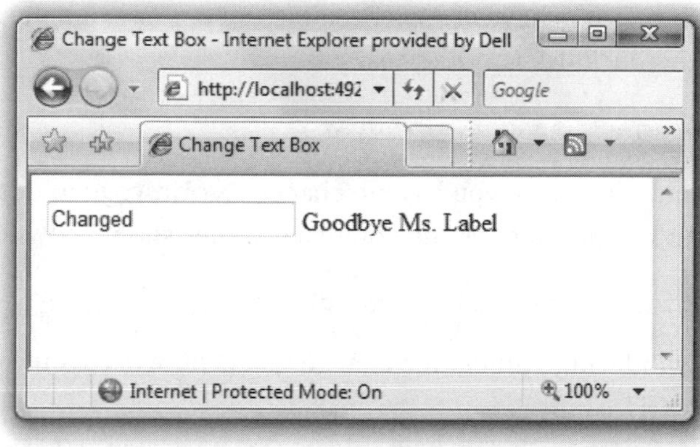

Figure 8-4   The Change event generates two new messages.

previous chapters you have seen event handling associated with different web controls and even with Web forms. However, these sections focus exclusively on the events and how to best use them.

Button Command Events

One of the more interesting events you can use with buttons is OnCommand. The Button web controls have two command-related properties: CommandName and CommandArgument. You can assign the OnCommand event any name you want, and that name will be used as the function name in the C# portion of the application. For all intents and purposes, the OnCommand event works just like an OnClick event.

Both the CommandName and CommandArgument are recognized in the Properties window when you are creating an application. The CommandName is a unique name that can be associated with the command, and the CommandArgument is a string containing whatever command argument you want to include. Both are generally included when you use the OnCommand event.

Changing the Event Handler Parameters

To get the command information, you have to change the event handling function parameters you've used up to this point. Also, you will need to add another namespace. In the entire automatic C# code rendering you may have done in creating your applications, the parameters have always been the same. For example, the default line every new C# listing includes is

```
Event_Handler(object sender, EventArgs e)...
```

To use the command properties, you have to change `EventArgs` to `CommandEventArgs`. The event handling function for reading command values should now read

```
Event_Handler(object sender, CommandEventArgs e)...
```

The difference is subtle, but without the change you cannot access the command data stored in the ASP.NET controls.

In addition, you must add a new namespace, `System.Web.UI.WebControls`. The new namespace includes objects that can deal with both `CommandName` and `CommandArgument`. For example, the following code segment shows the passing of values in both command properties:

```
using System;
using System.Web.UI.WebControls;
public partial class BVents : System.Web.UI.Page
{
    private string cName;
    private string cArg
    protected void Handle_Event(object sender, CommandEventArgs e)
    {
        cName = e.CommandName;
        cArg = e.CommandArgument;
....
```

Whatever values are stored in the command properties can now be passed to variables `cName` and `cArg` in the preceding code segment. The consequence of this is that a single event handler can deal with multiple buttons using the command properties.

One Event Handler, Many Controls

To begin, you will see how to access the Command property values. This next example uses three buttons, each with a different `CommandName` and `CommandArgument`. Both of the command properties' values are sent to a Label web control's Text property to show how to gain access to the command values. Use the following steps to create the application:

1. Open a new Web Site, and use the Solution Explorer to change the name from Default to **BtnEvents**.

2. In the ASP.NET editor, place three buttons in the `<div>` container, separated vertically by two lines.

Figure 8-5 Adding `CommandArgument` to source

3. In the each of the button tags, add a `CommandName` and a `CommandValue` string value. Figure 8-5 shows both the IntelliSense context menu with the two command properties and the Design view of the buttons.

4. Add a Label web control, and position it to the right of the middle button.

5. To complete the ASP.NET portion of the application, add the following source code:

ASP.NET BtnEvents.aspx

```
<%@ Page Language="C#" AutoEventWireup="true"  CodeFile="BtnEvents
.aspx.cs" Inherits="BVents" %>
<!DOCTYPE html PUBLIC "-//W3C//DTD XHTML 1.0 Transitional//EN"
"http://www.w3.org/TR/xhtml1/DTD/xhtml1-transitional.dtd">
<html xmlns="http://www.w3.org/1999/xhtml">
<head runat="server">
    <title>OnCommand with Buttons</title>
</head>
<body>
    <form id="form1" runat="server">
    <div>
```

```
        <asp:Button ID="Button1" runat="server"
         CommandName="Seek"
         CommandArgument="Forward"
         OnCommand="GenericClick"
         Text="First" />
        <p />
<asp:Button ID="Button2" runat="server"
         CommandName="Stop"
         CommandArgument="Halt"
         OnCommand="GenericClick"
        Text="Second" />
            
        <asp:Label ID="Label1" runat="server" Text="Ready" />
        <p />
        <asp:Button ID="Button3" runat="server"
        CommandName="Pause"
        CommandArgument="Will Resume"
        OnCommand="GenericClick"
        Text="Third" />
    </div>
    </form>
</body>
</html>
```

6. Check over your code and save it; open the C# portion of your application, and enter and save the following script:

C# BtnEvents.aspx.cs

```
using System;
using System.Web.UI.WebControls;
public partial class BVents : System.Web.UI.Page
{
    protected void GenericClick(object sender, CommandEventArgs e)
    {
        Label1.Text = e.CommandName + "--";
        Label1.Text += e.CommandArgument;
    }
}
```

When you test this application, you will see that both command properties in each of the three Button controls are passed to the Label control. The double dashes (- -) serve to separate the CommandName value on the left from the CommandArgument value on the right. Figure 8-6 shows the output generated by clicking the bottom button.

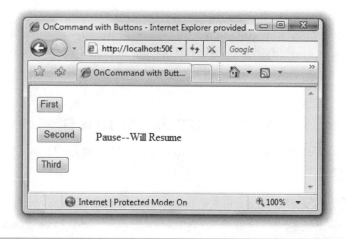

Figure 8-6 CommandName and CommandArgument values displayed in Label control

Using Command Events for Tasks

In organizing tasks for ASP.NET and C# in your site, the command properties allow you to develop multiple tasks using a single event handling function. Using the CommandName and/or the CommandArgument values with the OnCommand event trigger, you can use the different values in the command properties to select a specific action from within the C# event handler function. For example, you could place a switch statement in the event handler function to decide on a course of action based on the command values passed from the ASP.NET portion of the application. Writing separate methods for different kinds of events is perfectly fine, but with single statements used to complete a task sometimes, it's easier and just as functional to pass commands from the ASP.NET controls.

This next example shows how a single event handler in C# can distinguish between three kinds of activities depending on which button is pressed. Rather than simply display data, this next application completes one of three tasks:

- Sorts an array in ascending order
- Sorts an array in descending order
- Clears the TextBox used to display the array element values

All of these tasks are completed by a single event handling method. All of the selections are triggered in a single switch statement. A second private method configures the output for the display, but the main decision-making and task-assignment is done by the case selections in the switch statement.

To clear the TextBox, the operation uses the actual value of the CommandArgument. The value is converted to a string in the C# portion of the application and is assigned to the TextBox.Text property. This is a trivial operation, but as you will see further on in this section, far more complex strings could be used for an application.

Try This   Using the CommandArgument

Open up a new Web Site, and add the following code to the ASPX and C# elements of the application respectively:

ASP.NET CmdSort.aspx

```
<%@ Page Language="C#" AutoEventWireup="true" CodeFile="CmdSort.aspx.cs"
Inherits="DoCommand" %>
<!DOCTYPE html PUBLIC "-//W3C//DTD XHTML 1.0 Transitional//EN"
"http://www.w3.org/TR/xhtml1/DTD/xhtml1-transitional.dtd">
<html xmlns="http://www.w3.org/1999/xhtml">
<head runat="server">
    <title>Command List</title>
</head>
<body>
    <form id="form1" runat="server">
    <div>
        <asp:Button ID="Button1" runat="server"
            CommandName="Ascending"
            CommandArgument="Sort"
            OnCommand="CommandClick"
            Text="Sort" />
                                        <p />
        <asp:Button ID="Button2"
            OnCommand="CommandClick"
            CommandName="Backwards"
            CommandArgument="Reverse"
        runat="server" Text="Reverse" />
                                        <p />
        <asp:Button ID="Button3"
            OnCommand="CommandClick"
            CommandName="Erase"
            CommandArgument="Clear"
        runat="server" Text="Clear" />
                                        <p />
        <asp:TextBox ID="TextBox1" runat="server"
            Height="200px" ReadOnly="True"
            TextMode="MultiLine"/>
```

```
        </div>
        </form>
</body>
</html>
```

Before entering the C# section, you might want to quickly review how C# uses arrays in the section on arrays in Chapter 3. The purpose of using an array is to simulate dealing with data stored in a database. Beginning in Chapter 12 you will learn how to enter and extract data from a table in a database. Here you will get a feel of it by extracting and displaying data from an array.

C# CmdSort.aspx.cs

```csharp
using System;
using System.Web.UI.WebControls;
public partial class DoCommand : System.Web.UI.Page
{
    private string cmdArg;
    private string[] testList;
    private const int ARRAYSIZE=10;

    protected void CommandClick(object sender, CommandEventArgs e)
    {
        testList = new string[ARRAYSIZE];
        testList[0] = "Mouse";
        testList[1] = "Monitor";
        testList[2] = "Keyboard";
        testList[3] = "Processor";
        testList[4] = "Webcam";
        testList[5] = "Scanner";

        cmdArg = e.CommandArgument.ToString();
        switch (cmdArg)
        {
            case "Sort":
                Array.Sort(testList);
                outList();
                break;

            case "Reverse":
                Array.Reverse(testList);
                outList();
                break;

            case "Clear" :
                TextBox1.Text = cmdArg+"\n\n";
                break;
```

(continued)

```
        }
    }

    private void outList()
    {
        for (int goodie = 0; goodie < ARRAYSIZE;goodie++ )
        {
            if (testList[goodie] != null)
            {
                TextBox1.Text += testList[goodie] + "\n";
            }
        }
        TextBox1.Text += "\n";
    }
}
```

Figure 8-7 shows how the data from the array are sorted in one order (for example, ascending) or its reverse in a TextBox control. Both operations are handled in the same C# event handler method.

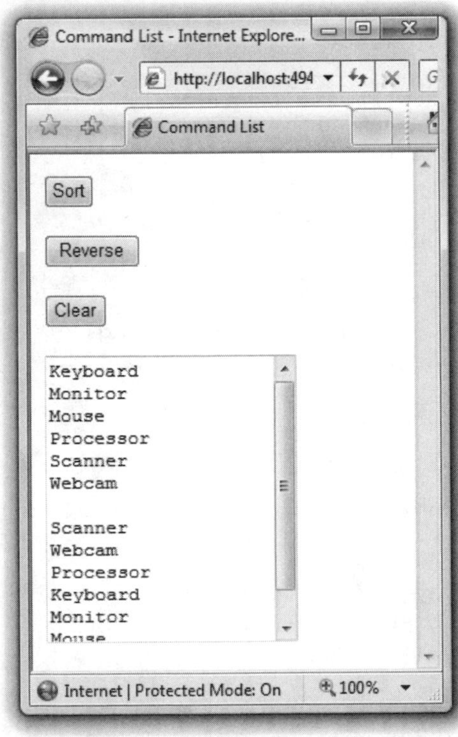

Figure 8-7 Sorted and reversed array data displayed using Command properties

Clicking the Clear button removes everything in the TextBox control except the word "Clear." The string "Clear" is the assigned value of the CommandArgument property in a Button control tag as shown in the following code snippet:

```
<asp:Button ID="Button3"
            OnCommand="CommandClick"
            CommandName="Erase"
            CommandArgument="Clear"
        runat="server" Text="Clear" />
```

Even though the assignment appears to be a string, it still must be converted to a string in the C# portion of the application. The following line makes that conversion:

```
cmdArg = e.CommandArgument.ToString();
```

Once that is done, you have successfully transferred the value of the CommandArgument from the ASP.NET Web form to a C# string variable. Instead of using a simple string like "Clear," you can also enter a more detailed command using Structured Query Language (SQL) such as the following:

```
CommandArgument="INSERT ENames (eName,eMail) Values (@eName, @eMail)";
```

By assigning different SQL statements to the web controls, you will be able to store query and nonquery SQL commands as values with the CommandArgument property in Button web controls. (Chapters 11 and 12 explain using SQL commands and working with data in database tables.)

Summary

In Chapters 5 and 6, the review of Web forms and web controls introduced events associated with the forms and controls. This chapter sought to isolate certain events and to look more closely at events and handling them. For the most part, the use of events and a control is a one-to-one operation. Each event has a unique event handler, and all C# code handles the event with a single method.

In this chapter you saw that not only can events come from unexpected places, but also that a single event handler can deal with more than a single control. TextBox controls can use Change events, and the Init event has similar properties and consequences as the Load events found in different controls. Further, using Button web controls and command events, you can use a single event handler to filter out the actions required for several different buttons. By assigning values to both CommandName and CommandArgument properties and using the C# CommandEventArgs object as a parameter in the event handler method, you can pass command values the ASP.NET Button controls to C#.

Chapter 9

Validation Controls

Key Skills & Concepts

- Where to validate

- Types of validation: RequiredFieldValidator, RangeValidator, RegularExpressionValidator, CompareValidator, CustomValidator

- Summarizing errors with ValidationSummary control

In your mind's eye, imagine people all over the world entering data into your ASP.NET creation. I like to think of someone in Timbuktu happily typing into a TextBox control. If the Timbuktu user does not enter the data correctly, he gets a reminder either that something is missing (like the @ sign from an e-mail address) or that he must fill in a certain box (a last name, for example). With this image in mind, I now go about creating a UI with validation that helps the user fill in everything correctly. In ASP.NET, several controls are available to make it easy to add any and all the validation that you need. Remember, that guy in Timbuktu is depending on you.

Where to Validate

Most developers automatically assume their application requires some kind of validation system when a diverse population enters web-based information. Even if your application is for fairly sophisticated users who are familiar with entering data, you still should consider some way to make sure that users do not accidentally omit an important piece of information or enter data incorrectly.

Client-Side Validation

To get the input they want, developers use some kind of *validation* process. For the most part, the validation is done on the client side. Client-side validation is preferred so that the server will not have to both process data and do validation. Imagine thousands of users entering data at the same time. If all those users had to first have their data verified by the server, the processing would be slowed as the server had the dual chores of verifying data entry and processing the data once it was verified. A more sensible approach is for users to have their data verified on their own computers before sending it to the server.

While client-side validation is more practical because the validation process is distributed to the clients, it does not offer the level of protection provided by the server. Clients can get around client-side validation. For example, you would not want credit-card validation done on the client-side even though you could design an application that could do so. So while some client-side validation with ASP.NET is possible, especially using Microsoft's Internet Explorer, even validated data are re-validated on the server side.

Types of Validation

ASP.NET 3.5 has five validation controls and a validation summary control. The Toolbox Validation menu displays all of the validation controls. Each can be dragged into the Visual Studio 2008 editor in the same way as the other controls. The following summarizes the controls in the order you will find them in the Validation menu:

RequiredFieldValidator	Checks to make sure specified field is filled in
RangeValidator	Checks to see if entry is within specified range
RegularExpressionValidator	Uses regular expressions to evaluate entry
CompareValidator	Compares entry with other entry fields
CustomValidator	User-developed C# method to evaluate entered data
ValidationSummary	Summarizes page validation

When you use these controls, use either the Split or Design mode. The validation controls generate error messages, and the space where that message appears is visible in the Design view. Basically, the Design mode shows what you will see if every single error message from a failed validation appears. As with other controls, you can use the Properties window to set values for the different properties. If you prefer, you can code in the values for the available properties just as you would any other control.

In the next several sections, you will see how to use the five different Validator controls. Each of the controls has a specific use, and by looking at each, you can distinguish which is the most appropriate for a specific task. For example, you may want to be sure that users fill in a form requesting their *last name*. Because of the range of last names, including ones with hyphens, looking for anything precise to ensure that the name is entered correctly is virtually impossible. Such a form only requires a `RequiredFieldValidator` that makes sure the field is completed. Conversely, even though email addresses are diverse, they all have certain features that must be included for them to be valid. For example, all emails have an @ symbol. If the @ symbol is missing from an entry, a validator that checks to see if the field is completed does not notice the omission, just that the field has been completed. However, using a `RegularExpressionValidator`, you can check to see if an email has been correctly entered. By looking at the five different Validator forms, you will better understand which would be the most appropriate.

RequiredFieldValidator

If you've ever registered for anything online, chances are that you ran into some kind of validator that checked to see if you had entered certain fields. The ASP.NET `RequiredFieldValidator` makes sure that the user fills in everything before the information is sent to a database table. For each field you want completed by a user, you can use a `RequiredFieldValidator` that includes the name of the control to validate and an error message using the following format:

```
ControlToValidate= "ControlName"
ErrorMessage="Error message informing user that the field needs to be
completed."
```

Importantly, any form that must be completed can be named as the control to be validated. So in addition to a TextBox control, others such as check boxes, radio buttons, and lists requiring selection can be validated as well.

Visual Validation

Before going though the process of creating an example using a required field validation control, first see what your Design view looks like when you develop in Visual Studio 2008. Figure 9-1 shows what you see once you have completed the ASP.NET portion of the application. The messages "Please enter your name." and "Please select your gender:" are both error messages that only appear if the user leaves a required field blank. However, when developing your application that uses a required field, the ability to see the error messages and their placement greatly aids in the design process.

If you prefer coding, you can use the Split mode and see the error message content and placement in the graphic portion of the Split window.

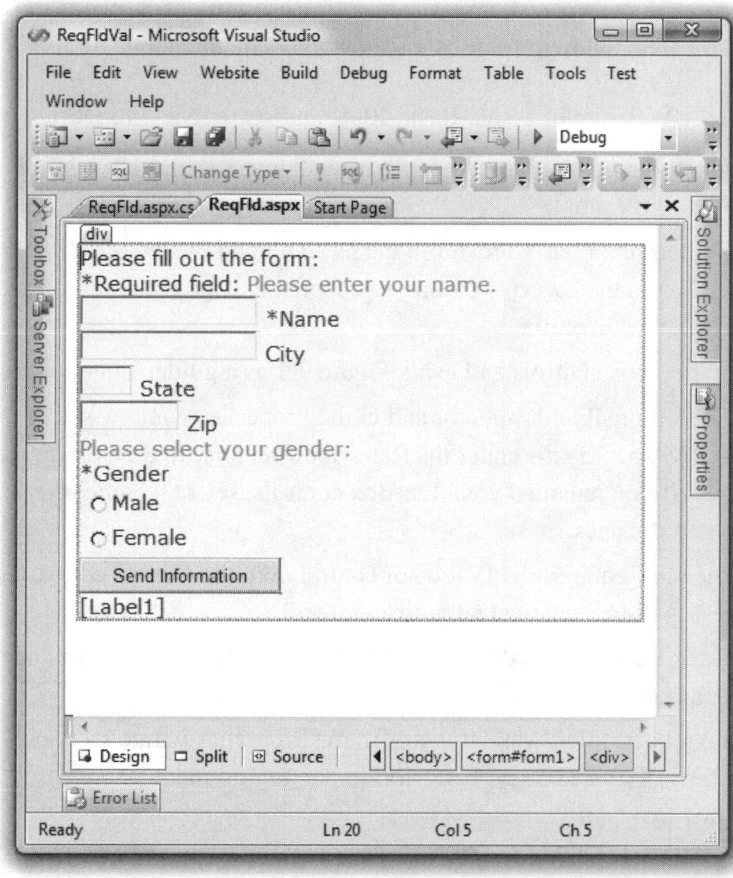

Figure 9-1 Design view shows all error messages and their placement.

Try This Creating a Page with Required Validation

To see how to use the `RequiredFieldValidator`, this first validation example shows how to validate TextBox and RadioButtonList controls. Keep in mind that while validation is important, equally important is that fields that do not require validation should not automatically require it and use up processing time. With five fields—Name, City, State, Zip, and Gender—only two will be subject to validation, Name and Gender. If any of the other fields is left blank, nothing happens. Each of the two fields with

(continued)

validation has separate error messages so that if one is left unfilled, it is the only one that throws an error. The following steps show how to create the application:

1. Open a new Web Site in Visual Basic 2008, and set the view to Design mode.

2. Open the Validation menu in the Toolbox, and drag a RequiredFieldValidator control onto the Design editor.

3. Select the RequiredFieldValidator in the Design window and open the Properties window. Next to the `ErrorMessage` property, change the default message to **"Please enter your name."**

4. Add four TextBox controls and using Figure 9-1 as a guide, label and resize them.

5. Select the RequiredFieldValidator and in the Properties window select `ControlToValidate` under the Behavior directory. In the pop-up menu, select TextBox1. (If you renamed your TextBox controls, select the one that will be used to accept entered names.)

6. Drag a second RequiredFieldValidator control onto the Design editor, and change the Error message to **"Please select your gender:"**.

7. Drag a RadioButtonList to the Design window, and place it directly under the validator you just placed.

8. Select the required field validator, and in the Properties window choose the `ControlToValidate` behavior; in the pop-up menu choose `RadioButtonList1`.

9. Add a Button control and change the `Text` property value to **"Send Information"**.

10. Double-click the Button to automatically generate an event handler.

11. Finally add a Label control at the bottom and remove the `Text` property. The following shows the code for the ASP.NET portion of the application:

ASP.NET ReqFld.aspx

```
<%@ Page Language="C#" AutoEventWireup="true"  CodeFile="ReqFld.aspx.cs"
Inherits="_Default" %>
<!DOCTYPE html PUBLIC "-//W3C//DTD XHTML 1.0 Transitional//EN"
"http://www.w3.org/TR/xhtml1/DTD/xhtml1-transitional.dtd">
<html xmlns="http://www.w3.org/1999/xhtml">
<head runat="server">
<style type="text/css">
div
{
    font-family:Verdana;
    font-size:11pt;
```

```
    color:#0000cc;
}
</style>
    <title>Required Field Validation</title>
</head>
<body>
    <form id="form1" runat="server">
    <div>
    Please fill out the form:<br />
    *Required field:

        <asp:RequiredFieldValidator ID="RequiredFieldValidator2"
        runat="server"
        ControlToValidate= "TextBox1"
        ErrorMessage="Please enter your name." /><br />
        <asp:TextBox ID="TextBox1" runat="server" />
         *Name<br />

        <asp:TextBox ID="TextBox2" runat="server" />
         City<br />
        <asp:TextBox ID="TextBox3" runat="server" Width="38px" />
         State<br />
        <asp:TextBox ID="TextBox4" runat="server" Width="72px" />
         Zip<br />

        <asp:RequiredFieldValidator ID="RequiredFieldValidator1"
         runat="server"
         ControlToValidate= "RadioButtonList1"
         ErrorMessage="Please select your gender:" />
         <br />
         *Gender
        <asp:RadioButtonList ID="RadioButtonList1" runat="server">
            <asp:ListItem>Male</asp:ListItem>
            <asp:ListItem>Female</asp:ListItem>
        </asp:RadioButtonList>

        <asp:Button ID="Button1" runat="server"
        onclick="Button1_Click" Text="Send Information" />
        <br />
        <asp:Label ID="Label1" runat="server" />
        <br />
    </div>
    </form>
</body>
</html>
```

The C# portion of the application is very short. All you need to do is to remove the default `Page_Load` function and add a single statement to the `Button_Click` event handler as shown in the following code listing:

(continued)

C# ReqFld.aspx.cs

```
using System;

public partial class _Default : System.Web.UI.Page
{
    protected void Button1_Click(object sender, EventArgs e)
    {
        Label1.Text = "Information sent successfully";
    }
}
```

Test the application by first filling in only the City and Zip fields. After you click the Send Information button, you should see the application respond with two error messages generated by the required field validation controls. Figure 9-2 shows what you can expect to see.

Notice that even though the State field was left unfilled, no error message has been generated. Only those fields where the required validator was at work was the error message generated when the field was left blank. Also note that no success notice at the bottom has been posted. Whenever a validation error occurs with the validation controls, C# methods associated with the ASP.NET portion of the application will not fire.

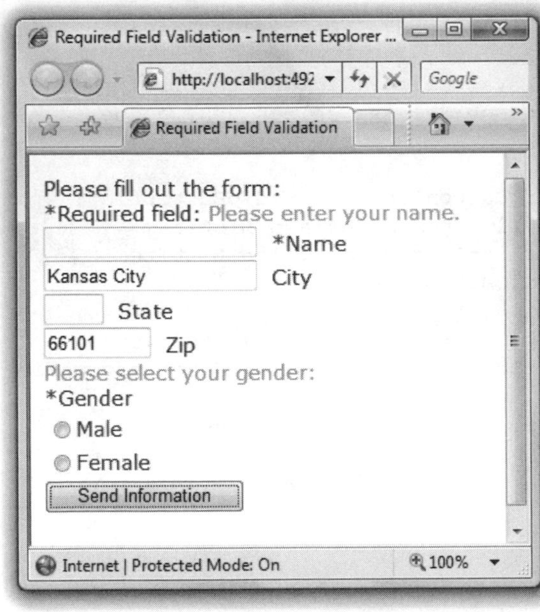

Figure 9-2 Error messages generated for required fields where no entries are made

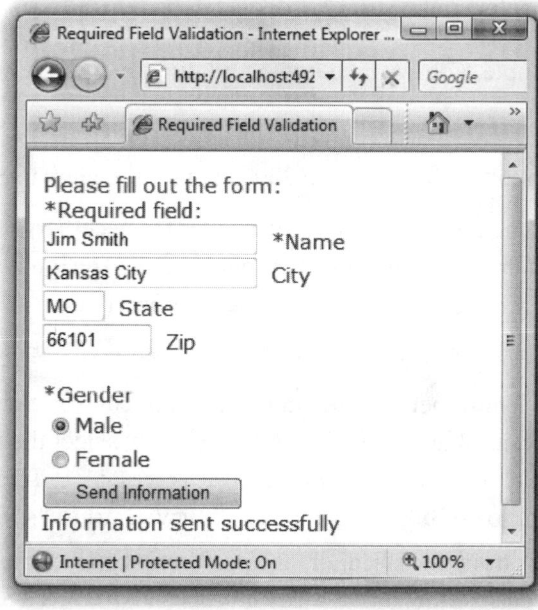

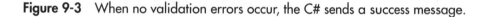

Figure 9-3 When no validation errors occur, the C# sends a success message.

Retest the application and fill in every field as shown in Figure 9-3.

As a rule of thumb, whenever information is successfully sent, you want to show the user that the submission has been successful.

RangeValidator

The second kind of validation available is the RangeValidator control. This validator evaluates data entry where a value range is expected. The two key properties of this validator are `MaximumValue` and `MinimumValue`. In the code, you will see the following elements required to connect and set these values to a form:

```
ControlToValidate="ControlName"
MaximumValue="150000"
MinimumValue="25000"
```

The values entered into the validated control are automatically treated as numeric values rather than text. When the user enters a value, as long it falls within the range specified, no error occurs.

Try This Validating on a Range of Values

Using a simple example, you will see how validating on a range works by following these steps:

1. Open a new Web Site in Visual Basic 2008, and set the view to Split mode.

2. Using the upcoming Figure 9-4 as a guide, enter the necessary text above the TextBox control, and then drag a RangeValidator control to the Design window, and place it beneath the text. Change the `ErrorMessage` property to:

   `"That is out of the position's salary range. <br/> Please revise."`

3. Drag a TextBox control beneath the RangeValidator control. Select the RangeValidator control and in the Properties window select the pop-up menu next to `ControlTolValidate` and choose `TextBox1`. Then change the `MaximumValue` to **"65000"** and the `MinimumValue` to **"45000"**.

4. Drag a Button control into the editor, and position it beneath the textbox. With the button selected, change the button's `Text` property to **"Enter Salary Request"**.

5. Double-click the button to generate an event handler. Change the `onclick` value to **"SalaryRequest"**.

6. Drag a Label into the editor and position it beneath the button. Remove the `Text` property in the Source portion of the Split mode. The following listing shows the entire ASP.NET portion of the application:

ASP.NET Range.aspx

```
<%@ Page Language="C#" AutoEventWireup="true"  CodeFile="Range.aspx.cs"
Inherits="Ranger" %>
<!DOCTYPE html PUBLIC "-//W3C//DTD XHTML 1.0 Transitional//EN"
"http://www.w3.org/TR/xhtml1/DTD/xhtml1-transitional.dtd">
<html xmlns="http://www.w3.org/1999/xhtml">
<head runat="server">
<style type="text/css">
div
{
        font-family:Verdana;
        font-size:11pt;
        color:Maroon;
}
</style>
    <title>Range Validation</title>
</head>
<body>
    <form id="form1" runat="server">
    <div>
```

```
    <strong>Dynamic ASP.NET Developer needed</strong><br />
      <br />
Enter the amount of your salary request.
      <br />
      Requests out of the position's range will not be processed.<br />
      <asp:RangeValidator ID="RangeValidator1" runat="server"
      ErrorMessage="That is out of the position's salary range.</br>Please revise."
      ControlToValidate="Salary"
      MaximumValue="65000"
      MinimumValue="45000" />
      <br /> 
      $<asp:TextBox ID="Salary" runat="server"/>
      <p />
      <asp:Button ID="Button1" runat="server" Text="Enter Salary Request"
         onclick="SalaryRequest" />

      <p />
         <asp:Label ID="Label1" runat="server"/>

    </div>
    </form>
</body>
</html>
```

7. Open the C# editor and remove the Page_Load function. Change the name of the button-click function to **SalaryRequest** as shown in the following C# listing.

C# Range.aspx.cs

```
using System;

public partial class Ranger : System.Web.UI.Page
{
    protected void SalaryRequest(object sender, EventArgs e)
    {
        Label1.Text = "Congratulations. Your salary will be: $" + Salary.Text;
    }
}
```

When you test the application, type in a value out of the assigned range. Test both below the minimum and above the maximum to make sure it works correctly. Figure 9-4 shows the error thrown when the amount is too high.

Note in Figure 9-4 that the <br /> tag in the error message causes a line break in the error message. You can format error messages with certain HTML tags. Once you have tested the application with too high and too low range values, enter any value within the established range. Figure 9-5 shows what you will see.

In this particular application, the value entered in the TextBox is used by C# to generate a message in the Label control.

(continued)

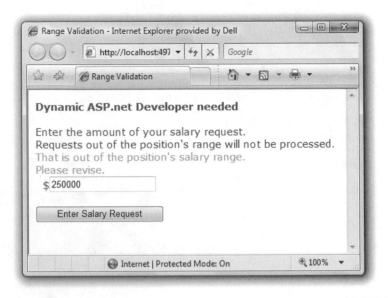

Figure 9-4 Error generated by out-of-range value

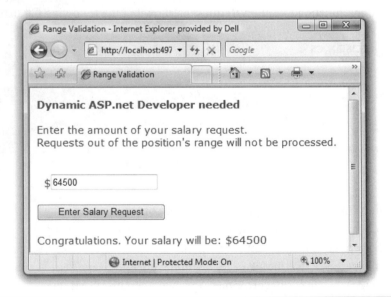

Figure 9-5 Acceptable range with RangeValidator

RegularExpressionValidator

Regular expressions are coded formulas that examine blocks of text for different elements. The term *regular expression* is a bit misleading because the expressions are anything but "regular" compared with natural language. For example, the regular expression

```
/[^ASP.NET]/
```

means to match any characters *except* "A", "S", "P", ".", "N", "E", or "T." It *would* match the lowercase version of those characters. To use those same characters as a match, just remove the caret (^) symbol. We could spend an entire chapter (or even an entire book) examining the nuances of regular expressions. However, rather than going into the rich world of regular expressions and their limitless possibilities, we will use the built-in regular expression menu in Visual Studio 2008.

Try This Working with Regular Expressions

To see how a RegularExpressionValidator works, this next example has a single data entry field where a regular expression examines the input and decides whether the entry is correctly formed. Because email addresses so commonly are requested, the example evaluates the data for a correctly formed email address. The following steps show how:

1. Open a new Web Site in Visual Basic 2008, and set the view to Split mode.

2. From the Validation directory of the Toolbox, drag a RegularExpressionValidator control into the Design portion of the Split window.

3. Select the RegularExpressionValidator control and open the Properties window.

4. Select `ValidationExpression` in the Properties window, and click on the pop-up menu arrow to open the Regular Expression Editor as shown in Figure 9-6.

5. In the Regular Expression Editor, scroll down to the Internet E-Mail Address selection and click OK. In the Validation Expression window, you will see the regular expression for checking for a properly formed email address.

6. Add a TextBox control, select the RegularExpressionValidator control, and in the Properties window select `ControlToValidate`; in the pop-up menu, select `TextBox1`. In the Appearance directory, enter **Yellow** for the `BackColor` and **Maroon** for the `ForeColor`. Your error message will pick up this color combination.

7. Add a Button control and change the `Text` property to **"Send Information"**. Beneath the button add a Label control, and remove the `Text` property or change it to blank.

(continued)

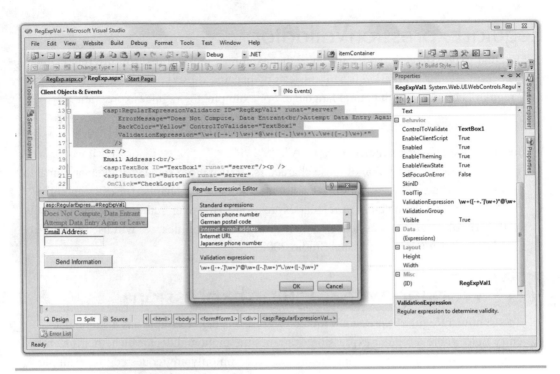

Figure 9-6 Adding a regular expression

8. Double-click the button to add an event handler in the C# portion of the application. Change the value of the onclick property to **"CheckLogic"**. The following code shows what your ASP.NET listing should look like at this point:

ASP.NET RegExp.aspx

```
<%@ Page Language="C#" AutoEventWireup="true"  CodeFile="RegExp.aspx.cs"
Inherits="RegExp" %>
<!DOCTYPE html PUBLIC "-//W3C//DTD XHTML 1.0 Transitional//EN"
"http://www.w3.org/TR/xhtml1/DTD/xhtml1-transitional.dtd">
<html xmlns="http://www.w3.org/1999/xhtml">
<head runat="server">
<style type="text/css">
.warn
{
    font-family:Courier New;
    font-size:10pt;
}
div
{
```

```
        font-family:Verdana;
        font-size:11pt;
        color:Navy;
    }
    </style>
        <title>Regular Expression Validation</title>
    </head>
    <body>
        <form id="form1" runat="server">
        <div>
        <span class="warn">
            <asp:RegularExpressionValidator ID="RegExpVal1" runat="server"
                ErrorMessage="Does Not Compute, Data Entrant<br/>Attempt
    Data Entry Again or Leave."
                BackColor="Yellow" ControlToValidate="TextBox1"
                ValidationExpression=
                "\w+([-+.']\w+)*@\w+([-.]\w+)*\.\w+([-.]\w+)*"
                ForeColor="Maroon"
            /></span>
            <br />
            Email Address:<br/>
            <asp:TextBox ID="TextBox1" runat="server"/><p />
            <asp:Button ID="Button1" runat="server"
             OnClick="CheckLogic"
            Text="Send Information" />
            <p />
                <asp:Label ID="Label1" runat="server" />
        </div>
        </form>
    </body>
    </html>
```

9. Open the C# portion of your application. Remove the Page_Load method, and change the button-click function name to **CheckLogic**. The following C# code shows the remaining code:

C# RegExp.aspx.cs

```csharp
using System;

public partial class RegExp : System.Web.UI.Page
{
    protected void CheckLogic(object sender, EventArgs e)
    {
        Label1.Text = "Thank you for correctly entering your email address.";
    }
}
```

(continued)

The first important feature to note is the regular expression that Visual Studio 2008 generates:

```
"\w+([-+.']\w+)*@\w+([-.]\w+)*\.\w+([-.]\w+)*"
```

If you spent several hours studying regular expressions, you could probably come up with the same expression. However, while learning ASP.NET and the associated C#, you have your hands full. Make a note to learn regular expressions later.

When you test your application, enter an email without the @ sign. When you click the Send Information button, you will see a dramatically different error warning than we've used up to this point as shown in Figure 9-7. Not only does it sound like what an alien computer might compose, the text is in a maroon monospaced font with yellow backing.

You also can leave out a domain (.net) or an initial identifier (billz), and the regular expression will catch it and throw an error. Figure 9-8 shows what you will see when you get it right.

Note the amount of space above the Email Address label. Even though the error message did not fire because no errors were detected, that space is still part of the RegularExpression Validator. As a result, you have to carefully plan your data entry design so that your page is not full of gaps where verbose error messages are meant to appear.

Appreciating Regular Expressions

If you are doing a lot of database development with ASP.NET and C#, you might want to consider investing some time learning regular expressions. The Regular Expression Editor only has 14 regular expressions, but you will find it uses far beyond those 14. You can configure very sophisticated regular expressions to get exactly what you want from a database table, or you can add to a validation control. If you know any Perl programmers, they live and breathe regular expressions and will readily lead you to the best learning materials on the topic. For a good quick start, check out www.regular-expressions.info/quickstart.html. You can find a nice regular expression "cheat sheet" at www.ilovejackdaniels.com/regular_expressions_cheat_sheet.pdf.

Figure 9-7 Catching an entry error using a regular expression

Figure 9-8 Correctly entered email address

CompareValidator

The CompareValidator control's main use is to compare two entry controls. For example, if you enter a password in a registration page, often you will be asked to enter the password a second time just to make sure that you have entered the password you want to use. The validator control uses the following operators:

- Equal
- NotEqual
- GreaterThan
- GreaterThanEqual
- LessThan
- LessThanEqual
- DataTypeCheck

Each operator does a comparison between controls identified as ControlToCompare and ControlToValidate. If all you want to do is to be sure they are the same or different, it doesn't really matter which control is assigned as the ControlToCompare or ControlToValidate; however, when using the other operators, you have to decide which will be the one to compare and which the one to validate.

Try This Comparing Fields for Validation

The application to illustrate how to use CompareValidator is a common one you may have encountered. It asks the users for a username and a password. Then they are required to reenter the password. The TextBox controls that accept passwords have their `TextMode` property set to `Password`, so all the users see are black dots as shown in Figure 9-9. The following steps show how to create the application:

1. Open a new Web Site in Visual Basic 2008, and set the view to Split mode.
2. Using the upcoming Figures 9-9 and 9-10 as guides, add three TextBox controls to the Design portion of the Split mode editor. From top to bottom, rename the TextBox IDs **"Username"**, **"Pass1"**, and **"Pass2"** respectively.
3. Beneath the bottom TextBox, add a CompareValidator control.
4. Select the CompareValidator control and open the Properties window. In the `ControlToCompare` open the pop-up menu and select `Pass1`.

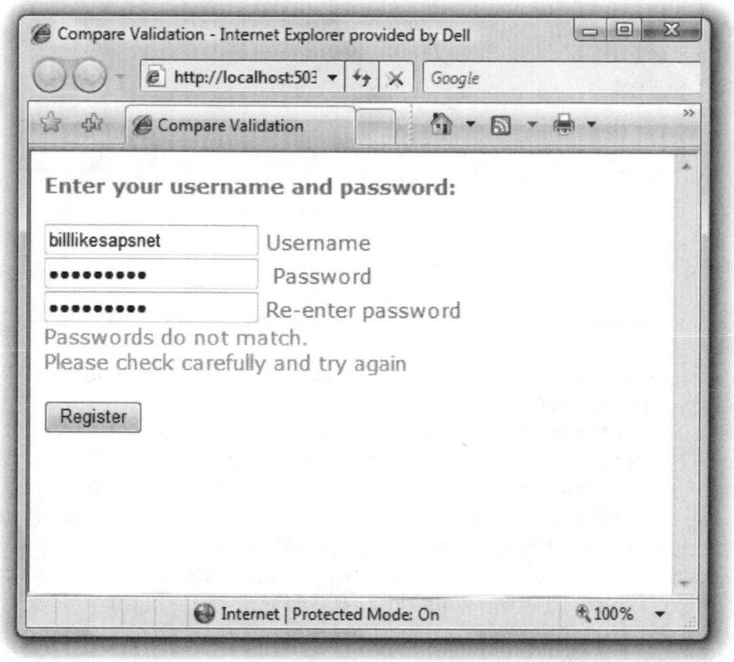

Figure 9-9 Comparison indicating no match

Next, in the `ControlToValidate`, select `Pass2`. The default operator is `Equal`, and if you do not indicate an operator, no operator will be shown in the code. However, it will compare for equality.

5. Add a Button and Label control using Figures 9-9 and 9-10 as guides. Double-click the Button control to generate an event handler for the button. Rename the `onclick` property to **"DoComparison"**. In the Source window, remove the `Text` property from the Label control. The following code shows the full source code for the ASP.NET portion of the application:

ASP.NET Compare.aspx

```
<%@ Page Language="C#" AutoEventWireup="true"  CodeFile="Compare.aspx.cs"
Inherits="Compare" %>
<!DOCTYPE html PUBLIC "-//W3C//DTD XHTML 1.0 Transitional//EN"
"http://www.w3.org/TR/xhtml1/DTD/xhtml1-transitional.dtd">
<html xmlns="http://www.w3.org/1999/xhtml">
<head runat="server">
<style type="text/css">
div
```

(continued)

```
{
    font-family:Verdana;
    color:Olive;
    font-size:11pt;
}
</style>
    <title>Compare Validation</title>
</head>
<body>
    <form id="form1" runat="server">
    <div>
        <strong>Enter your username and password:</strong><br />
        <br />
        <asp:TextBox ID="Username" runat="server"/> Username<br />
        <asp:TextBox ID="Pass1" runat="server"
        TextMode="Password"/>  Password<br />
        <asp:TextBox ID="Pass2" runat="server"
        TextMode="Password" /> Re-enter password<br />
        <asp:CompareValidator ID="CompareValidator1" runat="server"
        ErrorMessage="Passwords do not match.<br/>
        Please check carefully and try again" ControlToCompare="Pass1"
        ControlToValidate="Pass2" /><p />
        <asp:Button ID="Button1" runat="server"
         OnClick="DoComparison"
        Text="Register" />
        <p />
        <asp:Label ID="Label1" runat="server" />

    </div>
    </form>
</body>
</html>
```

6. Open the C# tab and delete the `Page_Load` default event handler function, and change the button-click event handler function name to **DoComparison**. The following listing shows the entire C# code listing:

C# Compare.aspx.cs

```
using System;

public partial class Compare: System.Web.UI.Page
{
    protected void DoComparison(object sender, EventArgs e)
    {
        Label1.Text = "Congratulations! You have successfully registered.";
    }
}
```

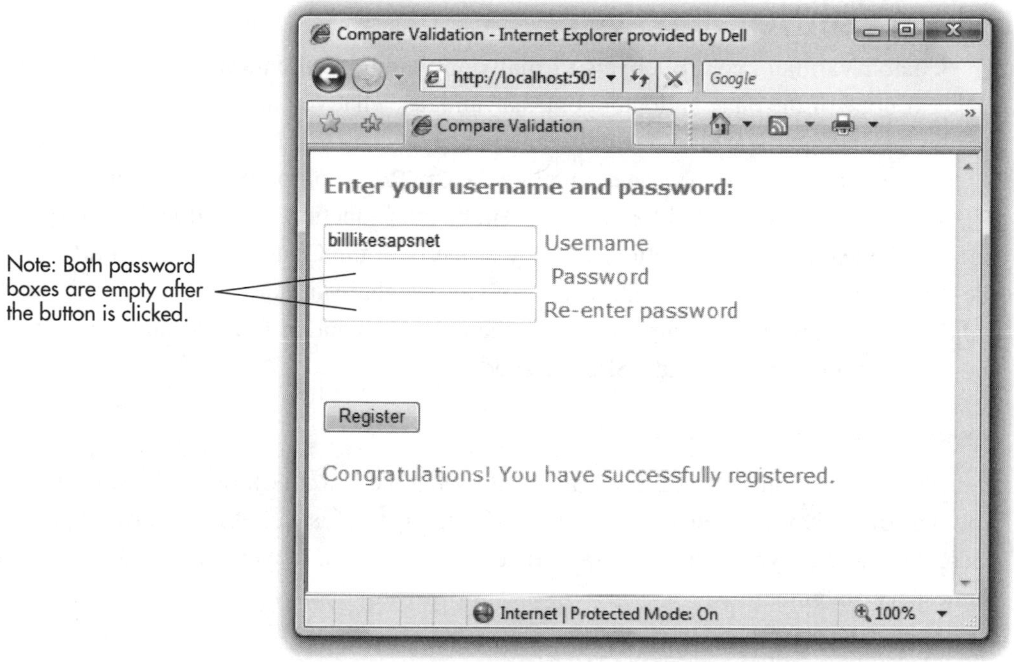

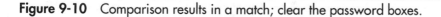

Note: Both password
boxes are empty after
the button is clicked.

Enter your username and password:

billlikesapsnet   Username

Password

Re-enter password

Register

Congratulations! You have successfully registered.

Figure 9-10   Comparison results in a match; clear the password boxes.

To test your application, you can put in anything you want for the username and
passwords. However, if the two passwords do not match, as shown in Figure 9-9, the
validator throws an error message.

The interesting thing about the CompareValidator control is that as long as the controls
match, you can enter anything you want. As a result, you can enter any combination of
upper- and lowercase letters, numbers, and symbols, and if the compared fields match,
they will verify.

Figure 9-10 shows what happens when the compare validation finds a match. Both
password fields are cleared, and the Label control shows a success message. Had the two
TextBox controls not been set to `Password TextMode`, the TextBox controls would
not have been cleared.

Try some of the different operators with the CompareValidator control. Experiment
with the greater- and less-than operators to see how text is handled with these controls.

CustomValidator

The CustomValidator control covers virtually any kind of validation case you wish to make. If none of the other validator controls validates what you need, you make your own validation routine.

Custom validation works something like the `OnClick` property in a Button control. The value assigned to `OnClick` is a C# event handler function. It can do whatever you put into the event handler function. The key property of the CustomValidator control is the `OnServerValidate` event. Instead of having a built-in function to deal with the validation process, it passes a parameter to the C# event handler function and then codes the outcome. For example, the ASP.NET code

```
OnServerValidate="MyValidation"
```

calls the C# function `MyValidation`. That's what the `OnClick` event does. However, you will find a key difference in the function's parameter. Instead of `EventArgs`, the second parameter type is `ServerValidateEventArgs`. It even requires an additional namespace statement:

```
using System.Web.UI.WebControls;
```

Once that is set up, you still need some way of handling the event generated by clicking the button. That's easy enough. Just add a regular event handler function the same as always. However, when both a validation event and a button event are in an ASP.NET script, the validation event is handled first. The following sequence shows what goes on:

```
Click button > Sets off validation function > Sets off button function
```

That sequence may seem counterintuitive. After all, the event handler called by the button is supposed to fire as soon as the user clicks the button. However, because the same ASP.NET listing has an event handler for a validation control, it launches the validation function instead.

Keep in mind that most of the typical validation you will need can be accomplished using one of the other validation controls, so it's only when you cannot use one of them that you will need a custom validator. This next example shows where you will need custom validation. The routine is used to find directions to different cities. (You will have to use your imagination that a database provides a wealth of detail and a number of locations instead of just three cities and fairly terse directions.) If the city the user enters is not in the "database," it throws an error message. Otherwise, it provides directions.

Ask the Expert

Q: Won't a button function fire first if I put it first in the C# code before I put in the validation function?

A: It does not matter in which order your C# methods are placed as far as a button function or validation function is concerned. The validation function uses the second parameter (`ServerValidateEventArgs e`) to establish validity. The `ServerValidateEventArgs` parameter has an `IsValid` property that you can set to true or false. (The default is true.) Once your validation function has determined whether the validation is successful, it launches the event associated with the button event handler. In this way, the button event can include the `Page.IsValid` statement and set up a response for the user to see. The `Page.IsValid` statement uses the value set with `ServerValidateEventArgs` instance, `e.IsValid`.

Try This   Customizing Validation

The ASP.NET side of the application includes a single TextBox control, a CustomValidator control, a button and two labels used for directions, and validation feedback. The following steps show how to develop the application:

1. Open a new Web Site in Visual Basic 2008, and set the view to Split mode.
2. Drag a TextBox control to the page in the Design window.
3. Place a CustomValidator control beneath the TextBox. In the Source mode add an `OnServerValidate` property, and assign it the value **"CityCheck"**.
4. Add a button beneath the validator. Change the text to **"Find City"**, and double-click the button to generate an event handler for the `OnClick` property. Change the `OnClick` value to **"DoValidation"**.
5. Place two Label controls beneath the button. Use Figures 9-11 and 9-12 as guides. Remove the `Text` property from both labels in the Source window of the Split mode.
6. Select the CustomValidator control and in the Properties window, change the error message to **"City not recognized. Try again."** Set `ControlToValidate` to **"TextBox1"**. The following listing shows all of the source code settings for the ASP.NET portion of the application:

(continued)

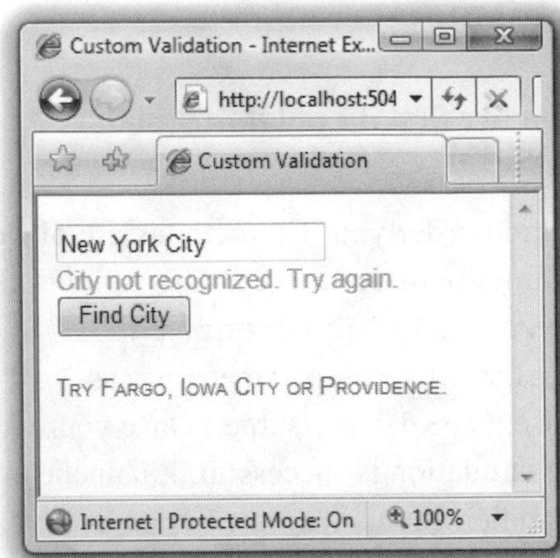

Figure 9-11 Error messages

ASP.NET CustomVal.aspx

```
<%@ Page Language="C#" AutoEventWireup="true"  CodeFile="CustomVal
.aspx.cs" Inherits="CusVal" %>
<!DOCTYPE html PUBLIC "-//W3C//DTD XHTML 1.0 Transitional//EN"
"http://www.w3.org/TR/xhtml1/DTD/xhtml1-transitional.dtd">
<html xmlns="http://www.w3.org/1999/xhtml">
<head runat="server">
```

Figure 9-12 Two responses for valid entries

```
<style type="text/css">
.val
{
font-family: Arial, Helvetica, sans-serif;
font-size: small;
font-variant: small-caps;
color: #aa0000;
}
div
{
    font-family: Arial, Helvetica, sans-serif;
          font-size: 11pt;
}
</style>
    <title>Custom Validation</title>
</head>
<body>
    <form id="form1" runat="server">
    <div>
<asp:TextBox ID="TextBox1" runat="server" />
<br />
<asp:CustomValidator ID="CustomValidator1"
        runat="server"
        ErrorMessage="City not recognized. Try again."
        OnServerValidate="CityCheck"
        ControlToValidate="TextBox1" />
        <br />
        <asp:Button ID="Button1" runat="server"
        Text="Find City" OnClick="DoValidation" /><p />
        <asp:Label ID="Label1" runat="server" />
      <p />
        <asp:Label ID="Label2" runat="server" CssClass="val" />
</div>
    </form>
</body>
</html>
```

7. Select the C# tab and remove the `Page_Load` function. Change the button-click default function name to DoValidation. Add the following code. (Make sure to include `using System.Web.UI.WebControls`.)

C# CustomVal.aspx.cs

```
using System;
using System.Web.UI.WebControls;
public partial class CusVal : System.Web.UI.Page
```

(continued)

```
{
protected void CityCheck(object sender, ServerValidateEventArgs e)
        {
     switch(TextBox1.Text)
     {
         case "Fargo":
             Label1.Text="Go to North Dakota and turn left.";
             break;
         case "Iowa City":
             Label1.Text="Go to Iowa and look for big university.";
             break;
         case "Providence":
           Label1.Text="Just go to Rhode Island. You can't miss it.";
             break;
         default:
             e.IsValid = false;
             break;
     }
   }
   public void DoValidation(object sender, EventArgs e)
   {
       if (Page.IsValid)
       {
           Label2.Text = "Your request is valid.";
       }
       else
       {
           Label2.Text = "Try Fargo, Iowa City or Providence.";
       }
   }
}
```

Despite the fact that the DoValidation method is triggered by pressing the button, it is processed *after* the CityCheck method. All validation functions are processed before the button functions. To see how the custom validation works, enter any city other than Fargo, Iowa City, or Providence. Figure 9-11 shows that in addition to an error message generated by the CustomValidator control, the function also recognizes a validation error and sends a helpful message for a second attempt.

When you enter a city recognized by the C# code, it results in the default validity method value of true. When the DoValidation method fires, the results are tested using the Page.IsValid method. Because the e.IsValid value *has not been* set to false, it resolves as true, and so does the Page.IsValid conditional test. Figure 9-12 shows that the `CustomValidator` does not throw an error, but the validation method (`IsValid`) can be used to generate C# messages.

With the CustomValidator control, the scope of validation events is limitless. Even with validators such as the RegularExpressionValidator that can have any number of different regular expressions used in the validation process, you still need a validator option where you can validate anything you want. Chances are, though, that most of the validation work you do will be with one of the simpler validation controls. However, the CustomValidator control is there when you need it.

Summarizing Validation Errors

As you have seen in the discussion of validation, wherever you have an error message, the space taken up by the message leaves a gap. With several different controls using some kind of validation control, a page could get cluttered and messy very quickly. An easy way to prevent this state of affairs is to use the ValidationSummary control. With this control all of the error messages for the page are stored in one place. The kind of message and validation control can be any you want. However, instead of the error message displayed in the location where you placed the validation control, all of the errors are displayed together. Usually, the summary errors are placed at the end of the form.

To see how this works, an application using two TextBox controls with a RequiredFieldValidator control and a RegularExpressionValidator control are set up as they have been in previous examples with one important difference—their `Display` property is set to `None`. When the display setting is `None`, the validation controls still show up in the Design mode as taking up space as shown in Figure 9-13. However, as you can see in Figures 9-14 and 9-15, no space at all is taken up by the area reserved for error messages. Instead, all of the messages appear at the bottom where the ValidationSummary control is positioned.

The example is easy to try. Just put in the controls and labels as shown in Figure 9-13. Where you see the bullet list of error messages is in the ValidationSummary control. Add the error messages to the two controls and controls to validate, and set the RegularExpressionValidator control's `ValidationExpression` to **"email"**. Remember to also set the display of both validators to **"None"**. When you place the `ValidationSummary`

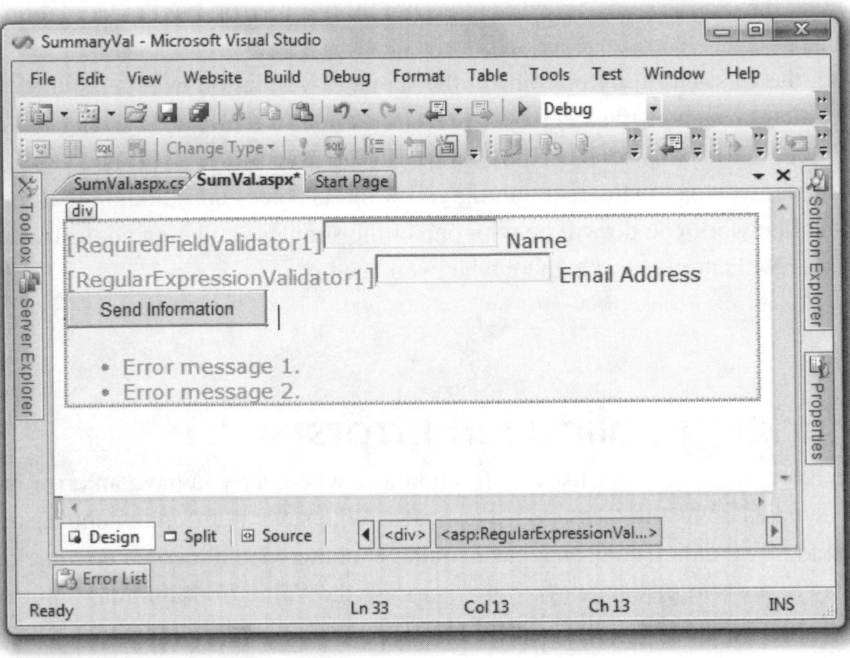

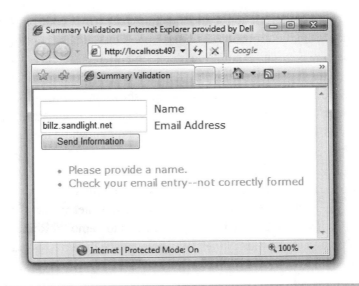

Figure 9-13 Validation error messages appear to take up space in Design mode.

Figure 9-14 Validation errors appearing in bullet list summary

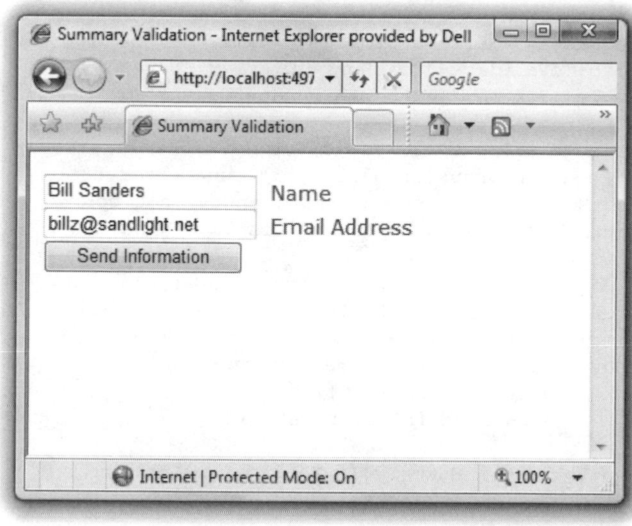

Figure 9-15 No errors found

control in the application, you don't have to change any of its properties. The following code listings show the source after you've built the application:

ASP.NET SumVal.aspx

```
<%@ Page Language="C#" AutoEventWireup="true"  CodeFile="SumVal.aspx.cs"
Inherits="_Default" %>

<!DOCTYPE html PUBLIC "-//W3C//DTD XHTML 1.0 Transitional//EN"
"http://www.w3.org/TR/xhtml1/DTD/xhtml1-transitional.dtd">

<html xmlns="http://www.w3.org/1999/xhtml">
<head runat="server">
<style type="text/css">
div
{
    font-family:Verdana;
    font-size:11pt;
    color:#770000;
</style>
    <title>Summary Validation</title>
</head>
<body>
    <form id="form1" runat="server">
    <div>
    <asp:RequiredFieldValidator ID="RequiredFieldValidator1"
```

```
         runat="server"
         ErrorMessage="Please provide a name."
         ControlToValidate="TextBox1" Display="None" />
         <asp:TextBox ID="TextBox1" runat="server"/>
     Name <br />
         <asp:RegularExpressionValidator
         ID="RegularExpressionValidator1" runat="server"
          ErrorMessage="Check your email entry--not correctly formed"
          ControlToValidate="TextBox2" Display="None"
          ValidationExpression=
   "\w+([-+.']\w+)*@\w+([-.]\w+)*\.\w+([-.]\w+)*"/>
         <asp:TextBox ID="TextBox2" runat="server" />
     Email Address<br />
         <asp:Button ID="Button1" runat="server"
                 onclick="Button1_Click"
                 Text="Send Information" />
    <br />
         <asp:ValidationSummary ID="ValidationSummary1"
                 runat="server" />
    </div>
    </form>
</body>
</html>
```

C# SumVal.aspx.cs

```
using System;
public partial class _Default : System.Web.UI.Page
{
protected void Button1_Click(object sender, EventArgs e)
    {
         //May add success statements if desired
    }
}
```

Go ahead and test the application. Leave the name blank, put in an incorrectly formed email address, and click the Send Information button.

As you can see in Figure 9-14, all of the error messages have been placed in a bullet list. You can combine different types of validation, and the error messages are all recognized by the ValidationSummary control.

When you have no errors, as seen in Figure 9-15, no space is used up by either the validator controls or the ValidationSummary control. For applications where you are adding validation after a page has already been designed, you will find that this will save you a huge amount of time because you do not have to reformat the basic design.

Summary

The validation process not only helps in preventing incomplete and invalid data from entering your database tables, but validation also assists users in putting in the information you want. It takes effort by users to do everything from register for a site to order an online product or service. If the sites you create have a clear user interface and good validation, users are more likely to return to the site and use it.

In Chapter 12 and beyond, you will be dealing with applications that accept data from users and store it in databases. As you work more and more with database tables, you will come to see the value of validation. Keep in mind that users who visit your site or your clients' sites have literally billions of URLs from which to choose. Provide them with a clear UI and easy-to-understand validation messages, and their experience will be one where the only thing they remember about your site is the content and not the data entry procedures.

Chapter 10

Rich Data Controls

Key Skills & Concepts

- Adding a Calendar to your application
- Calendar properties
- Calendar events
- Creating a calendar application
- Styling a Calendar
- Using Calendar events
- ASP.NET banner ads: AdRotator control
- XML file for data source
- AdRotator properties
- AdRotator events

Among the many web controls available with ASP.NET 3.5 are a number of rich data controls. These controls are highly functional and have a wide selection of properties, events, and features that make them quite flexible and adaptable. Two such controls, the Calendar and AdRotator, feature both ease of use and flexibility. Each is briefly examined next for some typical uses.

Calendar Web Control

All of the web controls examined up to this point have been quite rich in features and properties, but Calendar, with about 80 properties, eclipses most of the others reviewed up to this point. The Calendar is an extremely powerful while easy to use tool. When combined with C#, this ASP.NET control can become a dynamic part of your ASP.NET application.

One of the important features of the Calendar is its ability to be integrated into any web site. Having a functional calendar on one's web site can be quite useful, but if it clashes with the rest of the page it's on, it sticks out like a wart and needs to be fixed.

Given that most developers, including me, are not designers, one of the more useful features of the Calendar control is its ability to be formatted with a design scheme that is easy to alter.

Easy Style

To create a unique style for a calendar, all you need is a Calendar instance in the Design or Split mode editors. Then, by clicking the pop-up menu in the upper-right corner of the Calendar instance, you can access the AutoFormat window as shown in Figure 10-1.

From the AutoFormat window in Figure 10-1, you can see the selected scheme is Colorful 2. However, the color scheme in the image on the left is different even though the design is the same. So, using a scheme, you can first establish a nicely designed calendar for your site, and then add a color scheme that matches the rest of the page.

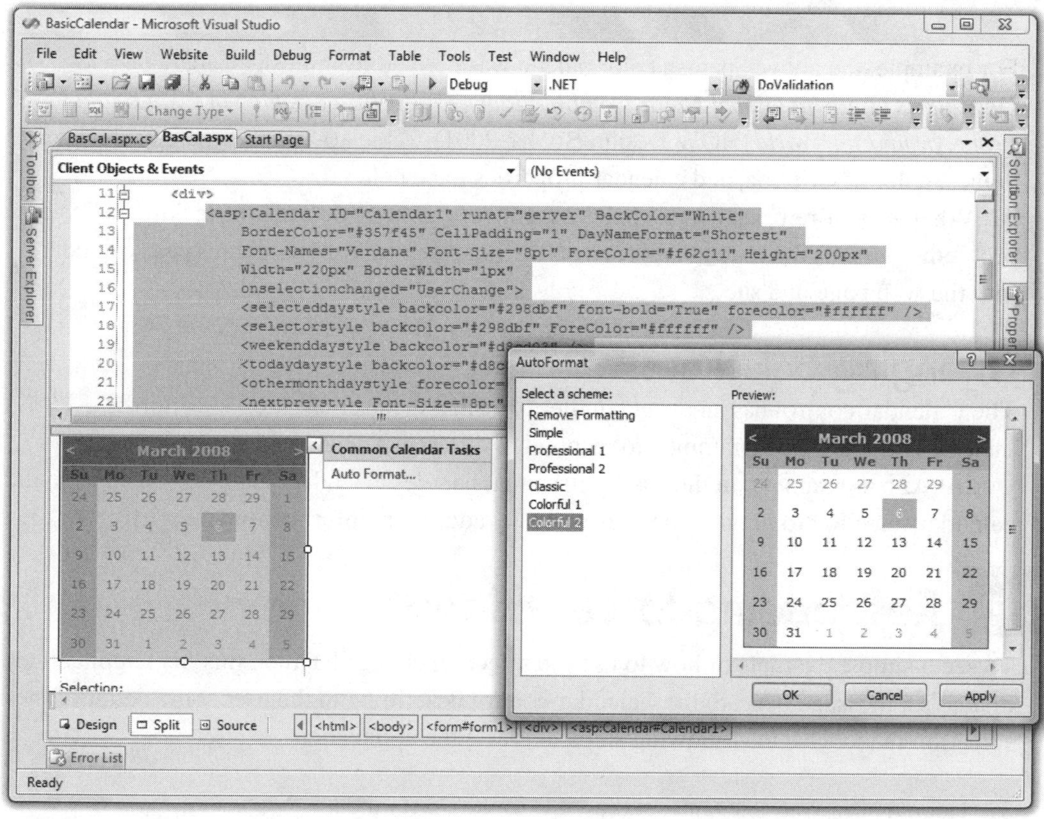

Figure 10-1   Automatic design

Hexadecimal	Color Description	Calendar Properties
D8CD03	Mustard	weekenddaystyle backcolor, todaydaystyle backcolor, nextprevstyle forecolor, titlestyle bordercolor, titlestyle forecolor
0F218B	Dark Blue	dayheaderstyle forecolor, Label1 forecolor
357F45	Dark Teal	titlestyle backcolor
6C8A29	Olive	dayheaderstyle backcolor
298DBF	Blue	selectorstyle backcolor, othermonthdaystyle forecolor, selecteddaystyle backcolor
F62C11	Brick Red	Calendar forecolor
FFFFFF	White	Calendar backcolor, selectorstyle forecolor, todaydaystyle forecolor, selecteddaystyle forecolor

Table 10-1 Calendar Color Palette

For example, the above Spanish color palette was derived from Leslie Cabarga's book, *The Designer's Guide to Global Color Combinations: 750 Color Formulas in CMYK and RGB From Around the World* (HOW Design Books, 2001). Table 10-1 shows the hexadecimal values, color description, and calendar properties to be colored.

Whether you're using a color palette from your graphic designer or tackling a design problem yourself, the Calendar gives you the flexibility to fully integrate your calendar into the web page and site.

Changing Selections

The Calendar control has an event handler for when the user changes selections; the calendar can be programmed to respond to different selections. Using a simple `EventArgs` parameter in the C# function that handles calendar changes, you can use the calendar selection to provide the user with any additional information you wish.

Try This Responding to Selections

To see a simple example of how to use the selection change handler, this next application displays a message beneath the Calendar control describing to the user some detail of the selection made. Use the following steps to create the application:

1. Open a new Web Site, and set the view to the Split mode.

2. Drag a Calendar control from the Standard menu in the Toolbox to the `<div>` container in the ASP.NET listing.

3. Double-click the Calendar in the Design portion of the Split mode. This automatically generates a function in C# for handling the `onselectionchanged` property of the Calendar object. Change the name of the handler from Calendar1_SelectionChanged to **UserChange** on both the ASP.NET and C# listings. (See the following listings, BasCal.aspx and BasCal.aspx.cs, for the complete listings.)

4. In the C# portion, delete the `Page_Load` function.

5. Select the Calendar in the Design portion, open the AutoFormat window, and select the Colorful 2 scheme.

6. Open the Properties window and using the values in Table 10-1, assign the appropriate color values to the listed properties. (Instead of using the colors shown in the table, this might be a good time to experiment with a color palette of your own choosing.)

7. Use the following listings to complete the application:

ASP.NET BasCal.aspx

```
<%@ Page Language="C#" AutoEventWireup="true" CodeFile="BasCal.aspx.cs"
Inherits="BaseCal" %>
<!DOCTYPE html PUBLIC "-//W3C//DTD XHTML 1.0 Transitional//EN"
"http://www.w3.org/TR/xhtml1/DTD/xhtml1-transitional.dtd">
<html xmlns="http://www.w3.org/1999/xhtml">
<head runat="server">
    <title>Basic Calendar</title>
</head>
<body>
    <form id="form1" runat="server">
    <div>
        <asp:Calendar ID="Calendar1" runat="server" BackColor="White"
            BorderColor="#357f45" CellPadding="1"
            DayNameFormat="Shortest"
            Font-Names="Verdana" Font-Size="8pt"
            ForeColor="#f62c11" Height="200px"
            Width="220px" BorderWidth="1px"
            onselectionchanged="UserChange">
            <selecteddaystyle backcolor="#298dbf" font-bold="True"
                forecolor="#ffffff" />
            <selectorstyle backcolor="#298dbf" ForeColor="#ffffff" />
            <weekenddaystyle backcolor="#d8cd03" />
            <todaydaystyle backcolor="#d8cd03" forecolor="White" />
            <othermonthdaystyle forecolor="#298dbf" />
            <nextprevstyle Font-Size="8pt" ForeColor="#d8cd03" />
            <DayHeaderStyle BackColor="#6c8a29" ForeColor="#0f218b"
                Height="1px" />
            <titlestyle backcolor="#357f45" bordercolor="#d8cd03"
```

(continued)

```
                    font-bold="True"
                    BorderWidth="1px" Font-Size="10pt"
                     ForeColor="#d8cd03" Height="25px" />
         </asp:Calendar>
         <br />
         <asp:Label ID="Label1" runat="server"
             Text="Selection:" Font-Names="Verdana"
            Font-Size="11px" ForeColor="#0F218B"/>
      </div>
    </form>
</body>
</html>
```

The C# portion of the code adds content to a Label control. In the ASP.NET portion, the Calendar property

```
OnSelectionChanged
```

is the event used to call the C# event handler. The content is determined by the Calendar instance properties. In particular, the method

```
ToLongDateString()
```

changes the selected date to a string that spells out the day and month—a long date string.

C# BasCal.aspx.cs

```
using System;

public partial class BaseCal : System.Web.UI.Page
{
    private string genString;

    protected void UserChange(object sender, EventArgs e)
    {
        genString=Calendar1.SelectedDate.ToLongDateString();
        Label1.Text = "You have selected: " + genString;
    }
}
```

Once you've completed setting up the calendar, test it. Figure 10-2 shows the output.

As you can see in Figure 10-2, the current date is March 4, and as soon as March 7 was selected, the Label control beneath the Calendar displayed a simple message using the Calendar's selected date in a long format as the data source.

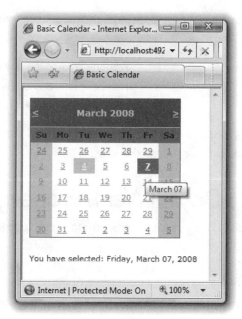

Figure 10-2   Selection event launches C# script

Soccer Mom's Calendar

Another useful feature of the Calendar control is the `OnDayRender` event. With it, you can pass a value from the ASP.NET control to a C# parameter. When the day-render event and handler are employed, you can dynamically add materials to the calendar. One example is a soccer mom's busy schedule running kids to and fro. This next application sets up tasks for Mondays, Wednesdays, and Fridays and repeats them for the days of the weeks that they occur.

To set up the calendar, two key elements are included. First, in ASP.NET 3.5, is the `OnDayRender` property. This property will pass an event value to the C# parameter in the event handler function `DayRenderEventArgs`. (This parameter replaces `EventArgs`.) The code segment, stored in the parameter instance (`e`), can be used to set up different types of reminders within the calendar. For example, the following three are among the values that are returned through the parameter (where e is the instance of DayRenderEventsArgs):

e.Day.Date.DayOfWeek	Property holding the day name (e.g., Monday)
e.Day.Date.Day	Number of the day of the month
e.Day.Date.Month	Number of the month (1–12)

You can use the values for creating in-calendar reminders of appointments, special days, or any other kind of one-time or repeated events.

Try This Using the DayOfWeek Property

This next example uses the DayOfWeek property to set up repeated events. The following steps get you started:

1. Open a new Web Site, and set the editor view to Split.

2. Drag a Calendar control into the editor, and place it in the <div> container.

3. Select the Calendar control and set the AutoFormat to **Classic**. Then change the Calendar's font-family to **Verdana** in the Properties window and its width to **800**. The width of the calendar is increased so that it has room to accommodate different text reminders.

4. In the Source portion, add **OnDayRender="CheckApps"** to the Calendar tag. Complete the application using the code in the following ASP.NET and C# listings:

ASP.NET CalMind.aspx

```
<%@ Page Language="C#" AutoEventWireup="true"  CodeFile="CalMind.aspx.cs"
Inherits="CalAppt" %>

<!DOCTYPE html PUBLIC "-//W3C//DTD XHTML 1.0 Transitional//EN"
"http://www.w3.org/TR/xhtml1/DTD/xhtml1-transitional.dtd">

<html xmlns="http://www.w3.org/1999/xhtml">
<head runat="server">
    <title>Birthday Note</title>
</head>
<body>
    <form id="form1" runat="server">
    <div>
        <asp:Calendar ID="Calendar1" runat="server" BackColor="White"
            BorderColor="Black" DayNameFormat="Shortest"
            Font-Names="Verdana"
            Font-Size="10pt" ForeColor="Black" Height="220px"
            NextPrevFormat="FullMonth"
```

```
       TitleFormat="Month" Width="800px" OnDayRender="CheckAppts">
       <SelectedDayStyle BackColor="#CC3333" ForeColor="White" />
       <SelectorStyle BackColor="#CCCCCC" Font-Bold="True"
           Font-Names="Verdana"
           Font-Size="8pt" ForeColor="#333333" Width="1%" />
       <TodayDayStyle BackColor="#CCCC99" />
       <OtherMonthDayStyle ForeColor="#999999" />
       <DayStyle Width="14%" />
       <NextPrevStyle Font-Size="8pt" ForeColor="White" />
       <DayHeaderStyle BackColor="#CCCCCC" Font-Bold="True"
         Font-Size="7pt"
           ForeColor="#333333" Height="10pt" />
       <TitleStyle BackColor="Black" Font-Bold="True"
        Font-Size="13pt"
           ForeColor="White" Height="14pt" />
     </asp:Calendar>
   </div>
   </form>
</body>
</html>
```

When adding the C# code, pay special attention to the `switch` statement. Often `switch` statements are used with arrays to filter out a single element, but here *all* of the days of the week are available when the calendar is rendered. The `switch` statement merely helps place the required materials. The `break` statements, while required for the `switch` structure, really are unnecessary. The `switch` does not break when it encounters the first `true` value in a case, but goes through the entire list, gets all of the instances, and places them in the calendar.

C# CalMind.aspx.cs

```
using System;
using System.Web.UI.WebControls;
public partial class CalAppt : System.Web.UI.Page
{
    private string dow;
    private string appt;
    private string soccer;
    private string ballet;
    private string baseball;
protected void CheckApps(object sender, DayRenderEventArgs e)
    {
        appt = "<br/>Drive to:<br/>";
        soccer = appt + "Soccer practice";
        ballet = appt + "Ballet lessons";
        baseball = appt + "Mom's baseball";

        dow=(e.Day.Date.DayOfWeek).ToString();
```

(continued)

```
switch (dow)
{
  case "Monday" :
    e.Cell.Controls.Add(new System.Web.UI.LiteralControl(soccer));
    break;
  case "Wednesday":
    e.Cell.Controls.Add(new System.Web.UI.LiteralControl(ballet));
    break;
  case "Friday":
  e.Cell.Controls.Add(new System.Web.UI.LiteralControl(baseball));
  break;
  }
}
}
```

Once you've finished, test it. Figure 10-3 shows what you should see.

As you can see from Figure 10-3, not only is the current month set up with the schedule, so too are the rest of the months. If you have a yearly schedule, this simple program is quite handy. Otherwise, you need to include the range of time that the schedule is applicable.

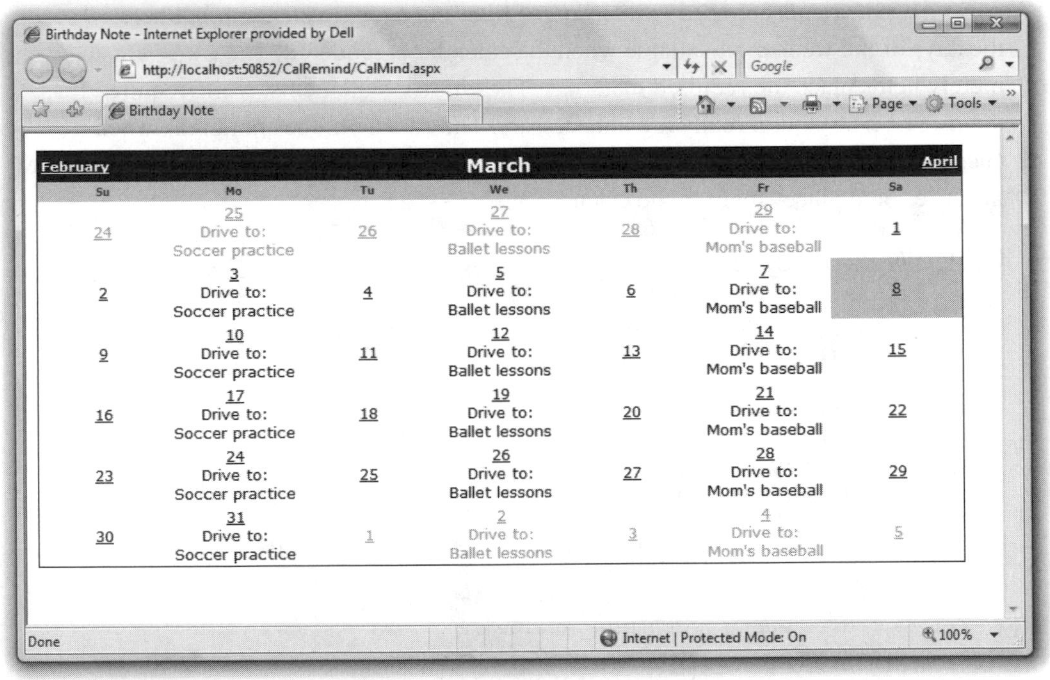

Figure 10-3 Adding text comments to Calendar

AdRotator Web Server Control

The AdRotator control can make the process of placing different announcements on your web site quite easy. The AdRotator displays different images and messages on the screen more or less randomly depending on the settings you have established in a data source. Each time a user visits your page with an AdRotator, a display randomly appears. By having different images and announcements appear on different visits, your site appears fresh and interesting rather than the same old thing all the time. The name of the control suggests that it has a marquee effect that rotates an ad, but "rotation" refers to the rotation of ads that it retrieves from a data source.

Of the different data sources at this stage of the book the one that will help you understand how the AdRotator uses stored data is an XML file. In the following example, you will see how to establish the necessary XML code and connect that code to the AdRotator.

XML and the Seven Tags

If you're not familiar with XML, it's something like HTML except that you can make up your own tags. (Actually, XML is an incredibly rich data-organization language, but this example employs only its most rudimentary aspects.) The XML scripts for the AdRotator control have seven tags:

Advertisements	General container for all ads
Ad	Individual ad container
ImageUrl	Location of image files
NavigateUrl	Address of web page
AlternativeText	Text you can pass to the event handler
Impressions	Relative probability that an ad is displayed (numeric value)
Keyword	Used as a filter for keywords

All of the tags must be within the `<Advertisements></Advertisements>` container. You can add two more tags, `<Height>` and `<Width>`, that override the default AdRotator settings. However, this next example uses the default AdRotator dimensions, so only the seven basic tags are employed.

Ask the Expert

Q: Don't you have to have a schema or Document Type Definition (DTD) in XML files?

A: XML files can be used either with or without a schema or DTD. In working with the built-in controls in ASP.NET 3.5, you do not need either. A schema or DTD defines the XML document's structure and lists the legal elements. If you want to add DTD, check out Brown University's Scholarly Technology Groups XML validation form at www.stg.brown.edu/service/xmlvalid/. Also, for issues surrounding validation and XML, see www.stg.brown.edu/service/xmlvalid/Xml.tr98.2.shtml, which explains why DTD is important.

To get started on this project, you need to open a new web site where you will be working on three code sets—ASP.NET, C#, and XML. All three of these files are placed within the default site directories. The XML file is placed in the App_Data folder that we have not yet used very much, but it has been a default directory in the web sites generated with Visual Studio 2008.

Try This Basic AdRotator

The following steps take you through the process of creating a page with an AdRotator Web Server control:

1. Open a new Web Site, and save it as **BasicAdRotator**.

2. Once you have opened the Web Site, select New | File, and when the Templates window appears, click on the XML file icon. In the Name window, type **AdCampaign.xml** as shown in Figure 10-4.

3. Create a folder on your web site named **ads**. Generate two different graphics ads, and save them as **ad1.jpg** and **ad2.jpg**. Figures 10-8 and 10-9 (later in this chapter) show a couple of examples. (Note: The message at the bottom of Figures 10-8 and 10-9 is generated by the AdRotator and a C# script, and should not be in the graphic image.)

4. When the XML window opens, enter the following code and save the file in the current web site's App_Data folder:

```
<Advertisements>
  <Ad>
    <ImageUrl>ads/ad1.jpg</ImageUrl>
```

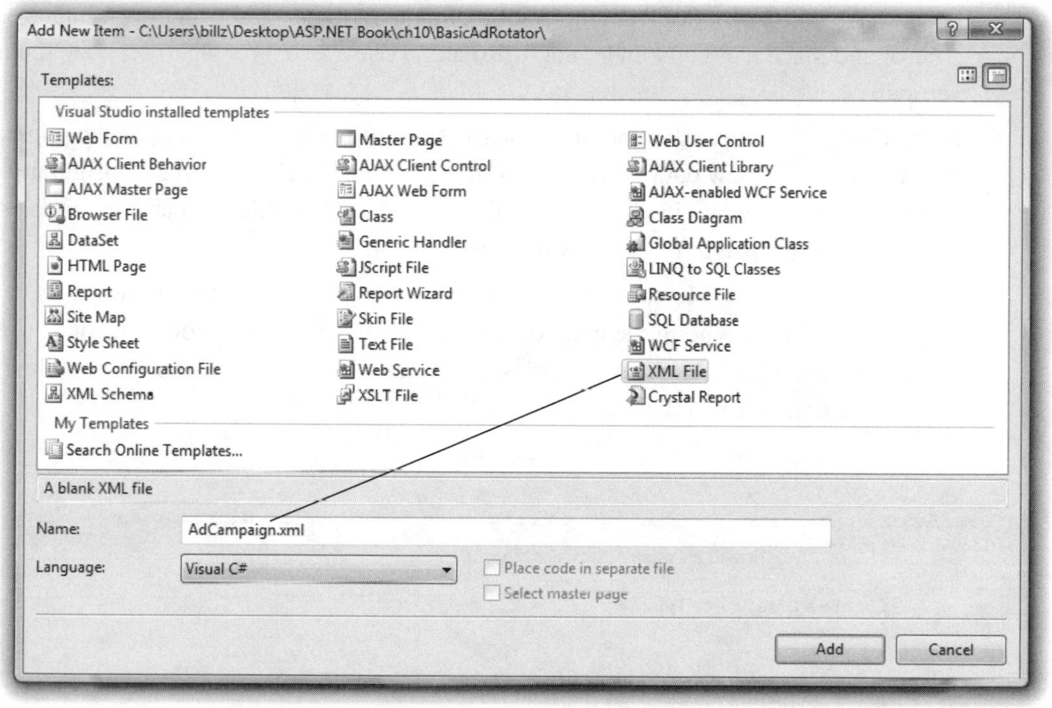

Figure 10-4   Adding XML file to web site

```
        <NavigateUrl>http://www.sandlight.net</NavigateUrl>
        <AlternateText>All backends in ASP.NET 3.5!</AlternateText>
        <Impressions>2</Impressions>
        <Keyword>Interactive Development</Keyword>
    </Ad>
    <Ad>
    <ImageUrl>ads/ad2.jpg</ImageUrl>
    <NavigateUrl>http://www.sandlight.net</NavigateUrl>
    <AlternateText>Powered by Ajax!</AlternateText>
    <Impressions>2</Impressions>
    <Keyword>Information Design</Keyword>
    </Ad>
</Advertisements>
```

5. Once your XML file is complete and stored in the App_Data folder, select the tab
   containing the ASPX template, and set the view to Split mode.

(continued)

6. Drag an AdRotator control from the Toolbox Standard menu, and then drag a Label control and place it directly under the AdRotator. (Use a `<br />` tag to separate them vertically.)

7. In the Design portion of the Split mode, select the AdRotator icon, and open the pop-up menu and select <New data source…> from the menu. The Data Source Configuration Wizard opens as shown in Figure 10-5. Click on the XML File icon and specify the ID as **AdCampaign**. Click OK when finished.

8. As soon as you click OK, the Configure Data Source window opens as shown in Figure 10-6. Either type in the path, or click the Browse button to locate it for you. You do not need to fill in either the Transform File or XPath Expression window. Just leave them both blank and click OK.

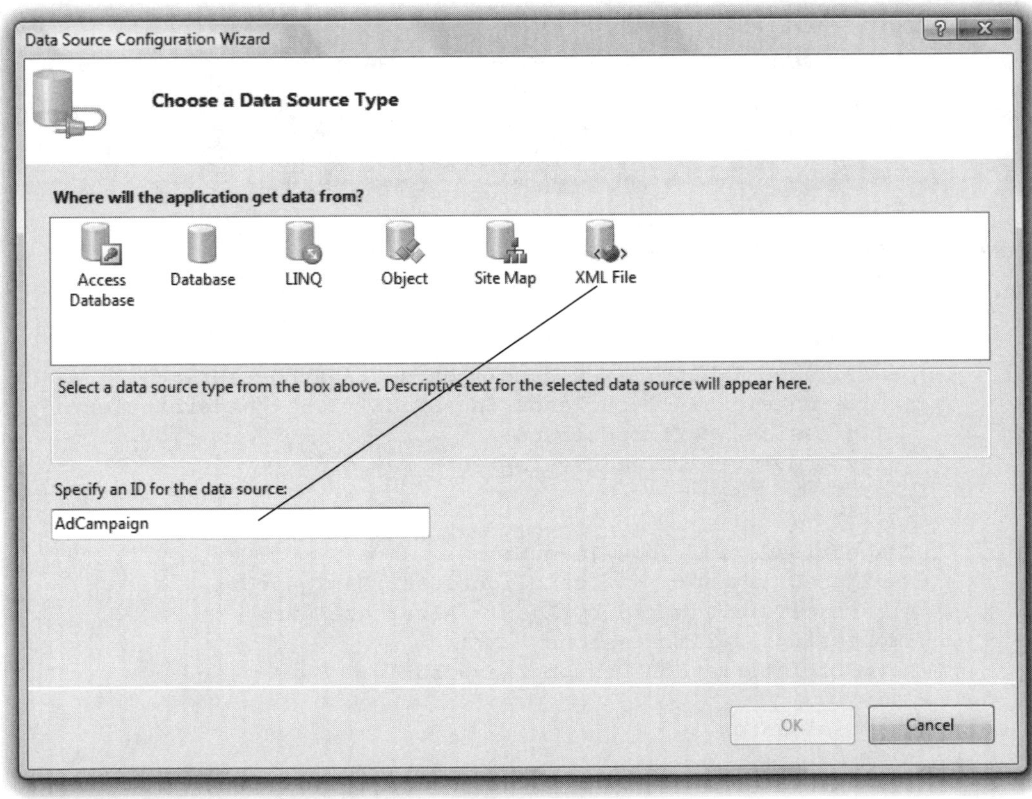

Figure 10-5   Selecting data source type

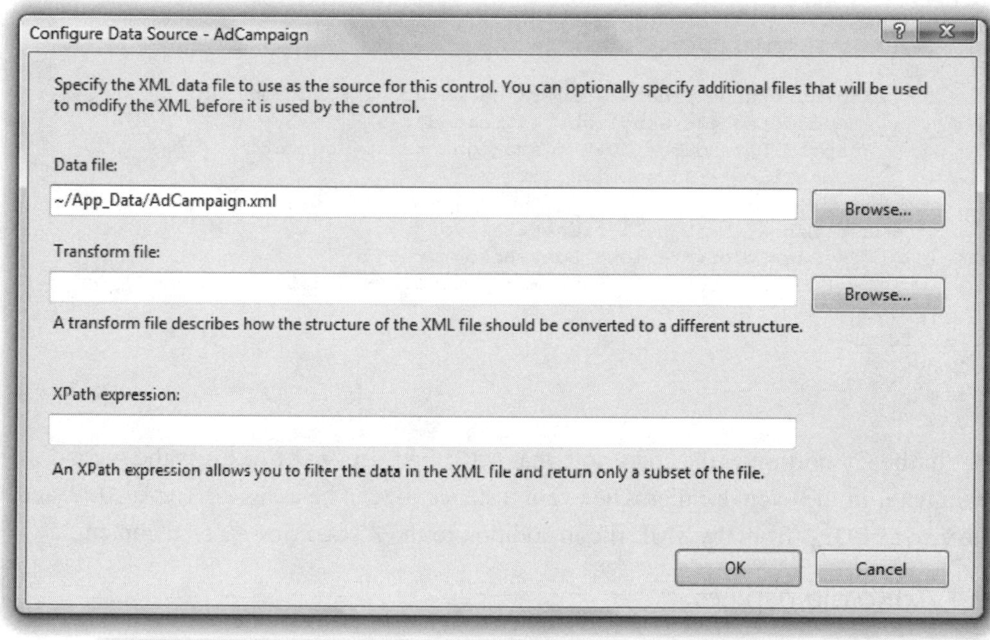

Figure 10-6 Specifying path to data source file

9. Double-click the AdRotator icon to generate the `onadcreated` attribute in the AdRotator tag and the C# event handler. Change the name of the event handler to **Sandlight_AdCreated** in both the ASP.NET and C# portions of the application. While you're at it, remove the `Page_Load` function from the C# portion of the application. The following listings provide the code for both the ASP.NET and C# portions of the application:

ASP.NET AdRotate.aspx

```
<%@ Page Language="C#" AutoEventWireup="true" CodeFile="AdRotate.aspx.cs"
Inherits="RollAd" %>
<!DOCTYPE html PUBLIC "-//W3C//DTD XHTML 1.0 Transitional//EN"
"http://www.w3.org/TR/xhtml1/DTD/xhtml1-transitional.dtd">
<html xmlns="http://www.w3.org/1999/xhtml">
<head runat="server">
    <title>ADRotator At Work</title>
</head>
```

(continued)

```
<body>
    <form id="form1" runat="server">
    <div>
        <asp:AdRotator runat="server" DataSourceID="AdCampaign"
            onadcreated="Sandlight_AdCreated" />
        <asp:XmlDataSource ID="AdCampaign" runat="server"
            DataFile="~/AdCampaign.xml" />
        <br />
        <asp:Label ID="Label1" runat="server"
            BackColor="Yellow" Font-Bold="True"
            Font-Names="Comic Sans MS" ForeColor="#036525" />
    </div>
    </form>
</body>
</html>
```

In the C# portion of the code, note that AdCreatedEventArgs is the second parameter in the event handler. The event instance, e, can be assigned ImageUrl and NavigateUrl from the XML file in addition to the AlternateText content.

C# AdRotate.aspx.cs

```
using System;
using System.Web.UI.WebControls;

public partial class RollAd : System.Web.UI.Page
{
    protected void Sandlight_AdCreated(object sender, AdCreatedEventArgs e)
    {
        Label1.Text=e.AlternateText.ToString();
    }
}
```

Once you have finished your application, check the directory where you have placed your web site files and folders. If you encounter any trouble, the cause may be due to misplacement of the files. Figure 10-7 shows a directory with the files and folders correctly placed.

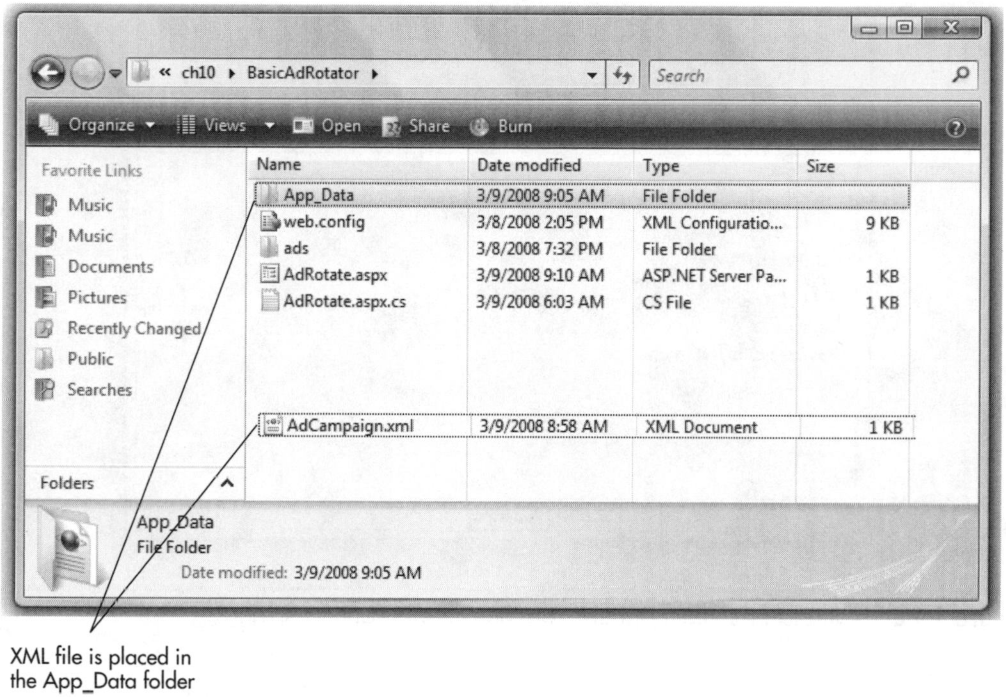

XML file is placed in
the App_Data folder

Figure 10-7   Files and folders for AdRotator application

Importantly, your data source, the XML file, goes into the App_Data file as indicated in Figure 10-7. You can add as many advertisement graphic files as you want in the ads folder. When more ads are placed in the ads folder, you will need to update your XML file for them to be shown. Alternatively, you can simply change the ad content by using the same graphic file names with new content, replacing the old ones in the ads folder. In that way, all you need to do is to replace the old set of graphic files with a new set and not change a thing in *anything* in the XML, ASP.NET, or C# files. Figures 10-8 and 10-9 show the two sample ads.

The order of the appearance of the ads does not depend on their placement in the XML file. The <impressions> tag sets up the relative frequency of the ad. In this example, both impression values are set to 2, so they should randomly appear the same number of times. Had one been set to 100 and the other to 185, the one set to 185 would appear 1.85 times for every one time the other did.

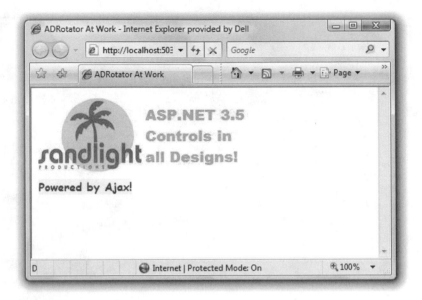

Figure 10-8 AdRotator content appears on the page in random order.

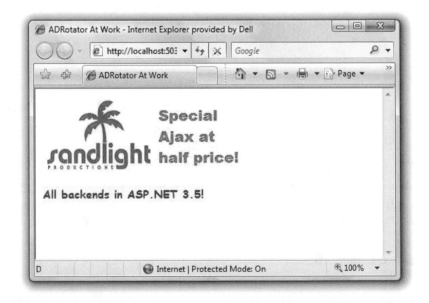

Figure 10-9 The first ad in the XML file appears first or second randomly.

If you have a good graphic artist on staff, the variety and quality of the messages generated by the `AdRotator` can be wonderfully varied. Further, using a database as a data source, you can have different `AdRotator` controls on every page and even on the same page that will provide your viewer with a wide and refreshed view of what your site has to offer.

Summary

Isolating only two of the ASP.NET 3.5 controls as rich data controls may be slightly misleading because so many of the controls can be considered rich data controls. Some of these controls are discussed elsewhere simply as "web controls," and others are specialized, such as the new LINQ controls that are examined in Chapter 14 and the special file controls discussed in Chapter 15. For now, though, the Calendar and AdRotator controls stand as examples of controls that are rich in properties and functionalities. They add a whole new level of functionality with a minimum of coding and configuration.

Part III

ASP.NET and Databases

Chapter 11

A SQL Primer

Key Skills & Concepts

- C# speaks SQL

- SQL commands

- C# data types and SQL data types

- Structured Query Language (SQL)

- Creating tables

- Adding data to tables

- Making table queries

- Filtering queries

- Adding fields to a table

- Deleting data

- Dropping tables

One of the most widely used languages in computing is Structured Query Language (SQL)—often pronounced "sequel." SQL is the language of the database, and you need to use it to communicate with the database and the tables that make up the part of the database where you will be arranging data for entry and retrieval. In Chapter 12 you will be using SQL to manipulate data and make queries, and here you will learn the basics of speaking SQL so that when it comes to use your database, you'll know the language it understands.

Data Types in SQL and C#: Essential Details and Differences

As with most other elements of ASP.NET and working with databases, Visual Studio 2008 has all of the SQL data types in a menu. However, to pass data to a table using SQL, you need to understand the type equivalences between C# and SQL types so you can handle the data typing of a C# variable. Table 11-1 shows the version of SQL used in Microsoft SQL Server 2008 (including SQLEXPRESS 3.5) and the equivalent types in C#.

Looking at Table 11-1, you will notice that some SQL/C# equivalencies are an exact match, like `int`, `float`, and `xml`. However, most are different, including common ones such as the SQL `text` and C# `string`. By spending a little time looking at Table 11-1, you will find that you can classify the types in terms of general characteristics, such as separating numeric from nonnumeric types, and string from non-string types. Once you do that, you may be able to see that while the typing may involve an `ArrayList`, for example, the array elements are of a string or non-string type. So in reality you may be dealing with nothing more than deciding whether you should handle data as a string or non-string.

Special kinds of types such as date and time types require more precise typing between SQL and C# when in use. However, most of these special types have very clear equivalencies. For instance, the SQL types `money` and `smallmoney` have the C# equivalent, `SqlMoney`. Likewise, SQL `datetime` and `smalldatetime` are matched by the C# `Datetime`.

SQL	C#	SQL	C#
bigint	Long	Real	Float
binary(50)	byte[]	smalldatetime	DateTime
bit	Bool	smallint	short
char(10)	Char	smallmoney	SqlMoney
datetime	Datetime	sql_variant	object
decimal(18,0)	Decimal	Text	string
float	Float	timestamp	byte ArrayList
image	Image	tinyint	byte
int	Int	uniqueidentifier	byte[16]
money	SqlMoney	varbinary(50)	byte ArrayList
nchar(10)	Char	varbinary(MAX)	byte ArrayList
ntext	String	varchar(50)	char ArrayList
numeric(18,0)	Decimal	varchar(MAX)	char ArrayList
nvarchar(50)	char ArrayList	xml	xml
nvarchar(MAX)	char ArrayList		

Table 11-1 SQL Type and C# Equivalent

The more you use SQL, the better you will be able to deal with the type matching between it and C#. For the purposes of getting started, the more general types are employed, and examples throughout the book will include a fuller set as you develop understanding and skills in working with SQL and C#.

Writing SQL Commands

Thus far in the book, you've had to switch between ASP.NET code and C# code. Getting to know a third coding language may seem like a bit of a challenge. This is especially true because you have SQL commands embedded as a parameter or value in a C# statement. Don't worry. Most SQL commands are relatively short, even if you're using Microsoft Notepad to write applications.

Using Visual Studio 2008 provides a lot of help. As you will see in more detail in the next chapter, as you develop tables and create queries, Visual Studio automatically generates code in a special Query editor. It's easy to copy the SQL code and paste it into your C# editor. Further on in this chapter you will see how to effectively use Visual Studio 2008 to do most of the query writing.

Conventions Used in Writing SQL Commands

One of the primary conventions that helps you separate C# code from SQL commands is the convention of writing SQL commands in all caps, just like a constant. For example, the following code segment from C# distinguishes the C# from the SQL:

```
sqlCmd = new SqlCommand("SELECT LastName, Donation FROM Supporters", hookUp);
```

Looking at that line of code, you can see the following language breakdown:

- `sqlCmd = new SqlCommand();` This is a C# statement.

- `"SELECT LastName, Donation FROM Supporters"` Terms in all caps are SQL keywords; others are labels for either fields or the name of the table.

- `hookUp` This is a C# `SqlConnection` instance name.

Figure 11-1 shows the precise breakdown you're likely to see in a SQL query. The SQL keywords can easily be distinguished from the C# code because the SQL keywords are written in all caps.

The other clue that code is SQL is if it is set as a string literal. The C# `SqlCommand` object's constructor accepts two parameters. The first is a string with all of the SQL commands, and a second parameter specifies the `SqlConnection` instance.

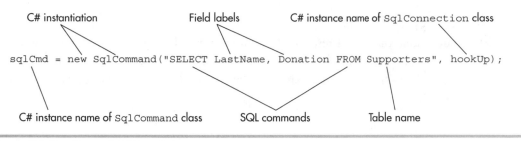

Figure 11-1 C# and SQL code

That arrangement also helps you to see where the SQL code is. Sometimes with a long SQL statement, the commands are placed in a string variable, and that variable is used as the first parameter in the SqlCommand instantiation.

CREATE: The SQL Command You Will Rarely Use

The first SQL command to examine is CREATE. This command is used to create a table in a database. However, because creating a table with Visual Studio 2008 is so easy, you will rarely use it. Nevertheless, understanding what it does helps to understand what goes into a table—particularly the SQL data types. The following shows the general format of the CREATE command:

```
CREATE TABLE TableName (fieldName1 TYPE, fieldname2 TYPE, etc.)
```

Which database the table will go into will have already been established through the connection statements. The TYPE must be a SQL data type even though it will be in the form of a string in a C# statement. The connection that exists to a database makes that particular database the default "owner" of the table you create. You can use the same table name for different databases, but every table in a single database must have a unique name. Once you have created a table, you can use it for any number of other applications that will access the table without having to create it more than once. In other words, you do not treat a table like a class where you have to create a new instance every time you want to use the class. Once it's created, all you need to do is to target the table in the database for adding, changing, reading, and deleting data.

Planning a Table

When you plan a table, you have to start with the practical question of what kind of information you will need. For example, if you want to create a table for a political candidate to keep track of fundraising, you may want to consider the following about the donor:

- Last name
- First name
- E-mail address
- Amount of donation
- Last time the donor was contacted

This is admittedly a simple set of requirements for a table, but it suffices for working out what has to go into a table. What you need to do first is to decide what kind of SQL data types you want to use. As just noted, you can start with the general categories of string and non-string types. The names and e-mail addresses are all string types, and the amount of donation and last time of contact are non-string.

The first impulse is to use the `text` SQL data type for the string types, but tables should be a bit more precise than the unspecified amount of space allocated in a table using the `text` type. Instead, the table uses the SQL `nvarchar()` type. First, the `nvarchar()` types allow you to specify a length for entries. The database reserves a specified length for each entry for more efficient table use. Second, the `nvarchar()` uses the Unicode format allowing for international languages. Thus, you have a more robust data type than either `text` or `varchar()` types. (The `varchar()` type uses ASCII instead of Unicode.)

Next, the first non-string type is the *amount of donation*. Initially, the best (even obvious) choice seems to be the `money` or `smallmoney` data type. Either is fine, and they provide the correct currency sign. However, the most important element is the actual amount received. So instead of using either of the money types, the `decimal()` type provides the advantage of being able to specify the number of decimal points, so it is selected for the financial data type.

Lastly, use the `datetime` type for the date and time. Fortunately, both SQL and C# have the same name for the type, except that C# references the type as a class, with the first letter capped (`Datetime`).

Specifying SQL Data Types

The next step is to decide what values to place in the type parameters. In breaking out the categories, the final requirement is to decide how much space is needed in the table to allocate each field. Table 11-2 shows field names with the parameter.

In a C# line, the CREATE statement with all of the fields and data types and parameters goes into a string. So, to use the values in Table 11-2, the C# string statement would look like the following:

```
string makeTable;
makeTable = "CREATE TABLE VoteWork (LastName nvarchar(20), FirstName
nvarchar(20), Email nvarchar(50), Donation decimal(6,2), LastContact datetime)";
```

The information in the parenthesis of the statement is nothing more than a set of field-type pairs. Each field has a SQL data type associated with it, and the list of pairs can be as long as you like.

Primary Key and Unique Values

In going over the list of information sources and the variables, one more item needs consideration. If you are successful in getting people to contribute, you may have duplicate names. For example, in the United States, the most common last name is *Smith* and the most common man's name is *Jim*. The most common woman's name is *Mary,* so the chances of having more than one Jim Smith or Mary Smith are pretty good. The more names you have, the greater the possibility of duplicates. To avoid this problem, most databases have what is called a *primary key*. The primary key indicates that the field (column) has unique values. That is, no two values can be the same. It's like social security numbers—each is unique. You specify a primary key with the code

```
fldName int PRIMARY KEY
```

Field Name	SQL Data Type	Parameter Value
LastName	nvarchar	20
FirstName	nvarchar	20
Email	nvarchar	50
Donation	decimal	6,2
LastContact	datetime	n/a

Table 11-2 Fields, Data Types, and Parameter Values

where `fldName` is the name of the field that you want as a primary key. First, you enter the SQL data type (`int`) and then the SQL statement, `PRIMARY KEY`.

To make life even simpler for whoever is going to be using the table, you can add an `IDENTITY` feature. Using `IDENTITY` provides an automatic increment in the value of the unique identifier. The `IDENTITY` element has two parameters, the increment value and the seed value. The *increment value* specifies how much to change the value of the field for each record, and the *seed value* specifies the starting value for the first record. For example, the statement

```
fldName int PRIMARY KEY IDENTITY(1,1)
```

sets up the table so that the first value for `fldName` is 1, and each subsequent record is 1 greater. With this arrangement, each record has unique values for every single record. In this way, you know that `Jim Smith ID=1234` is different from `Jim Smith ID=4321`.

TIP

In this book, the discussion of SQL and creating databases is elementary. The design of databases is a whole field unto itself. It is a vitally important one, and if you want to create more sophisticated databases, you should definitely pick up a book on database design. In particular, find a book that discusses both SQL and database design. When dealing with relational databases, your database will have multiple tables, and you will find red-hot controversy over the best way to design unique identifiers. When using multiple tables, the `IDENTITY` keyword probably is *not* the best choice for generating unique ID values. However, for the single-table examples you will find in this book, they're handy and will introduce you to the concept of a unique identifier.

Coding Table Creation

As noted, you're most likely to create your tables using Visual Studio 2008's *Server Explorer,* but by seeing the code in SQL in a C# context, you'll have a better sense of what goes into a table. (The VoteNow database is created in Chapter 12, and if you want to actually create the table used with the following code, you will first have to skip to Chapter 12 and create the database. However, simply by looking at the code in the next example, you should be able to see the structure of the table.)

The full ASP.NET and C# code is listed next. The ASP.NET portion simply provides a Label object to use for verification that the table was created. The key part of the C# code is the `createTable` string's assigned value—the full SQL code. Also, to keep things simple, only two of the fields shown in Table 11-2 are used.

ASP.NET CodeCreate.aspx

```
<%@ Page Language="C#" AutoEventWireup="true" CodeFile="CodeCreate.aspx.cs"
Inherits="CodeTable" %>
<!DOCTYPE html PUBLIC "-//W3C//DTD XHTML 1.0 Transitional//EN"
"http://www.w3.org/TR/xhtml1/DTD/xhtml1-transitional.dtd">
<html xmlns="http://www.w3.org/1999/xhtml">
<head runat="server">
 <title>Create Table</title>
</head>
<body>
 <form id="form1" runat="server">
 <div>
 <asp:Label ID="Label1" runat="server" Text="Outcome"/>
 </div>
 </form>
</body>
</html>
```

C# CodeCreate.aspx.cs

```csharp
using System;
using System.Data.SqlClient;

public partial class _Default : System.Web.UI.Page
{
 private string createTable;
 private SqlConnection hookUp;
 private SqlCommand sqlCmd;

 protected void Page_Load(object sender, EventArgs e)
 {
 hookUp = new SqlConnection("Server=localhost\\SqlExpress;Database=VoteNow;" +
 "Integrated Security=True");
createTable = "CREATE TABLE CodeTable (SupID int PRIMARY KEY IDENTITY
(1,1),LastName nvarchar(20),Donation decimal(6,2))";
 sqlCmd = new SqlCommand(createTable, hookUp);
 hookUp.Open();
 sqlCmd.ExecuteNonQuery();
 hookUp.Close();
 Label1.Text = "Table created";
 }
}
```

The connection to the database in the `SqlConnection` parameter points to the Visual Studio 2008 local host using the **SQL Express 2008** server, and the connection coding is all explained in Chapter 12. By looking at the line

```
createTable = "CREATE TABLE CodeTable (SupID int PRIMARY KEY IDENTITY
(1,1),LastName nvarchar(20),Donation decimal(6,2))";
```

you are able to see the entire set of SQL commands and properties to create a simple table with two fields—a last name (a string value) and the amount of a donation (a numeric value).

Ask the Expert

Q: **Why would you ever need to know how to create a table using code when it's so easy to do using Visual Studio 2008?**

A: For the most part, you would not. However, if you're ever using a computer that doesn't have Visual Studio 2008, you can easily create the code on virtually any computer by using a text editor or web page development application like Dreamweaver. Also, by understanding the SQL commands to create a table, you have a better understanding of the table's structure.

Adding Data to a Table with INSERT

As soon as you create a table, you have a matrix you can fill with data. The SQL command for adding data is INSERT with the following format:

```
INSERT INTO TableName (field1, field2, etc.) VALUES (valFld1, valFld2, etc.)
```

In the simple table created in the previous section, the SQL to add data would be

```
INSERT INTO CodeTable (LastName, Donation) VALUES ("Smith", 532.00)
```

That line provides the string literal value, *Smith,* for the LastName field and *532.00* for the Donation field.

You may wonder about the first field, SupID. Whenever you insert anything into a field (column) with an automatic increment, you do not need to name it. A field with a PRIMARY KEY and IDENTITY set for an increment handles everything. After the entry, Table 11-3 shows what the record in the table would be.

As each new record is entered into the table, the SupID automatically increments, so each record has at least one column (field) that is unique. In Chapter 12, you will see how to pass values from ASP.NET forms using C# variables, but for now all you need to know is the general process and to envision how data are added to tables one row at a time. Each row represents a unique record.

SupID	LastName	Donation
1	Smith	532.00

Table 11-3   Inserted Values in a Table

Looking into a Table with SELECT and FROM

Once you have a table and have added data, you can send a SQL query to look into a table and pull out whatever you want. The first SQL command for making queries is SELECT. It specifies the fields that you want to *query,* that is, to find out what their values are. The SELECT command needs a FROM clause to specify the table where the query will occur. The basic format is

```
SELECT field1, field2 FROM TableName
```

You can examine as many or as few fields as you want. In the example table shown, you might have

```
SELECT LastName, Donation FROM CodeTable
```

If you want to look at all of them, you can use the * wildcard symbol. For example,

```
SELECT * FROM CodeTable
```

examines all of the columns in the table, including the SupID field that was not specified in the first query of the table.

The WHERE Filter

Often a query is to locate certain elements in your database that have specific values or a range of values. The general format for the WHERE filter is

```
SELECT field1, field2 FROM TableName WHERE field condition
```

For example, you might want to find the donors in a political campaign who have donated at least $200. Using the example table, the filtered query would be

```
SELECT SupID, LastName FROM CodeTable WHERE Donation =>200
```

The query returns not only the LastName value of all donors who gave at least $200, it provides their ID. In this way, you can distinguish the *Mary Smith* who gave $50 from the *Mary Smith* who gave $5,000.

You can refine a query by adding an AND clause to the WHERE filter. For example, suppose you want to find all of the donors who gave $200 or more and have a last name of Smith:

```
SELECT SupID, LastName FROM CodeTable WHERE Donation >=200 AND LastName="Smith"
```

Translated, that statement expresses the following:

Return the ID and last name of anyone in the CodeTable who has donated $200 or more and has a last name "Smith."

If you look at both statements—one in SQL code and the other in plain English—you can begin to see that they are similar. Instead of using the term "return," the SQL uses SELECT, but otherwise, each has the same sense.

CAUTION

If you get a book on SQL and start trying out different query filters, you may find that you're getting errors that cannot be resolved. One possible reason is that SQL comes in different flavors. For example, the WITH clause does *not* work with the MS SQL server, even though it works fine with Oracle and DB2. Another common SQL can be found in MySQL, and it too has a set of supported commands and clauses that may not work with SQL commands you've used with the SQL server. So be sure that the SQL keyword that you're using works with the SQL server first.

Sorting Output with ORDER BY

In addition to making a query by specifying what fields you wish to search and other search conditions, you can also command the order of the output. Once you retrieve your data, using C# you can then sort the output. However, even before the data is sent to the client, you can set up the output order. The general format is:

```
SELECT field1, field2 FROM TableName WHERE field condition ORDER BY fieldX
```

The sort order is ascending by default, but you can change it to descending by adding on DESCENDING (or the abbreviation DESC) at the end. For example, the following code orders highest donations first:

```
SELECT SupID, LastName FROM CodeTable WHERE Donation >=200 ORDER BY Donation DESC
```

Even with a few SQL commands, you will find that the filters can give you a wide range of selected output. Once you have your table set up in Visual Studio 2008, you can test different SQL commands in the Query window and see how your output will be treated. For example, Figure 11-2 shows a similar set of SQL commands generated by selecting checkboxes and adding possible filters and sorting in a table.

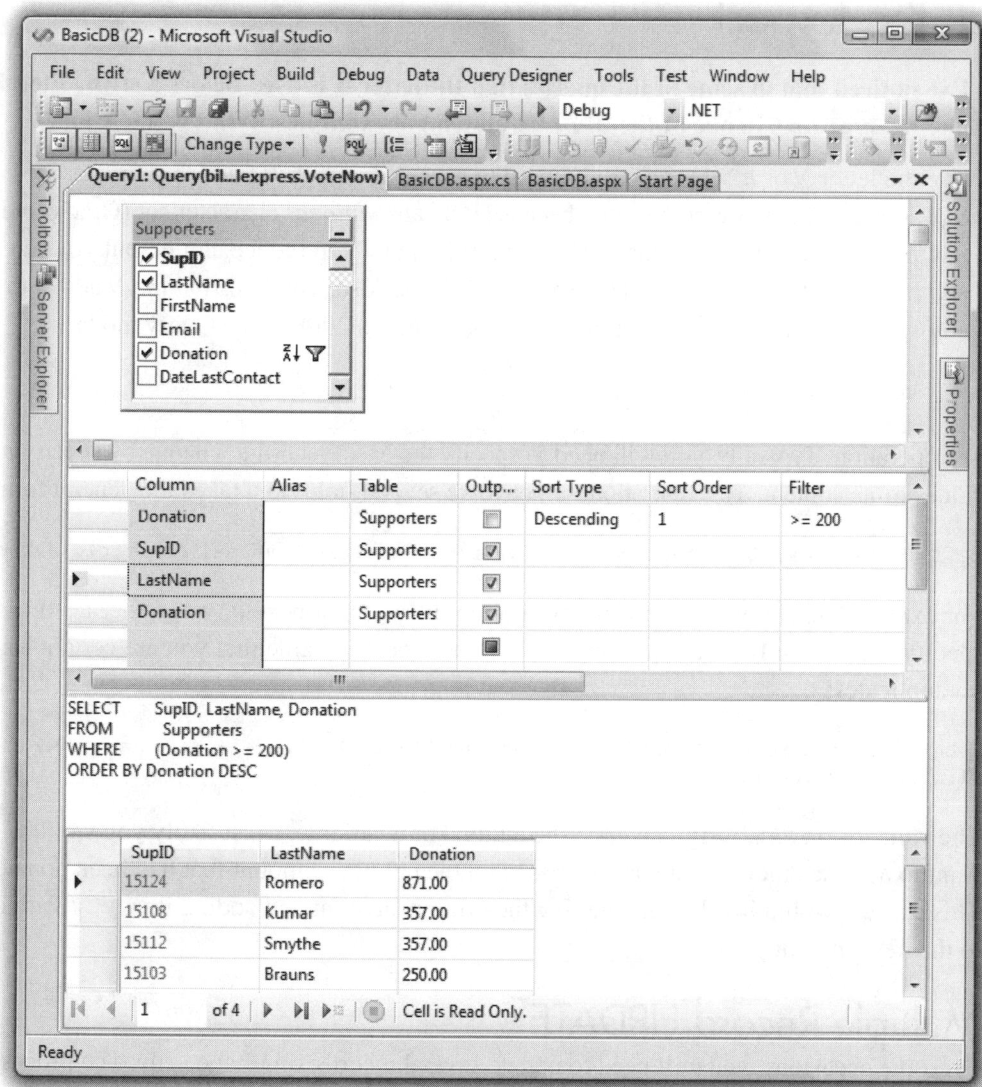

Figure 11-2   Testing SQL commands in Visual Studio 2008

Changing Data with UPDATE

Once you have established a table and added data to it, you may have to make changes. For instance, in the simple table used as an example, the value of a donation may change. In the case of the UPDATE command, often you will be dealing with a single record in any

Ask the Expert

Q: I've noticed that in some of the queries that the letter *N* is used before a string literal, like *N'*Brauns' in one of the UPDATE statement examples. What is the *N* for?

A: Use the letter *N* or *n* before a string literal to ensure it uses the Unicode character set in SQL server. The *N* was so selected because it means *national* character set (Oracle and ANSI). In the examples in this book, I've left it out to help reduce clutter, but you can add it to any of the examples that use string literals. Also, you will find the *N* added to any string literals in queries you make in Visual Studio 2008 in the Query mode.

one operation. Typically, you will need to specify the exact record to change by specifying values of its content. This operation may involve several fields and takes the general format

```
UPDATE TableName SET fieldToChange = newValue WHERE field1=value1 AND field2=value2
```

For example, if you want to update the amount in a donation field, you either need to specify the unique ID in the primary key or use a specific name that you are certain has no duplicates:

```
UPDATE Supporters SET Donation = newAmount WHERE (LastName = N'Brauns' AND
FirstName = N'Lelia')
```

The value of newAmount can either be a literal or a variable. Most likely you would want to add the amount as a variable based on the previous amount that had been donated. This process would involve first getting the original amount and adding it in a C# variable to the new amount.

Multiple Record UPDATE

On some occasions, you will need to update several records simultaneously. The process is exactly the same as when updating a single class. For example, suppose you have a table with one field for the company name. If one of your clients changes its name from "Sandlight" to "SandlightSoft," you can change the field name by setting the update with *fewer* parameters than when looking for a single record to update. The following SQL statement changes all records where the single change needs to be made but may affect multiple records:

```
UPDATE AcmeWareTable SET Company = 'SandlightSoft' WHERE Company = 'Sandlight'
```

The statement changes all records where the original name meets the search criteria. Because the name for that particular company is unique, a simple UPDATE statement with a single WHERE filter does the trick.

Making Multiple Partial Changes

Suppose one of your clients decides to spin off part of its company to a separate entity. The company, Sandlight, divides its operations into products and services. The product branch of the company will remain Sandlight, but the services are re-incorporated to the name SLServices. Because a whole new billing, marketing, and management structure has been put in place, if you don't make the changes quickly, billing and fulfillment will become entangled. Because your current database table includes a field for ContractType divided into products and services, you can use it as a filter and make multiple partial changes in your table:

```
UPDATE AcmeWareTable SET Company = 'SLServices' WHERE (Company =
'Sandlight' AND ContractType = 'service')
```

Because you are using more than a single filter, you can make multiple changes to records but only to those that meet the multiple criteria. Of course, those kinds of changes rely on the table having the necessary column (field) to use as a filter.

ADD a New Field with ALTER

Good planning is supposed to eliminate the need for adding a new field (column), but even the best planning cannot foresee everything, especially in technology. For example, imagine an audio/video chat address that becomes as common as e-mail. All of the A/V chats take place over the Web at unique A/V chat addresses, so you will need to add a field to reflect the new technology contact. Simply use the SQL ALTER command to make the changes using the following format:

```
ALTER TABLE TableName ADD NewFieldName SQLdataType
```

For example, to add a new column to the CodeTable, you would use the following statement where the new field named avChat will hold the URL to the audio/visual chat address using a 30-character NVARCHAR type:

```
ALTER TABLE CodeTable ADD avChat NVARCHAR(30)
```

That adds the field to the last column of the existing table. All of the data in the new field are *null* but can be changed using the UPDATE command.

Adding a single field is similar to the process where you create a table, but instead of adding a whole set of columns, you add only a single field. If you want, you can specify where the new field goes; you can either move it to the first column or place it after a specified column. Envision a table with the column (field) on the far left as the *first* position. When you alter a table by adding a new field, the default is to go to the *end*—the column on the rightmost position in the table. The following line shows how to add the new column to the first column:

```
ALTER TABLE CodeTable ADD avChat NVARCHAR(30) FIRST
```

Now that you can position the newly added field to the first or last position in the table, you need to know how to position it in some middle column position. Using the AFTER clause, you can place the new column after any other position in the table. The following line shows that the new field will go after (to the right of) the field LastName:

```
ALTER TABLE CodeTable ADD avChat NVARCHAR(30) AFTER LastName
```

As noted, good table planning will eliminate the necessity of using ALTER and ADD to insert a new field. However, if you need to add a new field, you are able to do so.

When You Must DELETE a Record

Have you ever received junk mail from a former workplace or organization that you no longer have any connection with? That is because a database table somewhere still has your name and address in a record that should be deleted. With very large databases, unwanted records can be as damaging to business as not having records you need. If your company does direct mail promotion like sending out catalogs and you have 1,000 records that are no longer valid, you save on the 1,000 unnecessary mailings if you can delete those invalid records. Your clients will appreciate any efforts you take to make deleting records manageable. Records should be made to be easy to delete intentionally but not accidentally.

Single DELETE

The best possible way to delete a record is to use the field that has a primary key. In this way, you know that you're getting rid of exactly the record you want and not another that may possibly be related. The general format for deleting a single record is

```
DELETE FROM TableName WHERE condition=someValue
```

That is fairly straightforward statement, but a typo could be disastrous. For example, the following drops a record identified by the primary key:

```
DELETE FROM CodeTable WHERE SupID=723
```

Because the ID is unique, you do not have to worry about deleting a whole set of records because the DELETE statement is filtered with a field where multiple records with the same value are stored. So when you have a DELETE statement to issue, you want to be sure that the user does some kind of double-check. For example, you might want to have a red warning label ask, "Are you sure that you want to delete record [*delete criteria*]?" Then the user must click a special button to delete the record.

Clear a Whole Table with DELETE

An even simpler (and deadlier) operation is to delete all of the records in a table. You keep the table, but all of the data is removed. In this way you keep all of the characteristics of the table, but you can clear it out. For example, you might have an annual cleanup of records for a certain type of transaction. On January 1st you clear out the previous year's records and begin anew.

The format for deleting the contents of an entire table is

```
DELETE FROM tableName
```

The good and bad news is that it's easy to clear the contents of a table. As a result, you definitely want a message that asks, "Are you sure you want to delete all of the records in the *tableName* table?" Even better, always make a backup of your data and table. Put it on an external hard drive or some other place. Remember the following:

If your data is important and it is not backed up, you will always accidentally delete it.

The corollary is

If your data is unimportant and backed up, it will be saved for eternity.

Deleting all the records from a table can be part of a regular maintenance routine, and you can save a good deal of database space by doing so. However, you need safeguards, because the SQL DELETE statement is so simple and final.

Removing a Table Using DROP

As you saw with the SQL DELETE command, you can delete all of the records stored in a table; however, that table stays in the database, even if you do not plan on using it ever again. To get rid of the unused table, the (deadly) DROP command is available. The format is exquisitely simple:

```
DROP TABLE tableName
```

So, if you want to tidy up your database and get rid of the example CodeTable created at the beginning of the chapter, you would use

```
DROP TABLE CodeTable
```

As noted with the DELETE command, you want to give the users fair warning that they are about to permanently eliminate a table and all of its data. So be sure to have some kind of button or label to wave a flag in front of the users to make certain they wish to eliminate the old table.

Summary

In this chapter you only saw a single listing that invoked ASP.NET and C# with SQL commands. That was by design to show how you could do so without the aid of Visual Studio 2008. Otherwise, this chapter's focus has been on SQL as a *language* in its own right. Similar SQL commands can be used with different types of languages and systems. For example, you could use Perl, PHP, or Adobe ColdFusion and the SQL language. Thus, to set off SQL as a language, this chapter saw very little of ASP.NET or C#.

In the next chapter, Chapter 12, all of this will change. Not only will you see a lot more ASP.NET and C# code with SQL statements embedded in C# strings, you will see Visual Studio 2008 in a much larger role. Most of the SQL you've learned in this chapter will make more sense in Chapter 12 because you can see it actually make changes in a database table.

Chapter 12

ADO.NET:
Hello Database

Key Skills & Concepts

- Creating databases

- Checking your database connection

- Planning tables

- Making a table

- Row and column matrix

- Specifying fields (columns)

- Selecting data types

- Entering data dynamically

- Retrieving data dynamically

- Changing data dynamically

- Deleting data dynamically

In many respects, ADO.NET (ActiveX Data Object.NET) is the *sine qua non* of ASP. NET. All of the web controls and forms are for naught without some way to work with them and a database. Work with any application that uses data input and/or recovery needs some mechanism for placing the data into a storage facility. E-business would be impossible without some way of entering data to store and retrieve orders and of keeping track of what has been processed and what is waiting to be processed. Working with ADO. NET, you can bring together all of the work you've done with web forms and controls and actually use the SQL commands from the previous chapter.

Creating a Database

The process of creating a database with Visual Studio 2008 is quite simple. Depending on the nature of your hosting service, you may be able to create your online database using Visual Studio 2008 in a remote site—such as your home or office not co-located with the SQL Server. However, to get started, we'll walk through the process of creating a database and of adding a table and data using the SQLEXPRESS server tucked into Visual Studio 2008. (If your Visual Studio does not have SQLEXPRESS, you may need to reconfigure it to include some access to a SQL server, express or otherwise.)

Working with the Server Explorer

The process of creating a little database on your computer is quite simple, but creating all of the different elements that go into your database requires attention to detail. The following steps show the path to getting started with true database computing:

1. Open Visual Studio 2008, and from the View menu select Server Explorer to open it.

2. At the top of the Server Explorer window, you will see Data Connections. Right-click on Data Connections, and select Create New SQL Server Database.

3. When the Create New SQL Server Database window opens, type in **localhost\ SQLEXPRESS** as shown in Figure 12-1. (Note: Be sure to use the backslash.)

Once your database is ready, you do not have to create it again. You can add several different tables to your database and use them independently or together to make a relational database.

Figure 12-1 Create a new database

Adding a Table to the Database

Databases hold all data in tables. To get started, you will need to place a new table in the VoteNow database. This particular table is to keep track of donors to a political campaign. It will contain fields for a supporter's unique ID: one field each for the last and first names. For contact, the table needs an e-mail field, one for the amount of donations, and finally one for the last time a supporter was contacted.

Resuming where we left off with the database, the following steps show how to add a table to your new database housed on your computer:

1. Once you have created your new database, it appears in the Server Explorer. The one named *billz-pc*\sqlexpress.VoteNow.dbo shown in Figure 12-2 gives you an idea of what you will see. (The first name of the database, rather than *billz-pc* as in the figure, is the name of your computer or server.) Click on the **+** icon next to the name of your new database to expand it to see the folders. The only one you will need now is the Tables folder shown as selected in Figure 12-2.

2. Right-click on the Tables folder, and select Add New Table. When you do so, the Table editor opens displaying a three-column work area and a Column Properties window. Figure 12-3 shows what you should see.

3. Click on the first row under Column Name and type in **SupID**. This is the name of your first field in the table.

4. Tab to the second column, Data Type. You will find a pop-up menu of all of the SQL data types. Select the default nchar(10).

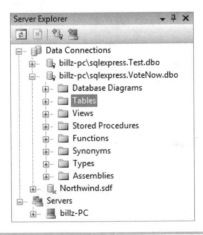

Figure 12-2 Folders in new database

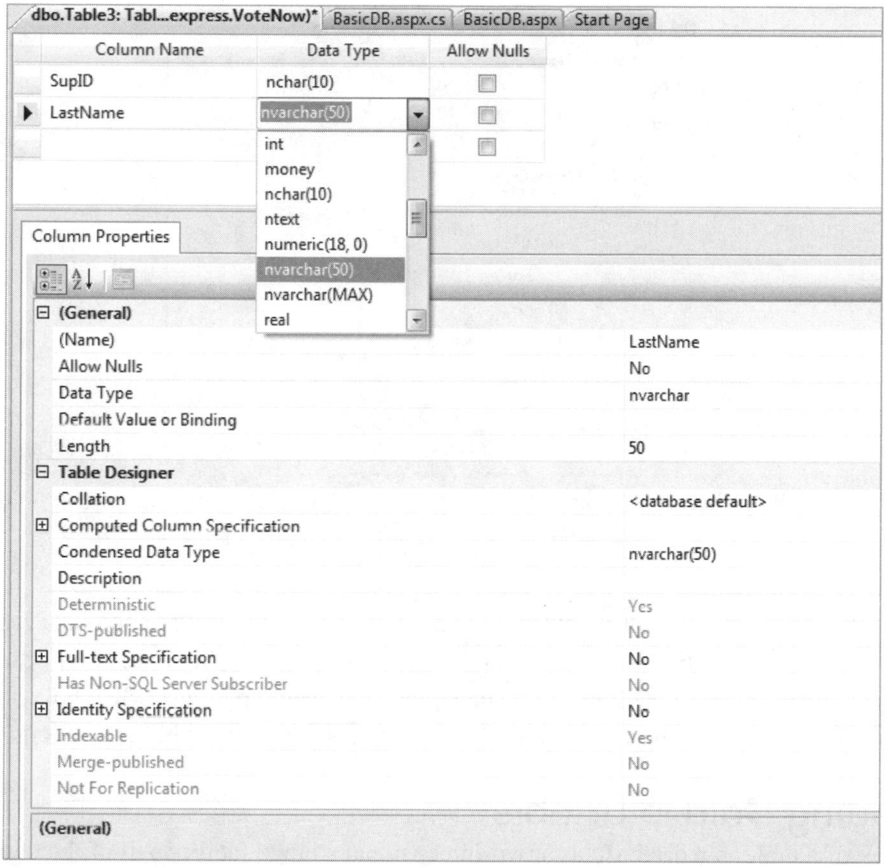

Figure 12-3   Adding a table field

5. Right-click on the SupID cell, and select Set Primary Key in the pop-up menu as shown in Figure 12-4.

6. Once you have added the first column and data type, uncheck the Allow Nulls box. Primary fields and several other fields will not allow nulls. To complete the table, add the remaining column names (fields) and data types, and indicate whether to allow nulls as shown in Figure 12-5.

7. When all of your columns and data information are entered, select File | Save. When you do, a dialog box appears where you enter the name of your table. Use the name **Supporters**. You will see a new table appear in the Tables folder in the Server Explorer.

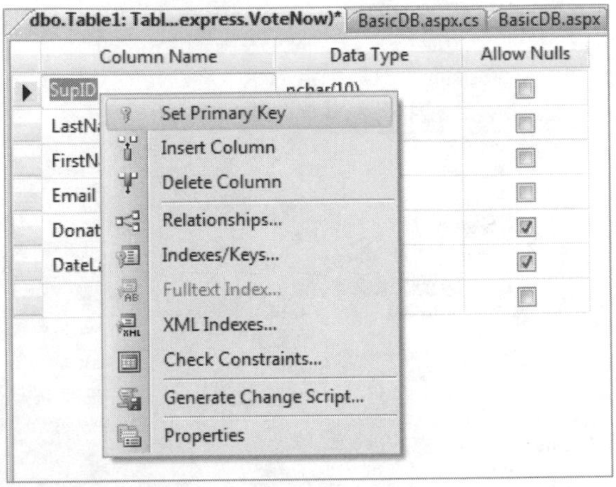

Figure 12-4 Setting the primary key

When you have all of the fields (columns) added, you will need to add data to the table. In the next section you will see how to do it using Visual Studio 2008. Further on in the chapter you will see how to add data that have been input into ASP.NET forms and sent to the database using C# and the SQL commands you learned in the previous chapter.

Adding Data to a Table

Think of a table in a database as a two-dimensional storage facility. All of the data you enter resides on a matrix made up of fields (columns) and records (rows). As you enter new data into your table, you create a new row. Eventually, you will want to set up your

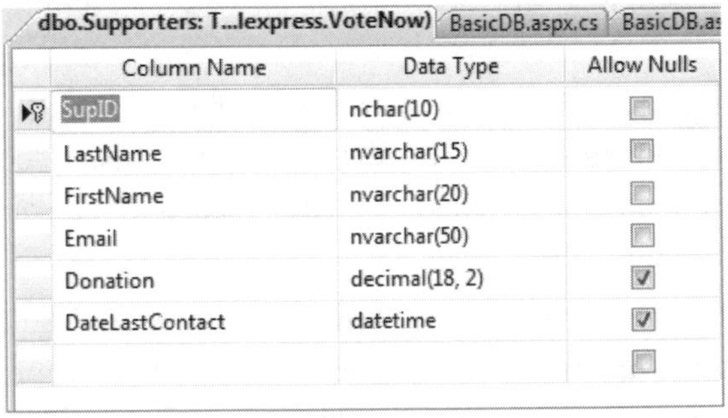

Figure 12-5 Entering fields and SQL data types

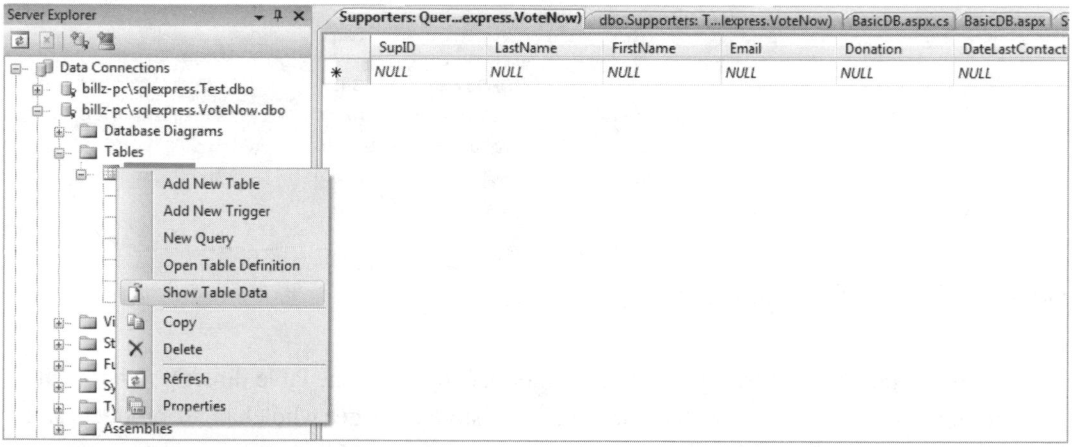

Figure 12-6 Adding data to table

application so that remote users anywhere in the world can enter data, but for now you can enter data simply by typing it in using Visual Studio 2008:

1. Right-click on the Supporters table, and in the pop-up menu select Show Table Data as shown in Figure 12-6. When the table opens, you will see NULL values for all of your fields in a single row as shown in Figure 12-6.

2. As you start entering data by typing the information into each cell, you will see a little red circle with an explanation point as shown in Figure 12-7. Once you are finished with each row, the red circles go away. If you enter data incorrectly, a dialog box appears once you are finished, indicating data entry error. Incorrect data entry is generally due to either putting in the wrong kind of data or exceeding the limits of one of the fields—a very long name might exceed the limit of 15 characters in the LastName field, for example.

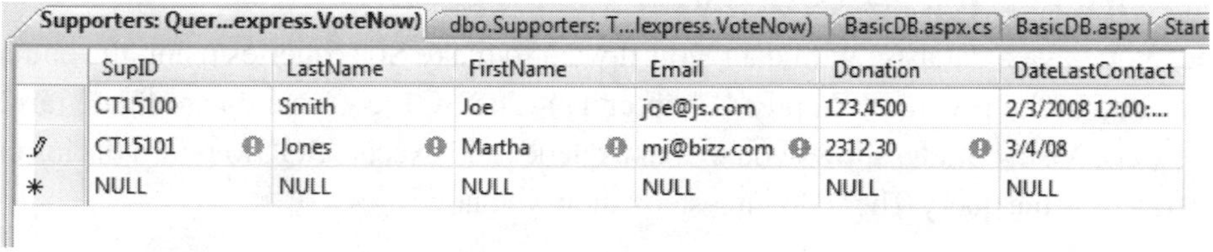

Figure 12-7 Entering table values

SupID	LastName	FirstName	Email	Donation	DateLastContact
Supporters: Quer...express.VoteNow)	dbo.Supporters: T...lexpress.VoteNow)	BasicDB.aspx.cs	BasicDB.aspx	Start Pa	
CT15100	Smith	Joe	joe@js.com	123.4500	2/3/2008 12:00:00 AM
CT15101	Jones	Martha	ms@ceo.com	234.0000	2/4/2008 12:00:00 AM
CT15102	Schafer	John	js2@df.com	1800.0000	1/31/2008 12:00:00 AM
CT15103	Brauns	Lelia	na@na.com	250.0000	3/1/2008 12:00:00 AM
NULL	NULL	NULL	NULL	NULL	NULL

Figure 12-8   Completed data entry

You might be wondering how you'd enter data by using the table directly rather than through a web portal. The web owner, such as a store manager who changes products and prices or some other information to which no one else should have access, updates certain kinds of databases. However, even for data upkeep and maintenance you will be better served by adding an administrative module for making changes to data in the table. For the most part, entering table data in the manner shown here is for becoming accustomed to the different data types and being able to see exactly what happens to data that you enter. For example, in the `DateLastContact` column, all of the data were entered using the format

```
m/d/yy (e.g., 5/22/08)
```

However, once the data are entered in the `DateLastContact` field, it changes the data to the format

```
m/d/yyyy time (e.g., 5/55/2008 12:00:00 AM)
```

Also, you learn about the kinds of data you can and cannot enter in certain fields. Figure 12-8 shows what your table looks like when you're finished entering the data.

You will always have an additional row with NULL values when you're done as shown in Figure 12-8, but that row is not saved to the table. It simply indicates that that table is ready to accept the next record.

Making a Table Query

Once you have a database with data, you'll want to make SQL queries using the commands described in the previous chapter (Chapter 11). The SQL commands are made targeting tables, and Visual Studio allows you to make queries and execute SQL to return the information generated by the query. The following steps show you how:

1. Select the Supporters table in the Tables folder.

2. Right-click on the table and select New Query.

3. When the dialog box appears, click the Add button to select the Supporters table for query practice. Once you have done so, you will see the Query editor as shown in Figure 12-9.

4. Click the `LastName`, `Donation`, and `DateLastContact` fields in the Supporters checkbox window in the top panel.

5. In the middle panel, in the `Filter` column of the `Donation` record, type in **>200**. When you do, you will see a set of SQL commands below the table:

```
SELECT LastName,Donation,DateLastContact
FROM Supporters
WHERE (Donation > 200
```

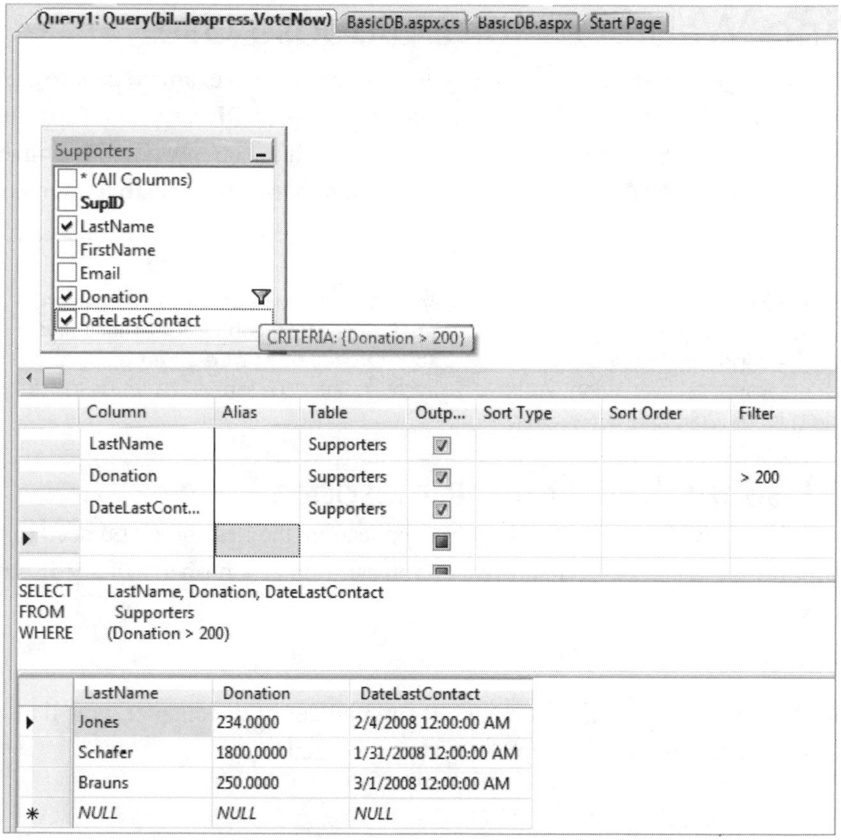

Figure 12-9 Working with a table query

That SQL query is the sequence you would use in a C# statement to make a database query to the Supporters table.

6. Finally, place the mouse anywhere on the Query editor and right-click it. Select Execute Query. At the bottom panel, you should see the output from your table as shown in Figure 12-9.

At this point you have a database, a table, and data with which to practice queries. Using the commands from Chapter 11, you should be able to use this to practice SQL queries. You might want to take a look at a good introduction to databases if you're not familiar with them. *Databases Demystified* by Andrew Oppel (McGraw-Hill, 2004) is a good jumping-off point. The next step is to get these commands arranged in a web site for real-world use.

Creating Web Sites for Database Use

Now that the table in the database is ready for use, we need to examine how to use ASP.NET and C# to work with ADO.NET in an application. Using a SQL server, you will find that the key SQL commands begin with—what else?—*Sql*. In this section we will examine what you need to connect to a database, to make a query, and to output the data to the screen.

NOTE

If you are working with Microsoft Access or with an Oracle database, you can use an `OdbcConnection` (Oracle) or `OleDbConnection` (Access) connection. Those must be set up by importing the `System.Data.Odbc` (Oracle) or `System.Data.OleDb` (Access) namespaces. Everything works very much like the `SqlConnection` as far as connecting to the database is concerned.

First Use the SqlClient Namespace

When you're ready to launch your database application, the first thing you need to remember is to import the `SqlClient` namespace. You set it up as a property of `System.Data` as follows:

```
using System.Data.SqlClient;
```

It's easy to forget, but in this section and the remainder of the chapter, you'll be using it for all of the different `Sql`... commands that you need to use.

TIP

The process in setting up a database is a one-time operation. Because of that, you're apt to forget the name of the database. Write it down and store it at someplace you can remember on your computer. This is vital if you create a database outside of Visual Studio 2008 that kindly stores the name of the database and related tables in the Server Explorer.

SqlConnection: The Command to Hook You Up

You're familiar with connections to a web server, and connecting to a SQL server is the same idea but a bit more involved. Using the `SqlConnection` command, you can connect to your SQL server that's built into Visual Studio 2008 or into the SQL Express that you can download from Microsoft. (This example uses the Visual Studio 2008 application as a database target.)

Depending on how your database is arranged, you have different ways to assign the `SqlConnection` parameters. For example, I have SQL server set up at a remote site with my database protected by a username and password. My connect parameter must include the following:

1. Server name (for example, myPlace.com)

2. User ID (the username for the database)

3. Password (the password for the database)

4. Name of database (only the database name—not a table name)

At the point of connection, I do not need the name of any tables. So when I get ready to work with my remote database, my focus is on the URL to the SQL server and database. I use the following:

```
private SqlConnection hookUp;
......
hookUp = new SqlConnection("Server=myPlace.com;uid=uname; pwd=pass;database=zero");
```

However, if using Visual Studio 2008, all I need is my `localhost` address and a reference to my `SqlExpress` server built into Visual Studio 2008. My connection target and database would be

```
Server=localhost\SqlExpress;Database=VoteNow;
```

However, because the expression will use a string, I have to place a backslash escape character in front of the backslash (\\), making it appear as double backslashes. Also, in the database creation process the logon selection is Windows Authentication (see Figure 12-1); the code must contain `Integrated Security` set to `True` to avoid a security problem when using Visual Studio 2008 on your computer. So now the connection statement is the following:

```
hookUp = new SqlConnection("Server=localhost\\SqlExpress;Database=Vote
Now;"+ "Integrated Security=True");
```

Once that has been completed, the C# operation is set to connect to the database.

SqlCommand: The Command to Query

In the previous chapter, you learned about the different SQL commands. In your C# code the `SqlCommand` is a class to gather up your SQL commands and send them to the server via the connection you have established using `SqlConnection`. The general format is

```
SqlCommand("SQL query", myConnection)
```

The SQL query (or non-query) is simply a string with the set of SQL commands and their targets. For example, the query shown in Figure 12-9 is simply laid out in a string as a SQL command:

```
"SELECT LastName,Donation,DateLastContact FROM Supporters WHERE (Donation > 200"
```

Bringing it together, the following shows a simple SQL query using the connection defined in the previous section. (Note that the query is a bit different than the example in Figure 12-9.)

```
private SqlCommand sqlCmd;
... .
sqlCmd = new SqlCommand("SELECT LastName, Donation FROM Supporters", hookUp);
```

Now the stage is set for opening a connection to the database and making a query. However, once the query is made, some mechanism must be available to show what the query has found. It's time for the next SQL command.

SqlDataReader Shows What You Found

The final SQL command required to read the results of a table query is one that can return the database contents in such a way that they can be passed to variables and sent to ASP. NET web controls. The `SqlDataReader` instance uses the `SqlCommand` instance to launch the reader that returns array elements of the query data from the table. The element values can then be passed to variables and on to web controls, or you can pass the element values directly to the controls. It has the following format:

```
private SqlDataReader reader;
...
reader = sqlCmd.ExecuteReader();
 while (reader.Read())
 {
 var1 = Convert.ToString(reader["Field1"]);
 var2 = Convert.ToString(reader["Field2"]);
 WebControl.Text += var1 + var2+ "<br/>";
 }
 reader.Close();
... .
```

In looking at the code, it's not too different than iterating through an array. By converting all output to a string, your data is ready to place into a web control's `Text` property.

Building a Web Site for Database Retrieval

Once you understand the basic SQL commands, you're all set to create an ASP.NET web site with a C# engine in code-behind mode. The sample application is designed to go with the VoteNow database and the Supporters table. The parameters are set for running in Visual Studio 2008 with and tested on the computer you developed the database on. If you have set up your database and tables on a remote location, just make the changes in the connection string.

The ASP.NET portion of the web site is very simple. All you have to do is to drag a Label web control between the `<div>` tags. Instead of going with the default Label name, use the ID name `DataOutput`. The following code shows the ASPX file:

ASP.NET BasicDB.aspx

```
<%@ Page Language="C#" AutoEventWireup="true" CodeFile="BasicDB.aspx.
cs" Inherits="BasicDB" %>
<!DOCTYPE html PUBLIC "-//W3C//DTD XHTML 1.0 Transitional//EN"
"http://www.w3.org/TR/xhtml1/DTD/xhtml1-transitional.dtd">
<html xmlns="http://www.w3.org/1999/xhtml">
<head runat="server">
 <title>Basic Database</title>
</head>
<body>
 <form id="form1" runat="server">
 <div>
 <asp:Label ID="DataOutput" runat="server" Text="Label" />
 </div>
 </form>
</body>
</html>
```

All the ASP.NET portion is going to do is act as a display for the data from the database table. In the C# portion, you will find the SQL commands and other code to funnel the output to the ASP.NET label. The following code shows what you'll need for the C# portion:

C# BasicDB.aspx.cs

```
using System;
using System.Data.SqlClient;

public partial class BasicDB : System.Web.UI.Page
{
 private string dona;
 private string ln;
 private SqlCommand sqlCmd;
 private SqlConnection hookUp;
 private SqlDataReader reader;

 protected void Page_Load(object sender, EventArgs e)
```

```
{
DataOutput.Text = "Supporter's Donations" + "<br/>";
DataOutput.Text += "--------------------------" + "<br/>";
hookUp = new SqlConnection("Server=localhost\\SqlExpress;Database=VoteNow;" +
"Integrated Security=True");

sqlCmd = new SqlCommand("SELECT LastName, Donation FROM Supporters", hookUp);
hookUp.Open();
reader = sqlCmd.ExecuteReader();
while (reader.Read())
{
dona = Convert.ToString(reader["Donation"]);
ln = Convert.ToString(reader["LastName"]);

DataOutput.Text += ln + " donated $" + dona + "<br/>";
}
reader.Close();
hookUp.Close();
}
}
```

Once you've entered and checked all the code, press CTRL-F5 to test the application.
Figure 12-10 shows what you can expect to see in a web page display.

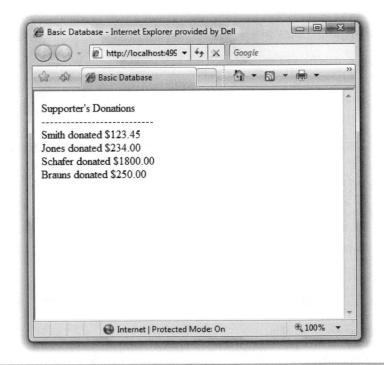

Figure 12-10 Displaying data from database

Once you have tested the application and gotten the expected output, try changing the query to test different combinations. Remember, the code is just a string of SQL queries.

Entering Data from a Web Site

One of the most important aspects of working with ADO.NET is its ability to store data entered from anywhere on the Internet. E-business is dependent on remote shoppers entering orders that can be stored for later retrieval for order processing. That means any e-business application is going to require a database that can accept input from someone other than the site administrator who sits with Visual Studio 2008 and enters data.

This section examines the different ways to enter data from a web site. Starting with basic code to enter data when the page loads to practical Web forms that let the user enter the data directly, this section gets you started on ways to add records to your database from the Web.

Automatic Data Entry

Sometimes you may want certain fields to be automatically filled. This is usually the case where you have a unique ID for each record. In the example table you have seen in this chapter, the `SupID` field is supposed to have unique values, but the way they are set up, somebody has to add a unique value. It could be the administrator, but such an entry system limits the entry process to a single person working from a list. Wouldn't it be better to have the unique ID value be entered no matter who enters the values for the other fields? To quote Curly, *soitenly*!

At this stage not too many entries have been made in the database table, so it should not be too difficult to make the necessary changes to set up an automatic unique value to be entered into the `SupID` field. The following steps guide you through this process:

1. In the Server Explorer open the VoteNow database in the Tables folder, and then double-click the Supporters table to open the Table Definition window.

2. Click on the Data Type cell in the `SupID` row. In the pop-up window, change the data type from `nchar(10)` to `int`. You need some kind of integer for automatic increment.

3. In the Column Properties window, open the Identity Specification directory, changing it from No to **Yes**. Change the (Is Identity) parameter to **Yes**, the Identity Increment to **1**, and the Identity Seed (the starting value) to **15100**. Figure 12-11 shows the new settings.

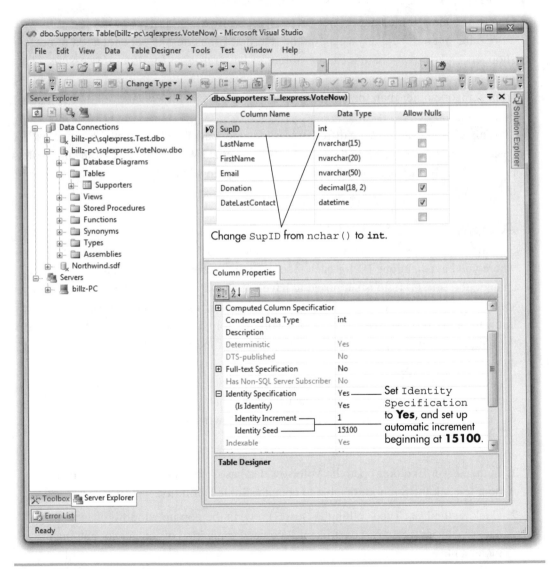

Figure 12-11 Settings for an automatic increment

4. Save the new table setup by pressing CTRL-S, or just click the close icon (X), and it will open a Save dialog box. You'll also get a little admonishment and warning that your data values may be toast. That makes perfect sense because you changed from character type data to numeric type.

5. Right-click the Supporters table, and select Show Table Data from the pop-up menu. When the table with the data appears, change all of the SupID values simply by removing the leading *CT* characters. For example, CT15100 would be changed to 15100. That's all you have to do.

TIP

Measure Twice, Cut Once. As a general rule, you should *not* change your data types in tables once you have entered data. The tailor's saying, *Measure twice, cut once,* applies to planning tables. Part of making a successful table is looking at the data you will be working with and what the user and site administrator both want in the data. Besides, it's time-consuming to have to change all of the data in a field once you have entered it. However, rather than getting stuck with a bad decision (and bad planning), if you have to change a field's data type, you can do it.

At this point, your new table is all set to automatically add a unique value to the SupID field. In the next section, you will see how to generate SQL commands to insert new data into the table.

Adding Data with INSERT

Beginning with Visual Studio 2008 tools, you will see how to add data to a table. The important element in this process is understanding what kinds of SQL commands you need to use. These commands then will be placed in a C# 3.0 script and used in a web site. The following steps show you how to get started:

1. Open the VoteNow database and right-click the Supporters table to open the context menu.

2. Select New Query from the context menu, click Add, and then click Close in the Add Table window.

3. Once the Query window is open, right-click anywhere in the window to open the Query context menu. Select Change Type | Insert Values as shown in Figure 12-12.

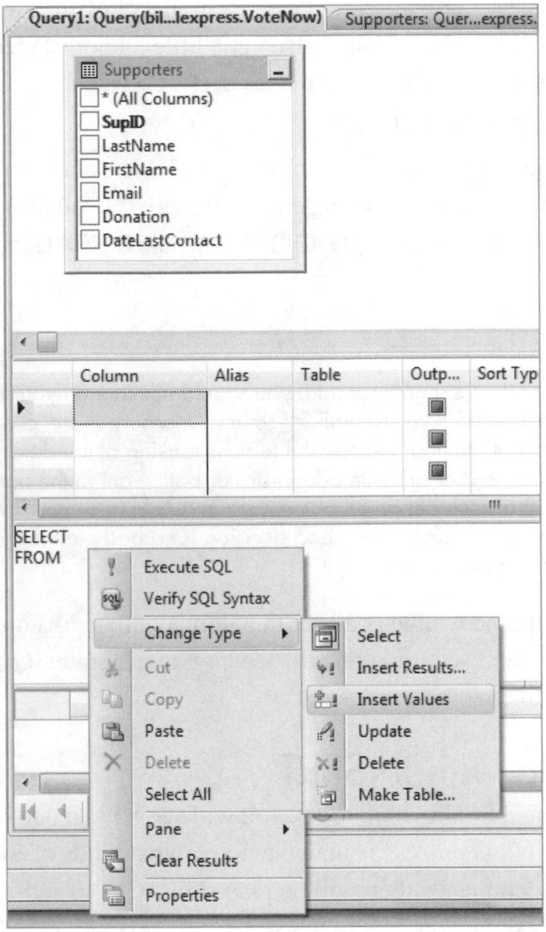

Figure 12-12 Changing a Query type to Insert Values

4. In the Supporters (table) window in the top panel, select all but the first field, SupID, as shown in Figure 12-13.

5. In the New Value field in the middle panel, add values for all of the Columns. When you enter a string, the letter *N* appears next to the entered value as shown in Figure 12-13. However, when the data is retrieved, the *N* is not shown. Also, when looking at the SQL commands in Figure 12-13, you can see the *N*, but you do not need it in your data entry code.

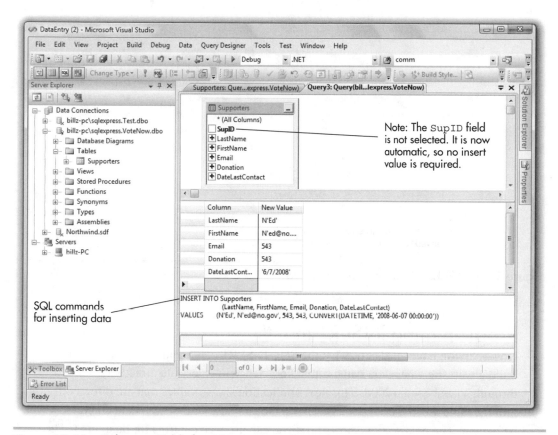

Figure 12-13 Selecting Fields for SQL Commands

6. Right-click anywhere on the window to open the context menu. Select Execute SQL. When you do so, the new data are added to the Supporters table as shown in Figure 12-14. You can see where the automatic numbering provided a value for the SupID column. It jumps from 15103 to 15107. That occurs because earlier records had been deleted.

This exercise shows you how the SQL statement looks for inserting data. In the following section you will see how to place that SQL command into a string and use it with C#.

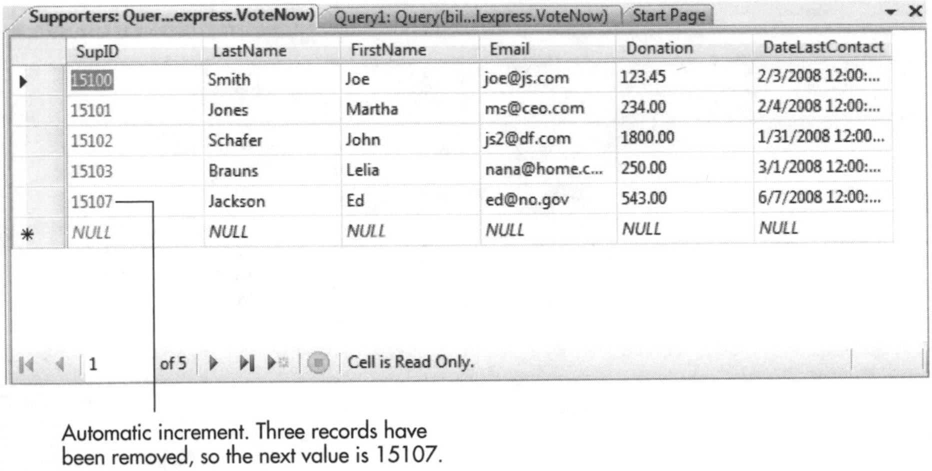

	SupID	LastName	FirstName	Email	Donation	DateLastContact
▶	15100	Smith	Joe	joe@js.com	123.45	2/3/2008 12:00:...
	15101	Jones	Martha	ms@ceo.com	234.00	2/4/2008 12:00:...
	15102	Schafer	John	js2@df.com	1800.00	1/31/2008 12:00...
	15103	Brauns	Lelia	nana@home.c...	250.00	3/1/2008 12:00:...
	15107—	Jackson	Ed	ed@no.gov	543.00	6/7/2008 12:00:...
✳	NULL	NULL	NULL	NULL	NULL	NULL

Supporters: Quer...express.VoteNow) Query1: Query(bil...lexpress.VoteNow) Start Page

|◀ ◀ | 1 | of 5 | ▶ ▶| ▶✱ | ◉ | Cell is Read Only.

Automatic increment. Three records have
been removed, so the next value is 15107.

Figure 12-14 Table showing inserted record

Programming INSERT in C#

Now that you have an idea of what the SQL INSERT command looks like, it's time to build a web site where you can use that knowledge to enter data directly rather than through Visual Studio 2008. This next application shows values that are directly inserted into the table when the page loads. This is the simplest kind of web data entry. However, be patient. The next section shows how you can use web controls for data input. The following steps walk you through the process:

1. Open a new Web Site, and name it **DataEntry**.

2. Change the Name file from Default.aspx to **BasicEntry.aspx** in the Solution menu. Then change the CodeFile assigned from _Default.aspx.cs to **BasicEntry.aspx.cs**. In the C# page, change the class name from _Default to **BasicEntry**. Save both files.

3. In the ASP.NET page, drag a single Label web control from the Toolbox to a position in the `<div>` container. Save the file. It should appear as the following:

ASP.NET BasicEntry.aspx

```
<%@ Page Language="C#" AutoEventWireup="true" CodeFile="BasicEntry.
aspx.cs" Inherits="BasicEntry" %>

<!DOCTYPE html PUBLIC "-//W3C//DTD XHTML 1.0 Transitional//EN"
"http://www.w3.org/TR/xhtml1/DTD/xhtml1-transitional.dtd">
```

```
<html xmlns="http://www.w3.org/1999/xhtml">
<head runat="server">
 <title>Data Entry</title>
</head>
<body>
 <form id="form1" runat="server">
 <div>
 <asp:Label ID="Label1" runat="server" Text="Label" />
 </div>
 </form>
</body>
</html>
```

As you can see, the ASP.NET portion is extremely simple. Its role is only to provide a label to indicate whether the operation is a success. First, take another look at the SQL statement that was generated by Visual Studio when the data was entered:

```
INSERT INTO Supporters
(SupID, LastName, FirstName, Email, Donation, DateLastContact)
VALUES (N'Jackson', N'Ed', N'ed@no.gov', 543, CONVERT(DATETIME, '2007-06-07 00:00:00'))
```

The task will be to turn that SQL directive into C# code. As you will see, it's almost identical except the *N* values have been removed and a new record is added. As a string the SQL command is

```
"INSERT INTO Supporters(LastName, FirstName, Email, Donation, DateLastContact)VALUES
('Kumar', 'Vladimir', 'pete@bmw.net', 357, CONVERT(DATETIME, '2008-10-15 00:00:00'))"
```

The format follows that which you learned about in Chapter 11; however, while you're learning to use SQL commands, the Query editor in Visual Studio 2008 is handy.

The connection procedures are the same as in the last example. In fact, the application has one fewer SQL command because it does not read the data—it only enters data. However, you will see a new method:

```
sqlCmd.ExecuteNonQuery();
```

When you enter data, you're doing just that; you're not querying the database. So the command is to execute a method that is not a query. The little message sent to the Label object is simply to let the user know that the operation was successful. The following shows the entire data entry code in C#:

C# BasicEntry.aspx.cs

```
using System;
using System.Data.SqlClient;
public partial class BasicEntry : System.Web.UI.Page
```

```
{
 private string dona;
 private string strInsert;
 private SqlCommand sqlCmd;
 private SqlConnection hookUp;

 protected void Page_Load(object sender, EventArgs e)
 {
 hookUp = new SqlConnection("Server=localhost\\SqlExpress;Database=VoteNow;" +
 "Integrated Security=True");
 strInsert = "INSERT INTO Supporters(LastName, FirstName, Email, Donation,
DateLastContact)VALUES('Kumar', 'Vladimir', 'pete@bmw.net', 357, CONVERT(DATETIME,
'2008-10-15 00:00:00'))";
 sqlCmd = new SqlCommand(strInsert, hookUp);
 hookUp.Open();
 sqlCmd.ExecuteNonQuery();
 hookUp.Close();
 Label1.Text = "Data Entered";
 }
}
```

Once you have saved the C# portion of the application, test it. All you will see is a little message that the data has been entered as shown in Figure 12-15.

While learning to work with ADO.NET, you should check to see whether the data that you entered are actually entered. The best way to do that is simply to use another web application. Since the first ADO.NET application reads all the data in the Supporters table, run it. You will see that Kumar made a donation of $357.00. Figure 12-16 shows what you should see.

To further check whether the data was entered correctly, you can open Visual Studio 2008 and look at the data in the Supporters table. As you can see in Figure 12-17 all of the new data have been entered correctly.

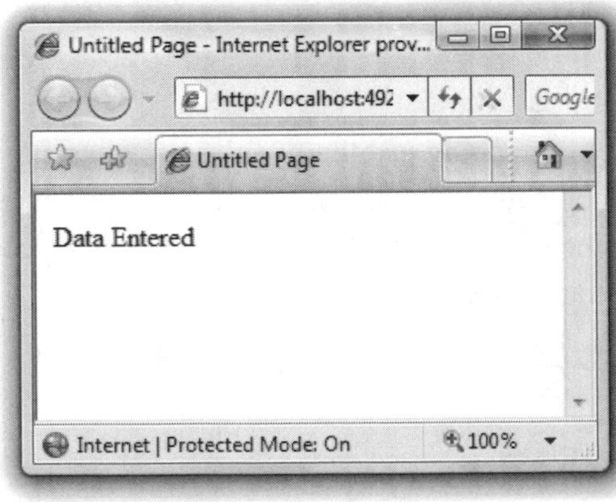

Figure 12-15 Message letting the user know that the operation was a success

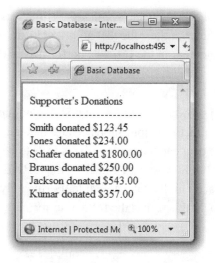

Figure 12-16   Output from data reader application shows added record.

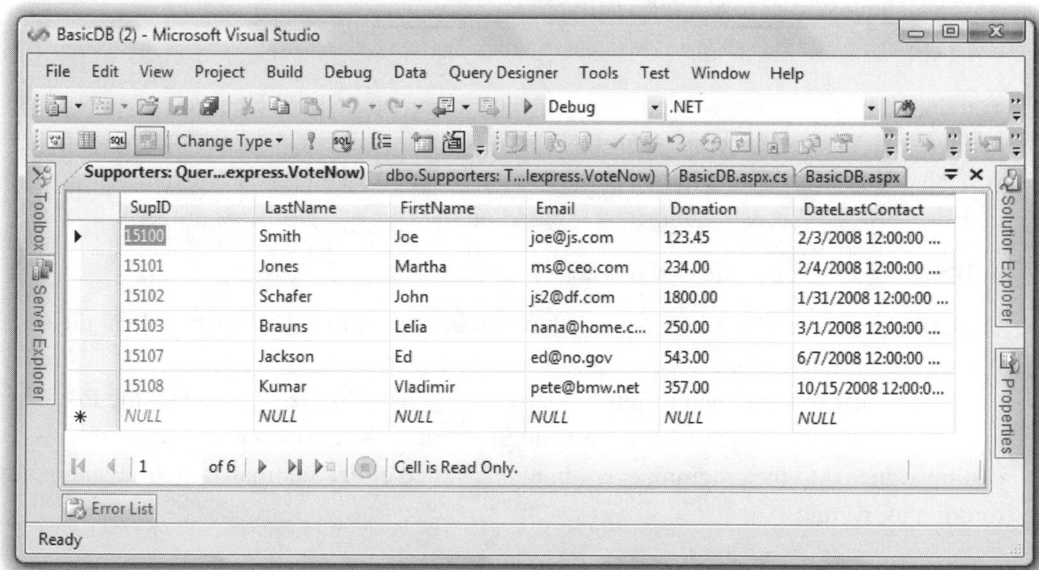

Figure 12-17   Table data showing new record

In looking at Figure 12-17, you can see that the `SupID` is automatically added even though there is no parameter in the code that adds a value to that field. Now you can rest assured that the SQL statement in the C# code performed as expected.

Dynamic Data Entry

The example application showed how to format a SQL command to insert data into a table. However, it is not a very practical application because the values are nondynamic. What you need is some way for the data entered using web controls to be passed on to the database.

The trick is to work out how to pass values from ASP.NET web controls or other sources to the values placed in the database table. Fortunately, a simple `SqlCommand` provides an easy way to do this. It has the following format where `sqlCmd` is the instance of the `SqlCommand`:

```
sqlCmd.Parameters.Add("@ValueName", Source);
```

The first parameter is the name of a placeholder that is used in the VALUE parameter, and the second is the source of the data that contains the values to be passed. For example, the following C# line of code uses the web control (a `TextBox`) named `LName.Text` as the source of data for the placeholder named `@LName`.

```
sqlCmd.Parameters.Add("@LName", LName.Text);
```

You do not have to use a web control or a value from the ASP.NET portion of your application. You can generate values using C# by using either calculated outcomes from ASP.NET controls or built-in objects such as the `DateTime` class. For example, the `currentDate` (second parameter) is based on the `DateTime.Now` property's value:

```
sqlCmd.Parameters.Add("@NowDate", currentDate);
```

Once the parameters have been added, they can be passed to the selected table in the same way as are literals.

To see how to use dynamic entry of data through an ASP.NET front-end, the following application uses the VoteNow database and Supporters table. However, instead of hard-coding values into the program, everything is handled either automatically or dynamically through user input.

ASP.NET DynamicEntry.aspx

```
<%@ Page Language="C#" AutoEventWireup="true" CodeFile="DynamicEntry.aspx.cs"
Inherits="DynamicEntry" %>
<!DOCTYPE html PUBLIC "-//W3C//DTD XHTML 1.0 Transitional//EN" "http://www
.w3.org/TR/xhtml1/DTD/xhtml1-transitional.dtd">
<html xmlns="http://www.w3.org/1999/xhtml">
```

```
<head runat="server">
<style type="text/css">
 div
 {
      font-family:Arial,Helvetica,Sans-Serif;
      color:#cc0000;
      line-height:normal;
 }
</style>
 <title>Dynamic Data Entry</title>
</head>
<body>
 <form id="form1" runat="server">
 <div>
 <h3>Please fill out the form:</h3>
 <asp:TextBox ID="LName" runat="server"/> Last Name<br />
 <asp:TextBox ID="FName" runat="server"/> First Name<br />
 <asp:TextBox ID="Em" runat="server"/> Email Address<br />
 <asp:TextBox ID="Donate" runat="server"/> Amount of Donation<p />

 <asp:Button ID="Button1" runat="server"
 Text="Send Information"
 onclick="EnterData"/><p />

 <asp:Label ID="Label1" runat="server"
 Text="Status"/>
 </div>
 </form>
</body>
</html>
```

Note the different web controls in the ASP.NET portion, and see how they are used to pass values to the table in the database in the C# part of the application.

C# DynamicEntry.aspx.cs

```
using System;
using System.Data.SqlClient;

public partial class DynamicEntry : System.Web.UI.Page
{
 private DateTime currentDate;
 private string strInsert;
 private SqlCommand sqlCmd;
 private SqlConnection hookUp;

 protected void EnterData(object sender, EventArgs e)
 {
 currentDate = DateTime.Now;
 hookUp = new SqlConnection("Server=localhost\\SqlExpress;Database=VoteNow;" +
 "Integrated Security=True");
 strInsert = "INSERT INTO Supporters(LastName, FirstName,";
```

```
strInsert +="Email, Donation, DateLastContact)VALUES";
strInsert +="(@LName,@FName,@Em,@Donate,@NowDate)";

sqlCmd = new SqlCommand(strInsert, hookUp);
sqlCmd.Parameters.Add("@LName", LName.Text);
sqlCmd.Parameters.Add("@FName", FName.Text);
sqlCmd.Parameters.Add("@Em", Em.Text);
sqlCmd.Parameters.Add("@Donate", Donate.Text);
sqlCmd.Parameters.Add("@NowDate", currentDate);

hookUp.Open();
sqlCmd.ExecuteNonQuery();
hookUp.Close();

Label1.Text = "Data has been sent";
 }
}
```

Once you get your application set up in Visual Studio 2008, test it. Figure 12-18 shows the dynamic interface where the user enters the data. Note that the form does *not* have an input `TextBox` for the date. The C# `DateTime` generated the correct date and time based on your computer's calendar and clock.

Figure 12-18 Dynamic input interface

The hand-entered dates show day, month, and year, and all the times are set to 12 A.M.

	SupID	LastName	FirstName	Email	Donation	DateLastContact
▶	15100	Smith	Joe	joe@js.com	123.45	2/3/2008 12:00:00 A...
	15101	Jones	Martha	ms@ceo.com	234.00	2/4/2008 12:00:00 A...
	15102	Schafer	John	js2@df.com	1800.00	1/31/2008 12:00:00 ...
	15103	Brauns	Lelia	nana@home.c...	250.00	3/1/2008 12:00:00 A...
	15107	Jackson	Ed	ed@no.gov	543.00	6/7/2008 12:00:00 A...
	15108	Kumar	Vladimir	pete@bmw.net	357.00	10/15/2008 12:00:0...
	15112	Smythe	Sandy	snd@beachy.c...	357.00	8/8/2008 12:00:00 A...
	15124	Romero	Jose	jose@ntech.com	871.00	2/2/2008 3:19:11 PM
*	NULL	NULL	NULL	NULL	NULL	NULL

Supporters: Quer...express.VoteNow)   DynamicEntry.aspx.cs   DynamicEntry.aspx   Start Page

◄◄ ◄ | 1 | of 8 | ► ►► ►▪ | ⬛ | Cell is Read Only.

Note: The time generated by the C# code provides precise time automatically.

Figure 12-19   Table showing the dynamic values added to the database

To see how the data look in the table, open the Supporters table in the VoteNow database. As you will see, the `DateLastContact` field has a very precise time. Instead of just showing the default 12:00:00 A.M., it shows the actual time down to the minute. Figure 12-19 shows the exact time—3:19:11 P.M.—in addition to the date.

At this point, you have most of the tools that you need to do just about anything you want with placing data into your database and reading them. However, you may want to change some values. For example, suppose one of your supporters changes her name. You'd definitely want to make the name changes. The next section shows how to change data.

Changing Data with UPDATE

You may remember from Chapter 11 that the UPDATE command is used to make changes in a field. To get an idea of how to work with UPDATE, start with the tools in Visual Studio. The following steps will guide you through the update process:

1. Open the Server Explorer, right-click on the Supporters table, and select New Query to open the Query window.

2. Then right-click on the window to open the context menu. Select Change Type | Update as shown in Figure 12-20.

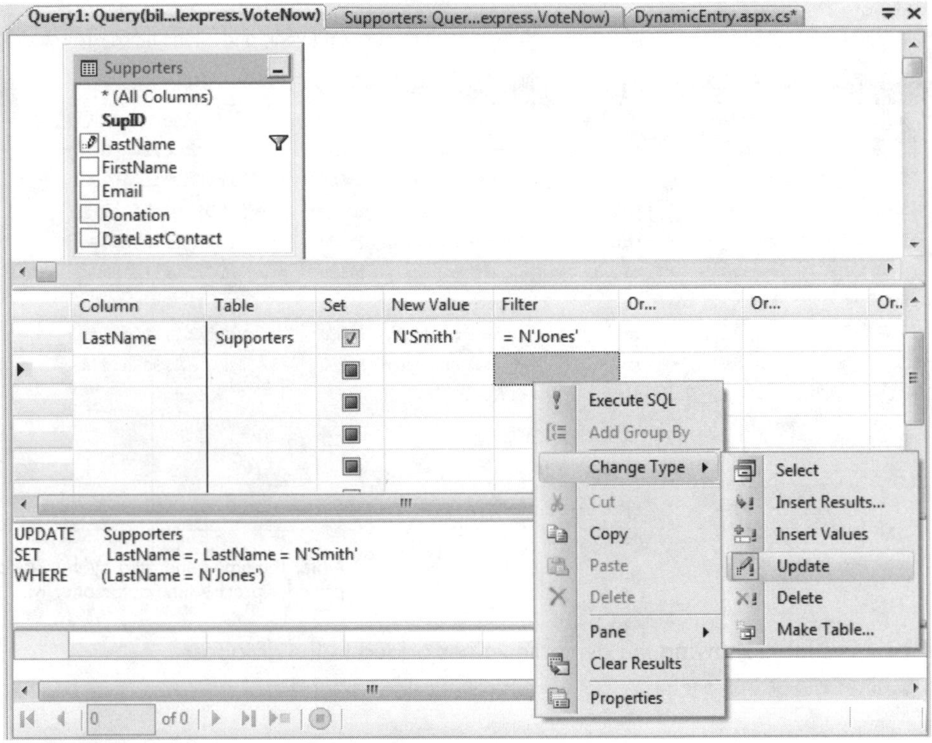

Figure 12-20 Updating a table

3. Once in the Update mode in the Query window, check the LastName column.

4. In the central panel in the New Value column, type in **Smith**. You will see "N'Smith'" as shown in Figure 12-20.

5. In the Filter column type in **Jones**. As soon as you tab out of the column, it shows "=N'Jones."

Those steps set up the UPDATE command you will need, but what does it mean? Essentially, the settings ask, "Look for the name *Jones,* and if you find it, change it to *Smith*." Because the update is taking place in a single field, the new value and filter share a common field.

To see how this works with a web site, the update application changes the last name of any name entered. It then tries to find the old last name, and if it finds it, it changes it to the new name. You will see that it uses the value parameters in the same way as did the application that is used for dynamic data entry.

ASP.NET Update.aspx

```
<%@ Page Language="C#" AutoEventWireup="true" CodeFile="Update.aspx.cs"
Inherits="Updater" %>
<!DOCTYPE html PUBLIC "-//W3C//DTD XHTML 1.0 Transitional//EN"
"http://www.w3.org/TR/xhtml1/DTD/xhtml1-transitional.dtd">
<html xmlns="http://www.w3.org/1999/xhtml">
<head runat="server">
<style type="text/css">
div
 {
      font-family:Arial, Helvetica, Sans-Serif;
      color:#005500;
      line-height:normal;
 }
 </style>
 <title>Update Last Name</title>
</head>
<body>
 <form id="form1" runat="server">
 <div>
 <h3>Enter Your Old and New Name</h3>
 Old Name:
 <asp:TextBox ID="LName" runat="server"/><p />
 New Name:
 <asp:TextBox ID="NewName" runat="server"/><p />
 <asp:Button ID="Button1" runat="server"
 onclick="UpdateData"
 Text="Make Change" /><p />
 <asp:Label ID="Label1" runat="server" Text="Status"/>
</div>
 </form>
</body>
</html>
```

The C# portion of the application is relatively short. Because only a single field is affected, less data are passed to the partial C# class. As you saw, the ASP.NET portion has only two data input controls, so the class requires less coding.

C# Update.aspx.cs

```
using System;
using System.Data.SqlClient;

public partial class Updater : System.Web.UI.Page
{
 private string strUpdate;
 private SqlCommand sqlCmd;
 private SqlConnection hookUp;
```

```
protected void UpdateData(object sender, EventArgs e)
{
hookUp = new SqlConnection("Server=localhost\\SqlExpress;Database=VoteNow;" +
"Integrated Security=True");
strUpdate = "UPDATE Supporters SET LastName=@NName WHERE (LastName=@LName)";

sqlCmd = new SqlCommand(strUpdate, hookUp);
sqlCmd.Parameters.Add("@LName", LName.Text);
sqlCmd.Parameters.Add("@NName", NewName.Text);

hookUp.Open();
sqlCmd.ExecuteNonQuery();
hookUp.Close();

Label1.Text = "Your Record is updated.";
}
}
```

Once you have completed the application, test it. Figure 12-21 shows how it looks when you run it using Visual Studio 2008. The sample Supporters table has one person with a last name of Jones, and it should change it to Smith.

Figure 12-21 Updating a field

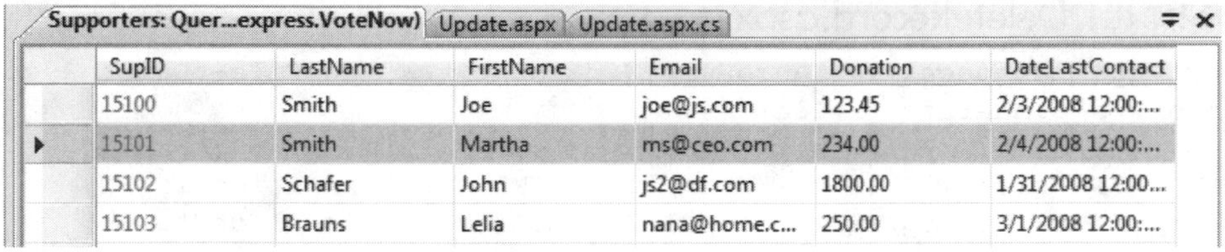

Supporters: Quer...express.VoteNow) | Update.aspx | Update.aspx.cs

SupID	LastName	FirstName	Email	Donation	DateLastContact
15100	Smith	Joe	joe@js.com	123.45	2/3/2008 12:00:...
15101	Smith	Martha	ms@ceo.com	234.00	2/4/2008 12:00:...
15102	Schafer	John	js2@df.com	1800.00	1/31/2008 12:00...
15103	Brauns	Lelia	nana@home.c...	250.00	3/1/2008 12:00:...

Figure 12-22 Data change seen in table

After you make the changes, be sure to check the data in the table to see if they have changed. Using the data in the Supporters table, you can see that the second record (row) in Figure 12-22 has changed the last name of Martha Jones to Smith.

At this point you are able to add data, change them, and read them. The only operation left to work on is the ability to remove an unwanted record.

Removing Data with DELETE

The SQL command `DELETE` is the final one examined in this chapter. Whenever destroying information, you need to be careful, and because `DELETE` launches an operation that removes records, you need to look at the consequences of its use. This doesn't mean that you should not use `DELETE`, but rather that you need to know what's going on when you do.

The first thing you need to know about `DELETE` is that whenever a field value is identified as specified for elimination, *all such records* in your database table will be removed. For example, you will see that if the name *Smith* is slated for deletion, all records with that name are removed. The first example you will see in this chapter is set up to remove all instances of a field value, but further on you will see how to filter a deletion so that only specific records are removed.

The general format of the `DELETE` command is

```
DELETE FROM TableName WHERE FieldName=Value
```

As you can see, even this simple command uses the `WHERE` filter to target all instances of a field with a given value. For example, suppose that several potential donors to a campaign never send donations. After a while you might want to delete all of them. So all you need to do is indicate in the filter that you want to purge your table of all records where the donation is Null.

To get started, the first delete application asks only for a value for a single field. If any records are found with the value, they will be removed. Start with the ASP.NET portion. It has a single `TextBox` web control for specifying the value slated for removal.

ASP.NET DeleteRecord.aspx

```
<%@ Page Language="C#" AutoEventWireup="true" CodeFile="DeleteRecord
.aspx.cs" Inherits="Killer" %>

<!DOCTYPE html PUBLIC "-//W3C//DTD XHTML 1.0 Transitional//EN"
"http://www.w3.org/TR/xhtml1/DTD/xhtml1-transitional.dtd">

<html xmlns="http://www.w3.org/1999/xhtml">
<head runat="server">
<style type="text/css">
div
 {
     font-family:Arial, Helvetica, Sans-Serif;
     color:#000099;
     line-height:normal;
 }
 </style>
 <title>Delete Record</title>
</head>
<body>
 <form id="form1" runat="server">
 <div>
 <h3>Clean Up: A Record Elimination Solution</h3>
 Last Name of Record to Delete:<br />
 <asp:TextBox ID="LName" runat="server"/><p />
 <asp:Button ID="Button1" runat="server"
 Text="Delete Record"
 onclick="DropIt"/><p />
 <asp:Label ID="Label1" runat="server" Text="Status"/>
 </div>
 </form>
</body>
</html>
```

The C# portion of the script is equally simple because the filter (WHERE) only specifies one value. That value is whatever the user types in the TextBox in the ASP.NET portion of the application.

C# DeleteRecord.aspx.cs

```
using System;
using System.Data.SqlClient;

public partial class Killer : System.Web.UI.Page
{
 private string strDelete;
 private SqlCommand sqlCmd;
 private SqlConnection hookUp;
```

```
protected void DropIt(object sender, EventArgs e)
{
hookUp = new SqlConnection("Server=localhost\\SqlExpress;Database=VoteNow;" +
"Integrated Security=True");
strDelete = "DELETE FROM Supporters WHERE LastName=@LName";

sqlCmd = new SqlCommand(strDelete, hookUp);
sqlCmd.Parameters.Add("@LName", LName.Text);

hookUp.Open();
sqlCmd.ExecuteNonQuery();
hookUp.Close();

Label1.Text = LName.Text +" was deleted.";
 }
}
```

When you test the program, you will see that whatever name you enter in the input window is repeated in a Label web control when you click the Delete Record button. If no such record exists, it still shows the message because the label simply takes the entered text and echoes it in the label output. Figure 12-23 shows what you can expect to see when you test the application.

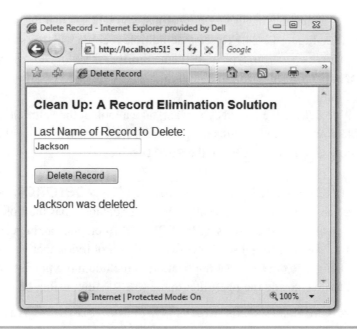

Figure 12-23 Interface for deleting database record

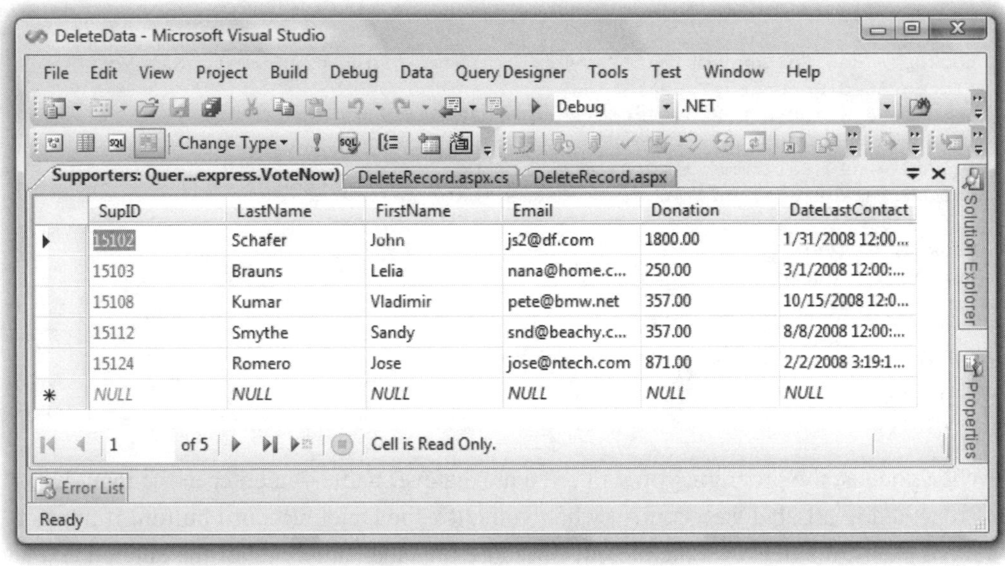

Figure 12-24 Table shows files have been deleted

If you check your table in Visual Studio 2008, you will see that the record is no longer there. (See Figure 12-24.) To see that multiple records with the same value can be removed in a single operation, type in the name **Smith**. As you recall, when the record for Martha Jones was changed to Martha Smith, the table contained two records where the last name is Smith.

Once you've deleted the records you want, take a look at the values left in the table. Figure 12-24 shows that both Smiths are gone as is Jackson. Also notice that when you eliminate records, you can get gaps in the `SupID` values.

Adding More Filters to the DELETE Operation with AND

A single filter can be a bit risky, especially when your database has multiple records that match values on a single field. By using the SQL AND filter, you can increase the precision of your record removal and not send records to silicon oblivion that you want to keep.

Making changes to the DELETE application to include more precise criteria is easy. All you need to do is to add the AND filter to the WHERE filter using the following format:

```
DELETE FROM TableName WHERE Field1=@Val1 AND Field2=@Val2
```

You can add as many AND filters as you want. The more filters in the SQL statements, the more precise the selection for deletion. This next web site is a variation on the previous DELETE example. It adds another TextBox and another field to be considered before deleting a record. You can create the following application by editing the first DELETE example:

ASP.NET FilterWipe.aspx

```
<%@ Page Language="C#" AutoEventWireup="true" CodeFile="FilterWipe
.aspx.cs" Inherits="Wipe" %>

<!DOCTYPE html PUBLIC "-//W3C//DTD XHTML 1.0 Transitional//EN"
"http://www.w3.org/TR/xhtml1/DTD/xhtml1-transitional.dtd">

<html xmlns="http://www.w3.org/1999/xhtml">
<head id="Head1" runat="server">
<style type="text/css">
div
 {
     font-family:Arial, Helvetica, Sans-Serif;
     color:Maroon;
     line-height:normal;
 }
 </style>
 <title>Multiple Filtered Delete Record</title>
</head>
<body>
 <form id="form1" runat="server">
 <div>
 <h3>Precise Delete: A Record Smart Bomb</h3>
 Last Name of Record to Delete:<br />
 <asp:TextBox ID="LName" runat="server"/><p />
 First Name of Record to Delete:<br />
 <asp:TextBox ID="FName" runat="server"/><p />
 <asp:Button ID="Button1" runat="server"
 Text="Wipe Out Record"
 onclick="WipeOut"/><p />
 <asp:Label ID="Label1" runat="server" Text="Status"/>
 </div>
 </form>
</body>
</html>
```

The C# portion of the application is very similar to the first delete code. Different class and event names are included to help differentiate the two. The key difference is the addition of the AND filter and second web control reference.

C# FilterWipe.aspx.cs

```
using System;
using System.Data.SqlClient;

public partial class Wipe : System.Web.UI.Page
{
 private string strDelete;
 private SqlCommand sqlCmd;
 private SqlConnection hookUp;

 protected void WipeOut(object sender, EventArgs e)
 {
 hookUp = new SqlConnection("Server=localhost\\SqlExpress;Database=VoteNow;" +
 "Integrated Security=True");
 strDelete = "DELETE FROM Supporters WHERE LastName=@LName AND
FirstName=@FName";

 sqlCmd = new SqlCommand(strDelete, hookUp);
 sqlCmd.Parameters.Add("@LName", LName.Text);
 sqlCmd.Parameters.Add("@FName", FName.Text);
 hookUp.Open();
 sqlCmd.ExecuteNonQuery();
 hookUp.Close();

 Label1.Text = FName.Text +" "+ LName.Text + " has left the table.";
 }
}
```

To test this application, you will need to add two records with the last name *Schafer*. So before testing it, add the necessary records. Once the records have been added, test the application and see what happens when you remove the record that matches the new filters. Figure 12-25 shows how the new interface looks when executed.

Figure 12-26 shows the Supporters table *before* the attempt was made to remove the record, and Figure 12-27 shows the table *after* it was tested. Notice that only *one* of the two Schafer records was removed by the application.

From this second example, you can see that even though a single record is removed, you can do so by using more than a single field as a filter control. Depending on what you need to delete, you can use as many or few fields as you need for a reference. Using C# as a control agent, you are able to make flexible and useful applications for a wide range of options for cleaning up your database table.

Figure 12-25   Entering values for two fields for DELETE operation

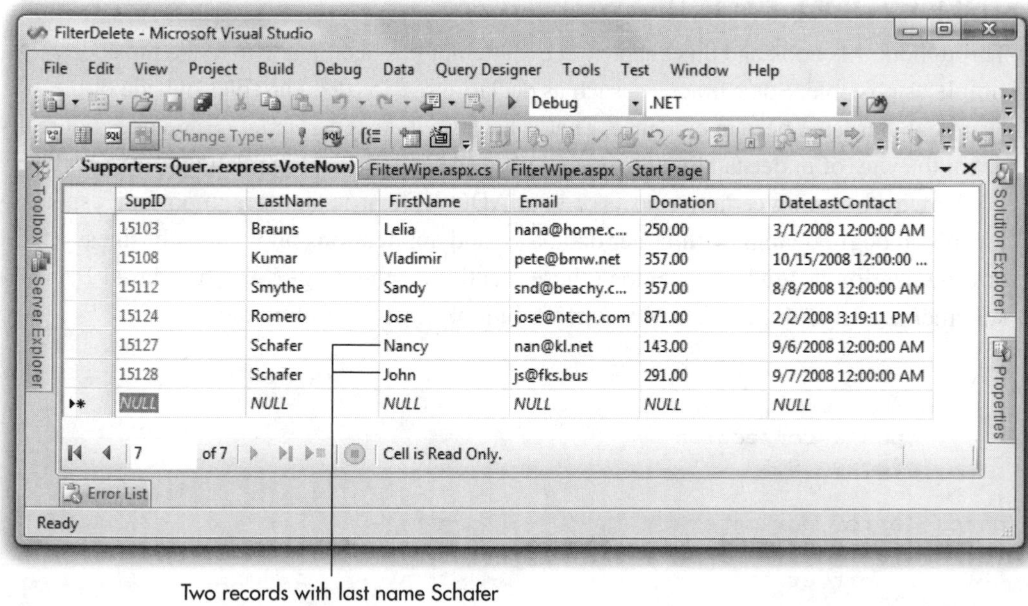

Two records with last name Schafer

Figure 12-26   Table before filter delete

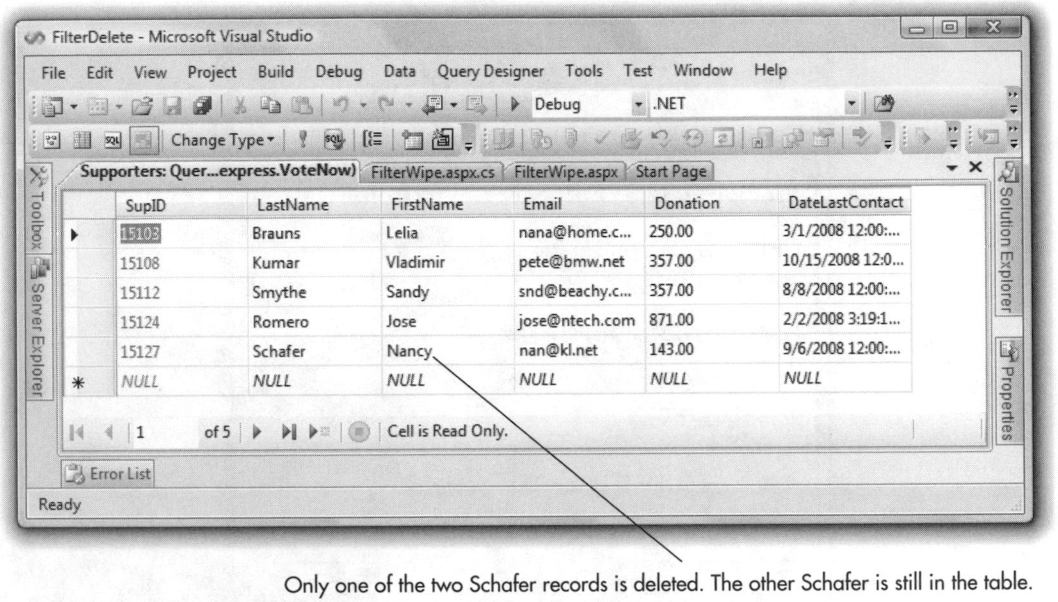

Only one of the two Schafer records is deleted. The other Schafer is still in the table.

Figure 12-27 Table after filter delete

Using Good Practices

Throughout this book and this chapter, every attempt has been made to make the code as simple as possible. Some practices such as declaring `private` variables outside of the event handler have been in evidence. That is because it is a good practice and does not really get in the way of understanding the other code, especially that code relating to ADO.NET.

However, testing certain aspects of your ADO.NET procedures is important, especially when you begin dealing with larger databases and applications on which a business or organization depends. Key among these practices is the `try-catch-finally` statement. Outlined, the ADO.NET operation looks like the following:

```
try
{
      open a connection
      process SQL
}
catch (error parameter)
{
      report error
}
finally
```

```
{
     close the connection
}
```

The `try-catch-finally` statement is meant to catch problems before they become a big problem or even corrupt data in your database tables. However, another way to look at it is as a reminder of what you need to do with an ADO.NET application:

- Open your connection
- Handle errors
- Close your connection

Looking at it that way, it's a reminder of what you have to do and an aid to learning rather than an added complexity.

To see how this works and what it looks like in an application, the BasicDB application has been rewritten to include the `try-catch-finally` statement. (You can find the original application in the section "Building a Web Site for Database Retrieval" near the beginning of the chapter.) As you will see, everything is the same except that the `try-catch-finally` statement has been added in the C# code and an additional Label web control has been added to the ASP.NET portion.

ASP.NET TryFirst.aspx

```
<%@ Page Language="C#" AutoEventWireup="true" CodeFile="TryFirst.aspx
.cs" Inherits="Catcher" %>

<!DOCTYPE html PUBLIC "-//W3C//DTD XHTML 1.0 Transitional//EN"
"http://www.w3.org/TR/xhtml1/DTD/xhtml1-transitional.dtd">

<html xmlns="http://www.w3.org/1999/xhtml">
<head runat="server">
 <title>Good Practice</title>
</head>
<body>
 <form id="form1" runat="server">
 <div>
 <asp:Label ID="DataOutput" runat="server" Text="Data"/><p />
 <asp:Label ID="ErrorCatcher" runat="server" Text="Error"/>
 </div>
 </form>
</body>
</html>
```

In the C# portion you will see how the `try-catch-finally` statement is woven into the original code. The `try` segment opens the connection and executes the code. The `catch` segment detects errors and reports them, and the `finally` segment closes everything. The keywords in the `try-catch-finally` statement have been placed in bold.

C# TryFirst.aspx.cs

```csharp
using System;
using System.Data.SqlClient;

public partial class Catcher : System.Web.UI.Page
{
 private bool catchMe;
 private string dona;
 private string ln;
 private SqlCommand sqlCmd;
 private SqlConnection hookUp;
 private SqlDataReader reader;

 protected void Page_Load(object sender, EventArgs e)
 {
 catchMe = false;
 DataOutput.Text = "Supporter's Donations" + "<br/>";
 DataOutput.Text += "--------------------------" + "<br/>";
 hookUp = new SqlConnection("Server=localhost\\SqlExpress;Database=VoteNow;" +
 "Integrated Security=True");
 sqlCmd = new SqlCommand("SELECT LastName, Donation FROM Supporters", hookUp);
 try
 {
 hookUp.Open();
 reader = sqlCmd.ExecuteReader();
 while (reader.Read())
 {
 dona = Convert.ToString(reader["Donation"]);
 ln = Convert.ToString(reader["LastName"]);

 DataOutput.Text += ln + " donated $" + dona + "<br/>";
 }
 }
 catch (Exception error)
 {
 catchMe = true;
 ErrorCatcher.Text = error.Message;
 }
 finally
 {
 if (!catchMe)
 {
 ErrorCatcher.Text = "No errors found";
 }
 reader.Close();
 hookUp.Close();
 }
 }
}
```

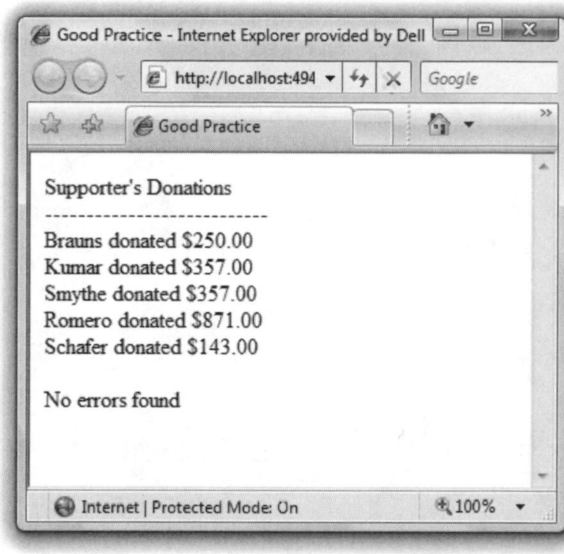

Figure 12-28   Error reporting

Other than adding a second label for reporting errors, the ASP.NET portion of the application is the same as the original BasicDB application. When everything is working right, you'll see the output shown in Figure 12-28.

Had an error occurred, the nature of the error would be reported with a description of the error following the Label that indicates an error has been found.

Summary

Now that you can deal with the fundamentals of ADO.NET, you can use the previous web controls, such as validation, to prevent the user from making errors with data input. Likewise, you can use C# to create more elaborate data handling, and in subsequent chapters you'll find valuable ASP.NET tools such as data binding to make data output more manageable and easier to format.

From this point on, most of the materials are some kind of enhancement of using ADO.NET and data stored in database tables. You will find other important features of the ASP.NET structure, but when all is said and done, without the capacity to read, write, and change data, none of these other structures are worth very much. So you may find yourself returning to this chapter for the basics of working with data.

Chapter 13

Data Binding

Key Skills & Concepts

- Data binding
- More options for data display
  - What is data binding?
  - Basic binding
  - Binding data to web controls
    - Binding to a Label
    - Binding with GridView control
    - Binding to a ListView
  - Binding to a table
    - Using the Repeater control
    - Headers and footers
    - Alternating styles
  - ListView binding

Data are as good as their accessibility. You can have all the great data stored in a table in your database, but if the user is confused or the data narrowly constricted in their display, the data might as well stay in the database. Data binding connects data sources with web controls, making it very easy to place your data into a clear presentation. In this chapter you will see how to connect data to everything from Labels to Lists and many controls in between.

What Is Data Binding?

Data binding is one of those terms that states exactly what it is. It is a process of binding data to an ASP.NET 3.5 control. The data source that makes the most sense to bind is the data from a table in a database, but any kind of data can be bound using data binding. For example, you can bind values from items in an array or from a simple variable. Likewise, you can usefully bind data from a relational database or a single table.

On the ASP.NET side of the equation, the binding tag is simplicity itself. The tag is assigned to a control property. It has the following format:

```
<%# dataSource %>
```

The data source can be as simple as a function called in the C# portion of the application, or it may use a special ASP.NET function. For example, further on in the chapter, you will see the following line that provides the source as one of the fields in a database table:

```
<%#DataBinder.Eval(Container.DataItem,"FieldName")%>
```

It is part of a larger data access application that uses a set of data binding tags employed with a Repeater control and multiple fields. If you prefer, you can use the shorter version that does not show the fuller object path:

```
<%# Eval("FieldName")%>
```

We'll start off using the longer version to provide a feel for the larger context and then use the shorter version when you're accustomed to the longer version. However, all of the data binding still comes back to the simple data source tag and its placement within the web controls.

Basic Binding

To get started using a single simple data source, this section walks through a basic application that calls a C# method that returns a string. The data source is bound to a Label web control, and text surrounding the web control helps distinguish which is bound and which is not. Using CSS styling statements in the C# code, the bound data are distinguished by boldface green text.

Try This Adding Data Binding

The following steps show how to create this first step into data binding:

1. Open a new Web Site with the name **DatBind**.

2. Open the ASP.NET portion of the application, and drag a Label web control to the editor.

3. Name the ID **BindMe** and set the text property to

   ```
   text=<%# boundMessage() %>
   ```

4. The following shows the entire ASP.NET code:

(continued)

ASP.NET DatBind.aspx

```
<%@ Page Language="C#" AutoEventWireup="true" CodeFile="DatBind.aspx.cs"
Inherits="Binder" %>
<!DOCTYPE html PUBLIC "-//W3C//DTD XHTML 1.0 Transitional//EN"
"http://www.w3.org/TR/xhtml1/DTD/xhtml1-transitional.dtd">
<html xmlns="http://www.w3.org/1999/xhtml">
<head runat="server">
    <title>Data Binder</title>
</head>
<body>
    <form id="form1" runat="server">
    <div>
    This text is not in a bind:<br />
      <asp:label
      ID="BindMe"
       text=<%# boundMessage() %>
       runat="server"/>
       <br />This text is back out of the binding.
    </div>
    </form>
</body>
</html>
```

5. Open the C# portion of the application. Using the `Page_Load()` event handler, you will need to enter the target of the bound web control's data source. For this simple example, a single method named `boundMessage()` returns a string. Also, to distinguish the bound from nonbound text, the BindMe web control instance is styled to generate boldface green text.

6. After entering the styling code, enter the important DataBind control. Figure 13-1 shows IntelliSense providing the DataBind option.

7. The following shows the entire C# code to finish up the application:

C# DatBind.aspx.cs

```
using System;

public partial class Binder : System.Web.UI.Page
{
    private string msg;

    protected void Page_Load(object sender, EventArgs e)
    {
        msg="This message is presented as a data binding example.<br>";
        msg+="Thanks for your attention.";
        BindMe.Style["color"] = "#00cc00";
        BindMe.Style["font-weight"] = "bold";
```

```
protected void Page_Load(object sender, EventArgs e)
{
    msg="This message is presented as a data binding example.<br> Thanks for your attention.";
    BindMe.
}
```

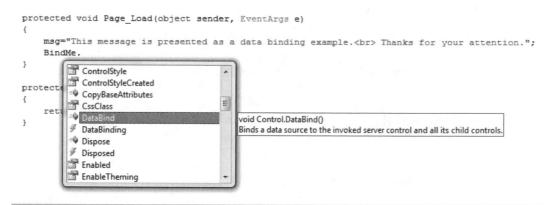

```
protect
{
    retu
}
```

```
void Control.DataBind()
Binds a data source to the invoked server control and all its child controls.
```

Figure 13-1   Adding DataBind to the Label web control

```
        BindMe.DataBind();
    }

    protected string boundMessage()
    {
        return msg;
    }
}
```

When you test the application, you should see both the text entered in the ASP.NET portion essentially as HTML text and the boldface green text entered using data binding as shown in Figure 13-2.

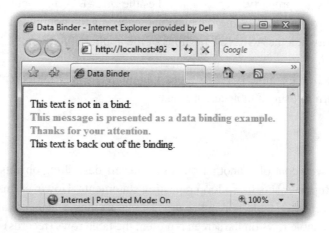

Figure 13-2   Output shows both bound and nonbound data

```csharp
C#
    protected void Page_Load(object sender, EventArgs e)
    {
        msg="This message is presented as a data binding example.<br>"
        msg+="Thanks for your attention.";
        BindMe.Style["color"] = "#00cc00";
        BindMe.Style["font-weight"] = "bold";
        BindMe.DataBind();
    }

    protected string boundMessage()
    {
        return msg;
    }
}
------------------------------------------
ASP.NET
<asp:label
  ID="BindMe"
  text=<%# boundMessage() %>
  runat="server"/>
```

Figure 13-3 C# and ASP.NET relations in establishing data binding

The Label's ID property, BindMe, invokes the DataBind() method to establish the binding. The Text property of the Label actually accepts the bound data. To better see the relationship between the ASP.NET portions of the application, Figure 13-3 shows how the two are related.

While this first example is very simple, it contains the key ingredients to data binding. Next, we'll turn to using a table and a repeater.

Repeater

The Repeater web control is another one of those self-describing objects. Used with data binding, the Repeater acts like a loop repeating statements. However, instead of repeating statements, it repeats a table-making routine so that as long as data are available, it repeats table rows. The table rows on the screen represent the table rows (records) in a table database.

This next example moves into the realm of reading tables from a database rather than data from any other source. In other words, we will be looking at binding ADO.NET database tables to ASP.NET controls. When dealing with ADO.NET data, you will quickly find that your best ASP.NET method is the `DataBinder.Eval()` method. It is combined with a `Container.DataItem` parameter to extract and bind a table field (column). The ASP.NET expression

```
<%#DataBinder.Eval(Container.DataItem,"FieldName")%>
```

makes identifying the data source very easy. Each field in the table has an identifier, and the data binding requires only that you know the name of the field. So rather than needing complex extraction code, the `DataBinder.Eval()` method for identifying a data source makes binding to a database table's data quite simple.

Basic Templates

This next example shows how to create a simple yet very clear and attractive table. To provide a row and column header, the application uses a `<HeaderTemplate>` that provides each column with a label using the table's column names. You do not have to use the column names supplied in the table, but can use any header name you want. In addition to a `<HeaderTemplate>`, you will also be using an `<ItemTemplate>` tag used in repeating rows for each record. The Repeater control is smart enough to know that the `<HeaderTemplate>` only expects one instance, while the `<ItemTemplate>` expects to be repeated until the table is exhausted.

Try This   Repeating a Table

The following steps show how to create data binding using a Repeater object:

1. Open a new Web Site with the name **TableRepeater**.

2. Open the ASP.NET portion of the application, and open the Data menu in the Toolbox.

3. Drag a Repeater web control to the editor in the `<div>` container.

4. Begin to type **<H** and IntelliSense provides you with the `<HeaderTemplate>` option to complete the tag as shown in Figure 13-4.

5. The header template expects some way of identifying the columns of data. The general format is the following:

```
<tr bgcolor=colorName>
    <th>Field#1</th>
    <th> Field#2</th>
    <th>etc</th>
</tr>
```

(continued)

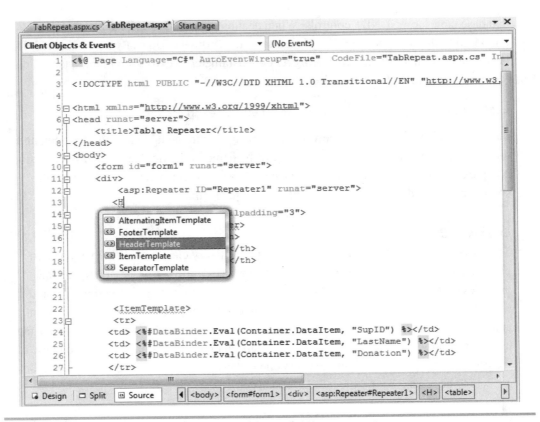

Figure 13-4 IntelliSense showing the HeaderTemplate option

Generally, the row for the header has a different background color to distinguish it from a record.

6. Following the header template is an item template. It is similar to the header template, except when using data binding, you will be repeating the template for every record. Also, in the item template, you must place the source data tags. You will see the following format:

```
<tr>
        <td> <%#DataBinder.Eval(Container.DataItem,"Field#1") %></td>
        <td> <%#DataBinder.Eval(Container.DataItem,"Field#2") %></td>
        <td> <%#DataBinder.Eval(Container.DataItem,"etc.") %></td>
</tr>
```

A key difference between the header and item templates is that in the data biding statements, you must use the actual names of the fields. The table tags, though, are the same.

7. The last tag that goes inside the Repeater control is the footer template. In this particular case, no table tags are included other than one that closes the table container. If you want a footer that will display more information, you can include it. Otherwise all you need is the following:

```
<FooterTemplate>
      </table>
</FooterTemplate>
```

One element often placed in a footer template is the date and time. Others use the footer for the location of a copyright notice.

The following listing shows the entire ASP.NET portion of the application:

ASP.NET TabRepeat.aspx

```
<%@ Page Language="C#" AutoEventWireup="true" CodeFile="TabRepeat
.aspx.cs" Inherits="TabRepeat" %>
<!DOCTYPE html PUBLIC "-//W3C//DTD XHTML 1.0 Transitional//EN"
"http://www.w3.org/TR/xhtml1/DTD/xhtml1-transitional.dtd">
<html xmlns="http://www.w3.org/1999/xhtml">
<head runat="server">
    <title>Table Repeater</title>
</head>
<body>
    <form id="form1" runat="server">
    <div>
        <asp:Repeater ID="Repeater1" runat="server">
      <HeaderTemplate>
      <table border="0" cellpadding="3">
          <tr bgcolor=silver>
              <th>SupID</th>
              <th>LastName</th>
              <th>Donation</th>
          </tr>
      </HeaderTemplate>

      <ItemTemplate>
      <tr>
<td> <%#DataBinder.Eval(Container.DataItem, "SupID") %></td>
<td> <%#DataBinder.Eval(Container.DataItem, "LastName") %></td>
<td> <%#DataBinder.Eval(Container.DataItem, "Donation") %></td>
      </tr>
      </ItemTemplate>

      <FooterTemplate>
        </table>
      </FooterTemplate>
```

(continued)

```
        </asp:Repeater>
      </div>
      </form>
  </body>
  </html>
```

Once you have finished entering the ASP.NET code, you are all set to enter the C# code and make the connection between the application and the database. You will find that the C# portion of the application looks very similar to the code you saw in Chapter 12 where ADO.NET was introduced, except that you will be using data binding.

8. Enter the connection information as you would for an application using ADO.NET except that the `SqlDataReader` is the data source for the binding operation from the data in the database table. Again, in setting this up in your code, you will get assistance from IntelliSense as shown in Figure 13-5.

You can finish up the application using the code in the following listing:

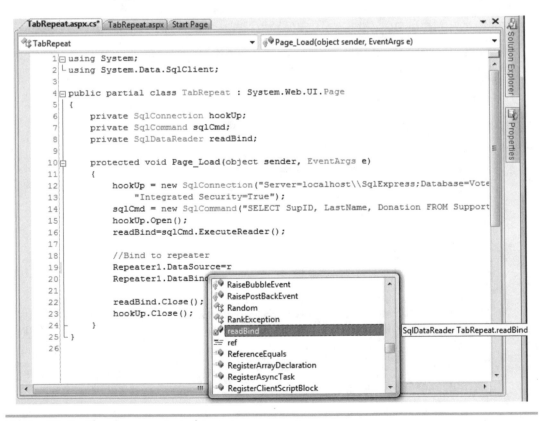

```
TabRepeat.aspx.cs*  TabRepeat.aspx  Start Page

TabRepeat                              Page_Load(object sender, EventArgs e)

 1  using System;
 2  using System.Data.SqlClient;
 3
 4  public partial class TabRepeat : System.Web.UI.Page
 5  {
 6      private SqlConnection hookUp;
 7      private SqlCommand sqlCmd;
 8      private SqlDataReader readBind;
 9
10      protected void Page_Load(object sender, EventArgs e)
11      {
12          hookUp = new SqlConnection("Server=localhost\\SqlExpress;Database=Vote
13              "Integrated Security=True");
14          sqlCmd = new SqlCommand("SELECT SupID, LastName, Donation FROM Support
15          hookUp.Open();
16          readBind=sqlCmd.ExecuteReader();
17
18          //Bind to repeater
19          Repeater1.DataSource=r
20          Repeater1.DataBind
21                                   RaiseBubbleEvent
22          readBind.Close();        RaisePostBackEvent
23          hookUp.Close();          Random
24      }                            RankException
25  }                                readBind            SqlDataReader TabRepeat.readBind
26                                   ref
                                     ReferenceEquals
                                     RegisterArrayDeclaration
                                     RegisterAsyncTask
                                     RegisterClientScriptBlock
```

Figure 13-5 The data source is the `SqlDataReader`

C# TabRepeat.aspx.cs

```
using System;
using System.Data.SqlClient;

public partial class TabRepeat : System.Web.UI.Page
{
    private SqlConnection hookUp;
    private SqlCommand sqlCmd;
    private SqlDataReader readBind;
    protected void Page_Load(object sender, EventArgs e)
    {
        hookUp =
new SqlConnection("Server=localhost\\SqlExpress;Database=VoteNow;" +
            "Integrated Security=True");
        sqlCmd = new SqlCommand("SELECT SupID, LastName, Donation FROM
Supporters", hookUp);
        hookUp.Open();
        readBind=sqlCmd.ExecuteReader();
//Bind to repeater
        Repeater1.DataSource = readBind;
        Repeater1.DataBind();
        readBind.Close();
        hookUp.Close();
    }
}
```

Once you're finished, go ahead and test it. Figure 13-6 shows what you should see.

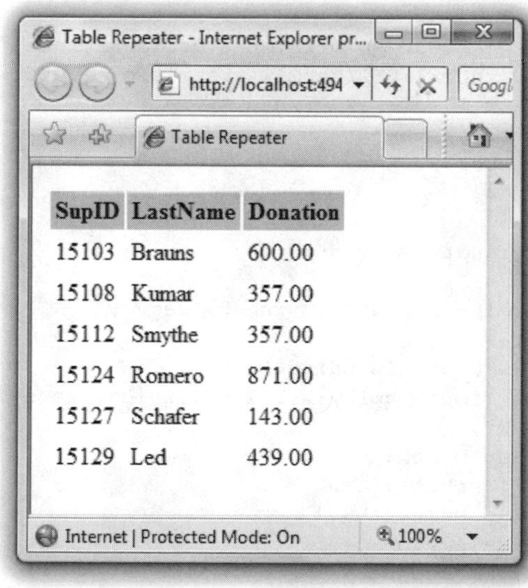

Figure 13-6   Data from table displayed in Repeater web control

Alternating Templates

Tables with a larger number of records can be difficult to read and even more difficult to find what you want easily. One way to make crisp distinctions between records is to use the `<AlternatingItemTemplate>` tag. When using the tag, you can add one or more alternate distinctive styles to your table. To see how the alternating templates work, the previous example is updated to include all of the sample table fields and a new header.

TIP

The great information designer Edward Tufte cautions against using high contrasts between data so as not to excite the background materials and make the data more difficult to read. In using alternate templates in a table, try to use what Tufte calls *minimum effective differences*. These are differences that distinguish objects but without blinding the user with high contrasts. The headers require a higher degree of contrast, but they only appear once and can stand out against the repetitions of the alternating rows of data. Note that the alternating value of the table row is FFFF66. This alternates with FFFFFF, the default white background color. As you can see, the difference is subtle but effective.

The following two listings show both the ASP.NET and C# portions of the coding:

ASP.NET Alternate.aspx

```
<%@ Page Language="C#" AutoEventWireup="true" CodeFile="Alternate.aspx.cs"
Inherits="AltRepeat" %>
<!DOCTYPE html PUBLIC "-//W3C//DTD XHTML 1.0 Transitional//EN"
"http://www.w3.org/TR/xhtml1/DTD/xhtml1-transitional.dtd">
<html xmlns="http://www.w3.org/1999/xhtml">
<head id="Head1" runat="server">
    <title>Table Repeater</title>
</head>
<body>
    <form id="form1" runat="server">
    <div>
        <asp:Repeater ID="Repeater1" runat="server">
        <HeaderTemplate>
        <table border="0" cellpadding="3">
            <tr style="font-family:Arial,Helvetical,sans-serif;color:
White;background:black">
                <th>SupID</th>
                <th>FirstName</th>
                <th>LastName</th>
                <th>Email</th>
                <th>Donation</th>
                <th>Last Contact</th>
            </tr>
        </HeaderTemplate>
```

```
    <ItemTemplate>
     <tr>
    <td> <%#DataBinder.Eval(Container.DataItem, "SupID") %></td>
    <td> <%#DataBinder.Eval(Container.DataItem, "FirstName") %></td>
    <td> <%#DataBinder.Eval(Container.DataItem, "LastName") %></td>
    <td> <%#DataBinder.Eval(Container.DataItem, "Email") %></td>
    <td> <%#DataBinder.Eval(Container.DataItem, "Donation") %></td>
    <td> <%#DataBinder.Eval(Container.DataItem, "DateLastContact") %></td>
     </tr>
     </ItemTemplate>

     <AlternatingItemTemplate>
     <tr bgcolor="#FFFF66">
    <td> <%#DataBinder.Eval(Container.DataItem, "SupID") %></td>
    <td> <%#DataBinder.Eval(Container.DataItem, "FirstName") %></td>
    <td> <%#DataBinder.Eval(Container.DataItem, "LastName") %></td>
    <td> <%#DataBinder.Eval(Container.DataItem, "Email") %></td>
    <td> <%#DataBinder.Eval(Container.DataItem, "Donation") %></td>
    <td> <%#DataBinder.Eval(Container.DataItem, "DateLastContact") %></td>
     </tr>
     </AlternatingItemTemplate>


     <FooterTemplate>
       </table>
      </FooterTemplate>
      </asp:Repeater>
    </div>
    </form>
  </body>
  </html>
```

C# Alternate.aspx.cs

```csharp
using System;
using System.Data.SqlClient;

public partial class AltRepeat : System.Web.UI.Page
{
    private SqlConnection hookUp;
    private SqlCommand sqlCmd;
    private SqlDataReader readBind;

    protected void Page_Load(object sender, EventArgs e)
    {
        hookUp = new SqlConnection("Server=localhost\\SqlExpress;Database=VoteNow;" +
            "Integrated Security=True");
        sqlCmd = new SqlCommand("SELECT * FROM Supporters", hookUp);
        hookUp.Open();
        readBind = sqlCmd.ExecuteReader();
```

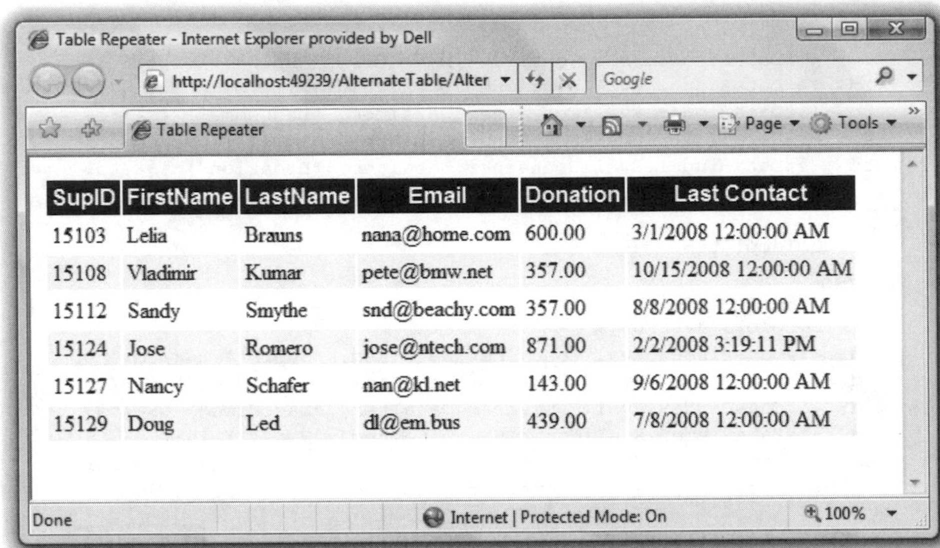
Table Repeater - Internet Explorer provided by Dell
http://localhost:49239/AlternateTable/Alter
Table Repeater
SupID FirstName LastName Email Donation Last Contact
15103 Lelia Brauns nana@home.com 600.00 3/1/2008 12:00:00 AM
15108 Vladimir Kumar pete@bmw.net 357.00 10/15/2008 12:00:00 AM
15112 Sandy Smythe snd@beachy.com 357.00 8/8/2008 12:00:00 AM
15124 Jose Romero jose@ntech.com 871.00 2/2/2008 3:19:11 PM
15127 Nancy Schafer nan@kl.net 143.00 9/6/2008 12:00:00 AM
15129 Doug Led dl@em.bus 439.00 7/8/2008 12:00:00 AM
Done
Internet | Protected Mode: On
100%

Figure 13-7 Alternating shading in rows helps differentiate records.

```
        //Bind to repeater
        Repeater1.DataSource = readBind;
        Repeater1.DataBind();
        readBind.Close();
        hookUp.Close();
    }
}
```

Figure 13-7 shows the alternating rows and the very different header. You do not want the alternating differences as sharply differentiated as the header. The header appears only once, so it does not generate a jarring contrast that repeats itself within the rows of data.

Experiment with alternating row shading by changing the value of the alternating row color. The base color does not need to be white, so you might also want to experiment with different colors for each `<ItemTemplate>` tag as well.

DataList

The DataList control is a lot like the Repeater control insofar as binding data is concerned. However, using a DataList control is when you need a single-column list. For example, suppose you're setting up a networking party with donors to a political campaign. Each donor will wear a nametag with his or her e-mail address so that the participants can easily exchange e-mail contact. The format for each nametag should look like the following:

Donor's Name: Mary Smith

Email: ms@msmith.com

Now everyone can see that the other people are fellow donors and can see their e-mail address for future contact.

You will find using the DataList control very simple compared with the Repeater in conjunction with HTML tables. Because you only have a single column, all of your formatting can be done without worry about multiple columns or any table tags. For example, you can format the text within the `<ItemTemplate>` container pretty much as you would HTML:

```
<ItemTemplate>
  <strong> Field Description:</strong>
  <%#Eval("FieldName")%>
</ItemTemplate>
```

Stacked up in a single column, each record needs to be separated. Using the `<SeparatorTemplate>`, you can make sure that the viewer can tell where one record begins and the previous one ends. Depending on what you're doing with your data, your separator can just add vertical space or provide instructions. For example, with the goal of making nametags, you might want to put in a "Cut Here" dashed line between records.

Try This Add a DataList

The steps for creating a DataList are pretty simple:

1. Open a new Web Site and save it as **DataList**.

2. In the ASP.NET portion of the application, drag a DataList control from the Data menu of the Toolbox, and place it in the `<div>` container.

3. Once you have the DataList control set up, enter the code in the following listing:

ASP.NET DataList.aspx

```
<%@ Page Language="C#" AutoEventWireup="true"  CodeFile="DataList
.aspx.cs" Inherits="DataList" %>
<!DOCTYPE html PUBLIC "-//W3C//DTD XHTML 1.0 Transitional//EN"
"http://www.w3.org/TR/xhtml1/DTD/xhtml1-transitional.dtd">
<html xmlns="http://www.w3.org/1999/xhtml">
```

(continued)

```
<head id="Head1" runat="server">
    <title>DataList Control</title>
</head>
<body>
    <form id="form1" runat="server">
    <div>
        <asp:DataList ID="DataList1" runat="server">
                <ItemTemplate>
                        <strong> Donor's Name:</strong>
                        <%#Eval("FirstName")%> 
                        <%#Eval("LastName") %><br />
                        <strong>Email:</strong>
                        <%#Eval("Email") %>
                </ItemTemplate>

                <SeparatorTemplate>
                        <h6>---------------------------Cut Here</h6>
                        <p/>
                </SeparatorTemplate>
        </asp:DataList>
    </div>
    </form>
</body>
</html>
```

Once you've entered the ASP.NET portion of the code, open the C# window. You can use most of the C# code for the previous two examples making minor but important changes. The following shows the complete C# listing:

C# DataList.aspx.cs

```
using System;
using System.Data.SqlClient;

public partial class DataList : System.Web.UI.Page
{
    private SqlConnection hookUp;
    private SqlCommand sqlCmd;
    private SqlDataReader readBind;

    protected void Page_Load(object sender, EventArgs e)
    {
        hookUp = new SqlConnection("Server=localhost\\SqlExpress;
Database=VoteNow;" +
            "Integrated Security=True");
        sqlCmd = new SqlCommand("SELECT FirstName, LastName, Email
FROM Supporters", hookUp);
        hookUp.Open();
```

```
        readBind = sqlCmd.ExecuteReader();
        //Bind to repeater
        DataList1.DataSource = readBind;
        DataList1.DataBind();
        readBind.Close();
        hookUp.Close();
    }
}
```

As you will see, the code for the DataList is much less than for the previous examples. You are limited to one column, but within that single column you can format the code any way you want. As you can see from Figure 13-8, the records are clearly separated, and when printed on nametag paper, could easily be used for the desired purpose.

Figure 13-8   DataList output for nametags

Whether to use the DataList control or some other control, such as the Repeater, wholly depends on what you need to do with the data.

DataGrid Made Easy

If you're in a big hurry and have to get a table produced *yesterday,* you'll like this next method of data binding. Use the following steps:

1. Open a new Web Site to be saved as **EZdataGrid**.

2. In the ASP.NET editor, open the Server Explorer. Drag a table of your choice from the Server Explorer to the `<div>` container as shown in Figure 13-9.

3. Save the file and test it by pressing CTRL-F5. You should see the table in Figure 13-10.

As you can see in Figure 13-10, the data are neatly laid out in rows and columns with a boldface header. You need not add a single line of C# code. In fact, you don't even have to open the C# portion of the application at all. It's completely done.

If you're wondering how this can be accomplished in ASP.NET with no call to the SQL table using C# statements, the answer lies in ASP.NET tags that automatically

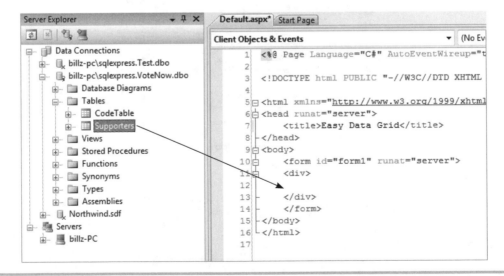

Figure 13-9   Drag table from Server Explorer to ASP.NET editor

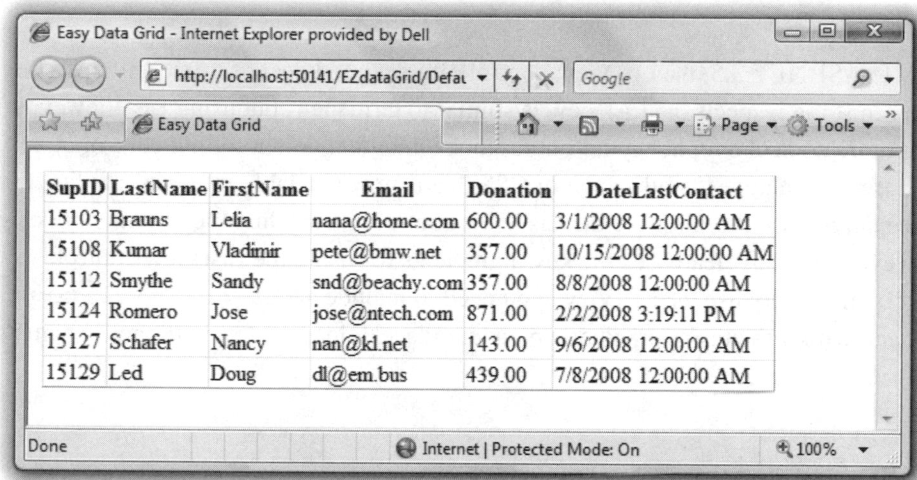

Figure 13-10 Data shown in the DataGrid control

identify the table's location and place the necessary SQL commands in ASP.NET controls that access the table:

```
<asp:SqlDataSource ID="SqlDataSource1" runat="server"
ConnectionString="<%$ ConnectionStrings:VoteNowConnectionString1 %>"
ProviderName="<%$ ConnectionStrings:VoteNowConnectionString1
.ProviderName %>"
```

Rather than the data source being identified by C# code, the ASP.NET provided the access.

Ask the Expert

Q: Using the DataGrid by dragging a table into the Visual Studio is so easy, why bother with the more complex methods when data binding?

A: If the output you want is provided by that method, then you can use it all you want. However, for more complex SQL queries and other work with tables and databases, this method is fairly limited. For busy developers, though, I can see why you ask!

ListView

New to ASP.NET 3.5, the ListView control offers a good deal of flexibility in styling a page. In some respects the ListView is similar to GridView, but using ListView, you get a lot more control over how your output looks. In effect, it is a styling control of sorts because you can use the full range of CSS that is now available in Visual Studio 2008. The example used to illustrate the ListView control is fairly humble in terms of design. However, you can clearly see the key ingredients for using the ListView control.

To effectively use the ListView, you need to include a `<LayoutTemplate>` tag, and within the tag's container, you add a PlaceHolder control with the ID named `itemContainer`:

```
<LayoutTemplate>
      <some style>
                  <asp:PlaceHolder ID="itemContainer" runat="server"/>
      </some style>
</LayoutTemplate>
```

All of the displayed data are styled by the style added in the `<LayoutTemplate>` and then placed in the `PlaceHolder` control.

Individual styling done in the `<ItemTemplate>` overrides the style from the `<LayoutTemplate>`, but with good planning and the full control that the ListView provides, the differences need not be at odds. In fact, the idea of the ListView is to give the designer both the flexibility and general layout features needed in design.

The sample application uses one CSS style within the layout (generating a yellow background) and another CSS style for the names to be listed. The e-mail addresses that accompany the names use the default style, but are still cast on a yellow background.

ASP.NET ListView.aspx

```
<%@ Page Language="C#" AutoEventWireup="true" CodeFile="ListView.aspx.cs"
Inherits="ListViewer" %>
<!DOCTYPE html PUBLIC "-//W3C//DTD XHTML 1.0 Transitional//EN"
"http://www.w3.org/TR/xhtml1/DTD/xhtml1-transitional.dtd">
<html xmlns="http://www.w3.org/1999/xhtml">
<head id="Head1" runat="server">
<style type="text/css">
.highlight
{
      background-color:Yellow;
}
.sans
{
      font-family:Arial,Helvetica,sans-serif;
      color:Maroon;
```

```
    }
</style>
    <title>ListView Control</title>
</head>
<body>
    <form id="form1" runat="server">
    <div>
        <asp:ListView ID="ListView1" runat="server">
        <LayoutTemplate>
        <p class="highlight">
          <asp:PlaceHolder ID="itemContainer" runat="server"/>
         </p>
        </LayoutTemplate>

        <ItemTemplate>
           <strong><span class=sans> <%#Eval("FirstName")%> 
             <%#Eval("LastName") %>:</span></strong>
             <%#Eval("Email") %><br />
        </ItemTemplate>

        <EmptyDataTemplate>
            <div>No records have been found.</div>
        </EmptyDataTemplate>

        </asp:ListView>
    </div>
    </form>
</body>
</html>
```

The C# portion of the application is just a standard C# partial class to open the database table and issue the SQL commands to gather up the requested data and bind it to the ListView control.

C# ListView.aspx.cs

```
using System;
using System.Data.SqlClient;
using System.Web.UI.WebControls;

public partial class ListViewer : System.Web.UI.Page
{
    private SqlConnection hookUp;
    private SqlCommand sqlCmd;
    private SqlDataReader readBind;

    protected void Page_Load(object sender, EventArgs e)
```

```
    {
        hookUp = new SqlConnection("Server=localhost\\SqlExpress;Datab
ase=VoteNow;" +
            "Integrated Security=True");
        sqlCmd = new SqlCommand("SELECT FirstName,LastName,Email FROM
Supporters", hookUp);
        hookUp.Open();
        readBind = sqlCmd.ExecuteReader();

        //Bind to repeater
        ListView1.DataSource = readBind;
        ListView1.DataBind();
readBind.Close();
        hookUp.Close();
    }
}
```

Once you have all of the code in the listings completed, you will see the output shown in Figure 13-11. The different styling with CSS is to hint at the possibilities of what can be done with styling options with the ListView control—and it's just a hint.

With more sophisticated CSS design options, the ListView control may well replace the GridView altogether—except where you need some kind of display quickly.

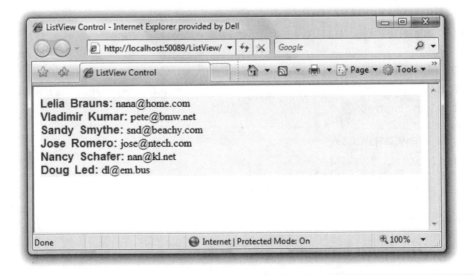

Figure 13-11 Data styled in Placeholder control and `ItemTemplate`

Summary

For busy developers and designers, data binding is not only a way to easily format your data for clarity, but it also is an opportunity to really think about the whole endeavor of making data clear and attractive. Huge tables of data can be confusing, and working to program the output format can be both time-consuming and daunting. With data binding, important data in a database table can be formatted as tables, lists, or nametags—depending on your client's needs.

Designers think long and hard about how data should appear in their design, while developers struggle to make sure that the data types all match the necessary output controls. With data binding, both development and design can come together to create displays of information that are clear and useful.

Chapter 14

LINQ

Key Skills & Concepts

- What is LINQ?

- Using LINQ with ASP.NET

This chapter concentrates on the ASP.NET 3.5 incorporation of Language Integrated Query, generally referenced as *LINQ*. A single chapter on this powerful new .NET Framework 3.5 tool only scratches the surface of LINQ. However, by looking at the basic functionality of LINQ and what it accomplishes in key examples, you will be able to see how SQL-type queries can be made using standard programming constructs. This chapter first examines how to use new LINQ controls available in ASP.NET 3.5 to create a powerful application for performing basic SQL commands using the LINQ framework. Secondly, with a simple C# example, you can see how a "normal" programming command structure issues LINQ queries.

LINQ Basics

Think of LINQ as a kind of replacement for SQL, and what LINQ does will begin to be clearer. All LINQ queries do the following:

- Obtain the data source.

- Create the query.

- Execute the query.

If you think that sounds a lot like what you do with SQL commands, you're absolutely right. However, instead of writing SQL strings that are passed to ASP.NET SQL controls or objects, you handle these queries in a way that looks just like standard programming in a wide variety of .NET Framework 3.5 languages. You write the queries in similar ways in such languages as C#, J#, Visual Basic, C++, and other .NET-supported languages. In other words, LINQ standardizes queries. The key examples in this chapter show you how to make those three steps using LINQ.

TIP

This single chapter about LINQ, a critically important new development in the .NET Framework 3.5, is the first step in a thousand-mile journey. You should be aware that more steps are available. In numerous blogs and online articles available from Microsoft, you can find some excellent and not-so-excellent discussions of LINQ. However, beware of some of the initial materials on LINQ and Visual Studio 2008. Many articles online, while initially accurate, are no longer so because of changes in Visual Studio 2008 or in the LINQ framework. At the time of this writing, several books are available where the authors have ample room to go into all of the intense detail of LINQ. After reading this chapter, if you wish to find out more about LINQ for your projects, check out some of these books that lead to the rest of the steps in the LINQ journey.

In a very fundamental way LINQ was designed to improve developer productivity. Because LINQ makes query statements more like standard language statements, developers are not sidetracked by incorporating a special flavor of SQL depending on the database system. Likewise, built-in tools in ASP.NET 3.5, such as the LinqDataSource control, make development easier through several properties used in LINQ queries. The next section examines how to use the controls in ASP.NET 3.5 to make queries as well as nonquery operations with LINQ.

ASP.NET 3.5 and LINQ

To see how to use the new LINQ control LinqDataSource, this example goes through a rather lengthy Visual Studio 2008 process. However, once everything is done, you may be surprised at how little ASP.NET code the process generates. Basically, the whole operation uses only two controls: LinqDataSource and DetailsView. If you are familiar with the DetailsView control from ASP.NET 2.0, you will be happy to hear that the new 3.5 version of control can use the LinqDataSource control as a data source. So while a lot of this will look new, the key display control is an old friend.

Try This   Getting Started with LINQ

This next set of steps to get you started requires Visual Studio 2008. If you are using one of the Express versions of Visual Studio, be sure that any add-ons for LINQ are in place. Also, you will need to:

1. Open a new Web Site, and name it **ShowLinq**.
2. Open Solution Explorer and rename Default.aspx to **ShowLinq.aspx**.

(continued)

3. Rename _Default to **DoLinq** in the C# script, and have it rename the ASP.NET inherit (**inherits DoLinq**).

4. Right-click the App_Data folder and select Add New Item.

5. Under Templates select SQL Server Database, and in the Name window change the default name to **ServiceReg.mdf** as shown in Figure 14-1. Click the Add button when finished.

6. Open the Server Explorer and you should see ServiceReg.mdf among the databases. Right-click the Tables folder icon, and select Add New Table as shown in Figure 14-2.

7. When the table window opens, add the information shown in Figure 14-3. RegID is a primary key field and an identity field, so values enter automatically.

8. Save the table using the name **RegClients**. You will see the table listed in the Tables folder of the ServiceReg.mdf database in the Server Explorer.

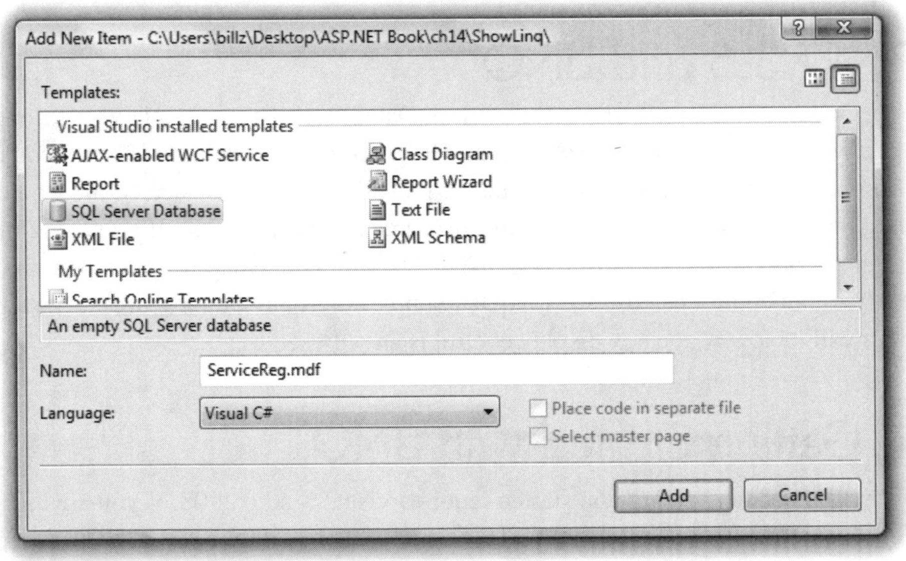

Figure 14-1 Selecting SQL database

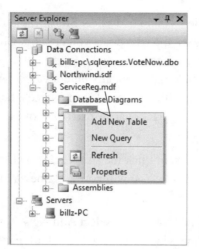

Figure 14-2 Adding a new table

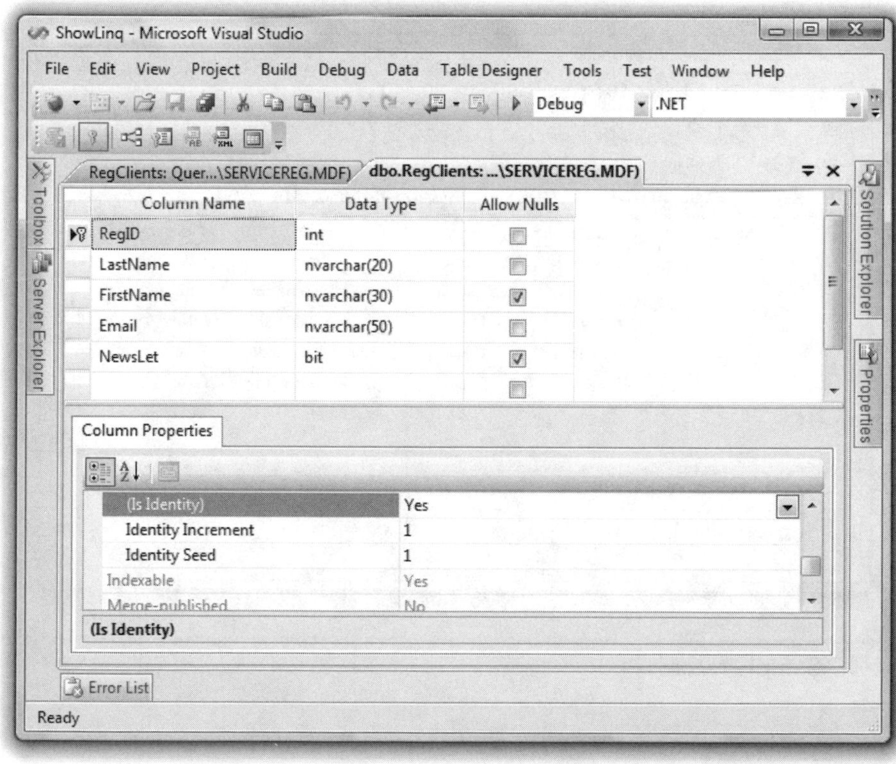

Figure 14-3 Setting the fields in a new table

(continued)

9. Right-click the RegClients table and select Show Table Data. The first time takes a little while. You will see the five fields you created. Click in the first field and press TAB to move to the `LastName` field. Begin entering records in this second field because the first field automatically enters values. Add about five records to have something to work with. Figure 14-4 shows an example. (Whenever you make changes in a record, the `ReqID` changes, so some of the `ReqID` values are out of sequence in Figure 14-4.)

10. In the Solution Explorer right-click the site (C:\..ShowLinq\), select Add ASP.NET Folder, and select App_Code. You will now see a new App_Code folder in the Solution Explorer.

11. Right-click the App_Code folder and select Add New Item. Select LINQ To SQL Classes, and in the Name window change the default name to **RegClients.dbml** and click Add. Figure 14-5 shows the correct settings.

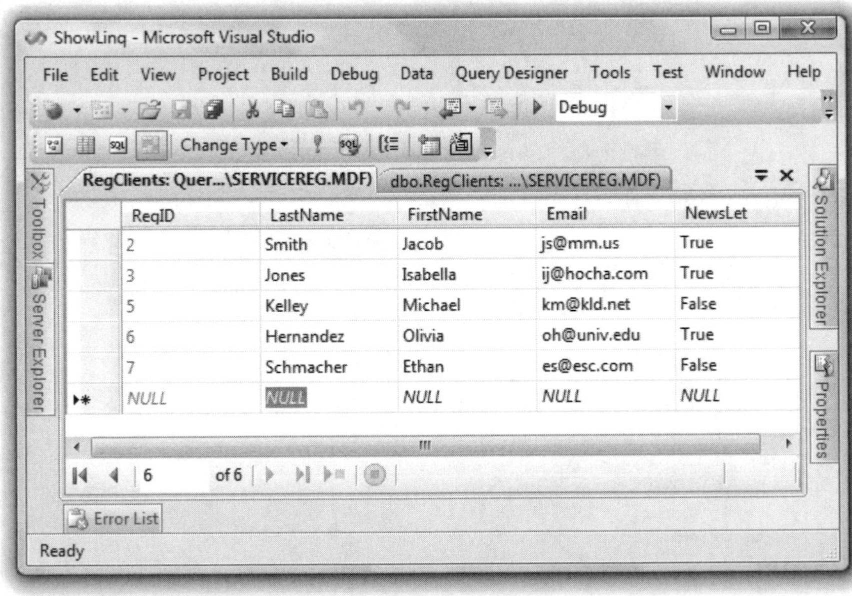

Figure 14-4 Sample records

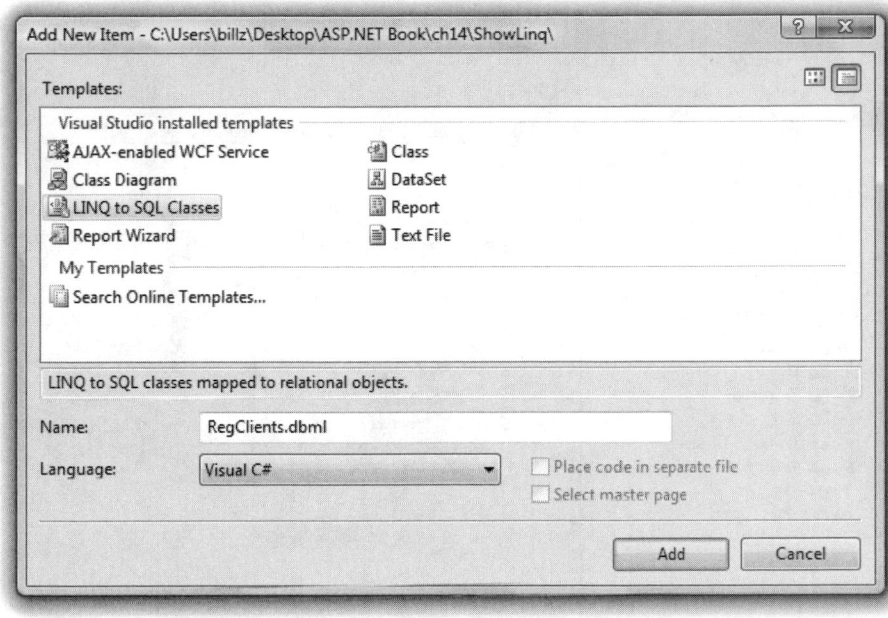

Figure 14-5 Adding the LINQ to SQL Classes template

12. After you click Add, a double window opens. This is the Object Relational Designer. Drag the RegClients table from the Server Explorer into the right window as shown in Figure 14-6.

13. From the Solution Explorer open the ShowLinq.aspx file. Then from the Toolbox Data menu drag a LinqDataSource control and drop it inside the `<div>` container. Switch to the Split mode or to Design mode.

(continued)

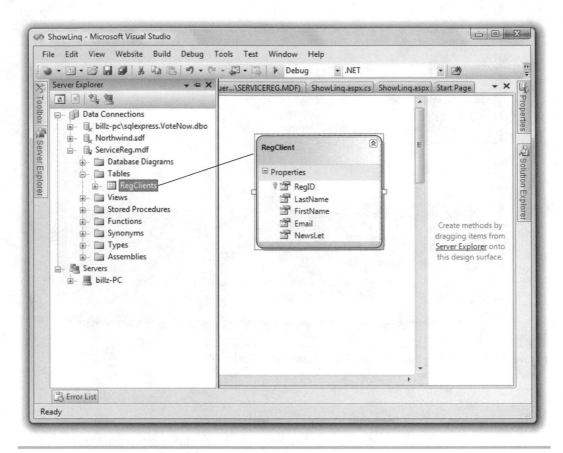

Figure 14-6 Dragging the table into the Object Relational Designer

14. Click the LinqDataSource object and open the Properties window. Next to
ContextTypeName, select RegClientsDataContext as shown in Figure 14-7.

15. Set the TableName property to RegClients and the AutoPage property
to True.

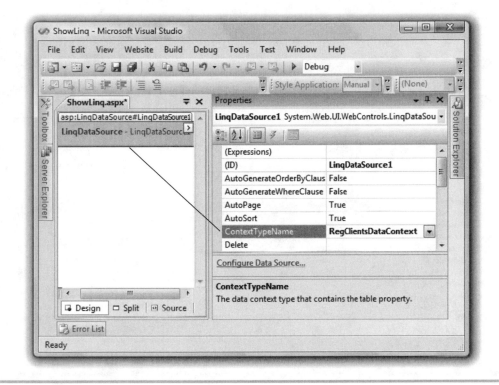

Figure 14-7 Setting the `ContextTypeName` property

16. Set the following `LinqDataSource1` properties to `True`:
    - `EnableDelete`
    - `EnableInsert`
    - `EnableUpdate`
17. From the Toolbox Data menu, drag a DetailsView control beneath the `LinqDataSource` object as shown in Figure 14-8.

(continued)

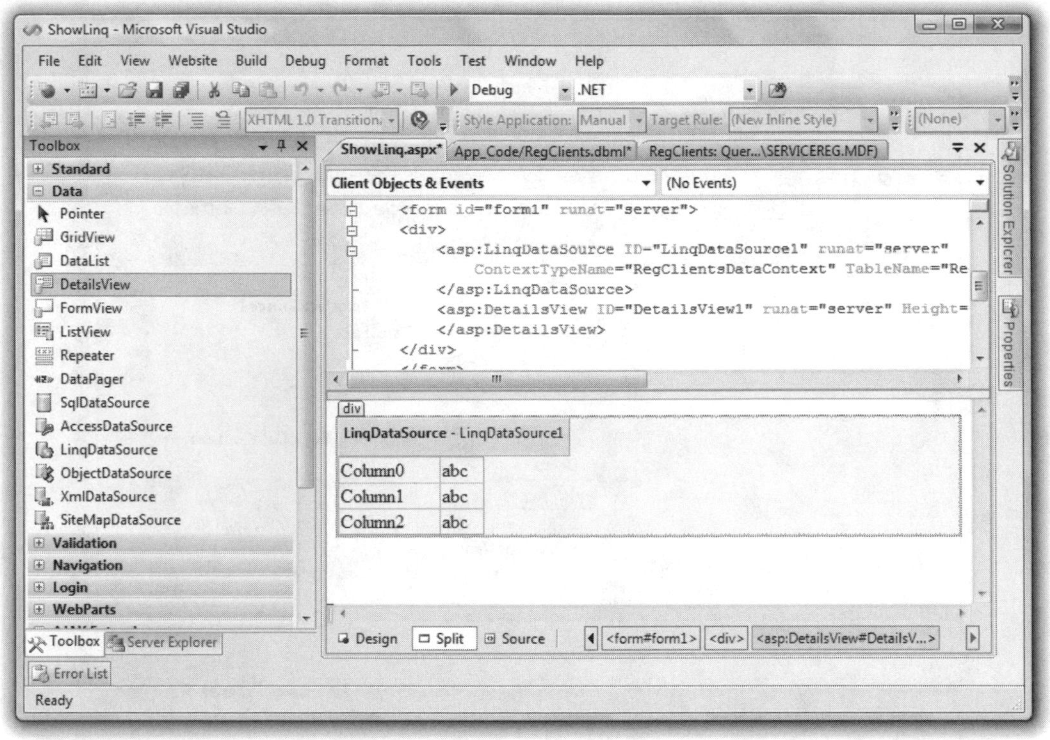

Figure 14-8 Adding the DetailsView control

18. Select the DetailsView control and in the Properties window select the `LinqDataSource1` as the `DataSourceID` as shown in Figure 14-9.

19. Widen the DetailsView control, and then in the Properties window set the following to `True`:

   - `AutoPage`

   - `AutoGenerateDeleteButton`

   - `AutoGenerateEditButton`

   - `AutoGenerateInsertButton`

20. Once you have the settings complete, press CTRL-F5 to test the application. Figure 14-10 shows what you should see.

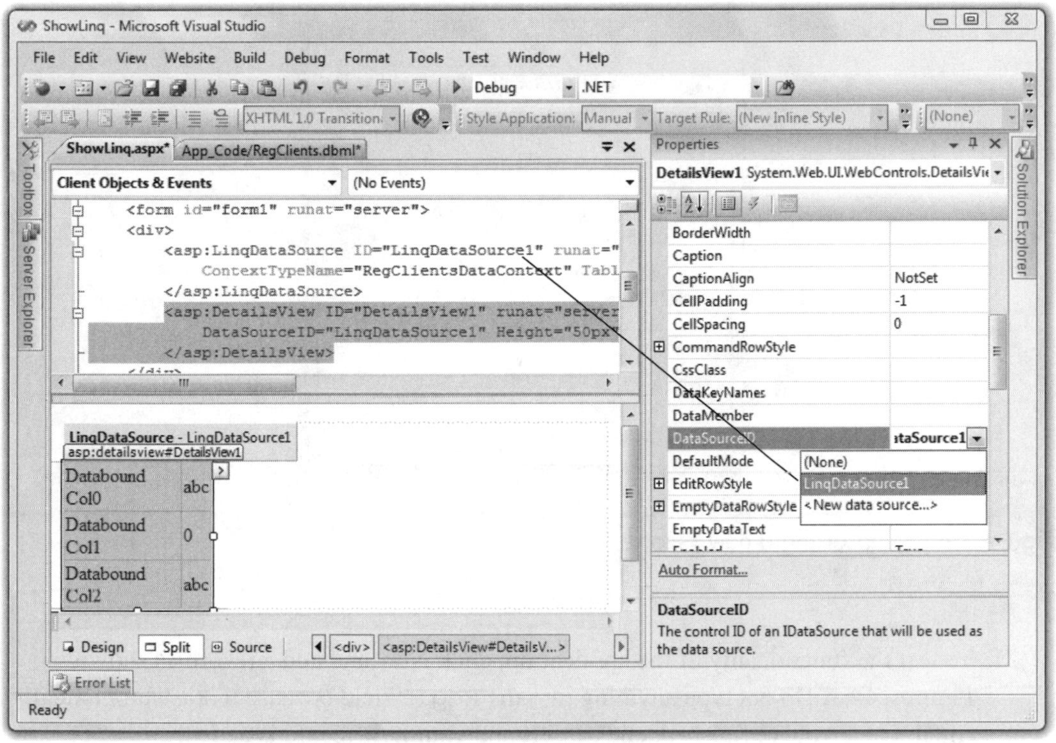

Figure 14-9 Setting the DetailsView control `DataSourceID` property to `LinqDataSource1`

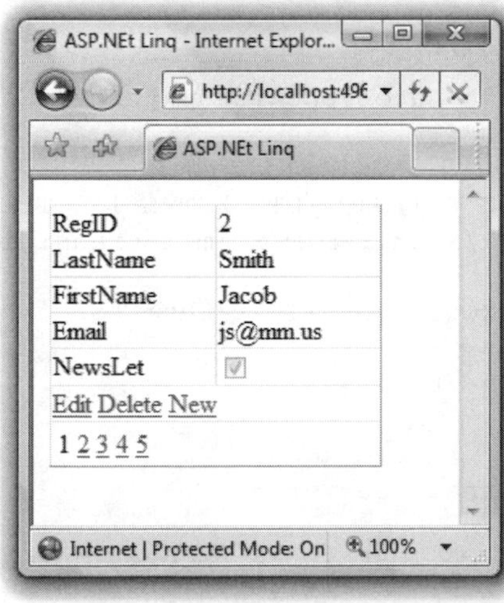

Figure 14-10 A LINQ-supported application

(continued)

Figure 14-11 Inserting a new record

21. To test the functionality of the application, click New and add a record as shown in Figure 14-11. Do not type anything into the RegID field because that is automatically filled. Once you've finished, click Insert and your new record is added.

All of those steps generated very little ASP.NET code. In looking at the ASP.NET portion of the application, all that you will see is shown in the following listing:

ASP.NET ShowLinq.aspx

```
<%@ Page Language="C#" AutoEventWireup="true" CodeFile="ShowLinq.aspx
.cs" Inherits="DoLinq" %>

<!DOCTYPE html PUBLIC "-//W3C//DTD XHTML 1.0 Transitional//EN"
"http://www.w3.org/TR/xhtml1/DTD/xhtml1-transitional.dtd">

<html xmlns="http://www.w3.org/1999/xhtml">
<head runat="server">
  <title>ASP.NET Linq</title>
</head>
<body>
  <form id="form1" runat="server">
  <div>
    <asp:LinqDataSource ID="LinqDataSource1" runat="server"
      ContextTypeName="RegClientsDataContext"
      EnableDelete="True" EnableInsert="True"
      EnableUpdate="True" TableName="RegClients">
```

```
    </asp:LinqDataSource>
    <asp:DetailsView ID="DetailsView1" runat="server"
      DataSourceID="LinqDataSource1"
      AllowPaging="True"
      AutoGenerateDeleteButton="True"
      AutoGenerateEditButton="True"
      AutoGenerateInsertButton="True"
      DataKeyNames="RegID"
      Height="50px" Width="205px">
    </asp:DetailsView>
  </div>
  </form>
</body>
</html>
```

As you can see, just two controls and a number of properties are involved in the entire application. If you look at the `ShowLinq.aspx.cs` portion of the application, all you see is the default C# generated with all new web sites. However, if you look in the App_Code folder, you will find that a good deal of C# was automatically generated by Visual Studio 2008 in a file named RegClients.designer.cs. By looking at this C# file, you can better see what is involved in the LINQ operations. First, take a look at the listing by opening it in Visual Studio 2008, and then see what is going on with the code.

In looking at the code, you can see a number of elements of C# that have been discussed in previous chapters. Some of the C# statements may be new. For example, note the `#region` and `#endregion` container-like statements. These statements let you specify a block of code that you can expand and collapse with the Visual Studio 2008 outlining feature. Load the file in Visual Studio 2008, and you will see how you can collapse and open those elements in the `#region` container.

You will see that all of the fields have been cast as private variables. The automatically generated C# uses the convention of underlining the variable names such as

```
private string _LastName;
```

In this way, the fields can be addressed like variables using the C# structures. In SQL alone, no such kind of "normal programming" reference would be possible. Further, when the states of those fields change, event handlers deal with those changes in the same way all events and event handlers work.

With the amount and type of code in the preceding C# listing, you may miss some of the fundamentals of coding C# for LINQ operations. As a beginner in ASP.NET and C#, don't worry about it. To help you better understand what is taking place, the next section takes a simple C# program and steps through a LINQ operation.

C# Uses LINQ

As you saw in the previous section, a rather lengthy C# script helped pull together an ASP.NET application with LINQ structures. It was able to access data from a database. However, besides a database, LINQ can be used with virtually any kind of data source. In this next example, you will see how to use LINQ to access data in a simple array.

Array Data Source

Rather than using a database as the source for data, the array provides a good simple place to put values to be extracted. Then using the LINQ functionality, you can see that while the statements look a lot like SQL statements, they are in fact set up in a standard C# fashion.

The IEnumerable<T> Interface

The `IEnumerable<T>` is a *lambda* expression. With a lambda expression, you can treat code like data. A lambda expression works something like an anonymous method where you can place several statements inside the method, but with a lambda, expressions are assigned to the lambda instance as you would assign data.

Using `IEnumerable<T>`, all of the LINQ query can be placed in a single assignment. It's something like placing a set of SQL commands in a string expression and then executing that expression as using a `SqlCommand` instance. However, instead of SQL, it's LINQ.

A Simple C# Example

This example requires only a single Label control in the ASP.NET portion of the application. The rest is purely C#. Note that the C# class imports both `System.Linq` and `System .Collections.Generic` namespaces. The `System.Linq` import allows for LINQ statements, and the `System.Collections.Generic` provides the foundation for the `IEnumerable<T>` expression.

Try This ## Working with the IEnumerable<T> Interface

This little example uses both LINQ and the special IEnumerable<T> interface. It will give you a better understanding of what happens with the interface and LINQ.

ASP.NET CSlinq.aspx

```
<%@ Page Language="C#" AutoEventWireup="true" CodeFile="CSlinq.aspx
.cs" Inherits="SeaLINQ" %>
```

```
<!DOCTYPE html PUBLIC "-//W3C//DTD XHTML 1.0 Transitional//EN"
"http://www.w3.org/TR/xhtml1/DTD/xhtml1-transitional.dtd">

<html xmlns="http://www.w3.org/1999/xhtml">
<head id="Head1" runat="server">
  <title>Basic LINQ</title>
</head>
<body>
  <form id="form1" runat="server">
  <div>
    <asp:Label ID="Label1" runat="server" Font-Names="Verdana" />
  </div>
  </form>
</body>
</html>
```

C# CSlinq.aspx.cs

```
using System;
using System.Linq;
using System.Collections.Generic;

public partial class SeaLINQ : System.Web.UI.Page
{
  private int lowerLimit;
  protected void Page_Load(object sender, EventArgs e)
  {
    lowerLimit = 30;
    int[] prices = new int[] { 50, 40, 55, 32, 18, 25, 63 };
    IEnumerable<int> priceQuery =
      from price in prices
      where price > lowerLimit
      select price;
    Label1.Text="Values greater than "+lowerLimit + ":<br />";
    foreach (int p in priceQuery)
    {
      Label1.Text += "$" + p + "<br />";
    }
  }
}
```

Using the "data" (element values) in the array named `prices`, a simple `foreach` loop iterates through the lambda expression to get values. However, the only elements available in the lambda expression are those that have been selected in the array based on a LINQ query statement. In looking at the `priceQuery`, you can see that only those elements in the array whose value is greater than the `lowerLimit` variable are sent to

(continued)

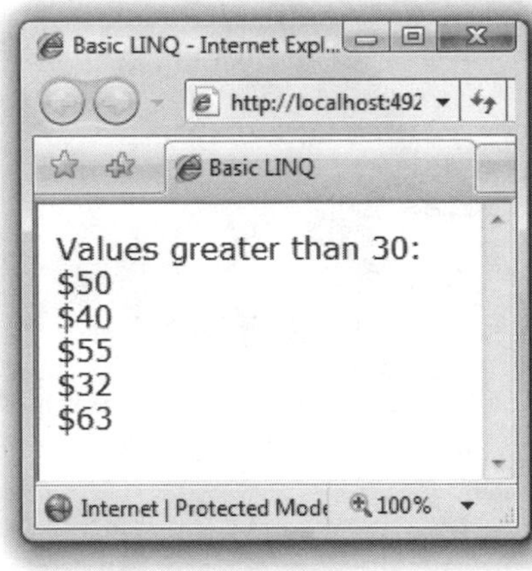

Figure 14-12 Output filtered through a LINQ query

the ASP.NET Label web control. When you test the application, Figure 14-12 shows what you should see.

While this is a simple example, it shows the functionality of a LINQ query used to filter data using the LINQ query statements. The fabulous `IEnumerable<int>` expression is assigned the values of the prices array if they meet the query requirements. Then the data are extracted using a `foreach` statement. Yet the entire process is remarkably simple. Applied to a database, the same structure can be used. The only difference is the data source.

Summary

For those who have toiled in the fields of database queries, LINQ will be a welcome relief from the peccadilloes characteristic of SQL. Not only can queries be made without having to concern oneself with which version of SQL is required, but also the queries use fairly normal programming constructs in C#.

With the new ASP.NET 3.5 LinqDataSource control, you can easily bind to a display control. The DetailsView control is ideal because of its `AutoGenerateDeleteButt on`, `AutoGenerateEditButton`, and `AutoGenerateInsertButton` properties. With these properties, all of the necessary query and nonquery operations that typically are used with a database are easily included. So instead of having to have a full table viewed simultaneously, you can have ASP.NET applications that can be constructed to provide the functionality in such a way that elaborate C# scripts automatically generated in Visual Studio 2008 can create an application with full query and nonquery functionality.

For C# programmers the combination of LINQ and the `IEnumerable<T>` expression makes it easy to use LINQ queries and nonqueries to extract filtered data from virtually any data source. Because this saves time, the developer can be far more productive, and reap the benefits of LINQ's goal of ease and standardization of data manipulation and use.

Chapter 15

Files

Key Skills & Concepts

- System.IO namespace

- Writing text files

- Appending text files

- Reading text files

- Displaying directories and files

Some web sites you build may need very little stored data or data access. As you have seen in the previous chapters examining ADO.NET, building databases and tables requires several steps to set up just what you need. Sometimes, though, all you need is a simple text file to store text for basic data entry and retrieval on the Web. Using no database, table, or special connection protocol, you can work with text files to store simple data and access that stored text using ASP.NET and C#. This chapter examines this relatively simple file writing and reading process for those applications where you need just a little data. Likewise, if you or your client does not have access to a database using files, you can create a rudimentary "pauper's database"!

Writing Files

At the outset you need to be aware that if you have a relatively complex set of data and data types and expect high-volume usage, you should use a database and tables. However, *solely* for simple, text-only projects, you can effectively use plain-text files for writing data and retrieving it. Compared with setting up a database and tables and writing data to different fields, creating, writing to, and appending text files is a simple procedure.

Using StreamWriter

The first file-writing web site shows how to use the `StreamWriter` class to create a text file and then store data in that file. A `StreamWriter` instance defaults to Unicode Transformation Format-8 (UTF-8) that encodes in the Unicode standard. It is backwardly compatible to ASCII format so that it can handle ASCII data sets. At this writing, UTF-8 is becoming the default text standard, so it should work well with just about any system.

The bulk of the work in these next several examples is done with C#, so the focus will be on working with `StreamWriter` in the C# partial class. The `StreamWriter` class is in the `System.IO` namespace, so that namespace needs to be imported. The general format for using a `StreamWriter` instance is unique, as can be seen in the following:

```
using(StreamWriter swInstance = new StreamWriter(@"C:\Folder\FileName.txt"))
{ …. }
```

Within the braces set up by the **using** statement, simply use either `StreamWriter` `.Write` or `StreamWriter.WriteLine` methods to add the text you want in the file. The only difference between using `Write()` and `WriteLine()` methods is that `WriteLine()` adds a line break at the end.

Try This Write a Text File

The following example shows how to write a file. The steps are quite simple:

1. Open a new Web Site, and save it as **WriteText**.

2. In your root C: folder, add a folder named **WriteStuff**.

3. Drag a Label control into the `<div>` container, and change the ID to **"writer"**. The following code shows the entire listing:

ASP.NET WriteTx.aspx

```
<%@ Page Language="C#" AutoEventWireup="true" CodeFile="WriteTx.aspx
.cs" Inherits="WriteTx" %>
<!DOCTYPE html PUBLIC "-//W3C//DTD XHTML 1.0 Transitional//EN"
"http://www.w3.org/TR/xhtml1/DTD/xhtml1-transitional.dtd">
<html xmlns="http://www.w3.org/1999/xhtml">
<head runat="server">
    <title>Basic Text Writer</title>
</head>
<body>
    <form id="form1" runat="server">
    <div>
    <asp:Label ID="writer" runat="server" Text="Label"></asp:Label>
    </div>
    </form>
</body>
</html>
```

The C# code is where all of the functionality can be found. Edit the C# portion of the web site using the following code:

(continued)

C# WriteTx.aspx.cs

```
using System;
using System.IO;

public partial class WriteTx : System.Web.UI.Page
{
    private StreamWriter sw;
    private string first;
    private string second;
    private string third;

    protected void Page_Load(object sender, EventArgs e)
    {
        using (sw = new StreamWriter(@"C:\WriteStuff\ASPNote.txt"))
    {
            first = "This has a line break at the end.";
            second = "No line break...";
            third = "so this is on the same line.";
            sw.WriteLine(first);
            sw.Write(second);
            sw.WriteLine(third);
            writer.Text = "Your file has been written.";
        }
    }
}
```

Once you have tested the program, open the target folder, WriteStuff, and you should see a new file as shown in Figure 15-1.

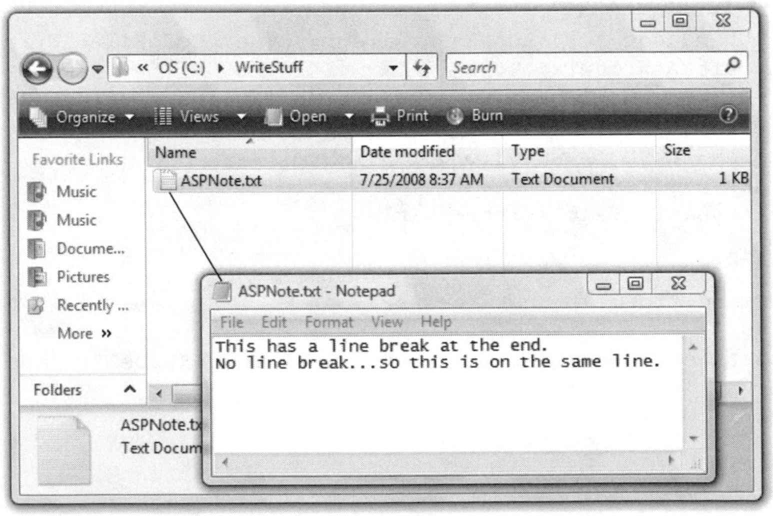

Figure 15-1 A new text file is created in the target director.

Ask the Expert

Q: **Wouldn't it be easier to use a word processor to save files? Then when they're loaded using ASP.NET 3.5, all of the formatting is preserved.**

A: I agree that it would be great if a client could update material on a web site simply by changing the contents of a word processor file. However, word processor files are binary files containing a lot of code that formats the text. Text files are typically *Unicode,* and most use the *UTF-8* encoding and can be written and read using the text methods in ASP.NET 3.5 and C# 3.0. Older text files use the ASCII format, but because Unicode is backwardly compatible with ASCII, they too can be read. Any formatting of the text is accomplished by treating the file as a string, and by parsing the string, you can dynamically format the text. However, that's not quite as easy as having the ability to bring in a wholly formatted word-processed file.

A crucial feature in specifying the path is the use of the **@** symbol. If it is not used, the backslashes (\) are assumed to be part of an escape sequence, and this generally causes an error. An alternative to using the **@** symbol is to use MapPath. The next section shows how and why it is probably a better choice in general.

Using MapPath

In the previous example using the **@** symbol, the exact path needs to be listed. That works out fine for files on your own system, but when you're working on a remote server, you may not know the exact path. Using the MapPath method, you can map a specified virtual path to a physical path. If you do not know the exact path, simply enter the name of the text file you wish to create, and it is created in your root directory with the ASPX and CS files of your web site. The format is

```
using(StreamWriter swInstance = new StreamWriter MapPath("Mapped.txt")))
{ ....}
```

As you can see, MapPath is used in setting up a StreamWriter operation. The following listings show how to use the MapPath method in an application:

ASP.NET MapFile.aspx

```
<%@ Page Language="C#" AutoEventWireup="true" CodeFile="MapFile.aspx.
cs" Inherits="MapFile" %>
<!DOCTYPE html PUBLIC "-//W3C//DTD XHTML 1.0 Transitional//EN"
"http://www.w3.org/TR/xhtml1/DTD/xhtml1-transitional.dtd">
```

```html
<html xmlns="http://www.w3.org/1999/xhtml">
<head runat="server">
    <title>Mapping File</title>
</head>
<body>
    <form id="form1" runat="server">
    <div>
        <asp:Label ID="writer" runat="server" Text="Label" />
    </div>
</form>
</body>
</html>
```

C# MapFile.aspx.cs

```csharp
using System;
using System.IO;

public partial class MapFile : System.Web.UI.Page
{
    private StreamWriter streamer;
    private string stuffMap;

    protected void Page_Load(object sender, EventArgs e)
    {
        stuffMap = "This is on a map path";
        using (streamer = File.CreateText(MapPath("Mapped.txt")))
        {
            streamer.Write(stuffMap);
            writer.Text = "Your text file has been mapped.";
        }
    }
}
```

When you run the application in a Visual Studio 2008 context, you will see the new file created right with your other files in the same directory as shown in Figure 15-2.

If you place the file on a remote system, you will see that your file is saved in the root directory with your C# and ASP.NET files (see Figure 15-3). You do not have to know the exact file path when using the `MapPath` methods.

If you double-click the text file, its contents appear in the browser. You may want better security for your content, so if you do have sensitive information in your text files, be sure to set the directory to keep out snoopers.

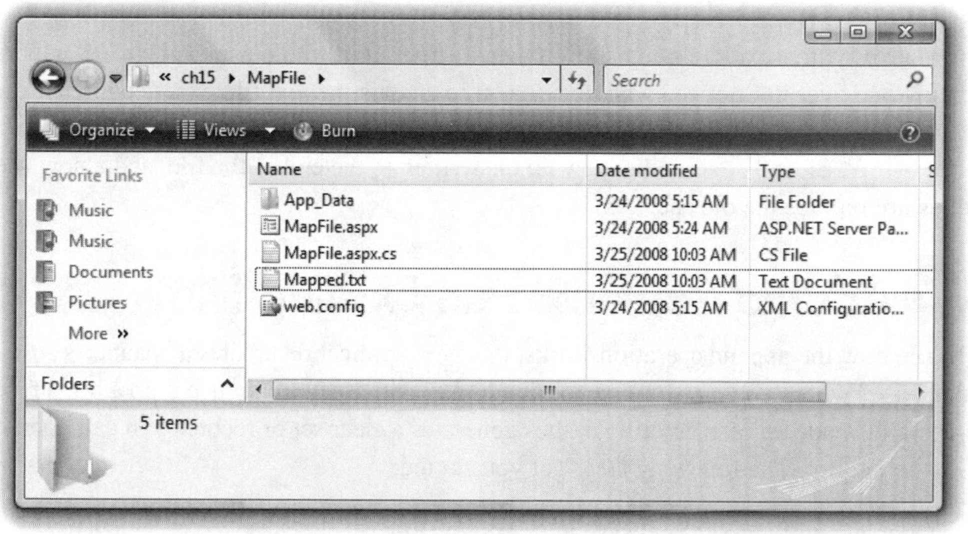

Figure 15-2 Text file in Visual Studio 2008 context

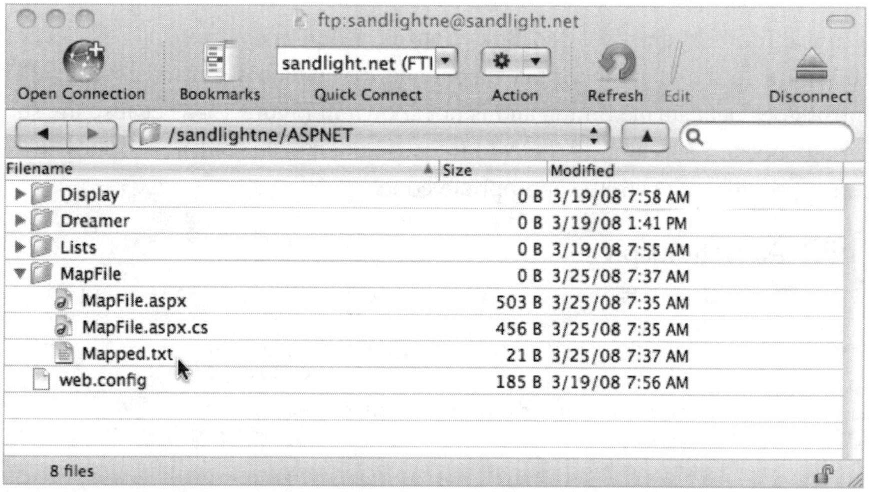

Figure 15-3 File created on remote server

Appending Files

Whenever you use a `File.CreateText()` operation, you erase the text file and create a new one over it. So if you want to add text to an existing text file, you need to use the `File.AppendText()` method. Everything about it is virtually the same as `File.CreateText()`, except that new text is written to the end of the file, and a new file does not replace the old one.

Try This ## Adding Content to an Existing File

To see how the append operation works, this next application creates a "pauper's database" where you can store names and e-mail addresses. To spruce it up a bit, a record separator made up of alternating dashes generates a clear set of records you can open in any text editor. The following steps get you started:

1. Open a new Web Site, and save it as **AppendFile**.

2. In the Solution Explorer change the ASPX name from Default.aspx to **AppFile.aspx**.

3. Open the C# file and change the partial class name to **AppFile**, and change the Inherits target in the AppFile.aspx file. (This can be done automatically in the C# file using the IntelliSense pop-up.)

4. From the Toolbox, drag two TextBox controls, a Button control, and a Label control. Use Figure 15-4 as a guide for placement and for text labels for the controls. (The Label control goes beneath the button and is not shown in Figure 15-4 because the success message doesn't appear until the Add Record button is clicked.) The following two listings provide you with the appropriate code.

ASP.NET AppFile.aspx

```
<%@ Page Language="C#" AutoEventWireup="true" CodeFile="AppFile.aspx
.cs" Inherits="AppFile" %>
<!DOCTYPE html PUBLIC "-//W3C//DTD XHTML 1.0 Transitional//EN"
"http://www.w3.org/TR/xhtml1/DTD/xhtml1-transitional.dtd">
<html xmlns="http://www.w3.org/1999/xhtml">
<head runat="server">
<style type="text/css">
body
{
    font-family: Verdana;
    color:Maroon;
}
</style>
    <title>Append File</title>
</head>
```

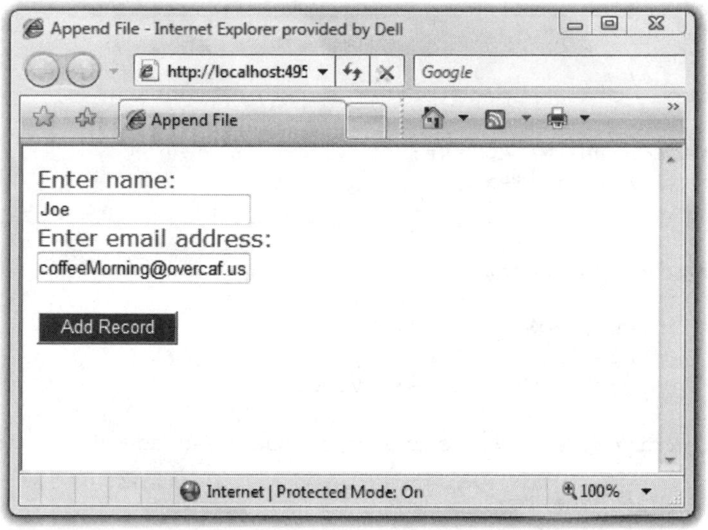

Figure 15-4 Entering data into a text file

```
<body>
    <form id="form1" runat-"server">
    <div>
        Enter name:<br />
        <asp:TextBox ID="UserName" runat="server" /><br />
        Enter email address:<br />
        <asp:TextBox ID="Email" runat="server" /><p />
        <asp:Button ID="Button1" OnClick="DoAppend"
            runat="server" Text="Add Record"
            BackColor="Maroon" ForeColor="White" /><p />
        <asp:Label ID="writer" runat="server"  />
    </div>
    </form>
</body>
</html>
```

C# AppFile.aspx.cs

```csharp
using System;
using System.IO;

public partial class AppFile : System.Web.UI.Page
{
    private StreamWriter pauperDB;
    private string uName;
```

(continued)

```
    private string eMail;
    private string divider;

    protected void DoAppend(object sender, EventArgs e)
    {
        uName = UserName.Text;
        eMail = Email.Text;
        divider = "-_-_-_-_-_-_-_-_-_-";

        using (pauperDB=File.AppendText(MapPath("pauperDataBase.txt")))
        {
            pauperDB.WriteLine(uName);
            pauperDB.WriteLine(eMail);
            pauperDB.WriteLine(divider);

            writer.Text = "Your record has been added to the text
file.";
            UserName.Text = "";
            Email.Text = "";
        }
    }
}
```

Once you've got your web site completed, test it. First, enter several names and e-mail addresses as shown in Figure 15-4.

After you've entered several records, open the text file you created. You will find the file named pauperDataBase.txt in the root folder of your web site. Figure 15-5 shows a sample of names entered.

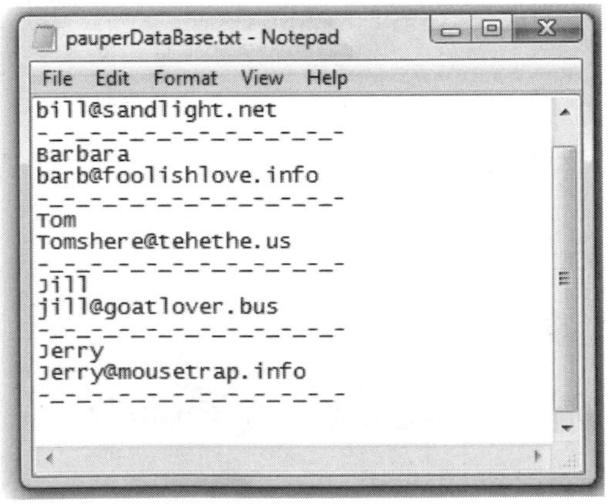

Figure 15-5 Data stored in text file opened in Notepad

As you can see, all of the records in the text file are clearly distinguishable. While simple, the file contains the information required in a clear, organized manner.

You may wonder how the file was created. After all, the `AppendText` instead of `CreateText` method is used to stream data to the file. That brings up one of the added features of `AppendText`. If no text file is found with the name provided, it creates a text file with the specified name. However, if it does find the text file addressed, then it opens the file and adds new materials to the end of the file.

Reading Text Files

Reading text files by opening them with Notepad or some other text editor is a simple way to see what you have stored. However, the whole purpose of having the ability to write data to a text file using ASP.NET is that the access is over the Web. A text file that can only be read by a text editor is not much help when your file is on a server and you're trying to access it using a browser. Fortunately, ASP.NET 3.5 and C# 3.0 have the necessary tools you will need to read the contents of a text file.

Using StreamReader

The `StreamReader` class is something like the mirror image of the `StreamWriter` class. The difference is that one reads the contents of a text file and the other writes to it. So, in looking at ways to read the contents of a text file, keep in mind what you have learned about `StreamWriter`.

The general format for `StreamReader` looks a lot like setting up `StreamWriter` in that both employ the **using** statement. The general format for establishing a `StreamReader` instance is

```
private StreamReader readMe;
using (readMe = new StreamReader("MyFile.txt"))
{....}
```

You will run into the same issues with the path to a text file, so using `MapPath` eases the problems in tracking down the absolute path to a text file.

The ReadLine Method

The key method to read the contents of a text file is `StreamReader.ReadLine()`. Text is treated as chunks of data demarcated by line breaks. More specifically, the line breaks are either a carriage return ("\r") or a line feed ("\n"), or a combination of a carriage return followed by a line feed ("\r\n").

When you enter data into a text file using the `WriteLine()` method, it automatically enters a line break, so when you use the `ReadLine()`, it knows what text is considered to be a separate line. Text entered in other ways marks the end of the line with either of the other two acceptable markers that `ReadLine()` can find. The following web site example reads the "Pauper Database" (pauperDataBase.txt), and it shows how you can retrieve and display the "records" from any text file:

ASP.NET FileReader.aspx

```
<%@ Page Language="C#" AutoEventWireup="true" CodeFile="FileReader.
aspx.cs" Inherits="FileRead" %>
<!DOCTYPE html PUBLIC "-//W3C//DTD XHTML 1.0 Transitional//EN"
"http://www.w3.org/TR/xhtml1/DTD/xhtml1-transitional.dtd">
<html xmlns="http://www.w3.org/1999/xhtml">
<head runat="server">
    <title>Read Text File</title>
</head>
<body>
    <form id="form1" runat="server">
    <div>
    <asp:Label ID="Label1" runat="server"
     Font-Names="Verdana" ForeColor="#990033" />
    </div>
    </form>
</body>
</html>
```

C# FileReader.aspx.cs

```
using System;
using System.IO;

public partial class FileRead : System.Web.UI.Page
{
    private StreamReader readMe;
    private String readLn;

    protected void Page_Load(object sender, EventArgs e)
    {
        try
        {
        using (readMe = new StreamReader(MapPath("pauperDataBase.
txt")))
            {
                while ((readLn = readMe.ReadLine()) != null)
                {
                    Label1.Text += readLn + "<br />";
```

```
            }
        }
    }
    catch (Exception ec)
    {
        Label1.Text = "Check the file name. It was not
found.<br/>";
        Label1.Text += ec.Message;
    }
  }
}
```

When you test the application, you will see something like Figure 15-6. Whatever is stored in the text file is displayed just as though you had opened the text file using a text editor. The only differences are that you can add your own style to the output, and you can access it from anywhere on the Web.

As you can see, the use of text files for storing and retrieving data is very simple. In cases where you do not want to use a database or do not have access to one, you can easily make a data storage system with the humble but flexible text file.

Figure 15-6 Text file displayed online

Viewing Directories and Files

Another useful feature of ASP.NET 3.5 and C# 3.0 is the ability to review your files and directories. For example, if you forgot the name of a file you want to view, you can scroll through your directories and files to locate it. Using the `DirectoryInfo` class, you can create, move, and display directories in addition to viewing files. For the purposes of reading text files, all you need to do is to find the directory with your files, so the focus will be on using the `DirectoryInfo.GetDirectories()` and `DirectoryInfo.GetFiles()` methods.

Locating and Displaying Directories

In using the `DirectoryInfo` class, an instance is created using a starting point in the directory structure. For example, the following shows the format for the root C: directory:

```
DirectoryInfo dir = new DirectoryInfo(@"C:\\");
```

To view the directories at the C: root, you can iterate through the `DirectoryInfo` instance to pull out the full set of directories using the following format:

```
foreach (DirectoryInfo dirInfoInstance in dirInfo.GetDirectories()) ....
```

Each of the elements in the `DirectoryInfo` instance has a `Name` property, and by converting the property to a string, you can display it as a text property in an ASP.NET web control. In this way, you are able to see all of the directories displayed on the screen.

Locating and Displaying Files

If you use files for storing different kinds of data, sometimes you might forget the location of the file or its name. Using the `DirectoryInfo.GetFiles()` method, you can retrieve the filenames in a given directory. The `FileInfo` class is similar to the `DirectoryInfo` class, except it is used with files rather than directories. However, you can work with both to locate a file within a directory. When iterating through a DirectoryInfo object, instead of using a `DirectoryInfo` instance to locate a specific directory, you use a FileInfo object as the element to retrieve the files in the directory. The format

```
foreach (FileInfo fileInfo in directoryInfoInstance.GetFiles())
```

finds the files in the specified instance of the `DirectoryInfo` method `GetFiles()`.

This next example application will give you a tour of your file structure. Using a variable root directory, you can explore your system to find any file you want.

The only caution is that you have to enter well-formed strings beginning with the root. For example, if you enter

c

you will get an error message. Any of the following will work to get you started:

```
C: or c:
C:\\ or C://
C:\\directoryName\\directoryName\
```

The following web site is set up so that you can explore your directory and file system:

ASP.NET ViewDir.aspx

```
<%@ Page Language="C#" AutoEventWireup="true" CodeFile="ViewDir.aspx.
cs" Inherits="ViewDir" %>
<!DOCTYPE html PUBLIC "-//W3C//DTD XHTML 1.0 Transitional//EN"
"http://www.w3.org/TR/xhtml1/DTD/xhtml1-transitional.dtd">
<html xmlns="http://www.w3.org/1999/xhtml">
<head runat="server">
    <title>Display Directories and Files</title>
</head>
<body>
    <form id="form1" runat="server">
    <div>
    Root Address:<br />
        <asp:TextBox ID="Root" runat="server" Width="200" /><p />
        <asp:Button ID="Button1" runat="server"
          Text="Show Files and Directories"
                OnClick="ShowInfo" /><p />
        <asp:Label ID="Label1" runat="server" />
    </div>
    </form>
</body>
</html>
```

C# ViewDir.aspx.cs

```
using System;
using System.IO;

public partial class ViewDir : System.Web.UI.Page
{
    private DirectoryInfo dir;
    private string divider;
    private string rootDir;
```

```
protected void ShowInfo(object sender, EventArgs e)
{
    rootDir = Root.Text;
    divider="<br />-----------------------------<br />";
    dir = new DirectoryInfo(@rootDir);
    Label1.Text = "Directories" + divider;
    try
    {
            foreach (DirectoryInfo sub in dir.GetDirectories())
            {
                Label1.Text += sub.Name.ToString() + "<br />";
            }
            Label1.Text += "<br />Files";
            Label1.Text += divider;
            foreach (FileInfo files in dir.GetFiles())
            {
                Label1.Text += files.Name.ToString() + "<br />";
        }
    }
    catch (Exception es)
    {
        Label1.Text = "That directory was not found or was formed
incorrectly.";
        Label1.Text += "<br />" + es.ToString();
    }
    }
}
```

Once you have it set up, try different roots and directories to view both the directories and the files within the directories. To get started, Figure 15-7 shows the root directory for an installed IIS server. (Because your computer may be different from the one used to develop these examples, what you see will likely be different.)

In the IIS server root directory, you will see all of the ASP.NET 3.5 web sites developed with Visual Studio 2008 and then placed in the IIS server root to be viewed remotely. Included in the list is the ReadFile web site. In that directory is a text file with stored data. Figure 15-8 shows the path to the web site and the files in that directory.

You can see the text file used to store information in Figure 15-8, pauperDataBase.txt. With other applications you create using Visual Studio 2008, the files and directory are fairly standard. Each has an App_Data directory and both an ASPX and an ASPX.CS file.

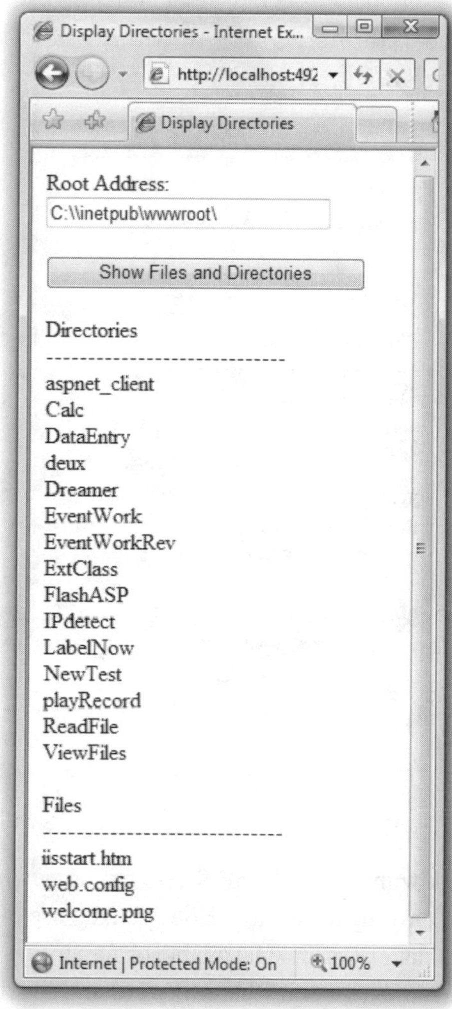

Figure 15-7 Viewing root directory of IIS server

However, you will not see the web.config file outside of the Visual Studio project files. That's because the web.config file is stored outside of the folder with the source files when used in a context where the file can be remotely accessed, such as a LAN or remote server.

Figure 15-8 Locating a text file

Summary

In some respects, the work with files and ASP.NET 3.5 is somewhat of a sideshow, especially compared with the power of using a database. However, the use of files provides an important functionality either where databases are unavailable or for storing small pieces of information that would make using a database somewhat awkward and overblown.

This chapter has only touched on a few of the uses for text files with ASP.NET 3.5; by knowing what they can do, you can employ them for a wide range of applications. Often, even with a database, you may want to have the ability to tap into stored data that can be used to select a database, a table, or some other small task required. So, while certainly not as powerful as a database, text files can be handy for storing details that may be required by a database.

Chapter 16

Security

Key Skills & Concepts

- Authentication

- Forms

- Windows

- Authorization

- Web.config

- Encryption

- Membership

- Database encryption

For anyone creating web sites in the current Internet environment, the issue of security is not whether to use it but *what kind* and *how much*. If you're working on relatively simple sites where you have nothing you want secured or hidden, security is a fairly simple matter—you don't use any. However, if you want materials to be available only to selected individuals, security becomes more important. When you begin making e-business sites, security is essential. You cannot allow unauthorized individuals to intercept information like credit card or social security numbers, or to freely enter a site whose income is derived from customers paying for a service provided by the site. Likewise, safeguarding other information such as medical or grade records that you want to be viewed only by authorized individuals requires a much higher level of security than you find available with simple HTML and JavaScript routines. Fortunately, because of server-side operations and built-in security features, ASP.NET 3.5 has very strong security features that are easy to use.

Putting Web.config to Work

The idea behind web security is to filter. You want those who are allowed access to get it easily, and you want to keep everyone else out. Picture an e-business application that requires more than one entry portal. The public portal is open to everyone. This is where customers and clients enter to purchase products and services. Other portals only allow certain people in. An administrative portal where orders are processed can be available only to certain people. Such portals need to be guarded against intrusion, and ideally, you don't even want others to know it exists. For example, if a user intentionally or accidentally accesses a general folder on the server, you do not want that person to see all of the files in that folder.

The first line of defense is the web.config file. It is an XML file with the .config extension. As you have been developing ASP.NET applications, one of the files automatically generated is a little web.config file with information about the web site's environment. If you open it, you will see all kinds of information. For example, you will see that your application has been developed by version 3.5.0.0 of ASP.NET. (Your information may be slightly different if you have a newer version of ASP.NET 3.5.) However, the most basic web.config file is one that comes up in an error message that reads as follows:

```
<!-- Web.config Configuration File -->
<configuration>
 <system.web>
 <customErrors mode="Off"/>
 </system.web>
</configuration>
```

If you place this file in the root directory of your IIS server, the general errors in a file are displayed, but your custom errors have been turned off. For the most part, that is a handy tool for testing on the Internet, but it is not the web.config file you want in a production environment.

Using Multiple Web.config Files

When you want users to have access to some files and not others, one way to control access is to use multiple web.config files. A web.config file in the root directory affects all of the files, but if you place a different web.config file in a subdirectory, it will override the root web.config file.

For example, suppose you have the following directory structure:

Root (web.config)
      ASPNET
               Display
               Dreamer
               MapFile
               Special
                    Lists (web.config)

All of the files and folders in the root directory are subject to the directives in the root web.config file. However, in the Special directory is another web.config file that is open to all users:

```
<configuration>
<system.web>
          <authorization>
               <allow users="*" />
          </authorization>
</system.web>
</configuration>
```

The `<allow>` node indicates which users have access, and the asterisk (*) is an "all" wildcard symbol. The files in the Lists directory are subject to this second web.config file. Figure 16-1 shows the actual files on a production server.

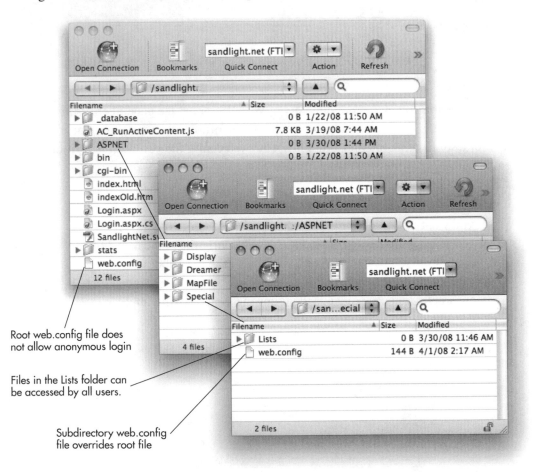

Root web.config file does not allow anonymous login

Files in the Lists folder can be accessed by all users.

Subdirectory web.config file overrides root file

Figure 16-1 Overriding root web.config

So while you can severely restrict user access to a wide range of files on your server, you also can isolate certain directories and files where you want users to have full access. In effect, you have the best of both worlds; control over user access on some files and wide-open access on others.

Developing a Forms Authentication Configuration

The first step in protecting your site is to develop a web.config file that has both an authentication and an authorization filter. If you use Forms authentication, all users are sent to a login page on their first visit. Once they have been authenticated, they can return to the site without having to go through a login process. For an e-business site, having ease of access is important for attracting and keeping customers.

With Forms authentication, no matter what page the user requests, he is automatically sent to a login page with the default name login.aspx. Once he fills out the login information, he is allowed to view the page requested initially. The following web.config file shows the required tags:

```
<configuration>
<system.web>
<authentication mode ="Forms" />
        <authorization>
                <deny users="?" />
        </authorization>
</system.web>
</configuration>
```

As noted, the authentication mode set to Forms automatically directs the browser to open a file named login.aspx, but if you want to change that to a specific file with a name you prefer, you can specify which one you want by using the tags

```
<authentication mode="Forms">
 <forms loginUrl="mySpecialFile.aspx" />
</authentication>
```

For the purposes of learning how to use the web.config set to Forms authentication, the rest of the examples use the default login.aspx, but feel free to make changes to another file if you wish.

First Login Application

To see how the web.config file from the previous section affects the flow, you will need to create a login file with the name **login.aspx**. The login web site that will be created is quite simple, but it has important consequences. Most importantly, the site uses the `FormsAuthentication` class from the `System.Web.Security` namespace. One of the methods is

`FormsAuthentication.RedirectFromLoginPage()`

which takes the original requested URL and sends the requested page if the login is successful. It uses the following format:

`FormsAuthentication.RedirectFromLoginPage(string, Boolean);`

The important feature of this method is that ASP.NET *automatically* adds the return URL when the browser is redirected to the login page. The string parameter is a username, and the Boolean is whether or not the login will store a persistent cookie. The false Boolean indicates that it will not store a cookie.

This whole state is set up when the web.config file indicates that anonymous users will not be permitted and the authentication mode is set to Forms. Figure 16-2 shows the intended path (dashed arrow) and actual path (solid arrow) of a request.

As noted earlier, if the web.config file has the authorization

`<authentication mode ="Forms" />`

the default redirection will be to a file named Login.aspx, so that will be the name of the login web site.

The login site is simply a bump in the road on the way to the desired site. This first example needs to be simple, but its purpose is important. In looking at the ASP.NET portion of the application, you will see absolutely nothing new from materials already covered. It consists of two TextBox controls, a Button control, and a Label control. The following code listing shows what you need to create the ASP.NET portion of the web site:

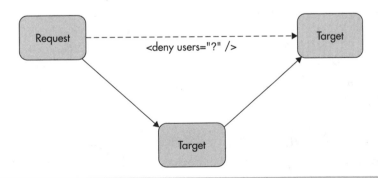

Figure 16-2 Request sent to Login before returning the target

ASP.NET Login.aspx

```
<%@ Page Language="C#" AutoEventWireup="true" CodeFile="Login.aspx.cs"
Inherits="LogNow" %>
<!DOCTYPE html PUBLIC "-//W3C//DTD XHTML 1.0 Transitional//EN"
"http://www.w3.org/TR/xhtml1/DTD/xhtml1-transitional.dtd">
<html xmlns="http://www.w3.org/1999/xhtml">
<style type="text/css">
    body
    {
      font-family:Verdana;
      font-size:11pt;
      color:Navy;
    }
    h1
    {
      font-size:18pt;
      font-weight:bold;
    }
</style>
<head runat="server">
    <title>Login</title>
</head>
<body>
    <form id="form1" runat="server">
    <div>
    <h1>Login Page</h1>
        <asp:TextBox ID="uname" runat="server" /> Name<p />
        <asp:TextBox ID="pw" runat="server" TextMode="Password"
/> Password<p />
        <asp:Button ID="Button1" runat="server" Text="Login"
onclick="DoLogin" /><p />
        <asp:Label ID="BadLog" runat="server"
          ForeColor="#FF3300" />
    </div>
    </form>
</body>
</html>
```

The C# portion of the web site is very simple as well. The event handler is a response to the button press, and an `if()` statement determines whether the login username and password are correct. If they are, the `FormsAuthentication` instance redirects the page to its original target URL. Otherwise, the user sees the message in the Label control.

C# Login.aspx.cs

```
using System;
using System.Web.Security;
public partial class LogNow : System.Web.UI.Page
```

```
{
protected void DoLogin(object sender, EventArgs e)
    {
        if (uname.Text == "snap" && pw.Text == "dragon")
        {
            FormsAuthentication.RedirectFromLoginPage(uname.Text, false);
        }
        BadLog.Text = "Check your username and password. Not logged in.";
    }
}
```

The tricky aspect of this example is that it should be placed on the root of an IIS server along with the web.config file. This can be on your own system as shown in Figure 16-3 or

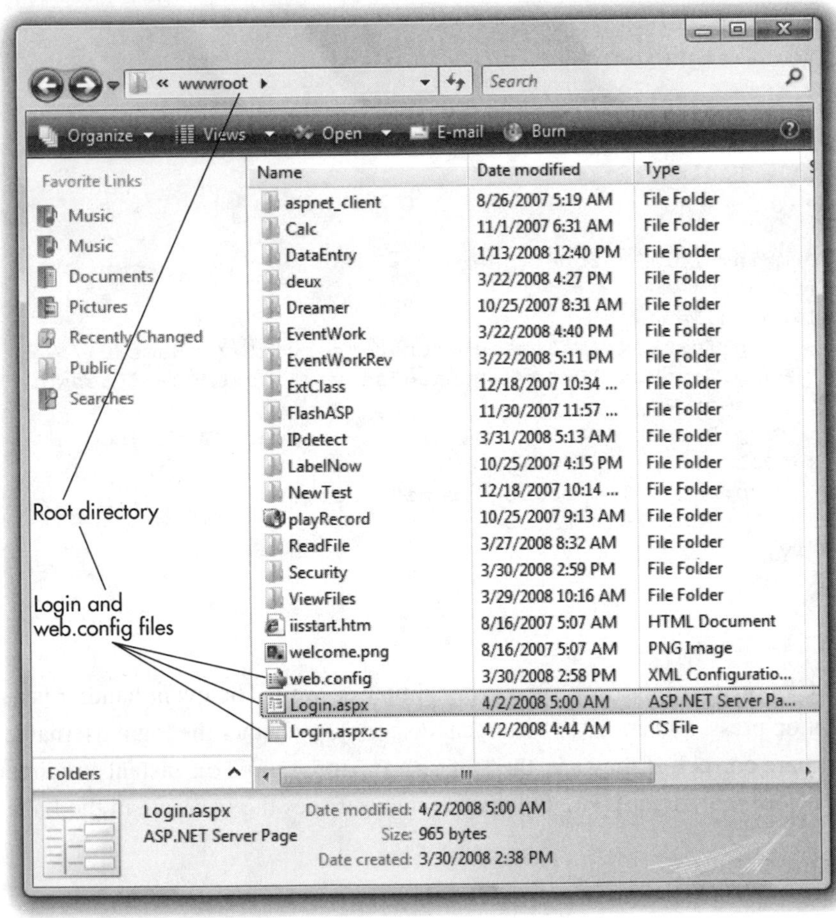

Figure 16-3 Placement of web.config and Login files in IIS root

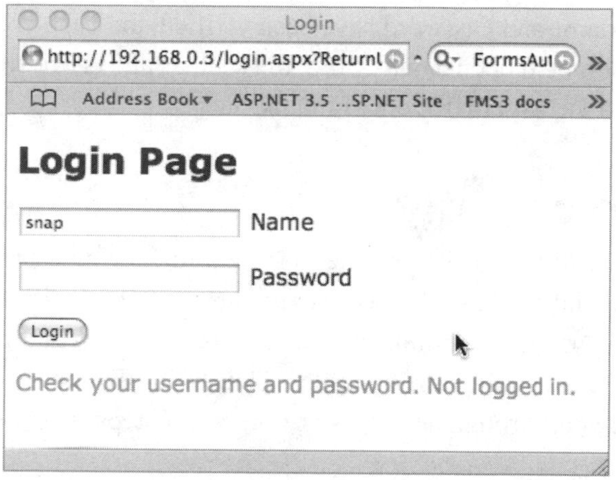

Figure 16-4   Login page appears automatically

on a production server. The full path for an IIS server on your computer would be `OS (C:)` `> inetpub > wwwroot`.

Once everything is in place, open your browser and navigate to an ASPX file. As soon as you do, you will be redirected to the Login file as shown in Figure 16-4. If you put in an incorrect username or password, you will see the message that your attempt failed.

Ask the Expert

Q: Isn't it risky to put the login name and password in the C# code? Wouldn't it be fairly easy for a hacker to get those?

A: You bet! The C# portion of the login example is to illustrate how the `FormsAuthentication` class can be used to send the requested URL to the user after she has successfully logged in. Besides being a fairly risky way of protecting a username and password, it's awkward to store username and password information in a coded format. Imagine a site that has thousands of users. So keep in mind that the login example is to show how the web.config file can redirect a request to a login page and how the `FormsAuthentication` class sends the logged-in user to the requested URL.

Once the username and password have been verified, the page you originally requested appears. If you attempt to open a non-ASPX file such as an HTML file, your request will not be filtered, and the target URL opens immediately.

Membership Security

For strong security, ASP.NET 3.5 provides a system for storing usernames and encrypted passwords in a special database. You can set up this security in different ways using Visual Studio 2008. Many of the most important elements are set up automatically, including the database with the default name of ASPNETDB.MDF. To see how everything works, a simple example goes through an extensive number of steps to add users and roles that can be created.

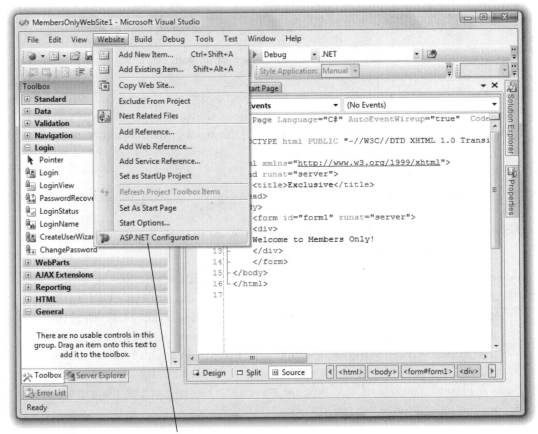

Select ASP.NET Configuration

Figure 16-5 Opening the Web Site Administration Tool

Try This A Member Based Security Web Site

To start this application, you will be using a simple site that does nothing more than let users know that a successful login has brought them to the requested site. However, while the destination site is very simple, you need several steps to get there. The following steps show how:

1. Create a new Web Site named **MembersOnlyWebSite1**. In the title, type in the word **Exclusive**, and in the `<div>` container, type in the greeting **Welcome to Members Only**. Save the ASPX file with the default name **Default.aspx**. That's all you need to do with the target site. It's completed.

2. From the Website menu select ASP.NET Configuration as shown in Figure 16-5.

3. You will see the Web Site Administration (WSA) Tool in your browser. When the WSA Tool first appears on the Home page, you will see four tabs and three links as shown in Figure 16-6. Click either the Security tab or the link.

Figure 16-6 Home page of the Web Site Administration Tool

(continued)

4. In the Security page of the WSA Tool, you will see the options shown in Figure 16-7. Click on the Select Authentication Type link under the Users column.

5. The two authentication options appear. Choose the From The Internet radio button as shown in Figure 16-8. Then click Done.

6. You will be returned to the main Security page. Note that the options have changed in the Users columns. Click on the Create User link. The Create User page shown in Figure 16-9 appears.

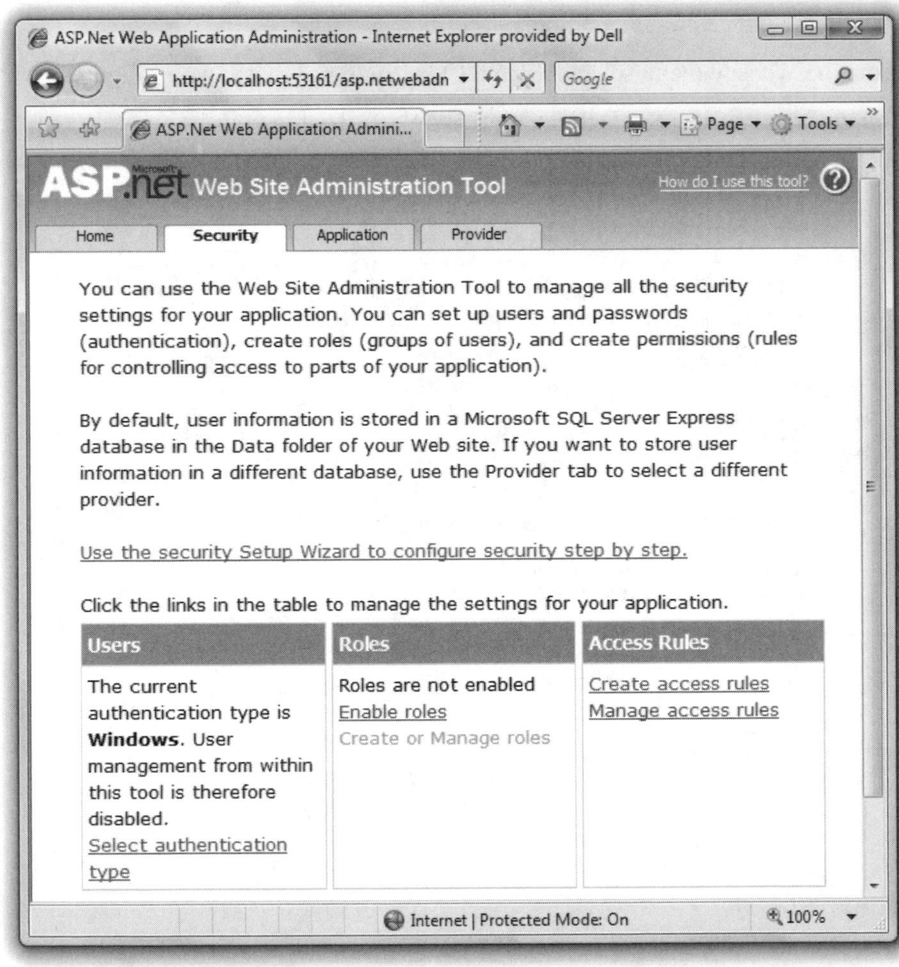

Figure 16-7   Web Site Administration Tool Security page

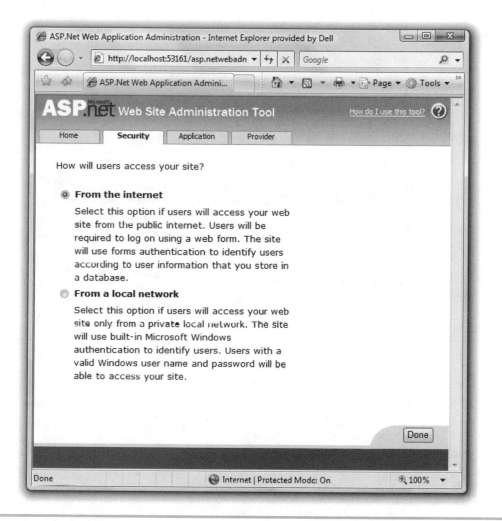

Figure 16-8   Choosing Internet authentication

7. Fill in the form to sign up for a new account. The password must be at least 7 characters and include a non-alphanumeric character. The password used for this example is *coffee!* with the exclamation point (!) being the sole non-alphanumeric character. Be sure to write down the username and password. The password is stored in a database, ASPNETDB.MDF, in a table named aspnet_Users. When you view the table, all of the passwords are encrypted, and if you don't have a record of them, you will likely forget them.

(continued)

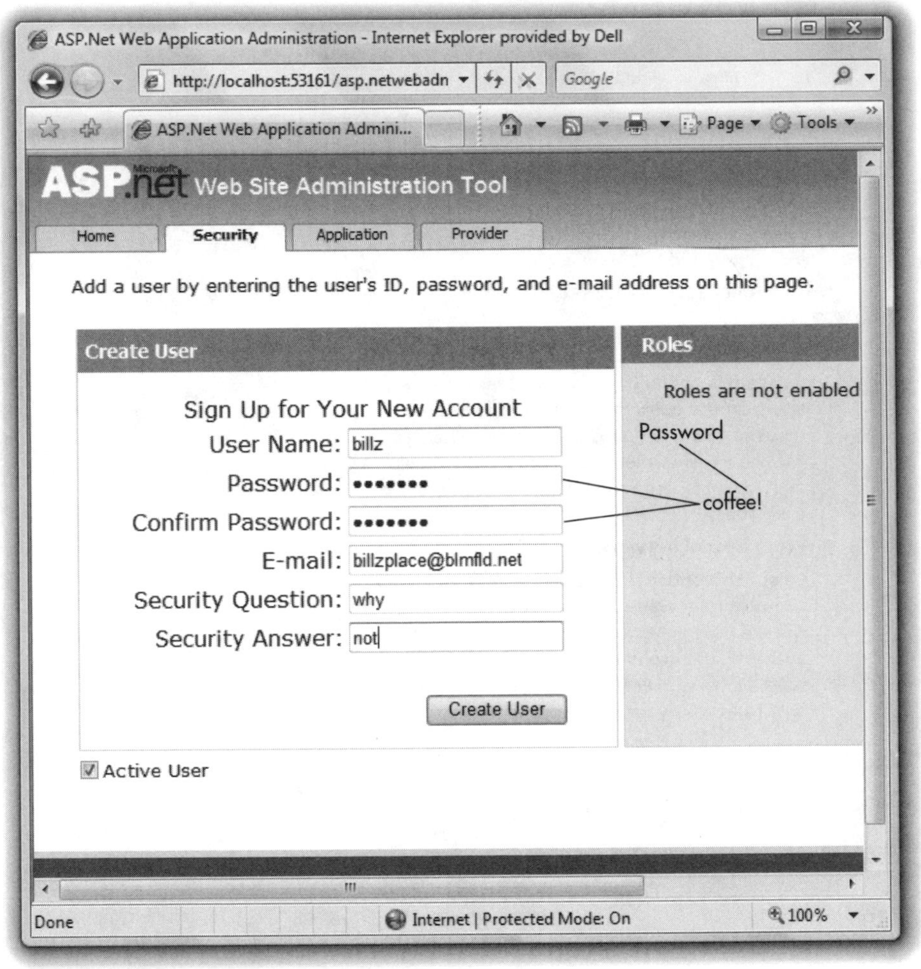

Figure 16-9 Creating a user account

8. When you have typed in the information, click on the Create User button. If you have successfully created an account, you will see the message page shown in Figure 16-10.

9. If you want to create more accounts, click the Continue button. (For now, add a few more unique accounts for practice.) When you've added a few more accounts, click the Security tab to return to the main Security page. Under the Roles column click on the Enable Roles link. When you do so, you will see two new links in the Roles column, Disable Roles and Create Or Manage Roles. Click on Create Or Manage Roles to create a new role. In the New Role Name window, type in **sysadmin** as shown in Figure 16-11. Click the Add Role button.

Figure 16-10 Successful creation of a user account

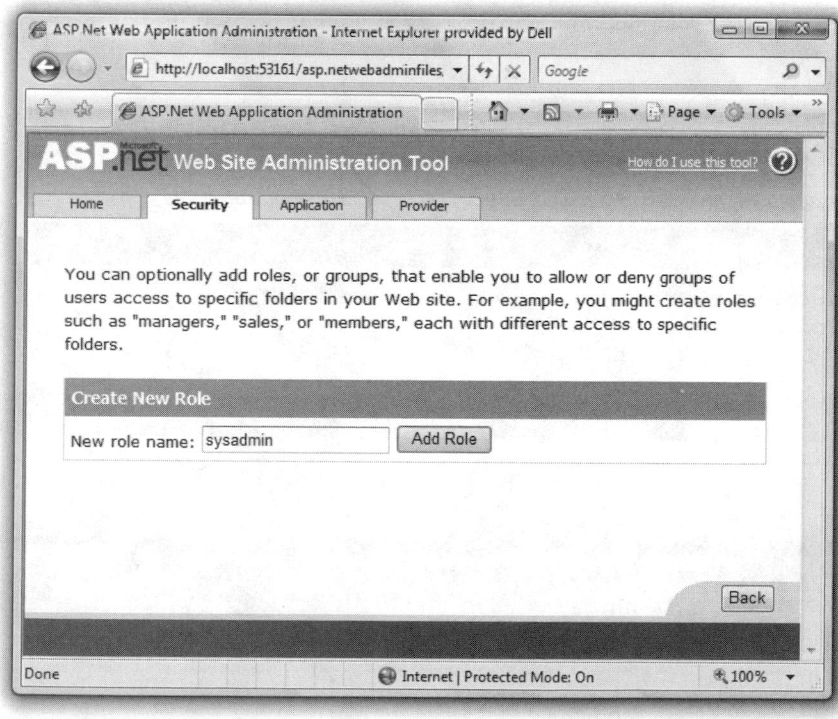

Figure 16-11 Adding a role

(continued)

10. After you click Add Role, the Role Name column appears. You will see a Manage link. Click it to bring up the role management page as shown in Figure 16-12.

11. Click on the letter that is the first letter in the username to which you wish to assign a role. It will appear in the User Name column. A second column, User Is In Role, has checkboxes that you click to include the user in the selected role. Figure 16-12 shows what you will see.

12. Click on the Security tab to return to the main Security page. In the Access Rules column you will see a link, Create Access Rules. Click that link to open the Add New Access Rule option as shown in Figure 16-13. Select the Role radio button in the Rule Applies To column and the Allow radio button in the Permission column and then click OK.

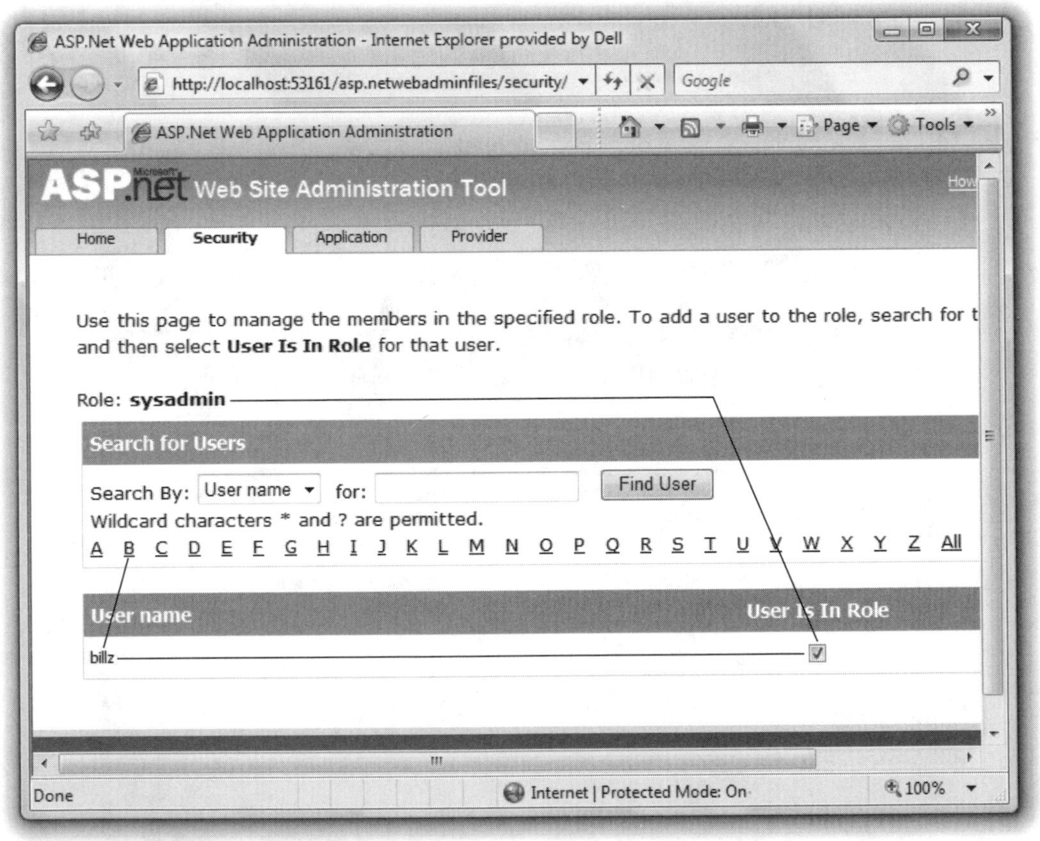

Figure 16-12 Adding role to user

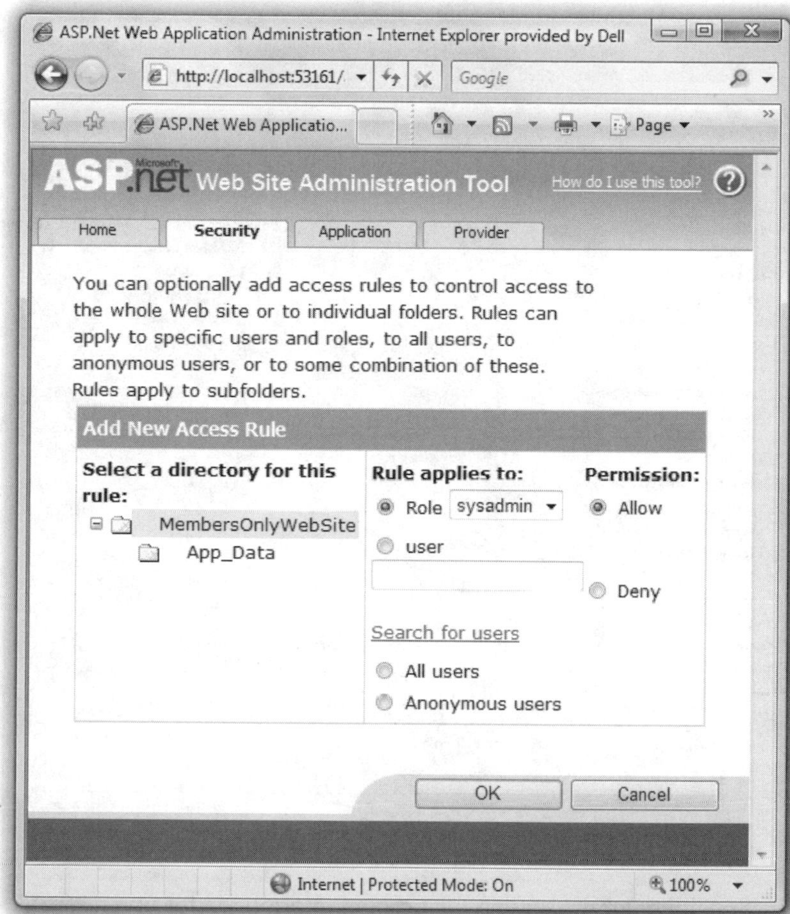

Figure 16-13 Adding access rules

13. Close the browser, open the Solution Explorer, and click on the App_Data folder. In it you will find the ASPNETDB.MDF database as shown in Figure 16-14. Double-click the ASPNETDB.MDF icon and open the Server Explorer. In the Server Explorer you will see ASPNETDB.MDF. Select it and open the Tables folder. In it you will see all of the different tables that have automatically been created and are used with the security system.

(continued)

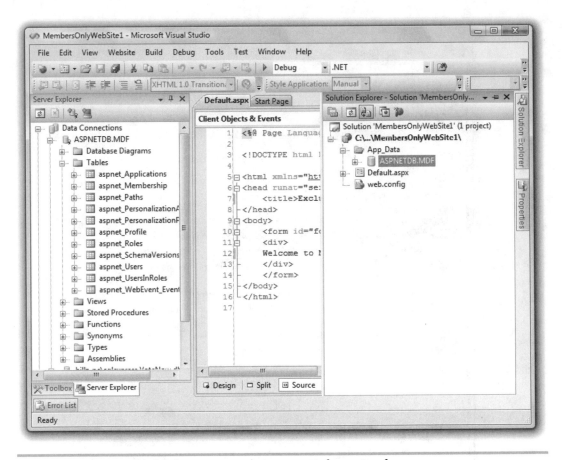

Figure 16-14 Special database storing the account information for users

14. Right-click the aspnet_Users table and select Show Table Data. Figure 16-15 shows the contents of the table. You can see the "billz" account in the UserName column, and another, "deez," in the same column. However, instead of the passwords, you see heavily coded ApplicationId and UserId columns. Not only is heavy encryption at work to discourage intruders, but also, unless you wrote down your password, you'd never be able to find it in the table.

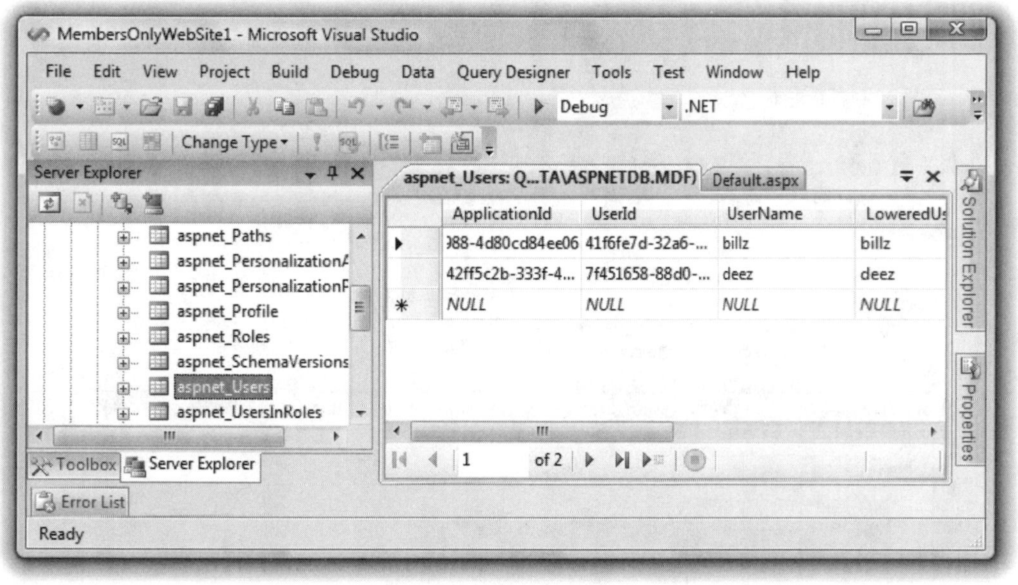

Figure 16-15 Table Data showing usernames and encrypted information

15. Open the Solution Explorer, right-click on the root name, and select Add New Item to open the Templates window. Select the Web Form template and enter the filename **login.aspx** in the Name window as shown in Figure 16-16. Click the Add button.

16. Select the login.aspx tab in Visual Studio 2008, and open the Login menu in the Toolbox. Choose the Split mode. Drag a Login control to the `<div>` container as shown in Figure 16-17.

17. In the Design portion of the Split mode, select the Login control, and from the pop-up menu, select Auto Format and choose the Elegant scheme as shown in Figure 16-18; then click OK. After this step your application should be good to go.

(continued)

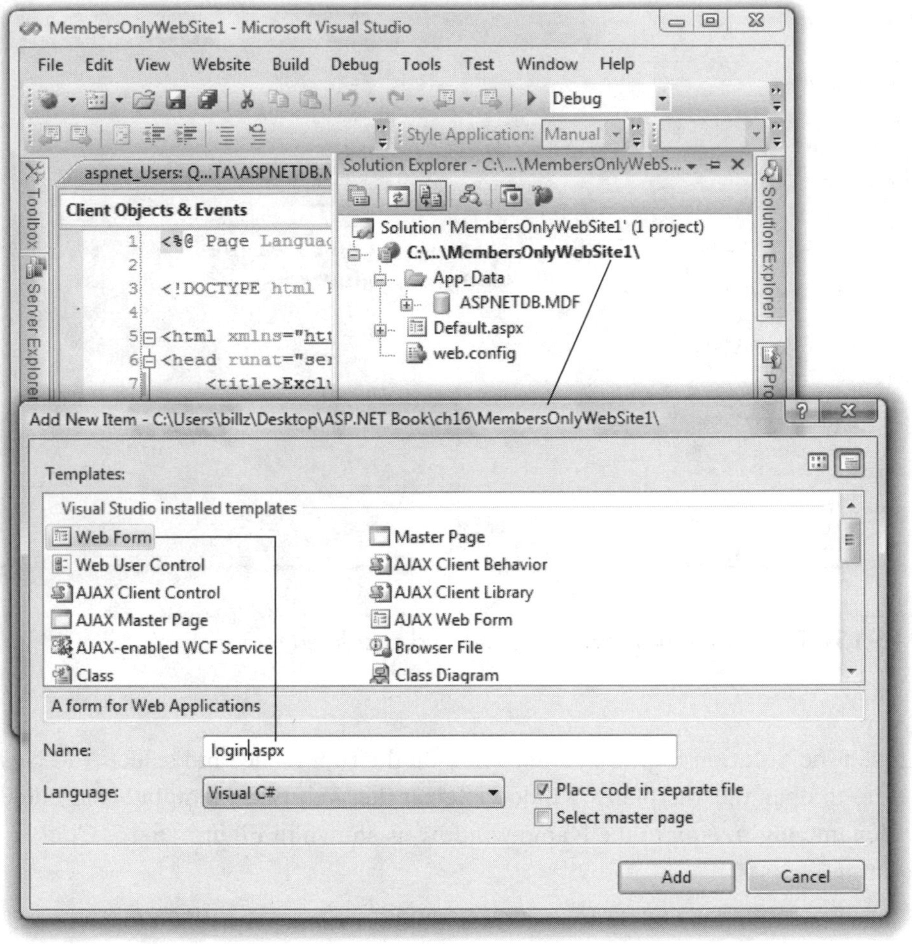

Figure 16-16   Adding a login file to the web site

To test the application, select the Default.aspx tab and press CTRL-F5. You will see the Login control appear as shown in Figure 16-19. When you enter the username and password of an account that you created in the Web Site Administration Tool, you will see the simple message "Welcome to Members Only!"

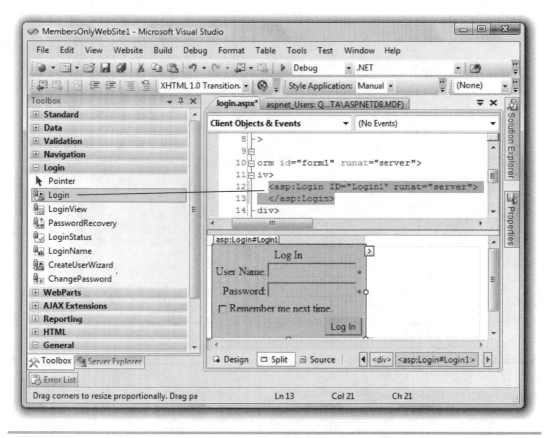

Figure 16-17 Adding a Login control

If you forgot your username or password or typed them in incorrectly, the Login control automatically returns an error message as can be seen in Figure 16-20.

You can change the error message by selecting the Login control and in the Properties window change the text in the `FailureText` property.

(continued)

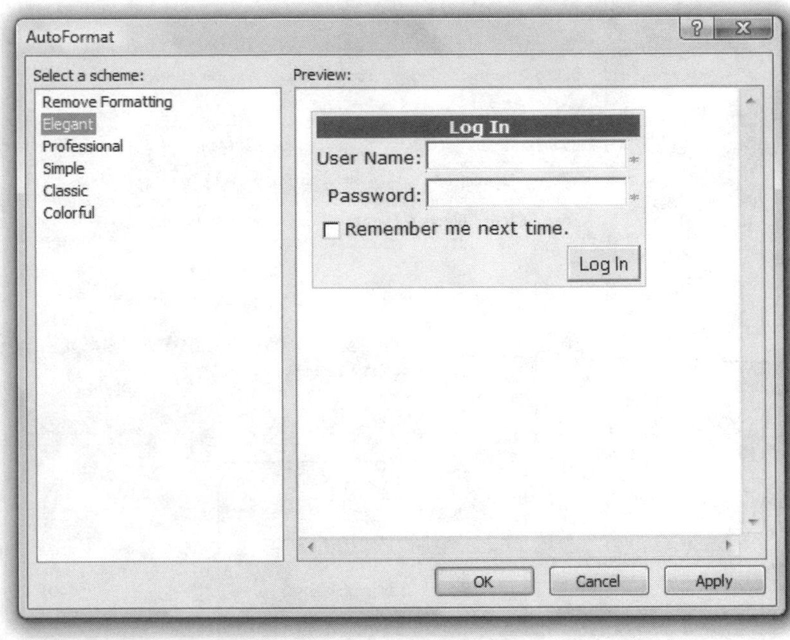

Figure 16-18 Applying autoformatting to the Login

Figure 16-19 Login page

Figure 16-20 Login error message

Remote Registration

The Web Site Administration Tool is fine for registering users, but what if your site gets thousands of inquiries? If registrants could register themselves, you could save a lot of time and speed up the process. Fortunately, in addition to a Login control, ASP.NET 3.5 also has a CreateUserWizard control that you can drag and drop right into the Visual Studio 2008 editor to easily allow users to set up their own accounts with very high security. The control includes a wealth of properties that you can use to customize the information you'd like to have when users register. In this section, we will be looking at the default set of properties and functionality built into the CreateUserWizard control.

How to Get to the Registration Page

The first issue that must be addressed when setting up a CreateUserWizard control is how a user will get to a registration page. Remember that the web.config file sends everything to the Login page because the authorization does not allow anonymous users. So the trick will be to first send the user to the Login page, and those who have not registered will be redirected to the Registration page.

However, as soon as you attempt to redirect the application to a registration page, the web.config settings return you to the Login page. To remedy that problem, keep in mind that a web site can have multiple web.config files with different authorization settings. (See the section "Using Multiple Web.config Files" at the beginning of this chapter.) If you place a second web.config file at a lower level in the hierarchy, the control can be accessed by a reference to a folder that allows anonymous logins. Figure 16-21 shows this arrangement in the Solution Explorer.

Basically, what you will be doing is starting off with the Default.aspx and login.aspx pages and adding the following code to the web.config file automatically generated with a new web site. (Find the `<system.web>` node and place the authentication and authorization nodes after it.)

```
...more code
<system.web>
    <authentication mode="Forms" />
    <authorization>
        <deny users="?"/>
    </authorization>
...more code
```

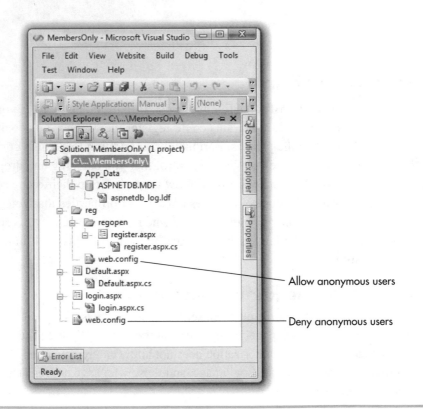

Figure 16-21 Register page in accessible position

Next, you need a web.config file in a separate folder where you will place the necessary files for the registration operation.

```
<!-- Web.config for Registration -->
<configuration>
    <system.web>
        <authorization>
            <allow users="*"/>
        </authorization>
    </system.web>
</configuration>
```

Basically, these two web.config files allow everyone to register, and the path to the registration page and back to the login page provides one technique for guiding users to the right place and back.

Try This   A Simple Login and Registration Application

The process for creating a web site that will both log in users and provide them with the opportunity to register is relatively easy once you understand the concept of using the two web.config files to help navigate in and out of restricted areas. In this next application, you may be very surprised to see the strong functionality of the two key controls used in creating the web site. After the arduous process of using the Web Site Administration Tool, this one is simple, requiring no C#, just two controls. The following steps show you how:

1. Create a new Web Site, and save it as **MembersOnly**. The Default.aspx file is nothing more than a target file. As in the previous example, just type in **Welcome to Members Only!**

2. Open the Solution Explorer and right-click on C:\...MembersOnly\. Select Add New Item, choose Web Form, and name it **login.aspx**. (If this sounds a lot like the previous application, just wait.)

3. Select the Design mode and drag a Login control from the Toolbox to the editor. Click on the pop-up menu on the control and choose Auto Format | Elegant. (If you open the App_Data folder, you will find the ASPNETDB.MDF database.)

4. From the Solution Explorer double-click on the web.config file, and then add the tags for authentication and authorization as shown in the previous section, "How to Get to the Registration Page." Save the web.config file and close it.

(continued)

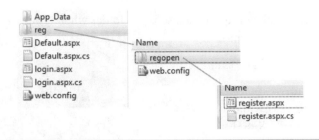

Figure 16-22 File structure from the Windows Explorer

5. This next section can be done outside of Visual Studio 2008. Figure 16-22 shows the relative folder and file directories that are the same as in Figure 16-21 except from the perspective of the Windows Explorer. First create a folder named **reg**, and place it in the same folder as the Default.aspx file. Then in the reg folder add the second web.config file shown in the previous section. This is the web.config file containing the `<allow users="*"/>` tag.

6. Inside the reg folder add another folder and name it **regopen**. Reopen MembersOnly in Visual Studio 2008 and open the Solution Explorer. In it you will find both the reg and regopen folders as well as the second web.config file.

7. In the Solution Explorer right-click on the regopen folder, and select Add New Item | Web Form. Name the new Web form **register.aspx**.

8. Set the editor to Design mode. Select the **login.aspx** tab in Visual Studio 2008, and drag a Login control into the editor.

9. Click the Login icon and in the Properties window find the `CreateUserUrl` property. Click on the navigation button (the rounded square button with the three dots) in the `CreateUserUrl` value column and navigate to the register.aspx file and select it. That will create a relative path to the registration page. Find the `CreateUserText` property and add the text **Register**. Once you have completed that, you should see the word "Register" at the bottom of the Login icon.

10. In the Properties window find the `DestinationPageUrl` property, click the navigation button, and navigate to the Default.aspx file. That will return users to the desired page after they log in.

11. In the Solution Explorer navigate to the register.aspx file, and double-click to open it. In the Design mode, drag a CreateUserWizard control to the `div` container in the editor. Select the control, open the pop-up menu, and select Auto Format | Elegant. Now your registration window has the same format as your login window.

12. With the CreateUserWizard control selected, open the Properties window and select the
`ContinueDestinationPageUrl`. Use the navigation button to navigate to login.aspx.
Switch to the Source mode and check your path. The `ContinueDestinationPageUrl`
property should show:

```
ContinueDestinationPageUrl="../../login.aspx
```

If it does not show that path, change the code so that it does. (Some versions of Visual
Studio 2008 put in the path `~/login.aspx` and that will not work.)

13. Select the Default.aspx tab in Visual Studio 2008 and press CTRL-F5. If all of your
web.config files are in place, instead of taking you to the Default.aspx page, Visual
Studio will open the Login page. Click on the Register link.

14. The registration page opens. Fill in the form as shown in Figure 16-23. All of this
information is automatically encrypted in the ASPNETDB.MDF database.

15. As soon as you click Create User, you will get either an error message or a box announcing
that you successfully created a new user. Figure 16-24 shows what you should see. Click
Continue.

16. You will now be returned to the Login page. Enter the new username and password,
and you will be taken to the default destination page.

   Using both the Login and CreateUserWizard controls, you can easily make a system
for logging in and registering users. As soon as you place the Login control in the Visual
Studio 2008 editor, it creates the ASPNETDB.MDF in the App_Data folder. Outside
of Visual Studio 2008, you lose much of the development functionality. For example,

Figure 16-23 Creating a new user

(continued)

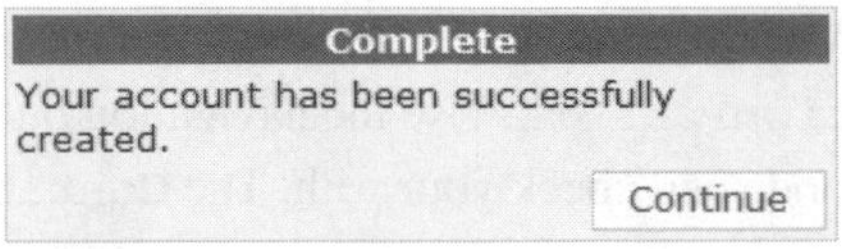

Complete
Your account has been successfully created.
Continue

Figure 16-24 "Complete" message shows if new user is in database

if you type in the code alone for the Login control, you will not get the ASPNETDB.MDF database and the aspnetdb_log.ldf files generated in the App_Data folder. Both of those are required for using the Login and CreateUserWizard controls.

Adding Roles

As you saw in the section on using the Web Site Administration Tool, you are able to add different roles and assign each an access rule (see Figure 16-13). You can add roles and rules using the Web Site Administration Tool directly from the Login control icon in the editor. From the Design mode, simply open the Login control's pop-up menu and select Administer Website. That will open the Web Site Administration Tool with direct access to the database you are working with for that web site. You have access to all of the users that have been generated with the CreateUserWizard control. This process must take place in the editor and cannot be used when the web site is up and running, even in Visual Studio 2008.

Warning

As much as I respect the strength of the encryption and protection afforded by ASP.NET 3.5, I *would not* recommend setting up any kind of financial-transfer web site using it. Whenever it comes to setting up an e-business site requiring financial transfers, I use (and recommend using) a security service that does financial security and nothing else. For both the purposes of legal protection against lawsuits and for smooth financial transactions, rely on a well-respected security firm that deals with credit card and bank transfers, not on beginning skills with ASP.NET.

With an e-business site, I am very comfortable using the ASP.NET encryption for logging in and registering users, but when it comes time to pay a bill, I use a separate page that logs into a security firm's financial transfer software. In this way, your clients have multiple protections and so do you.

Summary

Web site security is and will continue to be an important concern for developers. The number and sophistication of hackers gaining access to web sites to steal content, identities, and funds transferred over the Internet steadily grow. By using the strong encryption methods with identity information stored in a database discussed in this chapter, you virtually guarantee security. This is not to say someone won't come along and work out a way to break into a site protected with the methods discussed in this chapter, but the level of encryption is such that they'll have to get passwords from a source other than the database where accounts are created and stored. While creating example accounts, I was unable to retrieve the passwords of accounts I had forgotten. Even with total access to the ASPNETDB.MDF database, there was no way to find the forgotten password! Now that's strong protection.

Chapter 17

ASP.NET Ajax

Key Skills & Concepts

- What is Ajax?

- Slipping in just the data needed without reloading the page

- Changes without disruption

- Key Ajax Server controls

- ScriptManager

- UpdatePanel

- Timer

- Triggers

Ajax is a relatively new Internet technology that grew out of combining JavaScript and XML. The term itself is an acronym for "Asynchronous JavaScript And XML." The key feature of Ajax can be seen when the client requests new information. Instead of sending a whole new page, Ajax sends only the required new information. That means all of the buttons, text, graphics, and other objects that may be on a page do not have to be shipped over the Internet and reloaded into your browser. ASP.NET 3.5 includes all the controls you need, and you will find that using Ajax with ASP.NET is far easier than writing your own JavaScript programs.

ASP.NET Ajax

Virtually every control in ASP.NET uses a post-back to the server in that it is executed on the server and not on the browser. All of the form information from an ASP.NET page has the ability to post information to the server and return it to the same page. That's a good thing. The problem arises when everything in a page is returned to refresh just a little information. For example, text takes up very little Internet space and is pretty speedy to send all by itself. However, if you change just the text, the whole page along with the updated text still may get shipped back and that slows the process.

In the Marx Brothers movie *Duck Soup,* Chico inquired, "Well, who you gonna believe, me or your own eyes?" To show the efficiency of Ajax, two different applications will be used so that you will believe your eyes. One application, which will be called *Old School,* uses standard ASP.NET controls. The second application is virtually identical except that it uses Ajax and will be the *AjaxIntro* application.

Old School

The first web site is made up of three standard web controls: a TextBox, a Button, and a Label. When you press the button, the contents of the TextBox are passed to the Label. The following listings provide everything you need for this application:

ASP.NET Default.aspx

```
<%@ Page Language="C#" AutoEventWireup="true" CodeFile="Default.aspx.cs"
Inherits="_Default" %>
<!DOCTYPE html PUBLIC "-//W3C//DTD XHTML 1.0 Transitional//EN"
"http://www.w3.org/TR/xhtml1/DTD/xhtml1-transitional.dtd">
<html xmlns="http://www.w3.org/1999/xhtml">
<head runat="server">
    <title>Old School Update</title>
</head>
<body>
<h3>Update From the Old School</h3>
    <form id="form1" runat="server">
    <div>
        <asp:TextBox ID="TextBox1" runat="server" /><p />
        <asp:Button ID="Button1" runat="server" Text="Old School"
onclick="Button1_Click" /></p>
        <asp:Label ID="Label1" runat="server" Text="New Info Appears Here" />
    </div>
    </form>
</body>
</html>
```

C# Default.aspx.cs

```
using System;
public partial class _Default : System.Web.UI.Page
{
    protected void Button1_Click(object sender, EventArgs e)
    {
        Label1.Text = TextBox1.Text;
    }
}
```

When you test the application, Figure 17-1 shows what you will see.

What this application does is what ASP.NET was originally designed to accomplish—have pages that would post back to themselves. When you test it, you will notice that on the first test, it takes a while for any message to come back. That's because the post-back is sending more than just the message. It's old school. As you change the text, you can see

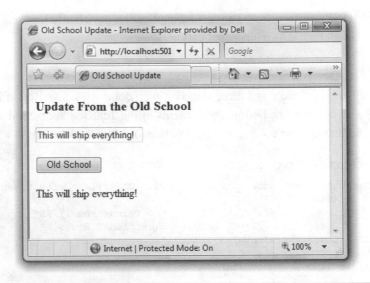

Figure 17-1 Sending a message back to the page

the delay bumps as everything is hauled back and forth over the Internet. (Actually, it's just going to the Visual Studio 2008 server on your machine, so it's not even subject to Internet traffic!)

Ajax and ASP.NET 3.5

ASP.NET 3.5 Ajax is easy to use and is efficient. Using Visual Studio 2008, you can create an Ajax web site using only two Ajax controls. The main Ajax control is what is called the *UpdatePanel,* where all of the elements in your Ajax application can be placed. The other control is the *ScriptManager.* The ScriptManager control is required to access the Ajax Library and partial page rendering without post-back.

TIP

The `<ContentTemplate>` property contains all of the content of an UpdatePanel control. If you drag an UpdatePanel using Visual Studio 2008 into the editor and then add a standard control inside the UpdatePanel from the Design mode, the `<ContentTemplate>` property is added automatically. However, if you do the same thing from the Source mode, no `<ContentTemplate>` property is added automatically, and you have to add the `<ContentTemplate></ContentTemplate>` tags by typing them. So, to get started in this next and subsequent examples in this chapter, start off using the Design mode, and once you have placed the Ajax and Standard controls inside the UpdatePanel, you can switch over to the Source mode if you wish.

Try This Upgrading to Ajax

To show how everything works, the first ASP.NET Ajax is an exact replica of the Old School example in the previous subsection. However, this new one uses Ajax so that you can see the difference in performance between it and the Old School example. The following steps show how:

1. Open a new Web Site, and name it **AjaxIntro**. (If you've used the Ajax plug-in in ASP.NET 2.0 and are looking for the special Ajax Web form from Visual Studio 2005, you will not find it in Visual Studio 2008. Just select ASP.NET Web Site as you would for any new web site.)

2. Switch to Design mode, open the Ajax Extensions menu in the Toolbox, and drag an UpdatePanel control inside the `<div>` container in the editor.

3. Open the Standard menu in the Toolbox and drag TextBox, Button, and Label controls into the editor. Use Figure 17-2 as a guide to where the parts are placed.

4. Switch to the Source mode, and right above the `<div>` tag drag a ScriptManager control. Delete the closing `ScriptManager` tag, and add a closing `/>` to the first `ScriptManager` tag. You should see the following:

```
<asp:ScriptManager ID-"ScriptManager1" runat="server" />
```

The following code listing shows the remaining elements to add to the web site:

ASP.NET Default.aspx

```
<%@ Page Language="C#" AutoEventWireup="true"  CodeFile="Default.aspx.cs"
Inherits="_Default" %>
<!DOCTYPE html PUBLIC "-//W3C//DTD XHTML 1.0 Transitional//EN"
"http://www.w3.org/TR/xhtml1/DTD/xhtml1-transitional.dtd">
<html xmlns="http://www.w3.org/1999/xhtml">
<head runat="server">
<style type="text/css">
body { background-color:#9cc7f4;
       color:#930b23;
       font-family:Verdana;
       font-size:12px;}
.btn { background-color:#930b23;
          color:#e2c7bc;
          font-size:14px;
          font-weight:bold;}
h2  {color:#930b23;}
</style>
    <title>Easy Ajax</title>
</head>
```

(continued)

```
<body>
    <form id="form1" runat="server">
    <asp:ScriptManager ID="ScriptManager1" runat="server" />
    <div>
        <asp:UpdatePanel ID="UpdatePanel1" runat="server">
            <ContentTemplate>
                <h2>This site has been Ajaxed!</h2>
                <asp:TextBox ID="TextBox1" runat="server" />
                     Favorite Web Application Framework<br />
                <asp:Button ID="Button1" runat="server"
                    Text="Ajax me!" CssClass="btn" />
                <p />
                <asp:Label ID="Label1" runat="server"
                    Text="Label" Font-Names="Verdana"
                    Font-Size="12px" Font-Bold="True" />
            </ContentTemplate>
        </asp:UpdatePanel>
    </div>
    </form>
</body>
</html>
```

You need only make a small change to the C# portion of the application that assigns the value of the TextBox to the Label control. Note that the only namespace used is System.

C# Default.aspx.cs

```
using System;
public partial class _Default : System.Web.UI.Page
{
    protected void Page_Load(object sender, EventArgs e)
    {
        Label1.Text = "Ajax presents=> " + TextBox1.Text;
    }
}
```

As you can see, other than the Ajax controls, everything else is like a normal web site. You use the same CSS, and the non-Ajax controls have the same properties as for a non-Ajax site. All this Ajax web site has that is different from others in this book is the UpdatePanel control, ContentTemplate property, and ScriptManager control.

When you test the web site in Visual Studio 2008, enter as much text as you want in the TextBox. Then click the button and watch the results appear in the Label control. Figure 17-2 shows what you should see.

The difference you will see is that the contents of the TextBox that you entered appear almost instantaneously in the Label control. Test the page a few more times to see how

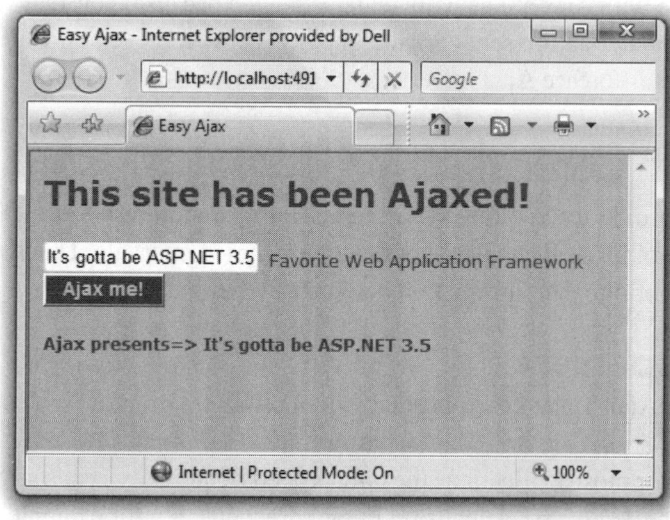

Figure 17-2 Ajax-enabled web site

quickly the text appears. Now load up and test the non-Ajax version, Old School, and compare the two. The difference is that only the text was posted back in the Ajax version, not the whole page.

When you run examples of your local host, they do not go through the routers and other time-consuming gates that typically happen in production use. As a result, the

Ask the Expert

Q: In the Ajax example, no event handling code was entered for the button. How is it possible for the button to keep passing the contents of the TextBox control to the Label control using the `Page_Load` event handler?

A: When the button is pressed, it generates a post-back. The page thinks that with the use of the default `Load_Page`, a new page is loaded, so it passes the values of the TextBox control to the Label control. By and large, that is not a recommended practice. See the section "Using Events with Ajax" later in this chapter.

savings you see with Ajax are actually underestimated because their real value lies in the fact that fewer materials are sent over the Internet. However, even on your local computer, you can see the difference Ajax makes.

Ajax Timer Control

The Timer control in the Toolbox's Ajax Extensions menu is very useful. Essentially, the Timer control is one that calls a C# function in timed intervals. This is a perfect application for bringing in information based on a timer but not reloading the entire page.

Timer Properties

Not only is the Ajax Timer control useful, but it also is easy to use. With only four properties, ID, Enabled, EnableViewState, and Interval, you can set it up very quickly. For most applications the only property that really needs setting is the Interval. The Interval value is set in microseconds. So, for example, if you want a 22-second interval, you would set the value to 22000.

The control has several different events as well, but for most uses, all you need is the OnTick event. The OnTick event calls a C# event handler (method) at the assigned Interval. By placing the Timer inside the UpdatePanel container, by default it is the Ajax event handler for the UpdatePanel. (See "Using Events with Ajax" for elaboration.)

To see a practical application of using the Ajax Timer control, this next web site shows how the contents of external text files can be loaded into an Ajax context. Keep in mind that by loading the text in the Ajax UpdatePanel container, you will ensure that only the text, not the entire page, will be reloaded.

Before building the web site, you will need to understand how C# generates random numbers. (They're actually pseudorandom numbers, and for the purposes of this application, pseudorandom will be fine.) The code for the random-number generator is simple, but very different from some other languages. For generating values within a given range, you use the following format:

```
Random random = new Random();
randomVar = random.Next(maxNumericValue);
```

For example, if you have 12 different elements in an application, to generate random values from 1 to 12, you would write

```
Random random = new Random();
randomVar = random.Next(12);
```

In the sample application, the random number is used to select an array element and is placed as a numeric key to select names of text files to load.

Try This Using the Ajax Timer to Load Text Files

Suppose your client has different services she wishes to offer. Rather than having several different links, she'd like to have a window on her home page that randomly loads a text file to describe each service. She wants to use text files because their content is easy to update. Knowing that the page might become unattractively jumpy if the page reloads every time a new text file loads, you decide to use ASP.NET 3.5 Ajax. In this way, everything stays put while just the text file content is displayed in a TextBox control. You decide to use a TextBox control so that you can keep the message area within the graphic and information design. Further, if your client wants to add a lengthy description, the user will be able to scroll to read the whole message. The following steps walk you through the application:

1. Before you get started, create four text files. You can use any text editor such as Microsoft's Notepad or Macintosh's TextEdit. Eventually, they will be placed along with your other ASP.NET web site files as shown in Figure 17-3.

2. Open a new ASP.NET web site in Visual Studio 2008 and save it as **AjaxTime**.

3. Open the Solution Explorer and rename Default.aspx to **AjaxTime.aspx**.

Figure 17-3 All text files are placed with the other ASP.NET files.

(continued)

4. Open the AjaxTime.aspx.cs file and change the name of the partial class from _Default to **AjaxTime**. Check to make sure the `Inherits` in the AjaxTime.aspx is now changed to **AjaxTime** as well.

5. Select the AjaxTime.aspx tab in the editor and select the Design mode.

6. Open the Ajax Extensions menu, and drag an `UpdatePanel` into the div container. Select the `UpdatePanel` that you just dragged into the editor.

7. Open the Standard Menu and drag a TextBox control into the `UpdatePanel`. In the Properties window set the `Height` to **180px**, `TextMode` to **Multiline**, `Width` to **247px**, `ReadOnly` to **True**, `BorderStyle` to **None**, `BackColor` to **#99FF33**, `ForeColor` to **#333333**, and `Font` to **Verdana**. (To double-check, review the code listing.)

8. Open the Ajax Extensions menu again, and drag a Timer control into the UpdatePanel. In the Properties window set the Interval to **5000**. (That provides a 5-second interval between events.) Switch to the Source view, and add **ontick="TimeShow"** to the Timer control tag.

9. Next, drag a ScriptManager to a space *above* the `<div>` tag. Review the following listing, add the CSS, and check your code against it.

ASP.NET AjaxTime.aspx

```
<%@ Page Language="C#" AutoEventWireup="true" CodeFile="AjaxTime.aspx.cs"
Inherits="AjaxTime" %>
<!DOCTYPE html PUBLIC "-//W3C//DTD XHTML 1.0 Transitional//EN"
"http://www.w3.org/TR/xhtml1/DTD/xhtml1-transitional.dtd">
<html xmlns="http://www.w3.org/1999/xhtml">
<head runat="server">
<style type="text/css">
#header
{
    font-family:Verdana;
    font-size:18pt;
    color:Gray;
    font-weight:bold;
}
</style>
    <title>Ajax Timer</title>
</head>
<body>
<form id="form1" runat="server">
    <asp:ScriptManager ID="ScriptManager1" runat="server" />
<div>
    <span id=header>Our Services</span><br/>
        <asp:UpdatePanel ID="UpdatePanel1" runat="server">
```

```
                    <ContentTemplate>
                        <asp:TextBox ID="TextBox1" runat="server"
                            Height="180px" TextMode="MultiLine"
                            Width="247px" BackColor="#99FF33"
                            Font-Names="Verdana,Arial,Helvetica,sans-serif"
                            ForeColor="#333333" ReadOnly="True"
BorderStyle="None" />
                        <asp:Timer ID="Timer1" runat="server"
                            Interval="5000" ontick="TimeShow" />
                    </ContentTemplate>
                </asp:UpdatePanel>
        </div>
        </form>
</body>
</html>
```

10. Once you have checked your ASP.NET file and saved it, open the AjaxTime.aspx.cs
    file and replace the default code with the following code. (Note that the code is very
    similar to what you learned in Chapter 15 for loading external text files.)

C# AjaxTime.aspx.cs

```csharp
using System;
using System.IO;
public partial class AjaxTime : System.Web.UI.Page
{
    private int counter;
    private StreamReader readAd;
    private String readLn;
    private String adNow;
    protected void TimeShow(object sender, EventArgs e)
    {
      Random Rand = new Random();
      counter = Rand.Next(4);
      string[] ads= {"Design.txt","Develop.txt","Ajax.txt", "Database.txt"};
      adNow= ads[counter];
      TextBox1.Text = "";
        try{
            using(readAd=new StreamReader(MapPath(adNow)))
            {
                while((readLn =readAd.ReadLine())!= null)
                {
                    TextBox1.Text+=readLn +"\n";
                }
            }
        }
        catch (Exception ec)
```

(continued)

```
        {
            TextBox1.Text="Check the file name. It was not found.";
            TextBox1.Text+=ec.Message;
        }
    }
}
```

Before you test your code, check the text filenames, *including the case,* and be sure they are placed in the same folder as the ASPX and ASPX.CS files as shown in Figure 17-3. As long as the filenames match those in the string array, ads, your application will function as expected. Figure 17-4 shows what you will see when you test your application.

You have to wait 5 seconds for the first message to appear because the interval is set to 5000 milliseconds (5 seconds). Then, every 5 seconds a different random message appears. If random chance twice or more in a row selects the same message, the change is so fast that it will look like no change at all occurred! That's because only the text is updating, not the whole page.

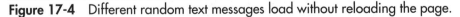

Figure 17-4 Different random text messages load without reloading the page.

NOTE

By default, you must have only one ScriptManager but you may need to add a proxy object (ScriptManagerProxy control) to ensure that the code, perhaps inside of a set of nested master pages, has the ScriptManager object present to execute properly.

Using Events with Ajax

Up to this point, all of the event-generating controls have been within the UpdatePanel control. If you call any events based on controls outside of the UpdatePanel, the whole page is reloaded unless you take certain steps to prevent that from happening.

You may wonder, why place controls outside of the `UpdatePanel` container if they are to be used for working with events inside the `UpdatePanel` container. You may be working with an existing site that originally did not have Ajax functionality. Instead of moving the different controls inside the `UpdatePanel` container, you just want their events to have an effect on the UpdatePanel controls.

Triggers

Fortunately, the solution for using Ajax with control events outside the `UpdatePanel` container is relatively simple. You can use the `<Triggers>` tag and the `AsyncPostBackTrigger` object to listen to the events of controls outside of the `UpdatePanel` container. The following shows the relevant code structure:

```
<Triggers>
    <asp:AsyncPostBackTrigger ControlID="ControlName"
      EventName="EventName" />
</Triggers>
```

By default, the trigger container goes *inside* the `UpdatePanel` container but *outside* of the `<ContentTemplate>` container. You can enter the code directly, or as you will see in the following example, do it using the Properties window.

In this context the `EventName` refers to the name of the event launched by the control, and not to the target function in the C# code. For example, a Button control may have a "Click" event, so the assignment

```
EventName="Click"
```

would mean that from inside the `UpdatePanel` container, the control outside the container is set up as a non-Ajax control. Then within the `UpdatePanel` container, the triggers just listen for the appropriate event from the named control; only the updated material, and not the whole page, is updated.

Try This Loading Images and Multiple Control Events with Ajax

A common feature of web sites is a series of images users can control. For example, a set of images showing different products, different views of a manufacturing plant, or different people who work for a company all require that different images be loaded and unloaded quickly. As you have seen, Ajax is great for loading text because just the text and not the whole page is reloaded. In the same way, Ajax is great for loading images as well.

The first thing to do is to create a set of eight images. (You need at least two and can have as many as you want, but the example is based on eight images.) You can use any image format recognized by a browser—GIF, JPEG, or PNG. Set them to all the same size. The example uses eight JPEG images set to 250×181. You can use any size you want, but for this exercise, keep them around that size. Name them **pix1.jpg** (or whatever graphic extension is appropriate) to **pix8.jpg**. If you use more or fewer than eight, you will have to change some of the code values to reflect the actual number used. Finally, place all of the images in a folder named **images**. You will be placing the images folder in the web site root folder with the Default.aspx file. The following steps show how to build the entire web site:

1. Open a new Web Site in Visual Studio 2008, and save it as **AjaxPix**. Set the mode to Design. In the Windows Explorer, drag the images folder with the images you have created for this sample into the AjaxPix folder where you see the Default.aspx file.

2. Drag an `UpdatePanel` control from the Ajax Extensions menu in the Toolbox, and place it in the div container.

3. From the Standard menu in the Toolbox, drag an Image control and place it in the `UpdatePanel` control container. With the Image control selected, open the Properties window and select ImageUrl. In the second column click the Browse button (the button with the three dots) and navigate to images | pix1.jpg. Once you select it, you will see `~/images/pix1.jpg` as the set value.

4. Drag a Label control and place it beneath the Image control with the picture you just assigned to the Image control. In the Properties window, set the Label's Text property to **1**. To the left of the Label, type in **Picture #**. You should see "Picture # 1" from the Design view.

5. Drag two Button controls into the `UpdatePanel` control container, placing them next to one another. Set the Text property of the left button control to "<= Previous" and the right button to "Next =>." Drag a third Button into the editor, but place it *outside*

of the `UpdatePanel` container but *inside* the div container. Set its Text property to **Original**. Double-click each of the buttons to establish an event handler for each in the C# portion of the code.

6. Right above the div container, drag a ScriptManager control from the Ajax Extensions menu, and place it above and outside of the div container as shown in Figure 17-5.

7. Above the ScriptManager icon, type in **Picture Selector** and set it to an `<h2>` style. Figure 17-5 shows how your application will look once you have placed everything in the editor. (See the CSS code in the listing for the style sheet.)

Figure 17-5   Button controls are inside and outside of the UpdatePanel control

(continued)

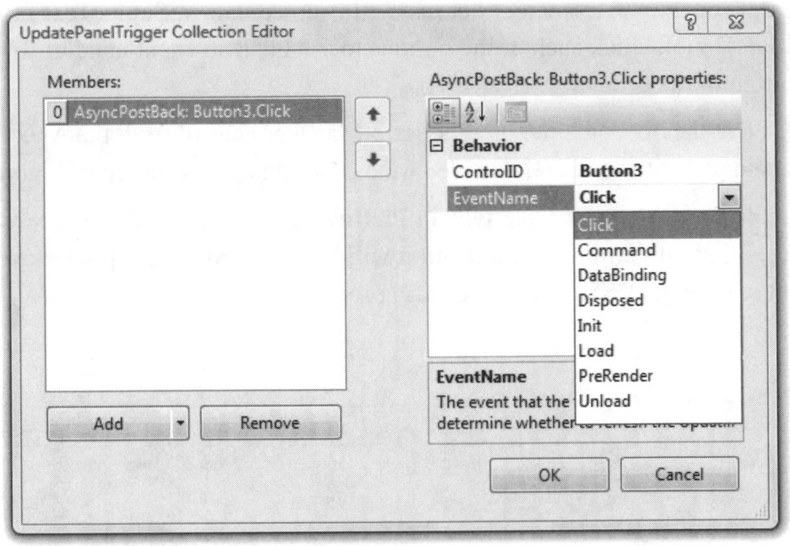

Figure 17-6 Adding a Trigger to a control outside of the UpdatePanel control

8. Click on the UpdatePanel icon to select it, and open the Properties window. In the Triggers row, click on the three-dot button in the (Collection) column. You should see the UpdatePanelTrigger Collection Editor open. Click the Add button. In the right panel, type in **Button3** for the ControlID, and select Click from the pop-up menu that appears in the EventName row. Figure 17-6 shows what you will see.

At this point all but the coding for the C# is complete. The following listings provide all of the code for both the ASP.NET and C# portions of the web site.

ASP.NET Default.aspx

```
<%@ Page Language="C#" AutoEventWireup="true" CodeFile="Default.aspx.cs"
Inherits="_Default" %>
<!DOCTYPE html PUBLIC "-//W3C//DTD XHTML 1.0 Transitional//EN"
"http://www.w3.org/TR/xhtml1/DTD/xhtml1-transitional.dtd">
<html xmlns="http://www.w3.org/1999/xhtml">
<head runat="server">
    <title>Ajax Picture Loader</title>
</head>
<style type="text/css">
```

```
body
{
      background-color:#cccccc;
      font-family:Verdana;
      font-size:small;
      color:Maroon;
}
h2
{

      font-size:16px;
      font-weight:bold;
}
.btn
{

      font-size:smaller;
      color:#cccccc;
      background-color:Maroon;
}
</style>
<body>
    <form id="form1" runat="server">
    <div>
    <center>
    <h2>Picture Selector</h2>
        <asp:ScriptManager ID="ScriptManager1" runat="server" />
        <asp:UpdatePanel ID="UpdatePanel1" runat="server">
            <ContentTemplate>
                <asp:Image ID="Image1" runat="server"
ImageUrl="~/images/pix1.jpg" />
                <br />Picture #
                <asp:Label ID="Label1" runat="server" Text="1" />
                <p />
                <asp:Button ID="Button1" runat="server" Text="&lt;= Previous"
                        onclick="Button1_Click" CssClass="btn" />
                <asp:Button ID="Button2" runat="server" Text="Next =&gt;"
onclick="Button2_Click"
                        CssClass="btn" />
            </ContentTemplate>
                <Triggers>
                    <asp:AsyncPostBackTrigger ControlID="Button3"
EventName="Click" />
                </Triggers>
        </asp:UpdatePanel>
        <asp:Button ID="Button3" runat="server" Text="Original"
onclick="Button3_Click"
                CssClass="btn" />
    </center>
    </div>
    </form>
</body>
</html>
```

(continued)

C# Default.aspx.cs

```csharp
using System;
public partial class _Default : System.Web.UI.Page
{
    private  int counter;
    private string pixName;
    protected void Button1_Click(object sender, EventArgs e)
    {
        //previous
        if (Convert.ToInt16(Label1.Text) >= 2)
        {
            counter = Convert.ToInt16(Label1.Text);
            counter--;
            Label1.Text = Convert.ToString(counter);
            pixName = "pix" + counter + ".jpg";
            Image1.ImageUrl = "~/images/" + pixName;
        }
    }
    protected void Button2_Click(object sender, EventArgs e)
    {
        //next
        if (Convert.ToInt16(Label1.Text) <= 7)
        {
            counter = Convert.ToInt16(Label1.Text);
            counter++;
            Label1.Text = Convert.ToString(counter);
            pixName = "pix" + counter + ".jpg";
            Image1.ImageUrl = "~/images/" + pixName;
        }
    }
    protected void Button3_Click(object sender, EventArgs e)
    {
        //original
        Label1.Text = "1";
        Image1.ImageUrl = "~/images/pix1.jpg";
    }
}
```

When you test the web site application, you should be able to select the next and previous images up to the limits you set in the C#. If you use exactly eight images and name them sequentially **pix1.jpg** through **pix8.jpg**, everything should run smoothly. Otherwise, you will need to make adjustments for the filenames and the limits in the Previous and Next button event handlers. Figure 17-7 shows the initial image without filters. It is also the image

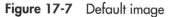

Figure 17-7 Default image

that appears when the Original button is clicked. Whenever the first image appears, the <= Previous button will not bring up a new image, and when the last image appears, the Next => button does not change images.

When you click the buttons to change the image, you will see the images change, but the page will not jump because the page is not reloaded. (If the images you use are different sizes, it appears jerky as the image changes the position of the other objects on the page.) Click the Next => button until you reach the last image as shown in Figure 17-8. At this

(continued)

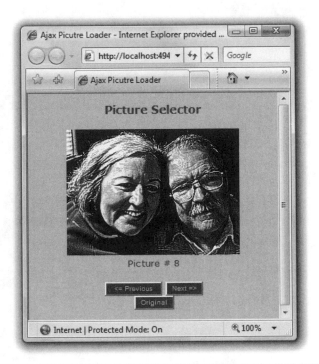

Figure 17-8 When images change, the page does not reload.

point the Next => button is inoperable. The picture number helps to show where you are in the sequence.

This web site example is meant to show how to seamlessly change images and to incorporate buttons for use with Ajax-enabled controls. Once you use changing images with Ajax, you will wonder why this great tool was not available before. If you want to update some old web sites using Ajax, instead of changing the entire site so that all of the controls are within an UpdatePanel control, you can just add triggers where needed.

While only a single UpdatePanel control was used in the example, you can add as many Ajax Extension controls as you want to a web site. In this way you can more easily distribute the other controls used in conjunction with Ajax. However, you only need a single ScriptManager control no matter how many UpdatePanel controls you use for a single page.

Summary

While Ajax functionality was added as a separate extension to ASP.NET 2.0, it is an integral part of ASP.NET 3.5. Using it with any kind of object that changes while the other objects on the page remain unchanged allows you to easily update just those elements of the web site that you want without reloading the entire page.

This functionality may seem trivial, but it has two distinct advantages. First, the viewer does not see jumpy images as the entire page reloads. That adds to an improved user experience and gives a far more professional look to the web sites you create. Secondly, your application uses less Internet resources, so it reduces the chances of a user's browser locking up or slowing down. Fewer resources are being sent to the client, so your site is experienced as trouble-free and one that can be trusted for return visits.

Index

X